ABOUT *Risk*

Risk is an entertaining, cutting-edge answer to a central paradox of our time: Why are the safest and healthiest people in history living in a culture of fear? Dan Gardner examines the psychology behind our perception of risk to reveal how irrational fear is influenced by politicians, corporations, activists, and the media – and how it is created by our own brains' hardwiring. We are safer than we think, and *Risk* shows us how to respond more logically and adaptively to our world.

ACCLAIM FOR
Risk

"Compelling. . . . Gardner aims to get us thinking more carefully about how we run our lives – and make it harder for politicians, the media and advertisers to lead us astray." — *New Scientist*

"Exceptionally good. . . . He takes you through a maze of difficult academic work, and makes it seem simple." — *Evening Standard*

"Gardner is forensic in his dissection of bogus claims in advertising and politics, just as he is lucid about the science explaining why they work." — *The Observer*

"A terrific book, full of wonderful insights, and offering cutting–edge social science in a reader–friendly package. The life you save may be your own!" – Cass Sunstein, director of the Program on Risk Regulation, Harvard University

"Excellent. . . . [Gardner's] take on terrorism in the book's penultimate chapter is refreshing." – *The Economist*

"[Gardner] is not content to blame the media, or blame corporations. He leads us through the evolutionary biology that underlies our sense of risk . . . and only then does he turn to the way these cognitive dispositions allow for political manipulation. In short, this is the best book out there on one of the most important subjects of our time." – Andrew Potter, author of *The Rebel Sell*

"Compelling story–telling backed up by hard facts gleaned from specialist research." – *The Guardian*

"Some books can change the world. This one might." – Paul Slovic, past president of The Society for Risk Analysis

risk

Why We Fear the Things We Shouldn't – and Put Ourselves in Greater Danger

Dan Gardner

EMBLEM

McClelland & Stewart

For Sandra

Cloth edition published 2008
Emblem edition published 2009

Emblem is an imprint of McClelland & Stewart Ltd.
Emblem and colophon are registered trademarks of McClelland & Stewart Ltd.

Library and Archives Canada Cataloguing in Publication

Gardner, Dan
Risk : why we fear the things we shouldn't –
and put ourselves in greater danger / Dan Gardner.

ISBN 978-0-7710-3259-2

1. Fear – Social aspects.   2. Fear – Political aspects.   3. Risk.
I. Title.

HM1101.G37 2009   302.'17   C2008-904238-7

We acknowledge the financial support of the Government of Canada through the
Book Publishing Industry Development Program and that of the Government of Ontario
through the Ontario Media Development Corporation's Ontario Book Initiative. We further
acknowledge the support of the Canada Council for the Arts and the Ontario Arts Council
for our publishing program.

Typeset in Nofret by M&S, Toronto
Printed and bound in Canada

ANCIENT FOREST
FRIENDLY

McClelland & Stewart Ltd.
75 Sherbourne Street
Toronto, Ontario
M5A 2P9
www.mcclelland.com

1 2 3 4 5   13 12 11 10 09

"Fear is implanted in us as a preservative from evil; but its duty, like that of the other passions, is not to overbear reason, but to assist it."

SAMUEL JOHNSON

CONTENTS

PROLOGUE

Anyone who saw it will never forget it. And almost everyone saw it.

When the first jet darted out of that crisp, blue September sky and crashed into the World Trade Center, only a single television camera – on the street filming city officials doing some mundane task now long forgotten – captured the image. But as the tower burned, alerts flashed through wires and airwaves. The world's electronic eyes turned, opened, and waited. When the second plane streaked in, an immense audience – perhaps hundreds of millions – saw the jet, the angry explosion, the gushing smoke, the glass and steel raining down like confetti in a parade. They saw it live. It was so clear, so intimate. It was like watching the whole awful spectacle through the living-room window.

Those who didn't see the attack live soon would. In the frantic hours and days that followed, the images were repeated over and over and over. They were everywhere. From London to Moscow and Tokyo. From the peaks of the Andes to the forests of Madagascar and the Australian desert. In every city, region, and village within reach of modern communications media – almost the entire planet – people witnessed the tragedy. Never in the history of the species had there been such a communal experience.

Almost 3,000 people died. Hundreds of thousands lost family and friends. It was an enormous crime. And yet, the attacks of September 11 did not inflict personal loss on the overwhelming majority of Americans, much less the population of the world at large. On September 12, the rest of us had to go back to the daily routine of living. But things had changed. How could they not after what we had seen?

Some of the changes were small, or at least they seemed trivial next to what had happened. People stopped flying, for one. When commercial air travel resumed several days after the attacks, the planes taking off were almost empty.

A big reason was those images. They were so visceral. Sure, there are lots of flights every day and the chances of being on one that gets hijacked and slammed into an office tower may be tiny. But that didn't seem to matter. Airports were unnerving. Flying felt strange and dangerous.

We all got to know the victims' families in the weeks and months after the attack. The media were filled with interviews, profiles, and terrible stories of loss, making the shocking event even more deeply personal. And there was so much talk of worse to come. Politicians, pundits, and experts talked about terrorism as if it were the Fifth Horseman of the Apocalypse. Death and destruction could come countless ways, we were warned: poison in town water supplies; planes crashing into nuclear reactors; genetically engineered small-pox virus unleashed in the subway; dirty bombs; suitcase nukes in the hold of some anonymous cargo ship.

Then came the news that several people had been killed by anthrax-infected mail. Anthrax. No one saw that coming. Months before, we were safe and prosperous. Suddenly, we were butterflies in a gale. Grim-faced politicians advised everyone to pay attention to colour-coded terror alerts. Stock up on emergency supplies. Don't forget to buy duct tape so you can seal windows and doors against chemical or biological attacks. And while you're at it, pray to God almighty that we might see the next day's dawn.

It was an unreal, frightening time and it was predictable that people would flee the airports. Perhaps surprisingly, though, they didn't start digging backyard bomb shelters. Instead, most went to work and carried on living. They just didn't fly. They drove instead.

Politicians worried what the mass exodus of Americans from planes to cars would do to the airline industry, so a bailout was put together. But no one talked about the surge in car travel. Why would they? It was trivia. There were deadly threats to worry about.

But what no politician mentioned is that air travel is safer than driving. Dramatically safer – so much so that the most dangerous part of a typical commercial flight is the drive to the airport.

The safety gap is so large, in fact, that planes would still be safer than cars even if the threat of terrorism were unimaginably worse than it actually is: An American professor calculated that even if terrorists were hijacking and crashing one passenger jet a week in the United States, a person who took one flight a month for a year would have only a 1-in-135,000 chance of being killed in a hijacking – a trivial risk compared to the annual 1-in-6,000 odds of being killed in a car crash.

Risk analysts knew all about this safety gap. And they understood what a large-scale shift from planes to cars would mean. It's simple mathematics. If one person gives up the relative safety of flying and drives instead, it's not a big deal. He will almost certainly survive. But if millions of people take the same risk, it is just as likely that some of them will lose the gamble and their lives.

But car crashes aren't like terrorist hijackings. They aren't covered live on CNN. They aren't discussed endlessly by pundits. They don't inspire Hollywood movies and television shows. They aren't fodder for campaigning politicians. And so in the months following the September 11 attacks, as politicians and journalists worried endlessly about terrorism, anthrax, and dirty bombs, people who fled the air-ports to be safe from terrorism crashed and bled to death on America's roads. And nobody noticed.

Or rather, few people noticed. Gerd Gigerenzer, a psychologist at the Max Planck Institute in Berlin, patiently gathered data on travel and fatalities. In 2006, he published a paper comparing the numbers five years prior to the September 11 attacks and five years after.

It turned out that the shift from planes to cars in America lasted one year. Then traffic patterns went back to normal. Gigerenzer also found that, exactly as expected, fatalities on American roads soared after September 2001 and settled back to normal levels in September 2002. With these data, Gigerenzer was able to calculate the number of Americans killed in car crashes as a direct result of the switch from planes to cars.

It was 1,595. That is more than one-half the total death toll of history's worst terrorist atrocity. It is six times higher than the total number of people on board the doomed flights of September 11. It is 319 times the total number of people killed by the infamous anthrax attacks of 2001.

And yet almost nobody noticed but the families of the dead. And not even the families really understood what had happened. They thought – they still think – that they lost husbands, wives, fathers, mothers, and children to the routine traffic accidents we accept as the regrettable cost of living in the modern world.

They didn't. It was fear that stole their loved ones.

1

THE RISK SOCIETY

Franklin Delano Roosevelt knew a thing or two about fear. When FDR raised his hand to take the oath that would make him the 32nd president of the United States, fear had settled like a thick, grey fog across Washington. It was the very bottom of the Great Depression. Banks were falling like dominoes and more than half the industrial production of the United States had evaporated. Prices for farm products had collapsed, one in four workers was unemployed, and two million Americans were homeless.

This was the country whose care was about to be entrusted to a partially paralyzed man who had narrowly escaped assassination only a month before. Eleanor Roosevelt understandably described her husband's inauguration as "terrifying."

In his first address as president, Roosevelt spoke directly to the mood of the day. "I am certain that my fellow Americans expect that on my induction into the presidency I will address them with a candor and a decision which the present situation of our nation impels," he began. "This is pre-eminently the time to speak the truth, the whole truth, frankly and boldly. Nor need we shrink from honestly facing conditions in our country today. This great nation will endure as it has endured, will revive and will prosper. So, first of all, let me assert my firm belief that the only thing we have to fear is fear itself – nameless, unreasoning, unjustified terror which paralyzes needed efforts to convert retreat into advance."

Of course Roosevelt knew there were plenty of things to fear aside from fear itself. But he also knew that serious as the nation's problems were, "unreasoning fear" would make things far worse by eroding faith in liberal democracy and convincing people to embrace the mad dreams of communism and fascism. The Great Depression could hurt the United States. But fear could destroy it.

It's an insight older than the United States itself. Roosevelt's line was lifted from Henry David Thoreau, and Thoreau in turn got it from Michel de Montaigne, who wrote, "The thing I fear most is fear" more than three and a half centuries ago.

Fear can be a constructive emotion. When we worry about a risk, we pay more attention to it and take action where warranted. Fear keeps us alive and thriving. It's no exaggeration to say that our species owes its very existence to fear. But "unreasoning fear" is another matter. It was unreasoning fear that could have destroyed the United States in the Great Depression. It was unreasoning fear that killed 1,595 people by convincing them to abandon planes for cars after the September 11 attacks. And it is the growing presence of unreasoning fear in all the countries of the Western world that is causing us to make increasingly foolish decisions in dealing with the risks we face every day.

Risk and fear are hot topics among sociologists, who have come to a broad consensus that those of us living in modern countries worry more than previous generations. Some say we live in a culture of fear. Terrorists, Internet stalkers, crystal meth, avian flu, genetically modified organisms, contaminated food: New threats seem to sprout like poisonous mushrooms. Climate change, carcinogens, leaky breast implants, the "obesity epidemic," pesticides, West Nile virus, SARS, avian flu, and flesh-eating disease. The list goes on and on. Open the newspaper, watch the evening news. On any given day, there's a good chance someone – a journalist, activist, consultant, corporate executive, or politician – is warning about an "epidemic" of something or other that threatens you and those you hold dear.

Occasionally, these fears burst into full-bore panics. The pedophile lurking in parks and Internet chat rooms is the latest. In the early 1990s, it was road rage. A decade earlier, it was herpes. Satanic cults, mad cow disease, school shootings, crack cocaine – all these have raced to the top of the public's list of concerns, only to drop as rapidly as they went up. Some surge back to prominence now and then. Others slip into the category of minor nuisances and are never heard from again. Farewell, herpes.

This is just the stuff of daily news. Authors, activists, consultants, and futurologists are constantly warning us about threats so spectacular and exotic they make scenarios of nuclear Armageddon look quaint. Genetically enhanced bio-weapons, self-replicating nanotechnology turning everything into "grey goo," weird experiments in physics that create a black hole, sucking in the planet and everyone on it. The millennium bug was a bust but that hasn't stopped theories of annihilation from piling up so quickly that it's become almost commonplace to hear claims that humanity will be lucky to survive the next century.

Ulrich Beck isn't quite that pessimistic. As the German sociologist and professor at the London School of Economics told *The Guardian* newspaper, he merely thinks it "improbable" that humanity will survive "beyond the 21st century without a lapse back into barbarism." Beck's opinion counts more than most because he was among the first to realize that modern countries were becoming nations of worriers. Back in 1986, he coined the term *risk society* to describe countries in which there is heightened concern about risk – particularly risks caused by modern technology – and where people are frightened like never before.

But why are we so afraid? That's the really tough question. Of course terrorism is a real risk. So are climate change, avian flu, breast cancer, child snatchers, and all the other things that have us wringing our collective hands. But humanity has always faced one risk or another. Why should we worry more than previous generations?

Ulrich Beck thinks the answer is clear: We are more afraid than ever because we are more at risk than ever. Technology is outstripping our ability to control it. The environment is collapsing. Social pressures are growing. The threat of cataclysm looms and people – like deer catching the scent of approaching wolves – sense the danger.

Many others agree with Beck. Peering into the future and imagining all the ways things could go horribly wrong has become something of a parlour game for intellectuals. The more ambitious of them turn their dark imaginings into best-selling books. But if these gloomy fantasists thought less about the future and more about the past, they would realize that it is *always* possible for things to go wrong and that to think the potential disasters facing us today are somehow more awful than those of the past is both ignorant and arrogant. A little more attention to history would also reveal that there have always been people crying "Doom!" – almost none of whom turned out to have any more ability to see into the future than the three blind mice of nursery rhyme fame.

And then there's the matter of basic facts. Here are a few to consider the next time someone claims with great certainty that the sky is crashing.

In England, a baby born in 1900 had a life expectancy of 46 years. Her great-grandchild, born in 1980, could look forward to 74 years of life. And the great-great-grandchild, born in 2003, can count on almost eight decades on the planet.

The story is the same in every other Western country. In the United States, life expectancy was 59 years in 1930. Seven decades later, it was almost 78 years. In Canada, life expectancy recently inched above 80 years.

For most of the history of our species, giving birth was one of the most dangerous things a woman could do. It is still a risky venture in much of the developing world, where 440 women die giving birth for every 100,000 children delivered. But in the developed world, that rate has plummeted to 20 – and we no longer think of birth and death as constant companions.

As for mothers, so for children. The experience of lowering a toddler-sized coffin into the earth was painfully common not so long ago, but the odds that a baby born today will live to blow out five candles on a birthday cake have improved spectacularly. In the United Kingdom in 1900, 14 per cent of all babies and young children died; by 1997, that number had fallen to 0.58 per cent. Since 1970 alone, the death rate among American children under five fell by more than two-thirds. In Germany, it dropped by three-quarters.

And we're not just living longer. We're living better. In studies across Europe and the United States, researchers have determined that fewer people develop chronic illnesses like heart disease, lung disease, and arthritis, that those who do develop them do so 10 to 25 years later in life than they used to, and that these illnesses are less severe when they strike. People are less physically disabled than ever. And they're bigger. The average American man is three inches taller and 50 pounds heavier than his ancestor of a century ago, which makes it difficult for Civil War re-enactors, who use only authentic kit, to fit in army tents. We're even getting smarter: IQs have been improving steadily for decades.

Humans in the developed world have undergone "a form of evolution that is unique not only to humankind, but unique among the 7,000 or so generations of humans who ever inhabited the earth," Robert Fogel, a Nobel laureate at the University of Chicago, told the *New York Times*. The good fortune of those alive today, and the promise of more to come, is summed up in the title of one of Fogel's books: *The Escape From Hunger and Premature Death, 1700–2100*.

The trends in humanity's political arrangements are also quite positive, despite what we read in newspaper headlines. In 1950, there were 22 full democracies. At the century's end, there were 120 and almost two-thirds of the people in the world could cast a meaningful ballot. As for the bloodshed and chaos that many people claim to see rising all around us, it just isn't so. "War between countries is much less likely than ever and civil war is less likely than at any time since 1960," Monty Marshall of George Mason University told the *New York Times* in 2005. A major study released later that year by the Human Security Centre at the University of British Columbia confirmed and expanded on that happy conclusion.

It is well known that those of us blessed to live in Western countries are the most prosperous humans in the history of the species but we feel a little guilty even mentioning it because we know so many others don't share our good fortune. Not so well known, however, is that there have been major improvements in the developing world, too.

In the two decades following 1980, the proportion of people in the developing world who were malnourished fell from 28 per cent to 17 per cent. That's still unconscionably high, but it's a lot better than it was.

Then there's the United Nations Human Development Index (HDI). It's probably the best measure of the state of humanity because it combines key data on income, health, and literacy. At the bottom of the HDI list of 177 countries is the African country of Niger – and yet Niger's 2003 HDI score is 17 per cent higher than it was in 1975. The same trend can be seen in almost all very poor countries. Mali is 31 per cent better off. Chad is up 22 per cent. Doom mongers like to point to the soaring populations of the poor world as a potential source of future catastrophe but what the doomsters never mention is that those populations aren't soaring because women are having far more babies than in the past. It's that the babies are far less likely to *die* than in the past – which everybody but the grumpiest Malthusian would consider to be very good news.

Put all these numbers together and what do they add up to? In a sentence: We are the healthiest, wealthiest, and longest-lived people in history. And we are increasingly afraid. This is one of the great paradoxes of our time.

So much of what we think and do about risk does not make sense. In a 1990 paper, researchers George Loewenstein and Jane Mather compared people's levels of concern about nine risks – including AIDS, crime, and teen suicide – with objective measures of those risks. The results can only be described as scrambled. In some cases, concern rose and fell as the risk rose and fell. In others, there was "wild fluctuation" in levels of concern that had absolutely no connection to the real risk. "There is no generally applicable dynamic relationship between perceived and actual risk," the researchers politely concluded.

There are countless illustrations of our confused and confusing relationship with risk. The single greatest risk factor for breast cancer is age – the older the woman, the greater the risk – but when a 2007 survey by Oxford University researchers asked British women when a woman is most likely to get breast cancer, more than half said, "Age doesn't matter." One in five thought the risk is highest when a woman "is in her 50s"; 9.3 per cent said the risk is highest "in her 40s"; and 1.3 per cent said "in her 70s." A grand total of 0.7 per cent of women chose the correct answer: "80 and older." Breast cancer has been a major public concern and topic of discussion since at least the early 1990s and yet the survey revealed that the vast majority of women still know nothing about the most important risk factor. How is that possible?

In Europe, where there are more cellphones than people and sales keep climbing, a survey found that more than 50 per cent of

Europeans believe the dubious claims that cellphones are a serious threat to health. And then there's the striking contrast between Europeans' smoking habits and their aversion to foods containing genetically modified organisms. Surely one of the great riddles to be answered by science is how the same person who doesn't think twice about lighting a Gauloise will march in the streets demanding a ban on products that have never been proven to have caused so much as a single case of indigestion.

In Europe and elsewhere, people tremble at the sight of a nuclear reactor but shrug at the thought of having an X-ray – even though X-rays expose them to the very same radiation they are terrified might leak from a nuclear plant. Stranger still, they pay thousands of dollars for the opportunity to fly somewhere distant, lie on a beach, and soak up the radiation emitted by the sun – even though the estimated death toll from the Chernobyl meltdown (9,000) is actually quite modest compared to the number of Americans diagnosed with skin cancer each year (more than one million) and the number killed (more than 10,000).

Or compare attitudes about two popular forms of entertainment: watching car races and smoking pot. Over a five-year period, NASCAR drivers crashed more than 3,000 times. Dale Earnhardt's death in 2001 was the seventh fatal smash-up in seven years. Governments permit NASCAR drivers to take these risks, and the public sees NASCAR as wholesome family entertainment. But if a NASCAR driver were to relieve post-race stress by smoking marijuana, he would be subject to arrest and imprisonment for possession of a banned substance that governments worldwide have deemed to be so risky not even consenting adults are allowed to consume it – even though it is impossible for someone to consume enough to cause a fatal overdose.

The same logic applies to steroids and other forms of doping: One of the reasons that these substances are banned in sports is the belief that they are so dangerous that not even athletes who know the risks should be allowed to take them. But in many cases, the sports those athletes compete in are far more dangerous than doping. Aerial skiing – to take only one example – requires a competitor to race down a hill, hurtle off a jump, soar through the air, twist, turn, spin, and return to earth safely. The slightest mistake can mean a head-first landing and serious injury, even a broken neck. But aerial skiing isn't banned. It's celebrated. In the 2006 Olympics, a Canadian skier who had broken her neck only months before was lionized when she and the metal plate holding her vertebrae together returned to the slopes to once again risk paralysis and death. "I would prefer my child take anabolic steroids and growth hormone than play rugby," a British scientist who studies doping told the *Financial Times*. "I don't know of any cases of quadriplegia caused by growth hormone." The same is all the more true of American football, a beloved game that snaps the occasional teenaged neck and routinely turns the stars of the National Football League into shambling, pain-wracked, middle-aged wrecks.

Handguns are scary, but driving to work? It's just a boring part of the daily routine. So it's no surprise that handgun killings grab headlines and dominate elections while traffic accidents are dismissed as nothing more than the unpleasant background noise of modern life. But in country after country – including the United States – cars kill far more people than handguns. In Canada, 26 people die in car crashes for every one life taken by a handgun. And if you are not a drug dealer or the friend of a drug dealer, and you don't hang out in places patronized by drug dealers and their friends, your chance of being murdered with a handgun shrinks almost to invisibility – unlike the risk of dying in a car crash, which applies to anyone who pulls out of a driveway.

Then there are the kids. There was a time when children were expected to take some knocks and chances. It was part of growing up. But no more. At schools, doors are barred and guarded against maniacs with guns, while children are taught from their first day in the classroom that every stranger is a threat. In playgrounds, climbing equipment is removed and unsupervised games of tag are forbidden lest someone sprain an ankle or bloody a nose. At home, children are forbidden from playing alone outdoors, as all generations did before, because their parents are convinced every bush hides a pervert – and no mere statistic will convince them otherwise. Childhood is starting to resemble a prison sentence, with children spending almost every moment behind locked doors and alarms, their every movement scheduled, supervised, and controlled. Are they at least safer as a result? Probably not. Obesity, diabetes, and the other health problems caused in part by too much time sitting inside are a lot more danger- ous than the spectres haunting parental imaginations.

And of course there is terrorism. It is the *bête noire* of our age. Ever since that awful day in September, terrorism has utterly dominated the agenda of the American government and, by extension, the agenda of the entire international order. George W. Bush has said nothing less than the survival of the United States is at stake. Tony Blair went further, saying the whole West faces a danger that is "real and existential."

And yet in the last century, fewer than 20 terrorist attacks killed more than a hundred people. Even the September 11 attacks – which were horribly unlike anything seen before or since – killed less than one-fifth the number of Americans murdered every year by ordinary criminals. As for the doomsday scenarios that get so much play in the media, the only time terrorists ever managed to acquire and use a genuine weapon of mass destruction was the 1995 nerve gas attack in Tokyo. The culprits, the Aum Shinrikyo cult, were wealthy and had the services of skilled scientists. The target, the crowded subway system, was ideal for a gas attack. Twelve people died.

Compare that to the toll taken by the considerably less frighten- ing spectres of obesity, diabetes, heart disease, and other common ail- ments. On average, 36,000 Americans are killed each year by the flu and related complications. Obesity may kill around 100,000 each year.

"Hundreds of thousands" die annually simply because they don't have access to "the most valuable preventive health services available," according to the Centers for Disease Control.

These risks are not new or darkly glamorous. They're not even terribly complicated or little-known. We have made enormous advances in human health but so much more could be done if we tackled them with proven strategies that would cost little compared to the benefits to be reaped. And yet we're not doing it. We are, however, spending gargantuan sums of money to deal with the risk of terrorism – a risk that, by any measure, is no more than a scuttling beetle next to the elephant of disease. As a direct result of this misallocation of resources, countless lives will be lost for no good reason.

That's what happens when our judgments about risk go out of whack. There are deadly consequences.

So it's important to understand why we so often get risk wrong. Why do we fear a proliferating number of relatively minor risks? Why do we so often shrug off greater threats? Why have we become a "culture of fear"?

Part of the answer lies in self-interest. Fear sells. Fear makes money. The countless companies and consultants in the business of protecting the fearful from whatever they may fear know it only too well. The more fear, the better the sales. So we have home-alarm companies frightening old ladies and young mothers by running ads featuring frightened old ladies and young mothers. Software companies scaring parents with hype about on-line pedophiles. Security consultants spinning scenarios of terror and death that can be avoided by spending more tax dollars on security consultants. Fear is a fantastic marketing tool, which is why we can't turn on the television or open a newspaper without seeing it at work.

Of course, private companies and consultants aren't the only merchants of fear. There are politicians who talk up threats, denounce their opponents as soft or incompetent, and promise to slay the wolf at the door just as soon as we do the sensible thing and elect them.

There are bureaucrats plumping for bigger budgets. Government-sponsored scientists who know the rule is "no problem, no funding." And there are the activists and non-governmental organizations who know they're only as influential as their media profile is big and that the surest way to boost that profile is to tell the scary stories that draw reporters like vultures to corpses.

The media, too, know the value of fear. The media are in the business of profit, and crowding in the information marketplace means the competition for eyes and ears is steadily intensifying. Inevitably and increasingly, the media turn to fear to protect shrinking market shares because a warning of mortal peril – "A story you can't afford to miss!" – is an excellent way to get someone's attention.

But this is far from a complete explanation. What about the serious risks we don't pay much attention to? There's often money to be made dealing with them, but still we are unmoved. And the media, to be fair, occasionally cast cold water on panics and unreasonable fears, while corporations, activists, and politicians sometimes find it in their interest to play down genuine concerns – as the British government tried and failed to do in the early 1990s, when there was growing evidence linking BSE ("mad cow disease") in cattle and a variant of the Creutzfeldt-Jakob disease in humans. The link was real. The government insisted it wasn't. A cabinet minister even went so far as to hold a press conference at which he fed his four-year-old daughter a hamburger made of British beef.

Clearly, there's much more than self-interest and marketing involved. There's culture, for one. Whether we fear this risk or that – or dismiss another as no cause for concern – often depends on our cultural values. Marijuana is a perfect example. Since the days of Depression-era black jazz musicians, pot has been associated with a hipster counter-culture. Today, the young backpacker wearing a T-shirt with the famous multi-leaf symbol on it isn't expressing his love of horticulture – it's a statement of cultural identity. Someone like that will have a very strong inclination to dismiss any claim that marijuana may cause harm as nothing more than old-fashioned reefer madness. The same is true in reverse: For social conservatives, that cluster of leaves is a symbol of the anarchic liberalism they despise, and they will consider any evidence that marijuana causes harm as vindication – while downplaying or simply ignoring evidence to the contrary.

Psychologists call this confirmation bias. We all do it. Once a belief is in place, we screen what we see and hear in a biased way that ensures our beliefs are "proven" correct. Psychologists have also discovered that people are vulnerable to something called group polarization – which means that when people who share beliefs get together in groups, they become more convinced that their beliefs are right and they become more extreme in their views. Put confirmation bias, group polarization, and culture together, and we start to understand why people can come to completely different views about which risks are frightening and which aren't worth a second thought.

But that's not the end of psychology's role in understanding risk. Far from it. The real starting point for understanding why we worry and why we don't is the individual human brain.

Four decades ago, scientists knew little about how humans perceived risks, how we judged which risks to fear and which to ignore, and how we decided what to do about them. But in the 1960s, pioneers like Paul Slovic, today a professor at the University of Oregon, set to work. They made startling discoveries and over the ensuing decades, a new body of science grew. The implications of this new science were enormous for a whole range of different fields. In 2002, one of the major figures in this research, Daniel Kahneman, won the Nobel Prize in economics, even though Kahneman is a psychologist who never took so much as a single class in economics.

What the psychologists discovered is that a very old idea is right. Every human brain has not one but two systems of thought. They called them System One and System Two. The ancient Greeks – who arrived at this conception of humanity a little earlier than scientists –

personified the two systems in the form of the gods Dionysus and Apollo. We know them better as Feeling and Reason.

System Two is Reason. It works slowly. It examines evidence. It calculates and considers. When Reason makes a decision, it's easy to put into words and explain.

System One – Feeling – is entirely different. Unlike Reason, it works without our conscious awareness and it is as fast as lightning. Feeling is the source of the snap judgments that we experience as a hunch or an intuition or as emotions like unease, worry, or fear. A decision that comes from Feeling is hard or even impossible to explain in words. You don't know why you feel the way you do, you just do.

System One works as quickly as it does because it uses built-in rules of thumb and automatic settings. Say you're about to take a walk at midday in Los Angeles. You may think, "What's the risk? Am I safe?" Instantly, your brain will seek to retrieve examples of other people being attacked, robbed, or murdered in similar circumstances. If it comes up with one or more examples easily, System One will sound the alarm: The risk is high! Be afraid! And you will be. You won't know why, really, because System One's operations are unconscious. You'll just have an uneasy feeling that taking a walk is dangerous – a feeling you would have trouble explaining to someone else.

What System One did is apply a simple rule of thumb: If examples of something can be recalled easily, that thing must be common. Psychologists call this the availability heuristic.

Obviously, System One is both brilliant and flawed. It is brilliant because the simple rules of thumb System One uses allow it to assess a situation and render a judgment in an instant – which is exactly what you need when you see a shadow move at the back of an alley and you don't have the latest crime statistics handy. But System One is also flawed because the same rules of thumb can generate irrational conclusions.

You may have just watched the evening news and seen a shock-ing report about someone like you being attacked in a quiet neigh-bourhood at midday in Dallas. That crime may have been in another city in another state. It may have been a very unusual, even bizarre, crime – the very qualities that got it on the evening news across the country. And it may be that if you think about this a little – if you get System Two involved – you would agree that this example really doesn't tell you much about your chance of being attacked, which, according to the statistics, is incredibly tiny. But none of that matters. All that System One knows is that the example was recalled easily. Based on that alone, it concludes the risk is high and it triggers the alarm – and you feel afraid when you really shouldn't.

Scientists have discovered that this Example Rule is only one of many rules and automatic settings used by System One. These devices often function smoothly and efficiently. But sometimes, they produce results that make no sense. Consider the terms *1 per cent* and *1 in 100*. They mean exactly the same thing. But as Paul Slovic discovered, System One will lead people to judge a risk to be much higher if they are told it is "1 in 100" than if it is described as "1 per cent."

The problem is that System One wasn't created for the world we live in. For almost the entire history of our species and those that came before, our ancestors lived in small nomadic bands that sur-vived by hunting animals and gathering plants. It was in that long era that evolution shaped and moulded System One. Having been forged by that environment, System One works quite well in it.

But today, very few human beings spend their days stalking ante-lope and avoiding lions. We live in a world transformed by technology – a world where risks are measured in microns and parts-per-million and we are bombarded with images and information from all over the planet.

Imagine a Stone Age hunter who falls asleep by the glowing embers of a campfire one night. When he opens his eyes in the morning, he is lying on a sidewalk in Times Square. That is System One, amazed, confused, and struggling to make sense of the world around him. It would be tough under any circumstances. Mistakes would be inevitable.

But the real trouble starts when this prehistoric refugee meets the merchants of fear.

2

OF TWO MINDS

On assignment in Lagos, Nigeria, several years ago, I went out late one night in a slum. If there were guidebooks to African slums, they would advise against this. I am visibly foreign, and in the slums of Africa foreigners are assumed to be wealthy people who carry large amounts of cash. In a poor, sprawling, tough city like Lagos, people who carry large amounts of cash have an unfortunate tendency to get robbed, murdered, or both.

As it turned out, my wallet was stolen in the gentlest manner possible – pickpocketed at a roadside canteen. I didn't discover this until after the fact but a local man I'd met said he thought he knew who did it. He also thought he knew where to find the culprit.

Together, we entered a maze of dirt paths and shanties where the only light came from campfires and kerosene lamps. Clusters of young men drank moonshine and stared at the foreigner. My new best friend asked around. No luck. But there was someone who could take me to a different place where the thief may be. And so in the company of another stranger, I plunged deeper into the humid, black night. I had lost all sense of where I was, and the sinking feeling in my stomach told me there was a good chance this was all going to end quite badly.

And yet, even as my skin grew clammy with sweat and fear, I kept going. It wasn't the money in the wallet. My newspaper would cover that. It was the photograph of my two young children that I couldn't get out of my mind. It was a cheesy Christmas photo done in a department-store studio with a painted backdrop of frosted windows and Santa's sleigh flying through the night sky. Both my toddlers have big, goofy grins, thanks to a very dedicated photographer who made silly faces while balancing a rubber duck on her head.

I had half a dozen just like it at home. I knew that. I also knew it was only a photograph. And yet I couldn't stop. I saw those grins. I imagined the wallet emptied of cash and tossed in a trash-filled gutter. I saw the photo lying in the filth, rotting, abandoned. I felt sick. Lost, miserable, and alone, I kept up the hunt for three hours. Finally someone told me I was a fool, that I could get my throat cut, and offered to guide me back to the hotel for a fee. I forced myself to accept.

The next morning, I shook my head in amazement. It still bothered me that my photo was gone, although the feeling wasn't so intense. But what I had done was so absolutely, fantastically stupid. Why had I done it? I didn't have a clue. It had been a long, exhausting day. It was late, I was tired, and I'd had a couple of beers. But surely that wasn't enough to skew my judgment so badly. There had to be something else at work. I just didn't understand what it was.

Indeed there was something else involved, as I discovered much later. It was my inner caveman – the ancient wiring of my unconscious mind – giving me some very bad advice.

We humans living in modern, wealthy countries like to think of ourselves as an advanced lot. We can read and write. We know the earth goes around the sun and not the other way round. We are clean, shaved, and perfumed. We're taller, healthier, and longer-lived than our ancestors. When we smile, the dental work we reveal would shock those who lived before the dawn of toothpaste and braces. And yet the one thing that is most responsible for making us who we are is not nearly so modern as our straight, gleaming teeth.

Between five and seven million years ago, the ancestors of chimpanzees and humans parted company on the primate family tree. Sometime around 2 or 2.5 million years ago, the brains of our ancestors ballooned from 400 cubic centimetres to about 650 cubic centimetres. That's only a fraction of the 1,400-cubic-centimetre brain of an average modern human, but it was enough to mark the real beginning of humanity. The genus *Homo* was born.

Around 500,000 years ago, the ancestral human brain took another big jump – to 1,200 cubic centimetres. The final step came sometime between 150,000 and 200,000 years ago when *Homo sapiens* first walked the plains of Africa. DNA analysis shows that every person alive today shares a common ancestor as recently as 100,000 years ago.

Evolution has two driving forces: natural selection and mutation. Natural selection favours traits that help an organism survive and reproduce, while weeding out those that hinder survival and reproduction. Other things being equal, a Paleolithic man with sharp eyesight and a strong arm had an edge over one who had neither. He was more likely to stay alive, to eat better, get a mate, and admire the keen eyesight and strong arm of his son. The short-sighted, skinny-armed man was more likely to end up in the belly of a lion. Over time, the eyes of the human population as a whole would become sharper, their arms stronger.

Genetic mutation is the source of the really major changes, however. In most cases, mutations have no obvious effect, or the effect is neither an advantage nor a disadvantage. These likely wouldn't change the odds of a person surviving and reproducing so natural selection would neither spread nor squelch them. Occasionally, a mutation produces a disaster – such as a deadly disease – that will make the person with the mutation much less likely to have children. A mutation like that is almost certain to vanish in a generation or two.

But then there is the very rare case in which the mutation produces a new trait that gives its fortunate owner an advantage in the fight to stay alive and bounce children on his knee. Given a little time, natural selection will pass on this spot of luck to many others, maybe even the entire species.

The line between positive and negative mutations isn't always clear, however. Some mutations do terrible harm to those who have them and yet they flourish because they also provide a benefit that outweighs the harm. The classic example can be found in West Africa, where about 10 per cent of the population carries a genetic mutation that causes sickle-cell anemia – a disease that, without modern medical intervention, is likely to kill the victim before adolescence. Ordinarily, natural selection would quickly eliminate this mutation. It hasn't because the mutation isn't always deadly. Only if a child is unlucky enough to get the mutant gene from both parents does it cause sickle-cell anemia. If she gets it from only one parent, it will instead boost the child's resistance to malaria – a disease that routinely kills children younger than five and that is rife all over West Africa. So the mutation kills in some circumstances and saves lives in others. As a result, natural selection has spread the mutation in the West African population, but only up to a certain level – because beyond that, more children would get the mutation from both parents and then it would take more lives than it saves.

Most people get this as far as physical traits go. The opposable thumb is mighty useful. Thank you, natural selection. And we also have no trouble talking this way about the brains and behaviour of other species. Why do chimpanzee mothers nurture and protect their children? Simple: Natural selection favoured this behaviour and, in time, it became hard-wired into chimp brains.

But the moment this conversation turns to human brains and actions, people get uncomfortable. The idea that much human thought is unconscious, and that evolutionary hard-wiring is its foundation, is too much for many to accept. "I am not willing to assume," wrote David Brooks, the *New York Times* columnist, "that our brains are like computers. . . . Isn't it just as possible that the back-stage part of the brain [meaning unconscious thought] might be more like a personality, some unique and nontechnological essence that cannot be adequately generalized about by scientists in white coats with clipboards?" What Brooks is saying here is what many of us vaguely sense: that the brain is a big, complex, physical organ at the centre of which is some indefinable thing or entity that makes decisions and issues commands for reasons scientists in white coats will never be able to fathom.

For this, we can thank René Descartes. Even those who have never heard of the French philosopher have imbibed his idea that body and mind are separate. The mind is not merely a lump of grey matter on our shoulders. It contains something we vaguely refer to as spirit, soul, or "nontechnological essence," to use Brooks's strange term. In 1949, three centuries after Descartes, philosopher Gilbert Ryle scornfully dubbed this idea "the ghost in the machine." In the almost six decades since, science has made enormous progress in under-standing how humans think, and everything we have learned sup-ports Ryle. There is no ghost, no spirit, no nontechnological essence. There is only the brain, and the brain is entirely physical. It was and is subject to the same pressures of natural selection that gave us the opposable thumb and sickle-cell anemia.

This is not to denigrate the brain, quite the opposite. The human brain is magnificent. We have to give it credit for everything our species has accomplished – from surviving and multiplying to putting a man on the moon and unlocking the secrets of the universe and even the brain itself – because, truth be told, we humans are the scrawny, four-eyed nerds in nature's schoolyard. Our senses of sight, smell, and hearing were never as good as those of the animals we wanted to catch and eat. Our arms, legs, and teeth were always puny compared to the muscles and fangs of the predators who competed with us for food and occasionally looked at us as lunch.

The brain was our only advantage. It alone kept us from becoming nature's Edsel. Relying on it so heavily, the dimmer among us lost out to the smarter. The brain developed new capabilities. And it got bigger and bigger. Between the time of our earliest hominid ancestors and the first appearance of modern man, it quadrupled in mass.

This radical transformation happened even though having huge brains caused serious problems. Housing them required skulls so large that when they passed through a woman's pelvis during childbirth, they put the life of the mother and her baby in peril. They made our heads so heavy that humans were put at much greater risk of broken necks than chimpanzees and other primates. They sucked up one-fifth of the body's entire supply of energy. But as serious as these drawbacks were, they were outweighed by the advantages humans got from having an on-board supercomputer. And so big brains were selected and the species survived.

The transformation of the human brain into its modern form occurred entirely during the "Old Stone Age" – the Paleolithic era that lasted from roughly two million years ago until the introduction of agriculture some 12,000 years ago. Not that the advent of agriculture suddenly transformed how most people lived. It took thousands of years for the new way of life to spread and it was only 4,600 years ago that the first city – not much more than a town by modern standards – was founded.

If the history of our species were written in proportion to the amount of time we lived at each stage of development, 200 pages would be devoted to the lives of nomadic hunter-gatherers. One page would cover agrarian societies. The world of the last two centuries – the modern world – would get one short paragraph at the end.

Our brains were simply not shaped by life in the world as we know it now, or even the agrarian world that preceded it. They are exclusively the creation of the Old Stone Age. And since our brains really make us what we are, the conclusion to be drawn from this is unavoidable and a little unsettling. We are cavemen. Or cavepersons, if you prefer. Whatever the nomenclature, we sophisticated moderns living in a world of glass, steel, and fibre optics are no different, in a fundamental sense, than the prehistoric humans for whom campfires were the latest in high tech and bison hides were haute couture.

This is the central insight of evolutionary psychology – a field that came into prominence only in the last 30 years, although Darwin himself saw the implications of evolution for the study of human thoughts and actions. Our minds evolved to cope with what evolutionary psychologists call the "Environment of Evolutionary Adaptation." If we wish to understand the workings of the mind today, we have to first examine the lives of ancient humans on the savannas of Africa.

Of course, the full truth is a little more complicated than this. For one thing, the brain that our oldest human ancestors had was a hand–me–down from earlier species. Human experience later rewired some of what was inherited and added greatly to it, but much of that original, prehuman brain remained. It's still there today, in the amygdala and other structures of what is sometimes called the reptilian brain, or even less elegantly, the lizard brain.

It's also true that not all of the Paleolithic history of ancient humans was spent hunting gazelles and dodging lions on the golden plains of Africa. Our ancestors were wanderers who moved from one strange land to another. So there wasn't one "Environment of Evolutionary Adaptation." There were many. And that meant humans and their giant brains had to learn and adapt. Flexibility became a quintessential human trait: The same brain that figured out how to chip flint into an arrowhead also learned how to keep warm in cold climates by stripping other animals of their hides and how to ensure a supply of breathable oxygen on the moon.

And yet for all the variability in the ancient environments that shaped the human brain, there were constants. We hunted and gathered. We lived in small bands. We mated and raised children. These are the universals that shaped the brain's developments.

The rather uncomfortable feeling most of us have when we're around snakes is evidence of how this ancient experience continues to influence us today. Throughout the long prehistory of our species and those that preceded it, snakes were a mortal threat. And so we learned our lesson: Beware snakes. Or, to be more precise, some of us learned that lesson. Others didn't, but they had a nasty habit of dying. So natural selection did its work and the rule – beware snakes – was ultimately hard-wired into every human brain. It's universal. Go any-where on the planet, examine any culture. People are wary of snakes. Even if – as in the Arctic – there are no snakes. Our primate cousins shared our long experience and they feel the same way: Even monkeys raised in laboratories who have never seen a snake will back away at the sight of one.

Of course not everyone is wary of snakes, much less afraid of them, and some people like snakes enough to keep a 12-foot Burmese python in the basement. It's also possible to be terrified of much cud-dlier animals, even dogs, which our ancient ancestors created by selectively breeding wolves for the traits they desired. Psychologists describe the natural human wariness of snakes as merely an *inclina-tion* to be afraid of snakes. If a person has positive experiences with snakes early in life, the phobia will not develop. Negative experiences will easily bring it out. People can also learn to be afraid of dogs, but those fears are not promoted by ancient hard-wiring. The difference in the two fears is revealed when psychologists attempt to treat phobias with "positive conditioning" (bringing the patient together with the feared animal in a safe and pleasant environment). Dog phobias typically disappear quickly. But snake phobias are often impossible to erase – thanks to lessons learned hundreds of thou-sands of years ago.

Our troubled relationship with snakes is an obvious example of how the environment of our ancient ancestors shaped the brain that is reading this sentence. It's also a fairly trivial one. More profound examples of ancient hard-wiring are not so easy to spot but, in many cases, they are also vastly more important to the operations of the brain.

One bit of very old wiring is sometimes called the Law of Similarity. In the late 19th century, anthropologists noticed that traditional cultures assumed that causes resembled their effects. The Zande people of Africa, for example, believed that ringworm was caused by fowl excrement because fowl excrement looks like ringworm. In European folk medicine, foxes were felt to have great stamina and so their lungs were used to treat asthma, while Chinese folk medicine treated eyesight ailments with ground-up bat eyes because it was (quite wrongly) believed that bats had superior eyesight. The fact that this same assumption – like causes like – could be found in culture after culture, all over the world, is a very strong indication that it has biological origins.

The Law of Similarity comes in an even more basic form: Appearance equals reality. If it looks like a lion, it is a lion. Or, to put it in the modern vernacular, if it walks like a duck and quacks like a duck, it's a duck. That may seem more like common sense than ancient wiring, but it is quite ancient. And it's not always so sensible.

Psychologists found that when they asked students to eat a piece of fudge shaped like dog feces, the students were – shall we say – reluctant. The students knew the fudge was fudge. But it looked like dog feces and that triggered a feeling of disgust – another bit of ancient hard-wiring – that they couldn't shake. The researchers got the same results when they asked people to put a piece of rubber shaped and coloured like vomit in their mouths. And when they asked students to choose an empty container, fill it with sugar, and label it "Sodium Cyanide, Poison," the students shrank from consuming the sugar. "In these studies," wrote psychologists Paul Rozin and Carol Nemeroff, "subjects realized that their negative feelings were unfounded, but they felt and acknowledged them anyway."

The appearance–equals–reality rule often surfaces in magical beliefs. Want to hurt someone? In voodoo, you torment a doll that looks like the target. The same connection was made when isolated tribes first encountered photographs and were terrified: These images were duplicates of the people they depicted, and that must mean cameras steal the spirit of the person being photographed.

Of course, I know that a photo of my children is not my children. On one level, that's easy to understand. I said so over and over as I stumbled around an African slum looking for that picture of my kids. But my inner caveman couldn't grasp this. For millions of years, he and his ancestors followed the appearance–equals–reality rule. If it looks like a deer, it is a deer: There's your lunch. If it looks like a lion, it is a lion: Run, or you will be lunch. That rule worked well. It worked so well it was wired into every human brain, where it remains to this day.

But the appearance–equals–reality rule clearly leads to the conclusion that a photograph of my children *is* my children. This is why my inner caveman panicked. I've lost my children! I can't abandon my children! And so off I went in a place where I stood a good chance of being robbed or killed or both, in search of a worthless scrap of chemical–covered paper.

This seems absurd only from the perspective of a modern human. For Paleolithic man, the appearance–equals–reality rule was useful and reliable. He could be quite confident that if he saw something that looked like his children, it was his children. Only when the environment changed as a result of the invention of photography would humans see images that looked like their children but were not their children – and that happened only 180 years ago.

Of course, our world is awash in photographic images that, presumably, could trigger ancient wiring and confuse our sense of reality. And yet that's not happening. A photo is not the thing it depicts. Most people don't have to think hard to get that. The reader may understandably conclude that it is only the author who's got faulty wiring, not the species.

Not so. To understand why, we must return to the two systems of thought introduced earlier.

System One is the more ancient. It is intuitive, quick, and emotional. System Two is calculating, slow, and rational. I'll call the two systems Gut and Head, because that's how we usually talk about them. "I have a gut feeling," someone may say when she has a vague sense that something is true for reasons she cannot quite explain. "Use your head," her friend may respond – meaning, that can't be true so stop and think carefully. (Bear in mind, however, that this is only a metaphor. Poets may say feelings come from the heart or the stomach but in reality the brain alone generates all thoughts and feelings.)

System Two, or Head, is conscious thought. When we examine the statistics and decide that the odds of being killed in a terrorist attack are far too small to worry about, Head is doing the work. Head is our best bet for accurate results but it has limitations. First, Head needs to be educated. We live in a world of complex information, and if Head doesn't learn the basics of math, stats, and logic – if it doesn't know the difference between an increase of 5 per cent and an increase of 5 percentage points, or that correlation does not prove causation – it can make bad mistakes. Head also works very slowly. That may not be a problem when you are reading the newspaper at the breakfast table, but it's a little troublesome when you see a shadow move in long grass and you have to decide what to do without consulting an encyclopedia to determine the prevalence and hunting habits of lions.

System One, or Gut, is unconscious thought, and its defining quality is speed. Gut doesn't need an encyclopedia to figure out what to do when something moves in the long grass. It makes a snap judgment and sounds the alarm instantly. There's a twinge in your stomach. Your heart beats a little faster. Your eyes zero in.

"The heart has its reasons," Blaise Pascal wrote more than three centuries ago, "which reason knows nothing of." So it is with the conscious and unconscious minds. Head cannot look into Gut and so it has no idea how Gut assembles its judgments, which is why psychologists believe that focus groups are far less insightful than some marketers think. If you put people together in a room, show them a car commercial, and ask them how they feel about the car, you will get clear answers. "I don't care for it," a man may say. Fine. Why not? He frowns. "Um, the styling on the front is ugly. And I want a more powerful engine." That looks like good insight, just the sort of thing a company can use to design and market its products. But it's not. This man's snap judgment – "I don't like that car" – came from Gut. But the interviewer is talking to Head. And Head doesn't have a clue why Gut doesn't like the car. So Head rationalizes. It looks at the conclusion and cobbles together an explanation that is both plausible and, quite possibly, wrong.

So we have, in effect, two minds working semi-independently of each other. Further complicating our thoughts is the constant, complex interaction between the two. It's possible, for example, that knowledge learned and used consciously by Head can sink into the unconscious mind, to be used by Gut. Every veteran golfer has experienced this process. When you first pick up a club, you consciously follow instructions. Keep head back, knees bent, right arm straight. Beginners think about each of these points consciously and carefully. They can't just step up to the tee and swing. But do this often and long enough, and you no longer have to think about it. Proper form just feels right and it happens much more quickly and fluidly. In fact, once it has been internalized, consciously thinking about what you're doing can interrupt the flow and hurt performance – which is why professional athletes are taught by sports psychologists to avoid thinking about the motions they have done thousands of times before.

Even the most cerebral actions can undergo this shift from Head to Gut. Neophyte doctors faced with a common ailment consciously and carefully think about the checklist of symptoms before making a diagnosis, but old hands "feel" the answer in an instant. Art historians whose job is to authenticate antiquities make the same transition.

In the now-famous anecdote that opens Malcolm Gladwell's book *Blink*, a Greek statue that had supposedly been authenticated by a battery of scientific tests was nonetheless instantly dismissed as a fraud by several art historians. Why? The experts couldn't say. They just *felt* that something was wrong – one called it "intuitive repulsion." Testing later confirmed the statue was indeed a fraud, a truth the experts were able to feel in an instant because they had studied and analyzed Greek statues for so long that their knowledge and skills had been absorbed into the unconscious operations of Gut.

Figuring out how those unconscious operations work is the job of cognitive psychologists. Over the last several decades, they've made enormous advances and learned many things that will forever change the way we think about thinking.

Heuristics and biases is the rather opaque name for one of the most exciting efforts to tease out the secrets of thinking. In this case, "bias" isn't meant to be an insult. It's a tendency, nothing more. If you read a shopping list on which one of the items was written in green ink while all the rest are blue, you will tend to remember the one green item. That's the Von Restorff effect – a bias in favour of remembering the unusual. It's only one of a long list of biases uncovered by psychologists. Some – like the Von Restorff effect – are pretty obvious. Others are more surprising, as we will see.

As for "heuristics," they're rules of thumb. One we've already encountered is the appearance–equals–reality rule. If it looks like a lion, it is a lion. Nice and simple. Instead of getting bogged down in information, Gut uses just a few observations and a handy rule to instantly conclude that the large cat–like animal walking this way is indeed a lion and perhaps it would be best if you were to depart forthwith. That's the kind of quick thinking that can keep you alive. Unfortunately, the same rule can also lead to the conclusion that the snapshot in your wallet is much more than a mere piece of paper and must be found even if that means wandering around an African slum after midnight. That's the kind of thinking that can get you killed. So Gut is good, but not perfect.

Fortunately, Gut isn't the only one trying to make decisions and get us to act accordingly. There's also Head. It monitors Gut's decisions and it can at least try to adjust or overrule them when it thinks Gut is wrong. Gut decides, Head reviews: This process is how most of our thoughts and decisions are made. "One of psychology's fundamental insights," writes Harvard psychologist Daniel Gilbert, "is that judgments are generally the products of non-conscious systems that operate quickly, on the basis of scant evidence, and in a routine manner, and then pass their hurried approximations to consciousness, which slowly and deliberately adjusts them."

Standing on a wide plain and looking at a mountain in the distance – to use an illustration devised by Daniel Kahneman – you will have an intuitive sense of how far away the mountain is. Where did that intuition come from? What is it based on? You won't know. You probably won't even know that you have an intuition, at least you won't think about it that way. You'll just look at the mountain and you'll have a rough sense of how far away the mountain is. As long as you don't have other information that suggests the intuition is completely out of whack, you'll accept it as a good measure of reality and act on it.

Unknown to you, that estimate came from the unconscious operation of Gut. It used a simple rule of thumb to come up with it: Objects appear increasingly blurry the farther away they are, so if the mountain looks very blurry, it is very far away. It's a good rule that generally provides reliable information in an instant. If it weren't, natural selection wouldn't have hard-wired it into our brains.

And yet, it can go wrong. What if the day happens to be particularly hot and humid? That will make the air hazy and all objects will appear more blurred than they would on a clear day. To get an accurate estimate of the distance, we have to adjust for that. But Gut doesn't adjust. It just applies the rule of thumb. And in this case, that will result in an error. So Head has to step in and tweak Gut's estimate to account for the hazy air.

But will it? Unfortunately, there's a good chance it won't.

Consider the following question: A bat and a ball cost $1.10 in total. The bat costs $1 more than the ball. How much does the ball cost?

Almost everyone who reads this question will have an immediate impulse to answer "10 cents." It just looks and feels right. And yet it's wrong. In fact, it's *clearly* wrong – if you give it some careful thought – and yet it is perfectly normal to stumble on this test. "Almost everyone we ask reports an initial tendency to answer 'ten cents,'" write psychologists Daniel Kahneman and Shane Frederick. "Many people yield to this immediate impulse. The surprisingly high rate of errors in this easy problem illustrates how lightly System Two [Head] monitors the output of System One [Gut]: people are not accustomed to thinking hard, and are often content to trust a plausible judgment that quickly comes to mind."

Head can be amazingly lax. Psychologists have repeatedly shown, for example, that when people are asked about their own sense of well-being, the weather makes a major difference: Sunny skies push the reported sense of well-being up, while rain drives it down. That's Gut talking. Everyone knows weather affects mood. But there's obviously far more to the question of one's well-being than a temporary mood caused by foul or fair weather. Head should step in and adjust Gut's answer accordingly. And yet it often doesn't. Numerous studies have even found that the weather is strongly correlated with gains or losses in stock markets. It's ludicrous that sunshine should have any bearing on the financial calculations of Wall Street stockbrokers and yet it clearly does. Head is like a bright but lazy teenager: capable of great things if he would just get out of bed.

And that's how things work under normal conditions. Psychologists have demonstrated that when people are in a rush, Head's monitoring of Gut's judgments becomes even looser and more mistakes get through. "Morning people" are sloppier in the evening, while evening people are at their worst in the morning. Distraction and exhaustion also reduce Head's focus. So does stress. And it's pretty obvious what happens after drinking a beer or three.

Now, if you happen to be in a stressful spot like an African slum after midnight, exhausted from a long day of work, a little woozy from drinking a few pints of Guinness, and upset by the theft of your wallet and the pictures inside – well, Head really isn't going to be at his best.

Summarizing the relationship between Head and Gut, Daniel Kahneman wrote that they "compete for the control of overt responses." One might say – with a touch less precision but a little more colour – that each of us is a car racing along a freeway and inside each car is a caveman who wants to drive and a bright-but-lazy teenager who knows he should keep a hand on the wheel but that's kind of a hassle and he'd really rather listen to his iPod and stare out the window.

That night in Nigeria, the caveman drove while the teen curled up in the back seat and went to sleep. I was lucky to get out alive.

3

STONE AGE MEETS INFORMATION AGE

"**R**ecent figures suggest some 50,000 pedophiles are prowling the Internet at any one time," says the website of Innocents in Danger, a Swiss–based NGO. No source is cited for the claim, which appears under the headline "Some Terrifying Statistics."

It is indeed a terrifying statistic. It is also well–travelled. It has been sighted in Britain, Canada, the United States, and points beyond. Like a new strain of the flu virus, it has spread from newspaper articles to TV reports to public speakers, websites, blogs, and countless conversations of frightened parents. It even infected Alberto Gonzales, the former attorney general of the United States.

Unfortunately, the mere fact that a number has proliferated, even at the highest levels of officialdom, does not demonstrate the number is true. So what about this number? Is it credible?

There's one obvious reason to be at least a little suspicious. It's a round number. A very round number. It's not 47,000, or 53,500. It is 50,000. And 50,000 is just the sort of perfectly round number people pluck out of the air when they make a wild guess.

And what method aside from wild guessing could one use to come up with the number of pedophiles on-line? Accurate counts of ordinary Internet users are tough enough. But pedophiles? Much as one may wish they were all identified and registered with the authorities, they aren't, and they aren't likely to be completely frank about their inclinations when a telephone surveyor calls to ask about on-line sexual habits.

Another reason for caution is the way this alleged fact changes from one telling to another. In Britain's *Independent* newspaper, an article stated there are "as many as" 50,000 pedophiles on-line. Other sources says there are precisely 50,000. A few claim "at least" 50,000.

There's also variation in what those pedophiles are supposed to be up to. In some stories, the pedophiles are merely "on-line" and the reader is left to assume they are doing something other than getting the latest headlines or paying the water bill. Others say the pedophiles are "looking for children." In the most precise account, all 50,000 pedophiles are said to have "one goal in mind: to find a child, strike up a relationship and eventually meet with the child." This spectacular feat of mind-reading can be found on the website of Spectorsoft, a company that sells frightened parents software that monitors their children's on-line activities for the low cost of $99.95.

Then there's the supposed arena in which those 50,000 pedophiles are said to be operating. In some versions, it's 50,000 around the world, or on the whole of the Internet. But an American blogger narrowed that considerably: "50,000 pedophiles at any one time are on MySpace.com and other social networking sites looking for kids." And a story in the magazine *Dallas Child* quotes two parent-activists – identified as "California's Parents of the Year for 2001" – who say, "The Internet is a wonderful tool, but it can also be an evil one, especially sites like MySpace.com. At any one given time, 50,000 pedophiles are on the site."

All this should have our inner skeptic ringing alarm bells. But there is a final, critical question that has to be answered before we can dismiss this number as junk: What is its source?

In most of the number's appearances, no source is cited. The author simply uses the passive voice ("It is estimated that . . . ") to paper over this gaping hole. Another way to achieve the same effect – one used far too often in newspapers – is to simply quote an official who states the number as fact. The number then takes on the credibility of the official even though the reader still doesn't know the number's source. After an article in the *Ottawa Citizen* repeated the 50,000 pedophiles figure within a quotation from Ian Wilms, the president of the Canadian Association of Police Boards, I called Wilms and asked where he got the number. It came up in a conversation with British police, he said. And no, he couldn't be more precise.

Fortunately, there are several versions of the "50,000 pedophiles" story – including the article in *The Independent* – that do point to a source. They all say it comes from the Federal Bureau of Investigation. So I called the FBI. No, a spokesperson said, that's not our number. We have no idea where it came from. And no, she said, the bureau doesn't have its own estimate of the number of pedophiles on–line because that's impossible to figure out.

Skepticism is rarely enough to finish off a dubious but useful number, however. In April 2006, U.S. Attorney General Alberto Gonzales gave a speech to the National Center for Missing and Exploited Children in which he said, "It is simply astonishing how many predators there are. . . . At any given time, 50,000 predators are on the Internet prowling for children." The source of this figure, Gonzales said, was "the television program *Dateline.*"

The attorney general should listen to National Public Radio more often. When journalists from NPR asked *Dateline* to explain where they got this number, they were told by the show's Chris Hansen that they had interviewed an expert and asked him whether this number that "keeps surfacing" is accurate. The expert replied, as paraphrased by Hansen: "I've heard it, but depending on how you define what is a predator, it could actually be a very low estimate."

Dateline took this as confirmation that the number is accurate and repeated it as unqualified fact on three different shows.

The expert *Dateline* spoke to was FBI agent Ken Lanning. When NPR asked Lanning about the magic number, he said, "I didn't know where it came from. I couldn't confirm it, but I couldn't refute it, either, but I felt it was a fairly reasonable figure." Lanning also noted a curious coincidence: 50,000 has made appearances as a key number in at least two previous panics in recent years. In the early 1980s, it was supposed to be the number of children kidnapped by strangers every year. At the end of the decade, it was the number of murders committed by Satanic cults. These claims, widely reported and believed at the time, were later revealed to be nothing more than hysterical guesses that became "fact" in the retelling.

Now, it may be that, as Lanning thinks, the 50,000 figure is close to the reality. But it may also be way off the mark. There may be five million pedophiles on the Internet at any given moment, or 500, or five. Nobody really knows. This number is, at best, a guess made by persons unknown.

I've taken the time to give this figure a thorough dissection because – as we will see later in the book – unreliable statistics are all too common in public discourse. And the influence of those numbers is not limited to the gullible. In fact, psychologists have demonstrated that even the toughest skeptics will find it difficult, or even impossible, to keep bogus statistics from worming into their brains and influencing their judgments.

The problem, as usual, lies in the division between Head and Gut. It's Head that scoffs at the "50,000 pedophiles" figure. Gut isn't so sure.

To illustrate, I'll ask a question that may at first seem somewhat unrelated to the subject at hand: Was Gandhi older or younger than nine when he died? Of course, that's a silly question. The answer is obvious. It is also irrelevant. Completely irrelevant. Please forget I asked.

Let's move along to another question: How old was Gandhi when he died? Now if you actually know how old Gandhi was when he died, you are excused from this exercise. Go get a cup of tea and come back in a few paragraphs. This question is for those who are uncertain and have to guess.

I wish I could amaze and astound the reader by writing precisely what you have guessed. I cannot. I can, however, say with great confidence that your answer to the second question was powerfully influenced by the number nine.

I know this because the questions I've asked come from a study conducted by German psychologists Fritz Strack and Thomas Mussweiler. They asked people two versions of the Gandhi questions. One version is what I've repeated here. The other began by asking people whether Gandhi was older or younger than 140 when he died, which was followed by the same direction to guess Gandhi's age when he died. Strack and Mussweiler found that when the first question mentioned the number nine, the average guess on the following question was 50. In the second version, the average guess was 67. So those who heard the lower number before guessing guessed lower. Those who heard the higher number guessed higher.

Psychologists have conducted many different variations on this experiment. In one version, participants were first asked to construct a single number from their own phone numbers. They were then asked to guess the year in which Attila the Hun was defeated in Europe. In another study, participants were asked to spin a wheel of fortune in order to select a random number – and then they were asked to estimate the number of African nations represented in the United Nations. In every case, the results are the same: The number people hear prior to making a guess influences that guess. The fact that the number is unmistakably irrelevant doesn't matter. In some studies, researchers have even told people that the number they heard is irrelevant and specifically asked them not to let it influence their judgment. Still, it did.

What's happening here is that Gut is using something psychologists call the anchoring and adjustment heuristic, or what I'll call the Anchoring Rule. When we are uncertain about the correct answer and we make a guess, Gut grabs hold of the nearest number – which is the most recent number it heard. Head then adjusts but "adjustments tend to be insufficient," write psychologists Nicholas Epley and Thomas Gilovich, "leaving people's final estimates biased toward the initial anchor value."

In the Gandhi quiz, Head and Gut first hear the number nine. When the question of Gandhi's age at the time of his death follows, the answer isn't known. So Gut latches onto the nearest anchor – the number nine – and passes it along to Head. Head, meanwhile, may recall the image of Gandhi as a thin, hunched old man, and so it adjusts upward from nine to something that fits what it knows. In this case, that turns out to be 50, which is a long way from nine.

But that is still much lower than the average guess of those who were given 140 as the anchor. What's happening here, in other words, isn't mind control. It's more like mind *influence*. And Head has no idea it's happening: When psychologists ask people if the first number they hear influences their guess, the answer is always no.

The Anchoring Rule is rich with possibilities for manipulation. Retail sales are an obvious example. A grocery store that wants to sell a large shipment of tomato soup in a hurry can set up a prominent display and top it off with a sign that reads "Limit 12 per customer," or "Buy 18 for your cupboard." The message on the sign isn't important. Only the number is. When a customer is deciding how many cans to buy, Gut will use the Anchoring Rule: It will start at 18 or 12 and adjust downward, settling on a number that is higher than it would have been without the sign. When psychologists Brian Wansink, Robert Kent, and Stephen Hoch carried out several variations on this scenario in actual supermarkets, they got startling results. Without a sign limiting purchases to 12, almost half the shoppers bought only one or two cans of soup; with a limit of 12, most shoppers bought between four and ten cans, while not one shopper bought only one or two cans.

Or imagine you're a lawyer and your client is about to be sentenced by a judge who has discretion as to how long the sentence will be. The Anchoring Rule suggests one way to put a thumb on the scales of justice. In a 2006 study, Strack and Mussweiler brought together a group of experienced German judges and provided them with a written outline of a case in which a man had been convicted of rape. The outline detailed all the facts of the case, including the evidence that supported the conviction. After the judges read the outline, they were asked to imagine that while the court was in recess they got a phone call from a journalist who asked if the sentence would be higher or lower than three years. Of course, the researchers told the judges, you properly refuse to answer and return to the courtroom. Now . . . what sentence will you give in this case? The average was 33 months in prison. But unknown to this group of judges, another group was run through precisely the same scenario – except the number mentioned by the imaginary journalist was one year, not three. In that case, the average sentence imposed by the judges was 25 months.

The Anchoring Rule can also be used to skew public opinion surveys to suit one's purposes. Say you're the head of an environmental group and you want to show that the public supports spending a considerable amount of money cleaning up a lake. You do this by conducting a survey that begins with a question about whether the respondent would be willing to contribute some money – say $200 – to clean up the lake. Whether people say yes or no doesn't matter. You're only asking this question to get the figure $200 into people's heads. It's the next question that counts: You ask the respondent to estimate how much the average person would be willing to pay to clean up the lake. Thanks to the Anchoring Rule, you can be sure the respondent's Gut will start at $200 and adjust downward, arriving at a figure that will still be higher than it would have been if that figure hadn't been handed to Gut. In a study that did precisely this, psychologists Daniel Kahneman and Jack Knetsch found that the average guess about how much people would be willing to pay to clean up the lake was $36. But in a second trial, the $200 figure was replaced with $25. When people were then asked how much others would be willing to pay to clean up the lake, the average guess was a mere $14. Thus a high anchoring number produced an average answer almost 150 per cent greater than a low number.

By now, the value of the Anchoring Rule to someone marketing fear should be obvious. Imagine that you are, say, selling software that monitors computer usage. Your main market is employers trying to stop employees from surfing the Internet on company time. But then you hear a news story about pedophiles luring kids in chat rooms and you see that this scares the hell out of parents. So you do a quick Google search and you find the biggest, scariest statistic you can find – 50,000 pedophiles on the Internet at any given moment – and you put it in your marketing. Naturally, you don't question the accuracy of the number. That's not your business. You're selling software.

And you're probably going to sell a lot of it thanks to the determined efforts of many other people. After all, you're not the only one trying to alarm parents – or alert them, as some would prefer to say. There are the child-protection activists and NGOs, police officers, politicians, and journalists. They're all out there waving the same scary number – and others like it – because, just like you, that scary number advances their goals and they haven't bothered to find out if it is made of anything more than chewing gum and dark fantasy.

Intelligent parents may be suspicious, however. Whether they hear this number from you or some other interested party, they may think this is a scare tactic. They won't buy it.

But the delightful thing – delightful from your perspective – is that their doubt won't matter. On-line stalking does happen, after all. And even the skeptical parent who dismisses the 50,000 number will find herself thinking, well, what *is* the right answer? How many pedophiles are on the Internet? Almost instantly, she will have a plausible answer. That's Gut's work. And the basis for Gut's judgment was the Anchoring Rule: Start with the number heard most recently and adjust downward.

Downward to what? Let's say she cut the number pretty dramatically and settled on 10,000. Reason dictates that if the 50,000 figure is nonsense, then a number derived by arbitrarily adjusting that nonsense figure downward is nonsense squared. The 10,000 figure is totally meaningless and it should be dismissed.

The parent probably won't do that, however. To her, the 10,000 figure will *feel* right for reasons she wouldn't be able to explain if she were asked to. Not even her skepticism about corporate marketing and bad journalism will protect her because, in her mind, this number didn't come from marketers or journalists. It came from her. It's what she *feels* is true. And for a parent, the thought of 10,000 pedophiles hunting children on-line at each and every moment is pretty damned scary.

Congratulations. You have a new customer.

The Anchoring Rule, as influential as it is, is only a small part of a much wider scientific breakthrough with vast implications. As always in science, there are many authors and origins of this breakthrough. But two who stand out are psychologists Daniel Kahneman and Amos Tversky.

Four decades ago, Kahneman and Tversky collaborated on research that looked at how people form judgments when they're uncertain of the facts. That may sound like a modest little backwater of academic work, but it is actually one of the most basic aspects of how people think and act. For academics, it shapes the answers to core questions in fields as diverse as economics, law, health, and public policy. For everyone else, it's the stuff of daily life: what jobs we take; who we marry; where we live; whether we have children and how many. It's also crucial in determining how we perceive and respond to the endless list of threats – from choking on toast to the daily commute to terrorist attacks – that could kill us.

When Kahneman and Tversky began their work, the dominant model of how people make decisions was that of *Homo economicus*. "Economic man" is supremely rational. He examines evidence. He calculates what would best advance his interests as he understands them, and he acts accordingly. The *Homo economicus* model ruled economics departments and was hugely influential in public policy circles as well, in part because it suggested that influencing human behaviour was actually rather simple. To fight crime, for example, politicians need only make punishments tougher. When the potential costs of crime outweigh the potential benefits, would–be criminals would calculate that the crime no longer advanced their interests and so they would not commit it.

"For every problem there is a solution that is simple, clean and wrong," wrote H.L. Mencken, and the *Homo economicus* model is all that. Unlike *Homo economicus*, *Homo sapiens* is not perfectly rational. Proof of that lies not in the fact that humans occasionally make mistakes. The *Homo economicus* model allows for that. It's that in certain circumstances, people *always* make mistakes. We are systematically flawed. In 1957, Herbert Simon, a brilliant psychologist/economist/political scientist and future Nobel laureate, coined the term *bounded rationality*. We are rational, in other words, but only within limits.

Kahneman and Tversky set themselves the task of discovering those limits. In 1974, they gathered together several years' work and wrote a paper with the impressively dull title of "Judgment Under Uncertainty: Heuristics and Biases." They published it in *Science*, rather than a specialist journal, because they thought some of the insights might be interesting to non–psychologists. Their little paper caught the attention of philosophers and economists and a furious debate began. It lasted for decades but Kahneman and Tversky ultimately prevailed.

The idea of "bounded rationality" is now widely accepted and its insights are fuelling research throughout the social sciences. Even economists are increasingly accepting that *Homo sapiens* is not *Homo economicus*, and a dynamic new field called "behavioural economics" is devoted to bringing the insights of psychology to economics.

Amos Tversky died in 1996. In 2002, Daniel Kahneman experienced the academic equivalent of a conquering general's triumphal parade: He was awarded the Prize in Economic Sciences in Memory of Alfred Nobel. He is probably the only winner in the history of the prize who never took so much as a single class in economics.

The amazing thing is that the *Science* article, which sent shockwaves out in every direction, is such a modest thing on its face. Kahneman and Tversky didn't say anything about rationality. They didn't call *Homo economicus* a myth. All they did was lay out solid research that revealed some of the heuristics – the rules of thumb – Gut uses to make judgments such as guessing how old Gandhi was when he died or whether it's safe to drive to work. Today, Kahneman thinks that's one reason that the article was as influential as it was. There was no grand theorizing, only research so solid it would withstand countless challenges in the years ahead.

Like the paper itself, the three rules of thumb it revealed were admirably simple and clear. The first – the Anchoring Rule – we've already discussed. The second is what psychologists call the representativeness heuristic, which I'll call the Rule of Typical Things. And finally, there is the availability heuristic, or the Example Rule, which is by far the most important of the three in shaping our perceptions and reactions to risk.

The Rule of Typical Things

Linda is 31 years old, single, outspoken, and very bright. She majored in philosophy. As a student, she was deeply concerned with issues of discrimination and social justice, and also participated in anti-nuclear demonstrations.

How likely is it that Linda

- is a teacher in elementary school?
- works in a bookstore and takes yoga classes?
- is active in the feminist movement?
- is a psychiatric social worker?
- is a member of the League of Women Voters?
- is a bank teller?
- is an insurance salesperson?
- is a bank teller and is active in the feminist movement?

Now, please rank these descriptions from most to least likely.

This is one of the most famous quizzes in psychology. When Kahneman and Tversky wrote the profile of "Linda" almost 40 years ago, they intended to make it strongly match people's image of an active feminist (an image that likely stood out a little more strongly at the time). Some of the descriptions on the list seem bang on. A member of the League of Women Voters? Yes, that fits. So it's very likely true and it will certainly be at or near the top of the list. Active in the feminist movement? Absolutely. It will also rank highly. But an insurance salesperson? A bank teller? There's nothing in the profile of Linda that specifically suggests either of these is correct so people taking this quiz rank them at or near the bottom of the list.

That's simple enough, but what about the final description of Linda as a bank teller who is also active in the feminist movement? Almost everyone who takes this quiz feels that, yes, this seems at least somewhat likely – certainly more likely than Linda being an insurance salesperson or a bank teller. When Kahneman and Tversky gave this quiz to undergraduate students, 89 per cent decided it was more likely that Linda was a bank teller who is active in the feminist movement than that she is a bank teller alone.

But if you stop and think about it, that makes no sense. How can it be more likely that Linda is a bank teller *and* a feminist than that she is solely a bank teller? If it turns out to be true that she is a bank teller *and* a feminist, then she is bank teller – so the two descriptions have to be, at a minimum, equally likely. What's more, there is always the possibility that Linda is a bank teller but *not* a feminist. So it has to be true that it is more likely that she is a bank teller alone than that she is a bank teller *and* a feminist. It's simple logic – but very few people see it.

So Kahneman and Tversky stripped the quiz down and tried again. They had students read the same profile of Linda. But then they simply asked whether it is more likely that Linda is (a) a bank teller or (b) a bank teller who is active in the feminist movement?

Here, the logic is laid bare. Kahneman and Tversky were sure people would spot it and correct their intuition. But they were wrong. Almost exactly the same percentage of students – 85 per cent – said it is more likely that Linda is a bank teller and a feminist than a bank teller only.

Kahneman and Tversky also put both versions of the "Linda problem," as they called it, under the noses of experts trained in logic and statistics. When the experts answered the original question, with its long list of distracting details, they got it just as wrong as the under-graduates. But when they were given the two–line version, it was as if someone had elbowed them in the ribs. Head stepped in to correct Gut and the error rate plunged. When the scientist and essayist Stephen Jay Gould took the test, he realized what logic – his Head – told him was the right answer. But that didn't change what intuition – his Gut – insisted was true. "I know [the right answer]," he recounted, "yet a little homunculus in my head continues to jump up and down, shout-ing at me – 'but she can't just be a bank teller; read the description.'"

What's happening here is simple and powerful. One tool Gut uses to make judgments is the Rule of Typical Things. The typical summer day is hot and sunny, so how likely is a particular summer day to be hot and sunny? Very. That's a simple example based on a simple notion of what's "typical" but we are capable of forming very complex images of typicality – such as that of a "typical" feminist or a "typical" bank teller. We make these sorts of judgments all the time and we're scarcely aware of them for the good reason that they usually work, and that makes the Rule of Typical Things an effective way to simplify complex situations and come up with reliable snap judgments.

Or at least, it usually is. The Linda problem demonstrates one way the Rule of Typical Things can go wrong. When there's something "typical" involved, our intuition is triggered. It just feels right. And as always with intuitive feelings, we tend to go with them even when doing so flies in the face of logic and evidence. It's not just ordinary people who fall into this trap, incidentally. When Kahneman and Tversky asked a group of doctors to judge probabilities in a medical situation, the Rule of Typical Things kicked in and most of the doctors chose intuition over logic.

Another problem is that the Rule of Typical Things is only as good as our knowledge of what is "typical." One belief about typical- ity that is unfortunately common in Western countries, particularly the United States, involves black men: The typical black man is a criminal and the typical criminal is a black man. Some people believe this consciously. Others who consciously reject this stereotype nonetheless believe it unconsciously – as even many black men do. Imagine someone who believes this – consciously or not – walking down a city sidewalk. A black man approaches. Instantaneously, this person's Gut will use the Rule of Typical Things to conclude that there is a good chance this black man is a criminal. If Head does not inter- vene, the person will experience anxiety and consider crossing the street. But even if Head does put a stop to this nonsense, that nagging worry will remain – which may produce the uneasy body language black men so often encounter on sidewalks.

There's another big downside to the Rule of Typical Things, one that is particularly important to how we judge risks. In 1982, Kahneman and Tversky flew to Istanbul, Turkey, to attend the Second

International Congress on Forecasting. This was no ordinary gathering. The participants were all experts – from universities, governments, and corporations – whose job was assessing current trends and peering into the future. If anyone could be expected to judge the chances of things happening rationally, it was this bunch.

The psychologists gave a version of the "Linda problem" to two groups, totalling 115 experts. The first group was asked to evaluate the probability of "a complete suspension of diplomatic relations between the USA and the Soviet Union, sometime in 1983." The second group was asked how likely it was that there would be "a Russian invasion of Poland, and a complete suspension of diplomatic relations between the USA and Poland, sometime in 1983."

Logically, the first scenario *has* to be more likely than the second scenario. And yet the experts' ratings were exactly the opposite. Both scenarios were considered unlikely, but the suspension–following–invasion scenario was judged to be *three times* more likely than the suspension scenario. A Soviet invasion of Poland was "typical" Soviet behaviour. It fit, in the same way "active feminist" fit with Linda's profile. And that fit heavily influenced the experts' assessment of the whole scenario.

Many other studies produced similar results. Kahneman and Tversky divided 245 undergrads at the University of British Columbia in half and asked one group to estimate the probability of "a massive flood somewhere in North America in 1983, in which more than 1,000 people drown." The second group was asked about "an earthquake in California sometime in 1983, causing a flood in which more than 1,000 people drown." Once again, the second scenario logically has to be less likely than the first but people rated it one–third *more* likely than the first. Nothing says "California" quite like "earthquake."

As Kahneman and Tversky later wrote, the Rule of Typical Things "generally favors outcomes that make good stories or good hypotheses. The conjunction 'feminist bank teller' is a better hypothesis about

Linda than 'bank teller', and the scenario of a Russian invasion of Poland followed by a diplomatic crisis makes a better narrative than 'diplomatic crisis.'" Gut is a sucker for a good story.

To see the problem with this, open any newspaper. They're filled with experts telling stories about what will happen in future, and those stories have a terrible track record. *Brill's Content*, a sadly defunct magazine that covered the media, had a feature that tracked the accuracy of simple, one-off predictions ("Senator Smith will win the Democratic nomination") made by famous American pundits like George Will and Sam Donaldson. The magazine compared their results to those of a prognosticator by the name of "Chippy," a four-year-old chimpanzee who made predictions by choosing among flash cards. Chippy was good. While the average pundit got about 50 per cent of his or her predictions right – as good as a flipped coin – Chippy scored an impressive 58 per cent.

Of course, pundits don't limit their futurology to simple predictions. They often lay out elaborate scenarios explaining how Senator Smith will take the Democratic nomination and the presidential election that follows, or how unrest in Lebanon could produce a long chain reaction that will lead to war between Sunni and Shia across the Middle East, or how the Chinese refusal to devalue the currency could send one domino crashing into the next until housing prices collapse in the United States and the global economy tips into economic recession. Logically, for these predictions to come true, each and every link in the chain must happen – and given the pundits' dismal record with simple one-off predictions, the odds of that happening are probably lower than Chippy's chances of becoming president.

But Gut doesn't process this information logically. Guided by the Rule of Typical Things, it latches onto plausible details and uses them to judge the likelihood of the whole scenario coming true. As a result, Kahneman and Tversky wrote, "a detailed scenario consisting of causally linked and representative events may appear more probable than a subset of those events." Add details, pile up predictions, construct elaborate scenarios. Logic says the more you go in this direction, the less likely it is that your forecast will prove accurate. But for most people, Gut is far more persuasive than mere logic.

Kahneman and Tversky realized what this meant for expert predictions. "This effect contributes to the appeal of scenarios and the illusory insight that they often provide," they wrote. "A political analyst can improve scenarios by adding plausible causes and representative consequences. As Pooh-Bah in the *Mikado* explains, such additions provide 'corroborative details intended to give artistic verisimilitude to an otherwise bald and unconvincing narrative.'"

Does this matter? In most cases, no. Much of the pundits' futurology may be as inaccurate as the horoscopes that appear on a different page of the newspaper but it is no more important. Occasionally, though, what opinion leaders are saying about the future does matter – as it did in the months prior to the 2003 invasion of Iraq – and in those moments Gut's vulnerability to a well-told tale can have very serious consequences.

The Example Rule

When a roulette wheel spins and the ball drops, the outcome is entirely random. On any spin, the ball could land on any number, black or red. The odds never change.

Tectonic plates are not roulette wheels and earthquakes are not random events. Heat generated by the earth's core relentlessly pushes the plates at the surface. Grinding against each other, the motion of the plates is stopped by friction, so the pressure from below steadily grows until the plates shudder and lurch forward in the violent moment we experience as an earthquake. With the pressure released, the violence stops and the cycle begins again.

For those whose bedrooms are perched atop one of the unfortunate places where tectonic plates meet, these simple facts say something important about the risk they face. Most importantly, the risk varies. Unlike the roulette wheel, the chances of an earthquake happening are not the same at all times. They are lowest immediately after an earthquake has happened. They rise as time passes and the pressure builds. And while scientists may not be able to precisely predict when an earthquake is about to happen – not yet, anyway – they do have a pretty good ability to track the rising risk.

Knowing this, there should be an equally clear pattern in sales of earthquake insurance. Since the lowest risk is immediately after an earthquake, that's when sales should be lowest. As time passes, sales should rise. When scientists start warning about the Big One, sales should soar. But earthquake insurance sales actually follow exactly the opposite pattern. They are highest immediately after an earthquake and they fall steadily as time passes. Now, the first part of that is understandable. Experiencing an earthquake is a frightening way to be reminded that, yes, your house could be flattened. But it's strange that people let their insurance lapse as time passes. And it's downright bizarre that people don't rush to get insurance when scientists issue warnings.

At least, it makes no sense to Head. To Gut, it makes perfect sense. One of Gut's simplest rules of thumb is that the easier it is to recall examples of something, the more common that something must be. This is the "availability heuristic," which I'll call the Example Rule.

Kahneman and Tversky demonstrated the influence of the Example Rule in a typically elegant way. First, they asked a group of students to list as many words as they could think of that fit the form _ _ _ _ _ n _. The students had 60 seconds to work on the problem. The average number of words they came up with was 2.9. Then another group of students was asked to do the same, with the same time limit, for words that fit the form _ _ _ _ ing. This time, the average number of words was 6.4.

Look carefully and it's obvious there's something strange here. The first form is just like the second, except the letters "i" and "g" have been dropped. That means any word that fits the second form must fit the first. Therefore, the first form is actually more common. But the second form is much more easily recalled.

Armed with this information, Kahneman and Tversky asked another group of students to think of four pages in a novel. There are about 2,000 words on those four pages, they told students. "How many words would you expect to find that have the form _ _ _ _ ing?" The average estimate was 13.4 words. They then asked another group of students the same question for the form _ _ _ _ _ n _. The average guess was 4.7 words.

This experiment has been repeated in many different forms and the results are always the same: The more easily people are able to think of examples of something, the more common they judge that thing to be.

Note that it is not the examples themselves that influence Gut's intuitive judgment. It is not even the *number* of examples that are recalled. It is how *easily* examples come to mind. In a revealing study, psychologists Alexander Rothman and Norbert Schwarz asked people to list either three or eight behaviours they personally engage in that could increase their chance of getting heart disease. Strangely, those who thought of three risk–boosting behaviours rated their chance of getting heart disease to be *higher* than those who thought of eight. Logically, it should be the other way around – the longer the list, the greater the risk. So what gives? The explanation lies in the fact – which Rothman and Schwarz knew from earlier testing – that most people find it easy to think of three factors that increase the risk of heart disease but hard to come up with eight. And it is the ease of recall, not the substance of what is recalled, that guides the intuition.

The Rothman and Schwarz study also demonstrated how complex and subtle the interaction of Head and Gut can be. The researchers divided people into two groups: those who had a family history of heart disease and those who didn't. For those who did not have a family history, the results were as outlined above. But those who did have a family history of heart disease got precisely the *opposite* results: Those who struggled to come up with eight risk-boosting behaviours they engage in rated their chance of getting heart disease to be higher than those who thought of three examples. Why the different result? People with no family history of heart disease have no particular cause for worry and nothing to base their judgment on, so they are more casual in their judgment and they go with the estimate that Gut comes up with using the Example Rule. But people with a family history of heart disease have a very compelling reason to think hard about this, and when they do Head tells them that Gut is wrong – that, logically, if you engage in eight risk-boosting behaviours, your risk is higher than if you engage in three such behaviours. A similar study by different researchers – this time quizzing women about the risk of sexual assault – got similar results: Those who did not think the risk was personally relevant went with Gut's estimate based on the Example Rule, while those who did corrected their intuition and drew a more logical conclusion.

As a rule of thumb for hunter-gatherers walking the African savannah, the Example Rule makes good sense. That's because the brain culls low-priority memories: time passes and if a memory isn't used, it is likely to fade. So if you have to think hard to remember that, yes, there was a time when someone got sick after drinking from that pond, chances are it happened quite a while ago and a similar incident hasn't happened since – making it reasonable to conclude that the water in the pond is safe to drink. But if you instantly recall an example of someone drinking that water and turning green, then it likely happened recently and you should find somewhere else to get a drink. This is how Gut makes use of experience and memory.

The Example Rule is particularly good for learning from the very worst sort of experiences. A snake coils and hisses inches from your hiking boot. An approaching truck slips onto the shoulder of the highway then weaves into your lane. A man presses a knife to your throat and tells you not to resist. In each case, the amygdala, a lump of brain shaped like an almond, will trigger the release of hormones, including adrenaline and cortisol. Your pupils dilate, your heart races, your muscles tense. This is the famous flight-or-fight response. It is intended to generate a quick reaction to immediate threats but it also contains one element intended to have a lasting effect: The hormones the amygdala triggers temporarily enhance memory function so the awful experience that triggered the response will be vividly encoded and remembered. Such traumatic memories last, and they are potent. Long after calm has returned, even years later in some cases, they are likely to be recalled with terrifying ease. And that fact alone will cause Gut to press the alarm that we experience as an uneasy sense of threat.

Even in circumstances much less dramatic than those that trigger the fight-or-flight response, the amygdala plays a key role. Neuro-scientists have found that the amygdalas of people sitting in a quiet, safe university laboratory will suddenly spark to life when frighten-ing or threatening images are shown. The level of activity corresponds with the level of recall people have later. As psychologist Daniel Schacter recounts in his book *The Seven Sins of Memory*, people who are shown a sequence of slides ranging from the ordinary – a mother walking her child to school – to the dreadful – the child is hit by a car – will remember the negative images far more readily than the others.

An image doesn't have to be as awful as a car hitting a child to have this effect, however. A face with a fearful expression will do. Neuroscientist Paul Whelan even found that flashing an image of a fearful face for such a short time that people aren't consciously aware that the face is fearful – they report that it looks expressionless – will trigger the amygdala. And that makes the memory more vivid, lasting, and recallable.

Fear is certainly the most effective way of gluing a memory in place, but there are others. Any emotional content makes a memory stickier. Concrete words – apple, car, gun – do better in our memories than abstractions like numbers. Human faces are particularly apt to stick in our minds, at least if they're expressing emotions, because scientists have found such images stir the amygdala just as frighten-ing images do. And all these effects are cumulative. Thus, a visually striking, emotion-drenched image – particularly one featuring a dis-traught person's face – is almost certain to cut through the whirl of sensations we experience every moment, grab our full attention, and burrow deep into our memories. A fallen child clutching her knee and heaving agonized sobs may just be a stranger on the sidewalk but I will see her and remember, at least for a while – unlike the boring conversation about taxes I had at that dinner party with a man whose name I forgot almost the moment I heard it.

Novelty also helps in getting something into memory. Psycholo-gists have found that people can usually give a detailed accounting of what happened at work the day before. But one week later most of the details are gone and in its place is an account of what happens on a typical workday. People guess, in other words. The problem here is what Daniel Schacter calls "interference." What you did Monday is similar to what you did on Tuesday and the other work days and so when you try to recall what you did on Monday a week later, expe-riences from the other work days interfere. But if Monday had been your last day of work before going on vacation, you would have much better recall of that day a week later because it would be more unusual.

Concentration and repetition also boost memory. If you see something – anything – and don't give it a second thought, there's a good chance it will never encode in memory and will vanish from your consciousness as if it had never happened. But if you stop and think about it, you make the memory a little stronger, a little more lasting. Do it repeatedly and it gets stronger still. Students do this when they cram for exams but the process can be much more infor-mal: Even a casual conversation at the water cooler will have the same effect because it, too, calls the memory back into consciousness.

There is obvious survival value in remembering personal experi-ences of risk. But even more valuable for our ancient ancestors – and us, too – is the ability to learn and remember from the experiences of others. After all, there's only one of you. But when you sit around the campfire after a long day of foraging, there may be 20 or 30 other people. If you can gather their experiences, you will multiply the information on which your judgments are based by 20 or 30 times.

Sharing experiences means telling stories. It also means visualizing the event the guy next to you at the campfire is telling you about: imagining the dimmest member of the tribe wading into the shallow waters of the river; imagining him poking a floating log with his walking stick; imagining the log suddenly turning into a crocodile; imagining the trail of bubbles that marks the demise of the tribe's dimmest member. Having envisioned the scene and committed it to memory, Gut can then use it to make judgments just as it uses memories from personal experiences. Risk of crocodile attack at water's edge? Yes. You can recall just such an incident. Chance that the log floating out there isn't what it appears? Considerable – that incident was easily recalled. You may not be consciously aware of any of this analysis, but you will be aware of the conclusion: You will have a feeling – a sense, a hunch – that you really shouldn't go any closer. Gut has learned from someone else's tragic experience.

But not all imagined scenes are equal. An event that comes from a story told by the person who actually experienced it provides valuable, real-world experience. But an imagined scene that was invented by the storyteller is something else entirely. It's fiction. Gut should treat it accordingly, but it does not.

One of the earliest experiments examining the power of imagination to sway intuition was conducted during the U.S. presidential election campaign of 1976. One group was asked to imagine Gerald Ford winning the election and taking the oath of office, and then they were asked how likely it was that Ford would win the election. Another group was asked to do the same for Jimmy Carter. So who was more likely to win? Most people in the group that imagined Ford winning said Ford. Those who saw Jimmy Carter taking the oath said

Carter. Later experiments have obtained similar results. What are your odds of being arrested? How likely is it you'll win the lottery? People who imagine the event consistently feel the odds of the event actually happening are higher than those who don't.

In a more sophisticated version of these studies, psychologists Steven Sherman, Robert Cialdini, Donna Schwartzman, and Kim Reynolds told 120 students of Arizona State University that a new disease was increasingly prevalent on campus. The students were split into four groups. The first group was asked to read a description of the symptoms of the new disease: low energy level, muscle aches, headaches. The second group was also asked to read the symptoms but this time the symptoms were harder to imagine: a vague sense of disorientation, a malfunctioning nervous system, and an inflamed liver. The third group was given the easily imaginable list of symptoms and asked to imagine in great detail that they had the disease and were experiencing the symptoms. The fourth group received the hard-to-imagine symptoms and was asked to imagine they had the disease. Finally, all four groups were asked to answer a simple question: "How likely is it that you would contract" the disease in future?

As expected, the students who got the easy-to-imagine symptoms and who imagined themselves contracting the disease rated the risk highest. Next came the two groups who did not do the imagining exercise. The lowest risk estimate came from those who got the hard-to-imagine symptoms and did the imagining exercise. This proved something important about imagining: It's not merely the act of imagining that raises Gut's estimate of how likely something is, it's how *easy* it is to imagine that thing. If imagining is easy, Gut's estimate goes up. But if it is a struggle to imagine, it will feel less likely for that reason alone.

It may be a little surprising to think that the act of imagining can so powerfully influence our thoughts, but in many different settings – from therapy to professional sports – imagining is used as a practical tool whose effectiveness is just as real as the famous placebo effect.

Imagination is powerful. When the ads of lottery corporations and casinos invite us to imagine winning – one lottery's slogan is "Just imagine" – they do more than invite us to daydream. They ask us to do something that elevates our intuitive sense of how likely we are to win the jackpot – which is a very good way to convince us to gamble. There is no "just" in imagining.

This isn't the only potential problem with Gut's use of the Example Rule. There's also the issue of memory's reliability.

Most people think memory is like a camera that captures images and stores them for future retrieval. Sure, sometimes the camera misses a shot. And sometimes it's hard to find an old photo. But otherwise, memory is a shoebox full of photos that directly and reliably reflect reality.

Unfortunately, this isn't even close to true. Memory is better described as an organic process. Memories routinely fade, vanish, or transform – sometimes dramatically. Even the strongest memories – those formed when our attention is riveted and emotions are pumping – are subject to change. A common experiment memory researchers conduct is tied to major news, such as the September 11 terrorist attacks. In the days immediately following these spectacular events, students are asked to write how they heard about it: where they were, what they were doing, the source of the news, and so on. Years later, the same students are asked to repeat the exercise and the two answers are compared. They routinely fail to match. Often the changes are small, but sometimes the entire setting and the people involved are different. When the students are shown their original descriptions and are told that their memories have changed, they often insist their current memory is accurate and the earlier account is flawed – another example of our tendency to go with what the unconscious mind tells us, even when doing so is blatantly unreasonable.

The mind can even fabricate memories. On several occasions, Ronald Reagan recalled wartime experiences that were later traced to Hollywood movies. These were apparently honest mistakes. Reagan's

memory simply took certain images from films he had seen and converted them into personal memories. Reagan's mistake was caught
because, as president, his comments were subjected to intense
scrutiny, but this sort of invention is far more common than we
realize. In one series of experiments, researchers invented scenarios
such as being lost in a shopping mall or staying overnight in a hospital with an ear infection. They then asked volunteers to imagine the
event for a few days or to write down how they imagine it played out.
Then, days later, the researchers interviewed the subjects and discovered that between 20 and 40 per cent believed the imagined scenarios
had actually happened.

A more basic problem with the Example Rule is that it is biased,
thanks to the way our memories work. Recent, emotional, vivid, or
novel events are all more likely to be remembered than others. In
most cases, that's fine because it's precisely those sorts of events that
we actually need to remember.

But the bias in our memory will be reflected in Gut's judgments
using the Example Rule – which explains the paradox of people
buying earthquake insurance when the odds of an earthquake are
lowest and dropping it as the risk rises. If an earthquake recently
shook my city, that memory will be fresh, vivid, and frightening. Gut
will shout: Be afraid! Buy insurance! But if I've been living in this
place for decades and there has never been an earthquake, Gut will
only shrug. Not even scientists issuing warnings will rouse Gut
because it doesn't know anything about science. It only knows what
the Example Rule says and the Example Rule says don't worry about
earthquakes if you have to struggle to remember one happening.

"Men on flood plains appear to be very much prisoners of their
experience," researcher Robert Kates wrote in 1962, bemoaning the fact
that people erect buildings despite being told that a flood must
inevitably come. We saw the same dynamic at work following the
terrible tsunami that swept across the Indian Ocean on December 26,
2004. Afterward, we learned that experts had complained about the

lack of a warning system. It didn't cost much, the experts had argued, and a tsunami was bound to come. It was a pretty esoteric subject, however, and no one was interested. Many people had never even heard the word *tsunami* until the day 230,000 lives were taken by one. And when that happened, the whole world started talking about tsunamis. Why was there no warning system in place? Could it happen here? Is our warning system good enough? It was the hot topic for a month or two. But time passed and there were no more tsunamis. Memories faded and so did the concern. For now, at least. A team of scientists has warned that one of the Canary Islands off the coast of Africa is fractured and a big chunk of the island will, some day, crash into the ocean – causing a mammoth tsunami to race across the Atlantic and ravage the coast from Brazil to Canada. Other scientists dispute these findings but we can safely assume that, should this occur, interest in this esoteric subject would revive rather abruptly.

Experience is a valuable thing and Gut is right to base intuitions on it, but experience and intuition aren't enough. "Experience keeps a dear school," Benjamin Franklin wrote, "but fools will learn in no other."

Franklin wrote those words in the mid–18th century. From the perspective of a human living in the early 21st century, that's a very long time ago but in evolutionary terms it might as well have been this morning. The brain inside Franklin's head was particularly brilliant but it was still, in its essentials, no different than yours or mine or that of the person who first put seeds in the ground 12,000 years ago – or that of the human who first daubed some paint on a cave wall 40,000 years ago.

As we have seen, the world inhabited by humans changed very little over most of that sweep of time. And then it changed almost beyond description. The first city, Ur, was founded only 4,600 years ago and it never got bigger than 65,000 people. Today, half of all humans live in cities – more than 80 per cent in some developed countries.

Even more sweeping than the transformation of the physical environment is the change in how we communicate. The first crude writing – with symbols scratched into soft clay – appeared about 5,000 years ago. Gutenberg invented modern printing a mere five and a half centuries ago and it was at this stage that Ben Franklin published his witticism about the limits of experience.

The first photograph was taken 180 years ago. Radio appeared a century ago, television 30 years later. It was only 48 years ago that the first satellite message was relayed – a Christmas greeting from U.S. President Eisenhower.

Then came cable television, fax, VCR, e-mail, cellphones, home video, digital, 24-hour cable news, and satellite radio. Less than 20 years ago, the rare journalist who knew of the Internet's existence and wrote about it would put quotation marks around the word and carefully explain the nature of this unfathomable contraption. Today, it is embedded in the daily lives of hundreds of millions of people and occasionally touches the lives of billions more. Google, iPod, Wikipedia, YouTube, Facebook, MySpace: All these words represent globe-spanning information channels with immense and unfolding potential to change societies and yet, as I write this sentence, only one – Google – has even existed for ten years.

When Saddam Hussein was executed at the end of 2006, official video was released by the Iraqi government. It appeared on television and the Internet minutes later. At the same time, another video clip appeared. Someone had smuggled a cellphone into the execution and recorded the entire hanging, including the taunts of guards and witnesses and the actual moment of execution that had been omitted from the official version. From phone to phone the video spread, and then to the Internet, putting uncensored images of a tightly guarded event in bedrooms, offices, and cafés in every country on earth.

But the really astonishing thing about that incident is that people didn't find it astonishing. During the Vietnam War, television news reports were filmed, put in a can, driven to an airport, and flown out to be shown days after they were shot – and they provided a startling immediacy unlike anything previously experienced. But when the tsunami of 2004 crashed into the coast of Thailand, tourists e-mailed video clips as soon as they got to high ground – accomplishing instantly and freely what sophisticated television networks could not have done with unlimited time and money just 30 years before. In 2005, when Londoners trapped in the wreckage of trains bombed by terrorists used cellphone cameras to show the world what they saw almost at the moment they saw it, the talk was almost exclusively of the content of the images, not their delivery. It was simply expected that personal experience would be captured and instantaneously distributed worldwide. In less than three human lifespans, we went from a world in which a single expensive, blurry, black–and–white photograph astonished people to one in which cheap colour video made instantly available all over the planet does not.

For the advance of humanity, this is a wondrous thing. For the promise it offers each individual to learn and grow, it is magnificent. And yet.

And yet the humans living amid this deluge of information have brains that believe, somewhere in their deepest recesses, that an image of our children *is* our children, that a piece of fudge shaped like dog poo is dog poo, and that a daydream about winning the lottery makes it more likely we will win the lottery.

We have brains that, in line with the Anchoring Rule, use the first available number as the basis for making an estimate about something that has absolutely nothing to do with the number. This is not helpful at a time when we are pelted with numbers like raindrops in a monsoon.

We have brains that defy logic by using the Rule of Typical Things to conclude that elaborate predictions of the future are more likely to come true than simple predictions. At a time when we are constantly warned about frightening future developments, this, too, is not helpful.

Most importantly, we have brains that use the Example Rule to conclude that being able to easily recall examples of something happening proves that it is likely to happen again. For ancient hunters stalking wildebeest on the savanna, that wasn't a bad rule. In an era when tourists can e-mail video of a tsunami to the entire planet in less time than it takes the wreckage to dry, it has the potential to drive us mad. Should we fear exotic viruses? Terrorists? Pedophiles stalking kids on the Internet? Any of the other items on the long and growing list of worries that consume us? The population of humans on the planet is approaching seven billion. On any given day, by sheer force of numbers, there's a good chance that some or all of these risks will result in people being hurt or killed. Occasionally, there will be particularly horrible incidents in which many people will die. And thanks to the torrent of instantaneous communications, we will all know about it. So, should we fear these things? Inevitably, Gut will attempt to answer that question using the Example Rule. The answer will be clear: Yes. Be afraid.

One of the most consistent findings of risk perception research is that we overestimate the likelihood of being killed by the things that make the evening news and underestimate those that don't. What makes the evening news? The rare, vivid, and catastrophic killers. Murder, terrorism, fire, and flood. What doesn't make the news is the routine cause of death that kills one person at a time and doesn't lend itself to strong emotions and pictures. Diabetes, asthma, heart disease. In American surveys conducted in the late 1970s by Paul Slovic and Sarah Lichtenstein, the gaps between perception and reality were often stunning. Most people said accidents and disease kill about equally – although disease actually inflicts about 17 times more deaths than accidents. People also estimated that car crashes kill 350 times more people than diabetes. In fact, crashes kill only 1.5 times as many. How could the results be otherwise? We see flaming wrecks every day on the news but only family and friends will hear of a life lost to diabetes.

Considerable research has tied skewed risk perception to skewed coverage in the news but information and images pour out of more sources than newspapers, magazines, and suppertime broadcasts. There are also movies and television dramas. These are explicitly designed to be emotional, vivid, and memorable. And risk is a vital component of countless dramas – prime-time television would be dead air if cop shows and medical dramas disappeared. Based on what psychologists have learned about the Example Rule, they should have just as powerful an effect on our judgments about risk as the news does. They may even have greater impact. After all, we see movies and TV dramas as nothing more than entertainment, so we approach them with lowered critical faculties: Gut watches while Head sleeps.

Unfortunately, almost no research has examined how fiction affects risk perception. One recent study, however, found just what psychologists would expect. Anthony Leiserowitz of Decision Research (a private research institute founded by Paul Slovic, Sarah Lichtenstein, and Baruch Fischhoff) conducted cross-country surveys in the United States before and after the release of *The Day After Tomorrow*, a disaster film depicting a series of sudden, spectacular catastrophes unleashed by global warming. The science in *The Day After Tomorrow* is dubious, to say the least. Not even the most frightening warnings about the effects of global warming come close to what the movie depicts. But that made no difference to the influence of the film. Across the board, more people who saw the film said they were concerned about global warming, and when they were asked how likely it was that the United States would experience various disasters similar to those depicted in the movie – flooded cities, food shortages, Gulf Stream shutdown, a new Ice Age, etc. – people who had seen the movie consistently rated these events more likely than those who didn't. The effects remained even after the numbers were adjusted to account for the political leanings of respondents.

Of course, Head can always step in, look at the evidence and overrule. As we have seen, it routinely does not. But even if it did, it could only modify or overrule Gut's judgment, not erase it. Head can't wipe out intuition. It can't change how we *feel*.

Most sociologists trace the beginning of Western countries' obsession with risk and safety to the 1970s. That was also when the near-exponential growth in media began and the information flood-waters started to rise. Of course, the fact that these two, profound shifts started together does not prove they are connected, but it certainly is grounds for suspicion and further investigation.

4

NOTHING MORE THAN FEELINGS

t is remarkable how many horrible ways we could die. Try making a list. Start with the standards like household accidents and killer diseases. After that, move into more exotic fare. "Hit by bus," naturally. "Train derailment," perhaps, and "stray bullet fired by drunken revellers." For those with a streak of black humour, this is where the exercise becomes enjoyable. We may strike a tree while skiing, choke on a bee, or fall into a manhole. Falling airplane parts can kill. So can banana peels. Lists will vary depending on the author's imagination and tolerance for bad taste, but I'm quite sure that near the end of every list will be this entry: "Crushed by asteroid."

Everyone knows deadly rocks can fall from the sky but outside space camps and science fiction conventions the threat of death-by-asteroid is used only as a rhetorical device for dismissing some worry as real but too tiny to worry about. I may have used it myself once or twice. I probably won't again, though, because in late 2004 I attended a conference that brought together some of the world's leading astronomers and geo-scientists to discuss asteroid impacts.

The venue was Tenerife, one of Spain's Canary Islands that lie off the Atlantic coast of North Africa. Intentionally or not, it was an ideal setting. The conference was not simply about rocks in space, after all. It was about understanding a very unlikely, potentially catastrophic risk. And the Canary Islands are home to two other very unlikely, potentially catastrophic risks.

First, there are the active volcanoes. All the islands were created by volcanic activity and Tenerife is dominated by a colossus called Teide, the third-largest volcano in the world. Teide is still quit active, having erupted three times in the last 300 years.

And there is the rift on La Palma mentioned in the last chapter. One team of scientists believes it will drop a big chunk of the island into the Atlantic and several hours later people on the east coast of North and South America will become extras in the greatest disaster movie of all time. Other scientists dispute this, saying a much smaller chunk of La Palma is set to go, that it will crumble as it drops, and that the resulting waves won't even qualify as good home video. They do agree that a landslide is possible, however, and that it is likely to happen soon in geological terms – which means it could be 10,000 years from now or tomorrow morning.

Now, one might think the residents of the Canary Islands would find it somewhat unsettling that they could wake to a cataclysm on any given morning. But one would be wrong. Teide's flanks are covered by large, pleasant towns filled with happy people who sleep quite soundly. There are similarly no reports of mass panic among the 85,000 residents of La Palma. The fact that the Canary Islands are balmy and beautiful probably has something to do with the residents' equanimity in the face of Armageddon. There are worse places to die. The Example Rule is also in play. The last time Teide erupted was in 1909, and no one has ever seen a big chunk of inhabited island disappear. Survivors would not be so sanguine the day after either event.

But that can't be all there is to it. Terrorists have never detonated a nuclear weapon in a major city but the mere thought of that happening chills most people, and governments around the world are working very hard to see that what has never happened never does.

Risk analysts call these low-probability/high-consequence events. Why would people fear some but not others? Asteroid impacts – classic low-probability/high-consequence events – are an almost ideal way to investigate that question.

The earth is under constant bombardment by cosmic debris. Most of what hits us is no bigger than a fleck of dust but because those flecks enter the earth's atmosphere at speeds of up to 72 kilometres per second, they pack a punch out of all proportion to their mass. Even the smallest fleck disappears in the brilliant flash of light that we quite misleadingly call shooting stars.

The risk to humans from these cosmic firecrackers is zero. But the debris pelting the planet comes in a sliding scale of sizes. There are bits no bigger than grains of rice, pebbles, throwing stones. They all enter the atmosphere at dazzling speed and so each modest increase in size means a huge jump in the energy released when they burn.

A rock one-third of a metre across explodes with the force of two tons of dynamite when it hits the atmosphere. About a thousand detonations of this size happen each year. A rock one metre across – a size commonly used in landscaping – erupts with the force of 100 tons of dynamite. That happens about 40 times each year.

At three metres across, a rock hits with the force of 2,000 tons of dynamite. That's two-thirds of the force that annihilated the city of Halifax in 1917, when a munitions-laden ship exploded in the harbour. Cosmic wallops of that force hit the earth roughly twice a year.

And so it goes up the scale, until, at 30 metres across, a rock gets a name change. It is now called an asteroid, and an asteroid of that size detonates in the atmosphere like two million tons of dynamite – enough to flatten everything on the ground within 10 kilometres. At 100 metres, asteroids pack the equivalent of 80 million tons of dynamite. We have historical experience with this kind of detonation. On June 30, 1908, an asteroid estimated to be 60 metres wide exploded eight kilometres above Tunguska, a remote region in Siberia, smashing flat some 2,000 square kilometres of forest.

Bigger asteroids get really scary. At one kilometre across, an asteroid could dig a crater 15 kilometres wide, spark a fireball that appears 25 times larger than the sun, shake the surrounding region with a 7.8 earthquake, and, possibly, hurl enough dust into the atmosphere to create a "nuclear winter." Civilization may or may not survive such a collision, but at least the species would. Not so the next weight class. A chunk of rock 10 kilometres across would add humans and most other terrestrial creatures to the list of species that once existed. This is what did in the dinosaurs.

Fortunately, there aren't many giant rocks whizzing around space. In a paper prepared for the Organization for Economic Cooperation and Development, astronomer Clark Chapman estimated that the chance of humanity being surprised by a doomsday rock in the next century is one in a million. But the smaller the rock, the more common they are – which means the smaller the rock, the greater the chance of being hit by one. The probability of the earth being walloped by a 300-metre asteroid in any given year is 1 in 50,000, which makes the odds 1 in 500 over the course of the century. If a rock like that landed in the ocean, it could generate a mammoth tsunami. On land, it would devastate a region the size of a small country. For a 100-metre rock, the odds are 1 in 10,000 in one year and 1 in 100 over the next 100 years. At 30 metres, the odds are 1 in 250 per year and 1 in 2.5 over the next 100 years.

Figuring out a rational response to such low-probability/high-consequence risks is not easy. We generally ignore one-in-a-million dangers because they're just too small and life's too short. Even risks of 1 in 10,000 or 1 in 1,000 are routinely dismissed. So looking at the probability of an asteroid strike, the danger is very low. But it's not zero. And what if it actually happens? It's not one person who's going to die, or even 1,000 or 10,000. It could be millions, even billions. At what point does the scale of the loss make it worth our while to deal with a threat that almost certainly won't come to pass in our lifetime or that of our children or their children?

Reason has a typically cold-hearted answer: It depends on the cost. If it costs little to protect against a low-probability/high-consequence event, it's worth paying up. But if it costs a lot, we may be better off putting the money into other priorities – reducing other risks, for example – and taking our chances.

For the most part, this is how governments deal with low-probability/high-consequence hazards. The probability of the event, its consequences, and the cost are all put on the table and considered together. That still leaves lots of room for arguments. Experts endlessly debate how the three factors should be weighted and how the calculation should be carried out. But no one disputes that all three factors have to be considered if we want to deal with these dangers rationally.

With regard to asteroids, the cost follows the same sliding scale as their destructive impact. The first step in mitigating the hazard is spotting the rock and calculating whether it will collide with the earth. If the alarm bell rings, we can then talk about whether it would be worth it to devise a plan to nudge, nuke, or otherwise nullify the threat. But spotting asteroids isn't easy because they don't emit light, they only reflect it. The smaller the rock, the harder and more expensive it is to spot. Conversely, the bigger the rock, the easier and cheaper it is to detect.

That leads to two obvious conclusions. First, asteroids at the small end of the sliding scale should be ignored. Second, we definitely should pay to locate those at the opposite end. And that has been done. Beginning in the early 1990s, astronomers created an international organization called Spaceguard, which coordinates efforts to spot and catalogue asteroids. Much of the work is voluntary but various universities and institutions have made modest contributions, usually in the form of time on telescopes. At the end of the 1990s, NASA gave Spaceguard annual funding of $4 million a year (from its $10-billion annual budget). As a result, astronomers believe that by 2008 Spaceguard will have spotted 90 per cent of asteroids bigger than one kilometre across.

That comes close to eliminating the risk from asteroids big enough to wipe out every mammal on earth, but it does nothing about smaller asteroids – asteroids capable of demolishing India, for example. Shouldn't we pay to spot them, too? Astronomers think so. So they asked NASA and the European Space Agency for $30 to $40 million a year for 10 years. That would allow them to detect and record 90 per cent of asteroids 140 metres and bigger. There would still be a small chance of a big one slipping through but it would give the planet a pretty solid insurance policy against cosmic collisions – not bad for a one-time expense of $300 million to $400 million. That's considerably less than the original amount budgeted to build a new American embassy in Baghdad and not a lot more than the $195 million owed by foreign diplomats to New York City for unpaid parking tickets.

But despite a lot of effort over many years, the astronomers couldn't get the money to finish the job. A frustrated Clark Chapman attended the conference in Tenerife. It had been almost 25 years since the risk was officially recognized, the science wasn't in doubt, public awareness had been raised, governments had been warned, but the progress was modest. He wanted to know why.

To help answer that question, the conference organizers brought Paul Slovic to Tenerife. With a career that started in the early 1960s, Slovic is one of the pioneers of risk perception research. It's a field that essentially began in the 1970s as a result of proliferating conflicts between expert and lay opinion. In some cases – cigarettes, seat belts, drunk driving – the experts insisted the risk was greater than the public believed. But in more cases – nuclear power was the prime example – the public was alarmed by things most experts insisted weren't so dangerous. Slovic, a professor of psychology at the University of Oregon, co-founded Decision Research, a private research corporation dedicated to figuring out why people reacted to risks the way they did.

In studies that began in the late 1970s, Slovic and his colleagues asked ordinary people to estimate the fatality rates of certain activities and technologies, to rank them according to how risky they believed them to be, and to provide more details about their feelings. Do you see this activity or technology as beneficial? Something you voluntarily engage in? Dangerous to future generations? Little understood? And so on. At the same time, they quizzed experts – professional risk analysts – on their views.

Not surprisingly, experts and laypeople disagreed about the seriousness of many items. Experts liked to think – and many still do – that this simply reflected the fact that they know what they're talking about and laypeople don't. But when Slovic subjected his data to statistical analyses it quickly became clear there was much more to the explanation than that.

The experts followed the classic definition of risk that has always been used by engineers and others who have to worry about things going wrong: Risk equals probability times consequence. Here, "consequence" means the body count. Not surprisingly, the experts' estimate of the fatalities inflicted by an activity or technology corresponded closely with their ranking of the riskiness of each item.

When laypeople estimated how fatal various risks were they got mixed results. In general, they knew which items were most and least lethal. Beyond that, their judgments varied from modestly incorrect to howlingly wrong. Not that people had any clue that their hunches might not be absolutely accurate. When Slovic asked people to rate how likely it was that an answer was wrong, they often scoffed at the very possibility. One-quarter actually put the odds of a mistake at less than 1 in 100 – although one in eight of the answers rated so confidently were, in fact, wrong. It was another important demonstration of why intuitions should be treated with caution – and another demonstration that they aren't.

The most illuminating results, however, came out of the ranking of riskiness. Sometimes, laypeople's estimate of an item's body count closely matched how risky they felt the item to be – as it did with the experts. But sometimes there was little or no link between "risk" and "annual fatalities." The most dramatic example was nuclear power. Laypeople, like experts, correctly said it inflicted the fewest fatalities of the items surveyed. But the experts ranked nuclear power as the 20th most risky item on a list of 30, while most laypeople said it was number one. Later studies had 90 items, but again nuclear power ranked first. Clearly, people were doing something other than multiplying probability and body count to come up with judgments about risk.

Slovic's analyses showed that if an activity or technology were seen as having certain qualities, people boosted their estimate of its riskiness regardless of whether it was believed to kill lots of people or not. If it were seen to have other qualities, they lowered their estimates. So it didn't matter that nuclear power didn't have a big body count. It had all the qualities that pressed our risk–perception buttons, and that put it at the top of the public's list of dangers.

1. Catastrophic potential: If fatalities would occur in large numbers in a single event – instead of in small numbers dispersed over time – our perception of risk rises.
2. Familiarity: Unfamiliar or novel risks make us worry more.
3. Understanding: If we believe that how an activity or technology works is not well understood, our sense of risk goes up.
4. Personal control: If we feel the potential for harm is beyond our control – like a passenger in an airplane – we worry more than if we feel in control – the driver of a car.
5. Voluntariness: If we don't choose to engage the risk, it feels more threatening.
6. Children: It's much worse if kids are involved.
7. Future generations: If the risk threatens future generations, we worry more.
8. Victim identity: Identifiable victims rather than statistical abstractions make the sense of risk rise.
9. Dread: If the effects generate fear, the sense of risk rises.

10. Trust: If the institutions involved are not trusted, risk rises.

11. Media attention: More media means more worry.

12. Accident history: Bad events in the past boost the sense of risk.

13. Equity: If the benefits go to some and the dangers to others, we raise the risk ranking.

14. Benefits: If the benefits of the activity or technology are not clear, it is judged to be riskier.

15. Reversibility: If the effects of something going wrong cannot be reversed, risk rises.

16. Personal risk: If it endangers me, it's riskier.

17. Origin: Man-made risks are riskier than those of natural origin.

18. Timing: More immediate threats loom larger while those in the future tend to be discounted.

Many of the items on Slovic's list look like common sense. Of course something that puts children at risk presses our buttons. Of course something that involves only those who choose to get involved does not. And one needn't have ever heard of the Example Rule to know that a risk that gets more media attention is likely to bother us more than one that doesn't.

But for psychologists, one item on the list – familiarity – is particularly predictable, and particularly important. We are bombarded with sensory input, at every moment, always. One of the most basic tasks of the brain is to swiftly sort that input into two piles: the important stuff that has to be brought to the attention of the conscious mind and everything else. What qualifies as important? Mostly, it's anything that's new. Novelty and unfamiliarity – surprise – grab our attention like nothing else. Drive the same road you've driven to work every day for the last 12 years and you are likely to pay so little conscious attention that you may not remember a thing you've seen when you pull into the parking lot. That is *if* the drive is the same as it always is. But if, on the way to work, you should happen to see a naked, pot-bellied man doing calisthenics on his front lawn, your consciousness will be roused from its slumber and you will arrive at work with a memory you may wish were a little less vivid.

The flip side of this is a psychological mechanism called habituation. It's the process that causes a stimulus we repeatedly experience without positive or negative consequences to gradually fade from our attention. Anyone who wears perfume or cologne has experienced habituation. When you buy a new scent and put it on, you catch a whiff of the fragrance all day long. The next day, the same. But if you wear it repeatedly, you gradually notice it less and less. Eventually, you may smell it only the moment you put it on and you will hardly pay attention to it even then. If you've ever wondered how the guy in the next cubicle at work can stand to reek of bad cologne all day, wonder no more.

Habituation is particularly important in coping with risk because risk is everywhere. Have a shower in the morning and you risk slipping and breaking your neck. Eat a poached egg and you could be poisoned. Drive to work and you may be crushed, mangled, or burned alive. Walk to work and carcinogenic solar radiation may rain down on you, or you may be hit by a bus, or have a heart attack, or be crushed by an asteroid. Of course, the chance of any of these horrible things happening is tiny – exposure to sunshine excepted, of course – and it would be a waste of our mental resources to constantly be aware of them. We need an "off" switch. That switch is habituation.

To carry out her famous observations of chimpanzees, primatologist Jane Goodall sat very still in their midst and watched them go about their ordinary business hour after hour, something that was possible only because the chimpanzees essentially ignored Goodall. To get the chimps to do that, Goodall had to show up and sit down, day after day, month after month, until the animals' alarm and curiosity faded and they stopped paying attention to her. The same process can be observed in other species. As I am writing this sentence, there is a black squirrel on my window sill eagerly chewing bird seed without the slightest regard for the large omnivore sitting in a chair barely one metre away. The birds that share the seed are equally blasé when I am in my backyard although I would need binoculars to see them up close in a forest. As for humans, simply recall the white-knuckle grip you had on the steering wheel the first time you drove on a freeway and then think of the last time the sheer boredom of driving nearly caused you to fall asleep at the wheel. If you had been asked on that first drive how dangerous it is to drive on a freeway, your answer would be a little different than it is now that habituation has done its work.

Habituation generally works brilliantly. The problem with it, as with everything the unconscious mind does, is that it cannot account for science and statistics. If you've smoked cigarettes every hour, every day, for years, without suffering any harm, the cigarette in your hand won't *feel* threatening. Not even your doctor's warnings can change that because it is your conscious mind that understands the warning but your conscious mind does not control your feelings. The same process of habituation can also explain why someone can become convinced it isn't so risky to drive a car drunk, or to not wear a seat belt, or to ride a motorcycle without a helmet. And if you live quietly for years in a pleasant Spanish town, you're unlikely to give a second thought to the fact that your town is built on the slopes of the world's third-largest active volcano.

For all the apparent reasonableness of Paul Slovic's list of risk factors, however, its value is limited. The problem is the same one that bedevils focus groups. People know what they like, what they fear, and so on. But what's the source of these judgments? Typically, it is the unconscious mind – Gut. The judgment may come wholly from Gut, or it may have been modified by the conscious mind – Head. But in either case, the answer to *why* people feel as they do lies at least partly within Gut. Gut is a black box; Head can't peer inside. And when a researcher asks someone to say why she feels the way she does about a risk, it's not Gut she is talking to. It is Head.

Now, if Head simply answered the researcher's question with a humble "I don't know," that would be one thing. But Head is a compulsive rationalizer. If it doesn't have an answer, it makes one up.

There's plenty of evidence for rationalization but the most memorable – certainly the most bizarre – was a series of experiments on so-called split-brain patients by neuroscientist Michael Gazzaniga. Ordinarily, the left and right hemispheres of the brain are connected and they communicate in both directions but one treatment for severe epilepsy is to sever the two sides. Split-brain patients function surprisingly well but scientists realized that because the two hemispheres handle different sorts of information, each side can learn something that the other isn't aware of. This effect could be induced deliberately in experiments by exposing only one eye or the other to written instructions. In one version of his work, Gazzaniga used this technique to instruct the right hemisphere of a split-brain patient to stand up and walk. The man got up and walked. Gazzaniga then verbally asked the man why he was walking. The left hemisphere handles such "reason" questions and even though that hemisphere had no idea what the real answer was, the man immediately responded that he was going for a soda. Variations on this experiment always got the same result: The left hemisphere quickly and ingeniously fabricated explanations rather than admit it had no idea what was going on. And the person whose lips delivered these answers believed every word.

When a woman tells a researcher how risky she thinks nuclear power is, what she says is probably a reliable reflection of her feelings. But when the researcher asks the person *why* she feels the way she does, her answer is likely to be partly or wholly inaccurate. It's not that she is being deceitful. It's that her answer is very likely to be, in some degree, a conscious rationalization of an unconscious judgment. So maybe it's true that what really bothers people about nuclear power are the qualities on Slovic's checklist. Or maybe that stuff is just Head rationalizing Gut's judgment. Or maybe it's a little of both. The truth is we don't know what the truth is.

Slovic's list was, and still is, very influential in the large and growing business of risk communication because it provided a handy checklist that allowed analysts to quickly and easily come up with a profile for any risk. Is it man-made? Is it involuntary? Its simplicity also appealed to the media. Newspaper and magazine articles about risk still recite the items on the list as if they explain everything we need to know about why people react to some dangers and not others. But Slovic himself acknowledges the list's limitations. "This was the mid-1970s. At the time we were doing the early work, we had no real appreciation for the unconscious, automatic system of thought. Our approach assumed that this was the way people were analyzing risks, in a very thoughtful way."

Ultimately, Slovic and his colleagues found a way out of this box with the help of two clues buried within their data. The first lay in the word *dread*. Slovic found that dread – plain old fear – was strongly correlated with several other items on the list, including *catastrophic*, *involuntary*, and *inequitable*. Unlike some of the other items, these are loaded with emotional content. And he found that this cluster of qualities – which he labelled "the dread factor" – was by far the strongest predictor of people's reaction to an activity or technology. This was a strong hint that there was more going on in people's brains than cool, rational analysis.

The second clue lay in something that looked, on the surface, to be a meaningless quirk. It turned out that people's ratings of the risks and benefits for the 90 activities and technologies on the list were connected. If people thought the risk posed by something was high, they judged the benefit to be low. The reverse was also true. If they thought the benefit was high, the risk was seen as low. In technical terms, this is an "inverse correlation." It makes absolutely no sense here because there's no logical reason that something – say, a new prescription drug – can't be *both* high risk *and* high benefit. It's also true that something can be low risk and low benefit – sitting on the couch watching Sunday afternoon football comes to mind. So why on earth did people put risk and benefit at opposite ends of a see-saw? It was curious but it didn't seem important. In his earliest papers on risk, Slovic mentioned the finding in only a sentence or two.

In the years to come, however, the model of a two-track mind – Head and Gut operating simultaneously – advanced rapidly. A major influence in this development was the work of Robert Zajonc, a Stanford psychologist, who explored what psychologists call affect – which we know simply as feeling or emotion. Zajonc insisted that we delude ourselves when we think that we evaluate evidence and make decisions by calculating rationally. "This is probably seldom the case," he wrote in 1980. "We buy cars we 'like', choose the jobs and houses we find 'attractive', and then justify those choices by various reasons."

With this new model, Slovic understood the limitations of his earlier research. Working with Ali Alhakami, a Ph.D. student at the University of Oregon, he also started to realize that the perceived link between risk and benefit he discovered earlier may have been much more than a quirk. What if people were reacting unconsciously and emotionally at the mention of a risky activity or technology? They hear "nuclear power" and . . . ugh! They have an instantaneous, unconscious reaction. This bad feeling actually happens *prior* to any conscious thought and because it comes first, it shapes and colours the thoughts that follow – including responses to the researchers' questions about risk.

That would explain why people see risk and benefit as if they were sitting at opposite ends of a see-saw. How risky is nuclear power? Nuclear power is a Bad Thing. Risk is also bad. So nuclear power must be very risky. And how beneficial is nuclear power? Nuclear power is Bad, so it must not be very beneficial. When Gut reacts positively to an activity or technology – swimming, say, or aspirin – it tips the see-saw the other way: Aspirin is a Good Thing so it must be low risk and high benefit.

To test this hypothesis, Slovic and Alhakami, along with colleagues Melissa Finucane and Stephen Johnson, devised a simple experiment. Students at the University of Western Australia were divided into two groups. The first group was shown various potential risks – chemical plants, cellphones, air travel – on a computer screen and asked to rate the riskiness of the item on a scale from one to seven. Then they rated the benefits of each. The second group did the same, except they had only a few seconds to make their decisions.

Other research had shown that time pressure reduces Head's ability to step in and modify Gut's judgment. If Slovic's hypothesis was correct, the see-saw effect between risk and benefit should be stronger in the second group than the first. And that's just what they found.

In a second experiment, Slovic and Alhakami had students of the University of Oregon rate the risks and benefits of a technology (different trials used nuclear power, natural gas, and food preservatives). Then they were asked to read a few paragraphs describing some of the benefits of the technology. Finally, they were asked again to rate the risks and benefits of the technology. Not surprisingly, the positive information they read raised students' ratings of the technology's benefits in about one–half of the cases. But most of those who raised their estimate of the technology's benefits also *lowered* their estimate of the risk – even though they had not read a word about the risk. Later trials in which only risks were discussed had the same effect but in reverse: People who raised their estimate of the technology's risks in response to the information about risk also lowered their estimate of its benefit.

Various names have been used to capture what's going on here. Slovic calls it the affect heuristic. I prefer to think of it as the Good–Bad Rule. When faced with something, Gut may instantly experience a raw feeling that something is Good or Bad. That feeling then guides the judgments that follow: "Is this thing likely to kill me? It feels good. Good things don't kill. So, no, don't worry about it."

The Good–Bad Rule helps to solve many riddles. In Slovic's original studies, for example, he found that people consistently underestimated the lethality of all diseases except one: The lethality of cancer was actually *over*estimated. One reason that might be is the Example Rule. The media pay much more attention to cancer than diabetes or asthma and so people can easily recall examples of deaths caused by cancer even if they don't have personal experience with the disease. But consider how you feel when you read the words *diabetes* and *asthma*. Unless you or someone you care about has suffered from these diseases, chances are they don't spark any emotion. But what about the word *cancer*? It's like a shadow slipping over the mind. That shadow is affect – the "faint whisper of emotion," as Slovic calls it. We use *cancer* as a metaphor in ordinary language – meaning something black and hidden, eating away at what's good – precisely because the word stirs feelings. And those feelings shape and colour our conscious thoughts about the disease.

The Good–Bad Rule also helps explain our weird relationship with radiation. We fear nuclear weapons, reasonably enough, while nuclear power and nuclear waste also give us the willies. Most experts argue that nuclear power and nuclear waste are not nearly as dangerous as the public thinks they are, but people will not be budged. On the other hand, we pay good money to soak up solar radiation on a tropical beach and few people have the slightest qualms about deliberately exposing themselves to radiation when a doctor orders an X–ray. In fact, Slovic's surveys confirmed that most laypeople underestimate the (minimal) dangers of X–rays.

Why don't we worry about sun–tanning? Habituation may play a role, but the Good–Bad Rule certainly does. Picture this: you, lying on a beach in Mexico. How does that make you feel? Pretty good. And if it is a Good Thing, our feelings tell us, it cannot be all that risky. The same is true of X–rays. They are a medical technology that saves lives. They are a Good Thing, and that feeling eases any worries about the risk they pose.

On the other end of the scale are nuclear weapons. They are a Very Bad Thing – which is a pretty reasonable conclusion given that they are designed to annihilate whole cities in a flash. But Slovic has found feelings about nuclear power and nuclear waste are almost as negative and when Slovic and some colleagues examined how the people of Nevada felt about a proposal to create a dump site for nuclear waste in that state, they found that people judged the risk of a nuclear waste repository to be at least as great as that of a nuclear plant or even a nuclear weapons testing site. Not even the most ardent anti-nuclear activist would make such an equation. It makes no sense – unless people's judgments are the product of intensely negative feeling to all things "nuclear."

Of course, the Example Rule also plays a role in the public's fear of nuclear power, given the ease with which we latch onto images of the Chernobyl disaster the moment nuclear power is mentioned. But popular fears long predate those images, suggesting there is another unconscious mechanism at work. This illustrates an important limitation in our understanding of how intuitive judgment works, incidentally. By carefully designing experiments, psychologists are able to identify mechanisms like the Example Rule and the Good–Bad Rule, and we can look at circumstances in the real world and surmise that this or that mechanism is involved. But what we can't do – at least not yet – is tease out precisely which mechanisms are doing what. We can only say that people's intuitions about nuclear power may be generated by either the Example Rule or the Good–Bad Rule or both.

We're not used to thinking of our feelings as the sources of our conscious decisions but research leaves no doubt. Studies of insurance, for example, have revealed that people are willing to pay more to insure a car they feel is attractive than one that is not, even when the monetary value is the same. A 1993 study even found that people were willing to pay more for airline travel insurance covering "terrorist acts" than for deaths from "all possible causes." Logically, that makes no sense, but "terrorist acts" is a vivid phrase dripping with bad feelings, while "all possible causes" is bland and empty. It leaves Gut cold.

Amos Tversky and psychologist Eric Johnson also showed the influence of bad feelings can extend beyond the thing generating the feelings. They asked Stanford University students to read one of three versions of a story about a tragic death – the cause being either leukemia, fire, or murder – that contained no information about how common such tragedies are. They then gave the students a list of risks – including the risk in the story and 12 others – and asked them to estimate how often they kill. As we might expect, those who read a tragic story about a death caused by leukemia rated leukemia's lethality higher than a control group of students who didn't read the story. The same with fire and murder. More surprisingly, reading the stories led to increased estimates for *all* the risks, not just the one portrayed. The fire story caused an overall increase in perceived risk of 14 per cent. The leukemia story raised estimates by 73 per cent. The murder story led the pack, raising risk estimates by 144 per cent. A "good news" story had precisely the opposite effect – driving down perceived risks across the board.

So far, I've mentioned things – murder, terrorism, cancer – that deliver an unmistakable emotional wallop. But scientists have shown that Gut's emotional reactions can be much subtler than that. Robert Zajonc, along with psychologists Piotr Winkielman and Norbert Schwarz, conducted a series of experiments in which Chinese ideographs flashed briefly on a screen. Immediately after seeing an ideograph, the test subjects, students at the University of Michigan, were asked to rate the image from one to six, with six being very liked and one not liked at all. (Anyone familiar with the Chinese, Korean, or Japanese languages was excluded from the study, so the images held no literal meaning for those who saw them.)

What the students weren't told is that just before the ideograph appeared, another image was flashed. In some cases, it was a smiling face. In others, it was a frowning face or a meaningless polygon. These images appeared for the smallest fraction of a second, such a brief moment that they did not register on the conscious mind and no student reported seeing them. But even this tiny exposure to a good or bad image had a profound effect on the students' judgment. Across the board, ideographs preceded by a smiling face were liked more than those that weren't positively primed. The frowning face had the same effect in the opposite direction.

Clearly, emotion had a powerful influence and yet not one student reported feeling any emotion. Zajonc and other scientists believe that can happen because the brain system that slaps emotional labels on things – nuclear power: bad! – is buried within the unconscious mind. So your brain can feel something is good or bad even though you never consciously feel good or bad. (When the students were asked what they based their judgments on, incidentally, they cited the ideograph's aesthetics, or they said that it reminded them of something, or they simply insisted that they "just liked it." The conscious mind hates to admit it simply doesn't know.)

After putting students through the routine outlined above, Zajonc and his colleagues then repeated the test. This time, however, the images of faces were switched around. If an ideograph had been preceded by a smiling face in the first round, it got a frowning face, and vice versa. The results were startling. Unlike the first round, the flashed images had little effect. People stuck to their earlier judgments. An ideograph judged likeable in the first round because – unknown to the person doing the judging – it was preceded by a smiling face was judged likeable in the second round even though it was preceded by a frowning face. So emotional labels stick even if we don't know they exist.

In earlier experiments – since corroborated by a massive amount of research – Zajonc also revealed that positive feeling for something can be created simply by repeated exposure to it, while positive feelings can be strengthened with more exposure. Now known as the mere exposure effect, this phenomenon is neatly summed up in the phrase "familiarity breeds liking." Corporations have long understood this, even if only intuitively. The point of much advertising is simply to expose people to a corporation's name and logo in order to increase familiarity, and, as a result, positive feelings toward them.

The mere–exposure effect has considerable implications for how we feel about risks. Consider chewing tobacco. Most people today have never been seen anyone chew a wad but someone who lives in an environment where it's common is likely to have a positive feeling for it buried within his brain. That feeling colours his thoughts about chewing tobacco – including his thoughts about how dangerous it is. Gut senses chewing tobacco is Good. Good things don't cause cancer. How likely is chewing tobacco to give you cancer? Not very, Gut concludes. Note that the process here is similar to that of habituation, but it doesn't require the level of exposure necessary for habituation to occur. Note also that this is not the warm glow someone may feel at the sight of a tin of tobacco because it brings back memories of a beloved grandfather who was always chewing the stuff. As the name says, the mere exposure effect requires nothing more than mere exposure to generate at least a little positive feeling. Beloved grandfathers are not necessary.

Much of the research about affect is conducted in laboratories but when psychologists Mark Frank and Thomas Gilovich found evidence in lab experiments that people have strongly negative unconscious reactions to black uniforms, they dug up corroboration in the real world. All five black–clad teams in the National Football League, Frank and Gilovich found, received more than the league–average number of penalty yards in every season but one between 1970 and 1986. In the National Hockey League, all three teams that wore black through the same period got more than the average number of penalty minutes in every season. The really intriguing thing is that these teams were penalized just as heavily when they wore their alternate uniforms – white with black trim – which is just what you would expect from the research on emotion and judgment. The black uniform slaps a negative emotional label on the team and that label sticks even when the team isn't wearing black. Gilovich and Frank even found a near–perfect field trial of their theory in the 1979–80 season of the Pittsburgh Penguins. For the first 44 games of the season, the team wore blue uniforms. During that time, they averaged eight penalty minutes a game. But for the last 35 games of the season, the team wore a new black uniform. The coach and players were the same as in the first half of the season, and yet the Penguins' penalty time rose 50 per cent to 12 minutes a game.

Another real–world demonstration of the Good–Bad Rule at work comes around once a year. Christmas isn't generally perceived as a killer. It probably didn't even make your list of outlandish ways to die. But it should. 'Tis the season for falls, burns, and electrocutions. In Britain, warns the Royal Society for the Prevention of Accidents (RSPA), holiday events typically include "about 1,000 people going to hospital after accidents with Christmas trees; another 1,000 hurt by trimmings or when decorating their homes; and 350 hurt by Christmas tree lights." The British government has run ad campaigns noting that people are 50 per cent more likely to die in a house fire during the holidays. In the United States, no less an authority than the under–secretary of Homeland Security penned an op–ed in which he warned that fires caused by candles "increase four–fold during the holidays." Christmas trees alone start fires in 200 homes. Altogether, "house fires during the winter holiday season kill 500 and injure 2,000 people," wrote the under–secretary, "and cause more than $500 million in damage."

Now, I am not suggesting we should start fretting about Christmas. Much of the public education around the holiday strikes me as a tad exaggerated and some of it – like the RSPA press release that draws our attention to the risk of "gravy exploding in microwave ovens" – is unintentionally funny. But compared to some of the risks that have grabbed headlines and generated real public worry in the past – shark attacks, "stranger danger," Satanic cults, and herpes, to name a few – the risks of Christmas are actually substantial. And yet these annual warnings are annually ignored, or even played for laughs (exploding gravy!) in the media. Why the discrepancy? Part of the answer is surely the powerful emotional content of Christmas.

Christmas isn't just a Good Thing. It's a Wonderful Thing. And Gut is sure Wonderful Things don't kill.

The fact that Gut so often has instantaneous, emotional reactions that it uses to guide its judgments has a wide array of implications. A big one is the role of justice in how we react to risk and tragedy.

Consider two scenarios. In the first, a little boy plays on smooth, sloping rocks at the seashore. The wind is high and his mother has told him not to go too close to the water. But with a quick glance to make sure his mother isn't looking, the boy edges forward until he can slap his hands on the wet rocks. Intent on his little game, he doesn't see a large wave roar in. It knocks him backward then pulls him tumbling into the ocean where strong currents drag him into deep water. The mother sees and struggles valiantly to reach him but the pounding waves blind her and beat her back. The boy drowns.

Now imagine a woman living alone with her only child, a young boy. In the community, the woman is perfectly respectable. She has a job, friends. She even volunteers at a local animal shelter. But in private, unknown to anyone, she beats her child mercilessly for any perceived fault. One night, the boy breaks a toy. The woman slaps and punches him repeatedly. As the boy cowers in a corner, blood and tears streaking his face, the woman gets a pot from the kitchen and returns. She bashes the boy's head with the pot, then tosses it aside and orders him to bed. In the night, a blood clot forms in the boy's brain. He is dead by morning.

Two lives lost, two sad stories likely to make the front page of the newspaper. But only one will prompt impassioned letters to the editor and calls to talk radio shows, and we all know which one it is.

Philosophers and scholars may debate the nature of justice but for most of us justice is experienced as outrage at a wrong and satisfaction at the denunciation and punishment of that wrong. It is a primal emotion. The woman who murdered her little boy *must* be punished. It doesn't matter that she isn't a threat to anyone else. This isn't about safety. She *must* be punished. Evolutionary psychologists argue that this urge to punish wrongdoing is hard-wired because it is an effective way to discourage bad behaviour. "People who are emotionally driven to retaliate against those who cross them, even at a cost to themselves, are more credible adversaries and less likely to be exploited," writes cognitive psychologist Steven Pinker.

Whatever its origins, the instinct for blame and punishment is often a critical component in our reactions to risks. Imagine there is a gas that kills 20,000 people a year in the European Union and another 21,000 a year in the United States. Imagine further that this gas is a by-product of industrial processes and scientists can precisely identify which industries, even which factories, are emitting the gas. And imagine that all these facts are widely known but no one – not the media, not environmental groups, not the public – is all that concerned. Many people haven't even heard of this gas, while those who have are only vaguely aware of what it is, where it comes from, and how deadly it is. And they're not interested in learning more.

Yes, it is an absurd scenario. We would never shrug off something like that. But consider radon. It's a radioactive gas that can cause lung cancer if it pools indoors at high concentrations, which it does in regions that scientists can identify with a fair degree of precision. It kills an estimated 41,000 people a year in the United States and the European Union. Public health agencies routinely run awareness campaigns about the danger but journalists and environmentalists have seldom shown much interest and the public, it's fair to say, have only a vague notion of what this stuff is. The reason for this indifference is clear: Radon is produced naturally in some rocks and soils. The deaths it inflicts are solitary and quiet and no one is responsible. So Gut shrugs. In Paul Slovic's surveys, the same people who shook at the knees thinking about radiation sources like nuclear waste dumps rated radon – which has undoubtedly killed more people than nuclear waste ever could – a very low risk. Nature kills, but nature is blameless. No one shakes a fist at volcanoes. No one denounces heat waves. And the absence of outrage is the reason that natural risks feel so much less threatening than man–made dangers.

The Good–Bad Rule also makes language critical. The world does not come with explanatory notes, after all. In seeing and experiencing things, we have to frame them this way or that to make sense of them, to give them meaning. That framing is done with language.

Picture a lump of cooked ground beef. It is a most prosaic object and the task of judging its quality shouldn't be terribly difficult. There would seem to be few, if any, ways that language describing it could influence people's judgment. And yet psychologists Irwin Levin and Gary Gaeth did just that in an experiment disguised as marketing research. Here is a sample of cooked beef, the researchers told one group. It is "75 per cent lean." Please examine it and judge it; then taste some and judge it again. With a second group, the researchers provided the same beef but they described it as "25 per cent fat." The result: On first inspection, the beef described as "75 per cent lean" got much higher ratings than the "25 per cent fat" beef. After tasting the beef, the bias in favour of the "lean" beef declined but was still evident.

Life and death are somewhat more emotional matters than lean and fat beef, so it's not surprising that the words a doctor chooses can be even more influential than those used in Levin and Gaeth's experiment. A 1982 experiment by Amos Tversky and Barbara McNeil demonstrated this by asking people to imagine they were patients with lung cancer who had to decide between radiation treatment and surgery. One group was told there was a 68 per cent chance of being alive a year after the surgery. The other was told there was a 32 per cent chance of dying. Framing the decision in terms of staying alive resulted in 44 per cent opting for surgery over radiation treatment, but when the information was framed as a chance of dying, that dropped to 18 per cent. Tversky and McNeil repeated this experiment with physicians and got the same results. In a different experiment, Tversky and Daniel Kahneman also showed that when people were told a flu outbreak was expected to kill 600 people,

people's judgments about which program should be implemented to deal with the outbreak were heavily influenced by whether the expected program results were described in terms of lives saved (200) or lives lost (400).

The vividness of language is also critical. In one experiment, Cass Sunstein – a University of Chicago law professor who often applies psychology's insights to issues in law and public policy – asked students what they would pay to insure against a risk. For one group, the risk was described as "dying of cancer." Others were told not only that the risk was death by cancer but that the death would be "very gruesome and intensely painful, as the cancer eats away at the internal organs of the body." That change in language was found to have a major impact on what students were willing to pay for insurance – an impact that was even greater than making a large change in the probability of the feared outcome. Feeling trumped numbers. It usually does.

Of course the most vivid form of communication is the photo-graphic image and, not surprisingly, there's plenty of evidence that awful, frightening photos not only grab our attention and stick in our memories – which makes them influential via the Example Rule – they conjure emotions that influence our risk perceptions via the Good–Bad Rule. It's one thing to tell smokers their habit could give them lung cancer. It's quite another to see the blackened, gnarled lungs of a dead smoker. That's why several countries, including Canada and Australia, have replaced text–only health warnings on cigarette packs with horrible images of diseased lungs, hearts, and gums. They're not just repulsive. They increase the perception of risk.

Even subtle changes in language can have considerable impact. Paul Slovic and his team gave forensic psychiatrists – men and women trained in math and science – what they were told was another clinician's assessment of a mental patient confined to an institution. Based on this assessment, the psychiatrists were asked, would you release this patient? Half the assessments estimated that patients similar to

Mr. Jones "have a 20 per cent chance of committing an act of violence" after release. Of the psychiatrists who read this version, 21 per cent said they would refuse to release the patient.

The wording of the second version of the assessment was changed very slightly. It is estimated, the assessment said, that "20 out of every 100 patients similar to Mr. Jones" will be violent after release. Of course, "20 per cent" and "20 out of every 100" mean the same thing. But 41 per cent of the psychiatrists who read this second version said they would keep the patient confined, so an apparently trivial change in wording boosted the refusal rate by almost 100 per cent. How is that possible? The explanation lies in the emotional content of the phrase "20 per cent." It's hollow, abstract, a mere statistic. What's a "per cent"? Can I see a "per cent"? Can I touch it? No. But "20 out of every 100 patients" is very concrete and real. It invites you to see a person. And in this case, the person is committing violent acts. The inevitable result of this phrasing is that it creates images of violence – "some guy going crazy and killing someone," as one person put it in post-experiment interviews – which make the risk feel bigger and the patient's incarceration more necessary.

People in the business of public opinion are only too aware of the influence seemingly minor linguistic changes can have. Magnetic resonance imaging (MRI), for example, was originally called "nuclear magnetic resonance imaging" but the "nuclear" was dropped to avoid tainting a promising new technology with a stigmatized word. In politics, a whole industry of consultants has arisen to work on language cues like these – the Republican Party's switch from "tax cuts" and "estate tax" to "tax relief" and "death tax" being two of its more famous fruits.

The Good–Bad Rule can also wreak havoc on our rational appreciation of probabilities. In a series of experiments conducted by Yuval Rottenstreich and Christopher Hsee, then with the Graduate School of Business at the University of Chicago, students were asked to imagine choosing between $50 cash and a chance to kiss their favourite movie star. Seventy per cent said they'd take the cash. Another group of students was asked to choose between a 1 per cent chance of winning $50 cash and a 1 per cent chance of kissing their favourite movie star. The result was almost exactly the reverse: 65 per cent chose the kiss. Rottenstreich and Hsee saw the explanation in the Good–Bad Rule: The cash carries no emotional charge and so a 1 per cent chance to win $50 feels as small as it really is; but even an imagined kiss with a movie star stirs feelings that cash does not and so a 1 per cent chance of such a kiss looms larger.

Rottenstreich and Hsee conducted further variations of this experiment that came to the same conclusion. Then they turned to electric shocks. Students were divided into two groups, with one group told the experiment would involve some chance of a $20 loss and the other group informed that there was a risk of "a short, painful but not dangerous shock." Again, the cash loss is emotionally neutral. But the electric shock is truly nasty. Students were then told the chance of this bad thing happening was either 99 per cent or 1 per cent. So how much would you pay to avoid this risk?

When there was a 99 per cent chance of losing $20, they said they would pay $18 to avoid this almost-certain loss. When the chance dropped to 1 per cent, they said they would pay just one dollar to avoid the risk. Any economist would love that result. It's a precise and calculated response to probability, perfect rationality. But the students asked to think of an electric shock did something a little different. Faced with a 99 per cent chance of a shock, they said they would pay $10 to stop it. But when the risk was 1 per cent, they were willing to pay $7 to protect themselves. Clearly, the probability of being zapped had almost no influence. What mattered is that the risk of being shocked is nasty – and they *felt* it.

Plenty of other research shows that even when we are calm, cool, and thinking carefully, we aren't naturally inclined to look at the odds. Should I buy an extended warranty for my new giant-screen television? The first and most important question I should ask is how likely it is to break down and need repair, but research suggests there's a good chance I won't even think about that. And if I do, I won't be entirely logical about it. Certainty, for example, has been shown to have outsize influence on how we judge probabilities: A change from 100 per cent to 95 per cent carries far more weight than a decline from 60 per cent to 55 per cent, while a jump from 0 per cent to 5 per cent will loom like a giant over a rise from 25 per cent to 30 per cent. This focus on certainty helps explain our unfortunate tendency to think of safety in black-and-white terms – something is either safe or unsafe – when, in reality, safety is almost always a shade of grey.

And all this is true when there's no fear, anger, or hope involved. Toss in a strong emotion and people can easily become – to use a term coined by Cass Sunstein – "probability blind." The feeling simply sweeps the numbers away. In a survey, Paul Slovic asked people if they agreed or disagreed that a one-in-10 million lifetime risk of getting cancer from exposure to a chemical was too small to worry about. That's an incredibly tiny risk – far less than the lifetime risk of being killed by lightning and countless other risks we completely ignore. Still, one-third disagreed; they *would* worry. That's probability blindness. The irony is that probability blindness is itself dangerous. It can easily lead people to overreact to risks and do something stupid like abandoning air travel because terrorists hijacked four planes.

It's not just the odds that can be erased from our minds by the Good-Bad Rule. It is also costs. "It's worth it if even one life is saved" is something we often hear of some new program or regulation designed to reduce a risk. That may be true, or it may not. If, for example, the program costs $100 million and it saves one life, it is almost certainly *not* worth it because there are many other ways $100 million could be spent that would certainly save more than one life.

This sort of cost-benefit analysis is itself a big and frighteningly complex field. One of the many important insights it has produced is that, other things being equal, "wealthier is healthier." The more money people and nations have, the healthier and safer they tend to be. Disaster relief people see this maxim in operation every time there is a major earthquake. People aren't killed by earthquakes. They are killed by buildings that collapse in earthquakes and so the flimsier the buildings, the more likely people are to die. This is why earthquakes of the same magnitude may kill dozens in California but hundreds of thousands in Iran, Pakistan, or India. The disparity can be seen even within the same city. When a massive earthquake struck Kobe, Japan, in 1995, killing 6,200 people, the victims were not randomly distributed across the city and region. They were overwhelmingly people living in poor neighbourhoods.

Government regulations can reduce risk and save lives. California's buildings are as tough as they are in part because building codes require them to be. But regulations can also impose costs on economic activity, and since wealthier-is-healthier, economic costs can, if they are very large, put more lives at risk than they keep safe. Many researchers have tried to estimate how much regulatory cost is required to "take the life" of one person but the results are controversial. What's broadly accepted, however, is the idea that regulations can inflict economic costs and economic costs can reduce health and safety. We have to account for that if we want to be rational about risk.

We rarely do, of course. As political scientist Howard Margolis describes in *Dealing With Risk*, the public often demands action on a risk without giving the slightest consideration to the costs of that action. When circumstances force us to confront those costs, however, we may change our minds in a hurry. Margolis cites the case of asbestos in New York City's public schools, which led to a crisis in 1993 when the start of the school year had to be delayed several weeks because work to assess the perceived danger dragged on into September. Parents had overwhelmingly supported this work. Experts had said the actual risk to any child from asbestos was tiny, especially compared to the myriad other problems poor kids in New York faced, and the cost would be enormous. But none of that mattered. Like the cancer it can cause, asbestos has the reputation of a killer. It triggers the Good–Bad Rule and once that happens, everything else is trivia. "Don't tell us to calm down!" one parent shouted at a public meeting. "The health of our children is at stake."

But when the schools failed to open in September, it was a crisis of another kind for the parents. Who was going to care for their kids? For poor parents counting on the schools opening when they always do, it was a serious burden. "Within three weeks," Margolis writes, "popular sentiment was overwhelmingly reversed."

Experiences like this, along with the research on the role of emotion in judgment, have led Slovic and other risk researchers to draw several conclusions. One is that experts are wrong to think they can ease fears about a risk simply by "getting the facts out." If an engineer tells people they shouldn't worry because the chance of the reactor melting down and spewing vast radioactive clouds that would saturate their children and put them at risk of cancer. . . . Well, they won't be swayed by the odds. Only the rational mind – Head – cares about odds and, as we have seen, most people are not accustomed to the effort required for Head to intervene and correct Gut. Our natural inclination is to go with our intuitive judgment.

Another important implication of the Good–Bad Rule is something it shares with the Rule of Typical Things: It makes us vulnerable to scary scenarios. Consider the story told by the Bush administration in support of the invasion of Iraq. It was possible Saddam Hussein would seek to obtain the materials to build nuclear weapons. It was possible he would start a nuclear weapons program. It was possible the program would successfully create nuclear weapons. It was possible Saddam would give those weapons to terrorists. It was possible that terrorists armed with nukes would seek to detonate them in an American city, and it was possible they would succeed. All these things were possible, but a rational assessment of this scenario would examine the odds of each of these events occurring on the understanding that if even one of them failed to occur, the final disaster would not happen. But that's not how Gut would analyze it with the Good–Bad Rule. It would start at the other end – an American city reduced to radioactive rubble, hundreds of thousands dead, hundreds of thousands more burned and sick – and it would react. This is an Awful Thing. And that feeling would not only colour the question of whether this is likely or not, it would overwhelm it, particularly if the scenario were described in vivid language – language such as the White House's oft-repeated line "We don't want the smoking gun to be a mushroom cloud."

Like terrorists armed with a nuclear weapon, an asteroid can also flatten a city. But asteroids are only rocks. They are not wrapped in the cloak of evil as terrorists are, nor are they stigmatized like cancer, asbestos, or nuclear power. They don't stir any particular emotion and so they don't engage the Good–Bad Rule and overwhelm our sense of how very unlikely they are to hurt us. The Example Rule doesn't help, either. The only really massive asteroid impact in the modern era was the Tunguska event, which happened a century ago in a place so remote only a handful of people saw it. There have been media reports of "near misses" and a considerable amount of attention paid to astronomers' warnings, but while these may raise conscious awareness of the issue, they're very different from the kind of concrete experience our primal brains are wired to respond to. Many people also know of the theory that an asteroid wiped out the dinosaurs but that's no more real and vivid in our memories than the Tunguska event, and so the Example Rule would steer Gut to conclude that the risk is tinier than it actually is.

There is simply nothing about asteroids that could make Gut sit up and take notice. We don't *feel* the risk. For that reason, Paul Slovic told the astronomers at the Tenerife conference, "it will be hard to generate concern about asteroids unless there is an identifiable, certain, imminent, dreadful threat." And of course, when there is an identifiable, certain, imminent, dreadful threat, it will probably be too late to do anything about it.

Still, does that matter? It is almost certain that the earth will not be hit by a major asteroid in our lifetime or that of our children. If we don't take the astronomers' advice and buy a planetary insurance policy, we'll collectively save a few bucks and we will almost certainly not regret it. But still – it could happen. And the $400–million cost of the insurance policy is very modest relative to how much we spend coping with other risks. For that reason, Richard Posner, a U.S. appeals court judge and public intellectual known for his hard–nosed economic analysis, thinks the astronomers should get their funding. "The fact that a catastrophe is very unlikely to occur is not a rational justification for ignoring the risk of its occurrence," he wrote.

The particular catastrophe that prompted Posner to write those words wasn't an asteroid strike, however. It was the Indian Ocean tsunami of 2004. Such an event had not happened in the region in all of recorded history and the day before it actually occurred experts would have said it almost certainly would not happen in our lifetime or that of our children. But experts would also have said – and in fact did say, in several reports – that a tsunami warning system should be created in the region because the cost is modest. The experts were ignored and 230,000 people died.

That disaster occurred three weeks after the Canary Islands conference on asteroids ended. Hours after waves had scoured coastlines from Indonesia to Thailand and Somalia, Slava Gusiakov, a Russian expert on tsunamis who had attended the conference, sent an emotional e-mail to colleagues. "We were repeatedly saying the words low–probability/high–consequence event," he wrote. "It just happened."

5

A STORY ABOUT NUMBERS

Japanese prostitutes were the first women to connect silicone and plumper breasts. It was the 1950s and American servicemen in Japan preferred breasts like they knew them back home so prostitutes had themselves injected with silicone or liquid paraffin.

The manufactured silicone breast implant followed in the early 1960s. In 1976, the United States Food and Drug Administration was given authority over medical devices, which meant the FDA could require manufacturers to provide evidence that a device is safe in order to get permission to sell it. Breast implants were considered medical devices but because they had been sold and used for so many years without complaints, the FDA approved their continued sale without any further research. It seemed the reasonable thing to do.

The first whispers of trouble came from Japanese medical journals. Some Japanese women were being diagnosed with connective-tissue diseases – afflictions like rheumatoid arthritis, fibromyalgia, and lupus. These women had also been injected, years before, with silicone, and doctors suspected the two facts were linked.

In 1982, an Australian report described three women with silicone breast implants and connective-tissue diseases. What this meant wasn't clear. It was well known implants could leak or rupture but could silicone seep into the body and cause these diseases? Some were sure that was happening. The same year as the Australian report, a woman in San Francisco sued implant manufacturers, demanding millions of dollars for making her sick. The media reported both these stories widely, raising concerns among more women and more doctors. More cases appeared in the medical literature. The number of diseases associated with implants grew. So did the number of stories in the media. Fear spread.

In 1990, an episode of *Face to Face With Connie Chung* aired on CBS. Tearful women told stories of pain, suffering, and loss. They blamed their silicone implants. And Chung agreed. First came the implants, then came the disease. What more needed to be said? The tone of the widely watched episode was angry and accusatory, with much of the blame focused on the FDA.

That broke the dam. Stories linking implants with disease – with headlines like "Toxic Breasts" and "Ticking Time Bombs" – flooded the media. A congressional hearing was held. Advocacy groups – including Ralph Nader's Public Citizen – made implants a top target. Feminists – who considered breast augmentation to be "sexual mutilation," in the words of best-selling writer Naomi Wolf – attacked implants as a symbol of all that was wrong with modern society.

Under intense pressure, the FDA told manufacturers in early 1992 that they had 90 days to provide evidence that implants were safe. The manufacturers cobbled together what they could but the FDA felt it was inadequate. Meanwhile, a San Francisco jury awarded $7.34 million to a woman who claimed her implants, manufactured by Dow Corning, had given her mixed connective-tissue disease.

The FDA banned silicone breast implants in April 1992, although it emphasized that the implants were being banned only because they had yet to be proved safe, as the manufacturers were required to do, not because they had been proved unsafe. The roughly one million American women with the implants shouldn't worry, the FDA chief insisted.

But they did worry. Along with the successful lawsuit, the FDA ban was seen as proof that the implants were dangerous. The media filled with stories of suffering, angry women and "the trickle of lawsuits became a flood," wrote Marcia Angell, editor of the *New England Journal of Medicine* at the time and the author of the definitive book on the crisis, *Science on Trial: The Clash Between Medical Science and the Law in the Breast Implant Case*.

In 1994, the manufacturers agreed to the largest class-action settlement in history. A fund was created with $4.25 billion, including $1 billion for the lawyers who had turned implant lawsuits into a veritable industry. As part of the deal, women would have to produce medical records showing that they had implants and one of the many diseases said to be caused by implants but they didn't have to produce evidence that the disease actually was caused by the implants – either in their case or in women generally. "Plaintiffs' attorneys sometimes referred clients to clinicians whose practice consisted largely of such patients and whose fees were paid by the attorneys," wrote Angell. "Nearly half of all women with breast implants registered for the settlement, and half of those claimed to be currently suffering from implant-related illnesses." Not even the mammoth settlement fund could cover this. Dow Corning filed for bankruptcy and the settlement collapsed.

The transformation of silicone implants was complete. Once seen as innocuous objects no more dangerous than silicone contact lenses, implants were now a mortal threat. In surveys Paul Slovic conducted around this time, most people rated the implants "high risk." Only cigarette smoking was seen as more dangerous.

And yet, at this point, there was still no scientific evidence that silicone breast implants actually cause connective-tissue disease or any

other disease. As late as 1994, there wasn't even a single epidemiological survey. "What we saw in the courtroom and in much of the media,"
wrote Angell, "were judgments based on anecdote and speculation."

This dramatic sequence of events was driven by many things,
naturally, but the most critical was not the chemistry of silicone, the
biology of breasts, the tenacity of activists, the rapaciousness of
lawyers, the callousness of corporations, or the irresponsible sensationalism of the media. No, the most fundamental factor was the
simple fact that humans are good with stories and bad with numbers.

Every journalist knows that people respond very differently to
numbers and stories. A news story that says an event has taken the
lives of many people may be able to get a reader's attention for a brief
moment, but it needs more to keep it. Think of reports like "A bus
overturned in the Peruvian Andes today, killing 35." Or "Flooding in
Bangladesh continues – aid groups believe thousands have perished."
These reports scarcely pause the coffee cup at our lips. They are
hollow, meaningless. The fact that they're often about people far away
may contribute to our lack of concern but more important is their
content: They are facts and numbers. If I add some graphic descriptions (the bus tumbled down a mountain pass) or vivid images
(survivors clinging to wreckage as corpses float by in the flood water)
I am far more likely to draw in readers or viewers.

But even that connection will be fleeting. To really grab people's
attention, to make them think and feel, the journalist has to make the
story personal. I once sat in a Mexican hotel room idly watching a
CNN story about severe flooding in the capital of Indonesia – scores
dead, hundreds of thousands homeless – when I turned the channel
and saw, at the bottom of the screen of a Spanish–language station,
this urgent bulletin: "Anna Nicole Smith *muere*." I know only a few
words of Spanish but *muere* is one of them. I was shocked. "Anna
Nicole Smith is dead," I called out to my wife in the bathroom. I did

not inform her of the Indonesian floods, needless to say, although by any rational measure that story was vastly more important than the untimely loss of a minor celebrity. But Anna Nicole Smith was an identifiable person; the dead in Indonesia were statistics. And the loss of an identifiable person can move us in ways that statistical abstractions cannot. That's just human nature.

Almost 3,000 people were killed that sunny morning in September 2001, but what does that statistic make us feel? It is big, certainly. But it is a cold, empty number. In itself, it makes us feel little or nothing. The best it can do is remind us of the images of the day – the explosion, the collapsing towers, the survivors shuffling through scattered paper and ash – that are infused with the emotions the number lacks. Still more potent are images of a single person, such as the horrifying photo of a man falling head first to his death or the businessman walking away with his briefcase and empty eyes.

Then there are the personal stories – like that of Diana O'Connor, 37, the 15th of 16 children in a Brooklyn family, who had worked at three jobs to pay her way through college and whose drive to succeed earned her an executive's office high up in the World Trade Center. Diana O'Connor may have been only one of thousands to die that day but her story, told in a way that allows us to imagine this one person, can move us in a way that the phrase "almost 3,000 were killed" never can. There's a reason that statistics have been called "people with the tears dried off."

The power of personal stories explains the standard format of most feature reports in newspapers and television: Introduce a person whose story is moving, connect that story to the larger subject at hand, discuss the subject with statistics and analysis, and close by returning to the person with the moving story. It's a sugar–coated pill and done well it is journalism at its best. It connects the reader emotionally but it also provides the intellectual substance needed to really understand an issue. It is, however, a lot easier to tell someone's touching story and skip the stuff in the middle, and the delightful

thing – delightful for the lazy journalist, that is – is that a touching
story minus analysis is just as likely to grab and hold the attention of
readers and viewers as a touching story with excellent analysis.

People love stories about people. We love telling them and we
love hearing them. It's a universal human trait, and that suggests to
evolutionary psychologists that storytelling – both the telling and the
listening – is actually hard-wired into the species.

For that to be true, there must be evolutionary advantages to storytelling. And there are. Storytelling is a good way to swap information, for one thing, which allows people to benefit from each other's
experiences. And storytelling is intensely social. Robin Dunbar of the
University of Liverpool noted that while chimpanzees don't tell
stories, they do spend about 20 per cent of each day picking ticks
from each other's fur. They aren't being fastidious; they're being
social. Grooming is what chimpanzees and other social primates do
to form and maintain personal bonds. Like chimps, humans are social
primates. But our hunter–gatherer ancestors lived in larger bands
than chimpanzees and our ancestors would have had to spend as
much as 50 per cent of their time picking ticks if they were to bond
as chimps do. Talking, on the other hand, is something we can do
with many people at the same time. We can even talk while doing
other things. That makes chat the ideal replacement for tick–picking.
Studies of the ordinary daily conversations of modern humans,
Dunbar notes, find little of it is instructional. Most is personal chit-
chat – people telling stories about people.

Storytelling can also be a valuable form of rehearsal. "If survival
in life is a matter of dealing with an often inhospitable physical universe, and [of] dealing with members of our own species, both friendly
and unfriendly, there would be a general benefit to be derived from
imaginatively exercising the mind in order to prepare it for the next
challenge," writes philosopher Denis Dutton. "Story–telling, on this
model, is a way of running multiple, relatively cost-free experiments
with life in order to see, in the imagination, where courses of action

may lead. Although narrative can deal with the challenges of the natural world, its usual home is, as Aristotle also understood, in the realm of human relations." Shakespeare may have as much to tell us about psychology as psychologists do, which is why we respond to his plays as we do. When Iago whispers in the ear of Othello and Othello's love for Desdemona turns to hate, and hate to murder, we sense that, yes, this could happen. This is what jealousy and distrust can do. This is true.

But sometimes stories are not true, or least they are an incomplete guide to what is true. The stories that led to the banning of silicone breast implants were deeply personal and painful. And there were so many. It seemed so obviously true that implants cause disease. It *felt* true. Gut said so. "There are thousands upon thousands of women who have breast implants and complain of terrible pain," Cokie Roberts reported on ABC News's *Nightline* in 1995. "Can they all be wrong?"

The answer to that was: possibly. At the time implants were banned, there were roughly 100 million adult women in the United States. Of those, about 1 per cent had implants and 1 per cent had connective-tissue disease. So "we could expect by coincidence alone that 10,000 would have both," Marcia Angell noted. The tragic stories of women who got silicone breast implants and who suffered connective-tissue disease did not, and could not, demonstrate that the implants caused the disease. What was needed were epidemiological studies to determine whether the rate of disease among women with implants was higher than it was among women without implants. If it was, that wouldn't definitively prove that implants cause disease – there could be a third factor connecting the two – but it would be solid grounds for suspicion and further investigation. But there weren't any epidemiological studies. Scientists opposed to the ban made this point repeatedly. So did the FDA, which insisted all along that it was only banning the implants while it awaited word from the epidemiologists. The risk hasn't been proved, the FDA emphasized.

There is no evidence. This outraged activist groups, whose slogan became "We are the evidence!" No one could doubt their sincerity but passion and pain are no substitute for reason, and reason said there was no evidence.

Anecdotes aren't data: That's a favourite expression of scientists. Anecdotes – stories – may be illuminating in the manner of Shakespeare. They may also alert us to something that needs scientific investigation. The proliferating stories of breast implants causing disease were certainly grounds for concern and aggressive research. But anecdotes don't *prove* anything. Only data – properly collected and analyzed – can do that.

This has always been true but the advance of science and technology has made it all the more important. We can now measure in microns and light–years and detect in parts per billion. Information and numbers are piling up. To really understand this proliferating information, we must do much more than tell stories.

Unfortunately, what isn't increasing is Gut's skill in handling numbers. Shaped in a world of campfires and flint spears, our intuition is as innately lousy with numbers as it is good with stories. Stanislas Dehaene, a neuroscientist at the Collège de France, notes that animals as varied as dolphins and rats have a very basic grasp of numbers. They can easily tell the difference between two and four and they "have elementary addition and subtraction abilities." But as the numbers go up, their abilities go down rapidly. Even numbers as low as six and seven require more time and effort to grasp and use than one or two.

It turns out humans' innate skill with numbers isn't much better than that of rats and dolphins. "We are systematically slower to compute, say, 4 + 5 than 2 + 3," writes Dehaene. And just as animals have to slow down and think to discriminate between close quantities such as 7 and 8, "it takes us longer to decide that 9 is larger than 8 than to make the same decision for 9 versus 2." Of course humans also have the capacity to move beyond this stage but the struggle every schoolchild has learning the multiplication tables is a reminder of the limits of our natural grasp of numbers. "Sadly enough, innumeracy may be our normal human condition," writes Dehaene, "and it takes considerable effort to become numerate."

How many of us make that effort isn't clear. A Canadian polling company once asked people how many millions there are in a billion. Forty-five per cent didn't know. So how will they react when they're told that the arsenic levels in their drinking water are three parts per billion? Even an informed layperson will have to gather more information and think hard to make sense of that information. But those who don't know what a billion is can only look to Gut for an answer and Gut doesn't have a clue what a billion is. Gut does, however, know that arsenic is a Bad Thing: Press the panic button.

The influence of our ancestral environment is not limited to the strictly innumerate, however. Physicist Herbert York once explained that the reason he designed the nuclear warhead of the Atlas rocket to be one megaton was that one megaton is a particularly round number. "Thus the actual physical size of the first Atlas warhead and the number of people it would kill were determined by the fact that human beings have two hands with five fingers each and therefore count by tens."

Numeracy also fails to give numbers the power to make us feel. Charities long ago learned that appeals to help one, identifiable person are far more compelling than references to large numbers of people in need. "If I look at the mass, I will never act," wrote Mother Teresa. "If I look at the one, I will." The impotence of numbers is underscored by our reactions to death. If the death of one is a tragedy, the death of a thousand should be a thousand times worse, but our feelings simply do not work that way. In the early years of the 1980s, reporting on AIDS was sparse despite the steadily growing number of victims. That changed in July 1985, when the number of newspaper articles on AIDS published in the United States soared 500 per cent. The event that changed everything was Rock Hudson's announcement that he had AIDS: His familiar face did what no statistic could. "The death of one man is a tragedy, the deaths of millions is a statistic," said that expert on death, Joseph Stalin.

Numbers may even hinder the emotions brought out by the presence of one, suffering person. Paul Slovic, Deborah Small, and George Loewenstein set up an experiment in which people were asked to donate to African relief. One appeal featured a statistical overview of the crisis, another profiled a seven-year-old girl, and a third provided both the profile and the statistics. Not surprisingly, the profile generated much more giving than the statistics alone, but it also did better than the combined profile-and-statistics pitch – as if the numbers somehow interfered with the empathetic urge to help generated by the profile of the little girl.

Of course, big numbers can impress, which is why activists and politicians are so keen on using them. But big numbers impress by size alone, not by human connection. Imagine standing at mid-field of a stadium filled with 30,000 people. Impressive? Certainly. That's a lot of people. Now imagine the same scenario but with 90,000 people. Again, it's impressive, but it's not three times more impressive because our feelings aren't calibrated to that scale. The first number is big. The second number is big. That's the best Gut can do.

A curious side effect of our inability to feel large numbers – confirmed in many experiments – is that proportions can influence our thoughts more than simple numbers. When Paul Slovic asked groups of students to indicate, on a scale from 0 to 20, to what degree they would support the purchase of airport safety equipment, he found they expressed much stronger support when told that the equipment could be expected to save 98 per cent of 150 lives than when they were told it would save 150 lives. Even saving "85 per cent of 150 lives" garnered more support than saving 150 lives. The explanation lies in the lack of feeling we have for the number 150. It's vaguely good, because it represents people's lives, but it's abstract. We can't picture 150 lives and so we don't *feel* 150 lives. We can feel proportions, however. Ninety-eight per cent is almost all. It's a cup filled nearly to overflowing. And so we find saving 98 per cent of 150 lives more compelling than saving 150 lives.

Daniel Kahneman and Amos Tversky underscored the impotence of statistics in a variation of the famous "Linda" experiment. First, people were asked to read a profile of a man that detailed his personality and habits. Then they were told that this man was drawn from a group that consisted of 70 engineers and 30 lawyers. Now, the researchers asked, based on everything you know, is it more likely this man is a lawyer or an engineer? Kahneman and Tversky ran many variations of this experiment and in every one, the statistics – 70 engineers, 30 lawyers – mattered less than the profile.

Statistical *concepts* may be even less influential than numbers. Kahneman once discovered that an Israeli flight instructor had concluded, based on personal experience, that criticism improves performance while praise reduces it. How had he come to this strange conclusion? When student pilots made particularly good landings, he praised them – and their subsequent landings were usually not as good. But when they made particularly bad landings, he criticized them – and the subsequent landings got better. Therefore, he concluded, criticism works but praise doesn't. What this intelligent, educated man had failed to account for, Kahneman noted, was "regression to the mean": If an unusual result happens, it is likely to be followed by a result closer to the statistical average. So a particularly good landing is likely to be followed by a landing that's not as good, and a particularly bad landing is likely to be improved on next time. Criticism and praise have nothing to do with the change. It's just numbers. But because we have no intuitive sense of regression to the mean, it takes real mental effort to catch this sort of mistake.

The same is true of the statistical concept of sample bias. Say you want to know what Americans think of the job the president is doing. That should be simple enough. Just ask some Americans. But which Americans you ask makes all the difference. If you go to a Republican rally and ask people as they leave, it's pretty obvious that your sample will be biased (whether the president is a Republican or a Democrat) and it will produce misleading conclusions about what "Americans" think. The same would be true if you surveyed only Texans, or Episcopalians, or yoga instructors. The bias in each case will be different and sometimes the way it skews the numbers may not be obvious. But by not properly sampling the population you are interested in – all Americans – the results you obtain will be distorted and unreliable. Pollsters typically avoid this hazard by randomly selecting telephone numbers from the entire population whose views are being sought, which creates a legitimate sample and meaningful results. (Whether the sample is biased by the increasing rate at which people refuse to answer surveys is another matter.)

In the silicone breast implant scare, what the media effectively did was present a deeply biased sample. Story after story profiled sick women who blamed their suffering on implants. Eventually, the number of women profiled was in the hundreds. Journalists also reported the views of organizations that represented thousands more women. Cumulatively, it looked very impressive. These were big numbers and the stories – I got implants then I got sick – were fright-eningly similar. How could you not think there was something to this? But the whole exercise was flawed because healthy women with implants didn't have much reason to join lobby groups or call reporters, and reporters made little effort to find these women and profile them because "Woman Not Sick" isn't much of a headline. And so, despite the vast volume of reporting on implants, it no more reflected the health of all women with breast implants than a poll taken at a Republican rally would reflect the views of all Americans.

Our failure to spot biased samples is a product of an even more fundamental failure: We have no intuitive feel for the concept of randomness.

Ask people to put 50 dots on a paper in a way that is typical of random placement and they're likely to evenly disperse them – not quite in lines and rows but evenly enough that the page will look balanced. Show people two sets of numbers – 1, 2, 3, 4, 5, 6 and 10, 13, 19, 25, 30, 32 – and they'll say the second set is more likely to come up in a lottery. Have them flip a coin and if it comes up heads five times in a row, they will have a powerful sense that the next flip is more likely to come up tails than heads.

All these conclusions are wrong because they're all based on intuitions that don't grasp the nature of randomness. Every flip of a coin is random – as is every spin of the roulette wheel or pull on a slot machine's arm – and so any given flip has an equal chance of coming up heads or tails; the belief that a long streak increases the chances of a different result on the next go is a mistake called gambler's fallacy. As for lotteries, each number is randomly selected and so something that looks like a pattern – 1, 2, 3, 4, 5, 6 – is as likely to occur as any other result. And it is fantastically unlikely that 50 dots randomly distributed on paper would wind up evenly dispersed; instead, thick clusters of dots will form in some spots while other portions of the paper will be dot-free.

Misperceptions of randomness can be tenacious. Amos Tversky, Tom Gilovich, and Robert Vallone famously analyzed basketball's "hot hand" – the belief that a player who has sunk his last two, three, or four shots has the "hot hand" and is therefore more likely to sink his next shot than if he has just missed a shot – and proved with rigorous statistical analysis that the "hot hand" is a myth. For their trouble, the psychologists were mocked by basketball coaches and fans across the United States.

Our flawed intuitions about randomness generally produce only harmless foibles like beliefs in "hot hands" and Aunt Betty's insistence that she has to play her lottery numbers next week because the numbers she has played for 17 years have never come up so they're due any time now. Sometimes, though, there are serious consequences.

One reason that people often respond irrationally to flooding – why rebuild in the very spot where you were just washed out? – is their failure to grasp randomness. Most floods are, in effect, random events. A flood this year says nothing about whether a flood will happen next year. But that's not what Gut senses. A flood this year means a flood next year is less likely. And when experts say that this year's flood is the "flood of the century" – one so big it is expected to happen once every 100 years – Gut takes this to mean that another flood of similar magnitude won't happen for decades. The fact that a "flood of the century" can happen three years in a row just doesn't make intuitive sense. Head can understand that, with a little effort, but not Gut.

Murder is a decidedly non-random event but in cities with millions of people the distribution of murders on the calendar is effectively random (if we set aside the modest influence that seasonal changes in the weather can have in some cities). And because it's random, clusters will occur – periods when far more murders than average happen. Statisticians call this Poisson clumping, after the French mathematician Simeon-Denis Poisson, who came up with a calculation that distinguishes between the clustering one can expect purely as a result of chance and clustering caused by something else. In the book *Struck by Lightning*, University of Toronto mathematician Jeffrey Rosenthal recounts how five murders in Toronto that fell in a single week generated a flurry of news stories and plenty of talk about crime getting out of control. The city's police chief even said it proved the justice system was too soft to deter criminals. But Rosenthal calculated that Toronto, with an average of 1.5 murders per week, had "a 1.4 per cent chance of seeing five homicides in a given week, purely by chance. So we should expect to see five homicides in the same week once every 71 weeks – nearly once a year!" The same calculation showed that there is a 22 per cent chance of a week being murder-free purely by chance, and Toronto often does experience murder-free weeks, Rosenthal noted. "But I have yet to see a newspaper headline that screams 'No Murders This Week!'"

Cancer clusters are another frightening phenomenon that owes much to our inability to see randomness. Every year in developed countries, public health authorities field calls from people convinced that their town's eight cases of leukemia or five cases of brain cancer cannot possibly be the result of mere chance. And people always know the real cause. It is pesticides on farm fields, radiation from the region's nuclear plant, or toxins seeping out of a nearby landfill. In almost every case, they don't have any actual evidence linking the supposed threat to the cancers. The mere fact that a suspicious cancer rate exists near something suspect is enough to link them in most people's minds.

In the great majority of these panics, officials do some calculations and find that the rate of illness can easily be the result of chance alone. This is explained and that's the end of it. But sometimes – usually when residents who don't trust the official explanation take their worries to the media and politicians get involved – full-scale investigations are launched. Almost always, nothing is found. Residents and activists have been known to reject even these findings but their suspicions say far more about the power of Gut-based judgments than they do about cancer.

I don't want to overstate Gut's failings. Even in this world of satellites and microchips, intuition still gets many things right. It's also important to remember that science and statistics have their own limitations. They never fully eliminate uncertainty, for one. Statistics may tell us that an apparent cancer cluster *could* be a product of chance but they can't tell us that it *is* a product of chance. And even the most thorough epidemiological studies cannot absolutely *prove* that farmers' pesticides are or are not causing cancer – they can only suggest it, sometimes weakly, sometimes strongly, but always with some degree of uncertainty. In all forms of scientific inquiry, hard facts and strong explanations are built up slowly, and only with great effort. "Sometimes Gut does get it right, even before science does," Paul Slovic notes. "Other times Gut's intuitions turn science on to a problem that needs examining. Often, science's best answer contains much uncertainty. In such cases, if the benefits are not great and the risks are scary, it may be best to go with Gut." At least until science tells us more.

It's also heartening to know there is evidence that we can, with a little effort, make ourselves much less vulnerable to Gut's weaknesses. In a series of four studies, a team of psychologists led by Ellen Peters, a colleague of Slovic's at Decision Research, examined whether numeracy makes any difference to the mistakes Gut tends to make. It did, in a big way. The studies repeated several well-known experiments – including some mentioned earlier in this book – but this time participants were also tested to see how skilled they were with numbers and math. The results were unequivocal: The more numerate people were, the less likely they were to be tripped up by Gut's mistakes. It's not clear whether this effect is the result of a numerate person's Head being better able to intervene and correct Gut or if numeracy, like golf, is a skill that can be learned by the conscious mind and then transferred, with lots of practice, to the unconscious mind. But in either case, numeracy helps.

Much less encouraging is what Ms. Peters found when she tested the numeracy levels of the people in her experiments. Only 74 per cent were able to answer this question correctly: "If Person A's chance of getting a disease is 1 in 100 in 10 years, and Person B's risk is double that of Person A, what is B's risk?" Sixty-one per cent got this question right: "Imagine that we roll a fair, six-sided die 1,000 times. Out of 1,000 rolls, how many times do you think the die will come up even (2, 4, or 6)?" And just 46 per cent figured out this one: "In the Acme Publishing Sweepstakes, the chance of winning a car is one in 1,000. What per cent of tickets of Acme Publishing Sweepstakes win a car?" Peters's test subjects were university students. When even a nation's university-educated elite has such a weak grasp of the numbers that define risk, that nation is in danger of getting risk very wrong.

The breast-implant panic was at its peak in June 1994, when science finally delivered. A Mayo Clinic epidemiological survey published in the *New England Journal of Medicine* found no link between silicone implants and connective-tissue disease. More studies followed, all with similar results. Finally, Congress asked the Institute of Medicine (I.O.M.), the medical branch of the National Academies of Science, to survey the burgeoning research. In 1999, the I.O.M. issued its report. "Some women with breast implants are indeed very ill and the I.O.M. committee is very sympathetic to their distress," the report concluded. "However, it can find no evidence that these women are ill because of their implants."

In June 2004, Dow Corning emerged from nine years of bank-ruptcy. As part of its reorganization plan, the company created a fund of more than $2 billion in order to pay off more than 360,000 claims. Given the state of the evidence, this might seem like an unfair wind-fall for women with implants. It was unfair to Dow Corning, certainly, but it was no windfall. Countless women had been tormented for years by the belief that their bodies were contaminated and they could soon sicken and die. In this tragedy, only the lawyers won.

In November 2006, the Food and Drug Administration lifted the ban on silicone breast implants. The devices can rupture and cause pain and inflammation, the FDA noted, but the very substantial evidence to date does not indicate that they pose a risk of disease. Anti-implant activists were furious. They remain certain that sili-cone breast implants are deadly and it seems nothing can convince them otherwise.

6

THE HERD SENSES DANGER

You are a bright, promising young professional and you have been chosen to participate in a three-day project at the Institute of Personality Assessment and Research at the University of California in sunny Berkeley. The researchers say they are interested in personality and leadership and so they have brought together an impressive group of 100 to take a closer look at how exemplary people like you think and act.

A barrage of questions, tests, and experiments follows, including one exercise in which you are asked to sit in a cubicle with an electrical panel. Four other participants sit in identical cubicles next to you, although you cannot see each other. Slides will appear on the panel that will ask you questions, you are told, and you can answer with the switches on the panel. Each of the panels is connected to the others so you can all see each other's answers, although you cannot discuss them. The order in which you will answer will vary.

The questions are simple enough at first. Geometric shapes appear and you are asked to judge which is larger. At the beginning, you are the first person directed to respond. Then you are asked to be the second to answer, which allows you to see the first person's response before you give yours. Then you move to the number three spot. There's nothing that takes any careful consideration at this point so things move along quickly.

Finally, you are the last of the group to answer. A slide appears with five lines on it. Which line is longest? It's obvious the longest is number four but you have to wait before you can answer. The first person's answer pops up on your screen: number five. That's odd, you think. You look carefully at the lines. Number four is obviously longer than number five. Then the second answer appears: number five. And the third answer: number five. And the fourth: number five.

Now it's your turn to answer. What will it be?

You clearly see everyone is wrong. You shouldn't hesitate to flip the switch for number four. And yet there's a good chance you won't. When this experiment was conducted by Richard Crutchfield and colleagues in the spring of 1953, 15 people out of 50 ignored what they saw and went with the consensus.

Crutchfield's work was a variation on experiments conducted by Solomon Asch in the same era. In one of psychology's most famous experiments, Asch had people sit together in groups and answer questions that supposedly tested visual perception. Only one person was the actual subject of the experiment, however. All the others were instructed, in the later stages, to give answers that were clearly wrong. In total, the group gave incorrect answers 12 times. Three-quarters of Asch's test subjects abandoned their own judgment and went with the group at least once. Overall, people conformed to an obviously false group consensus one-third of the time.

We are social animals and what others think matters deeply to us. The group's opinion isn't everything; we can buck the trend. But even when the other people involved are strangers, even when we are anonymous, even when dissenting will cost us nothing, we want to agree with the group.

And that's when the answer is instantly clear and inarguably true. Crutchfield's experiment involved slightly more ambiguous questions, including one in which people were asked if they agreed with the statement "I believe we are made better by the trials and hardships of life." Among subjects in a control group that was not exposed to the answers of others, everyone agreed. But among those in the experiment who thought that everyone else disagreed with the statement, 31 per cent said they did not agree. Asked whether they agreed with the statement "I doubt whether I would make a good leader," every person in the control group rejected it. But when the group was seen to agree with the statement, 37 per cent of people went along with the consensus and agreed that they doubted themselves.

Crutchfield also designed three questions that had no right answer. They included a series of numbers that subjects were asked to complete, which was impossible because the numbers were random. In that case, 79 per cent of participants did not guess or otherwise struggle to come up with their own answer. They simply went with what the group said.

These studies of conformity are often cited to cast humans as sheep, and it certainly is disturbing to see people set aside what they clearly know to be true and say what they know to be false. That's all the more true from the perspective of the early 1950s, when Asch and Crutchfield conducted their classic experiments. The horror of fascism was a fresh memory and communism was a present threat. Social scientists wanted to understand why nations succumbed to mass movements, and in that context it was chilling to see how easy it is to make people deny what they see with their own eyes.

But from an evolutionary perspective, the human tendency to conform is not so strange. Individual survival depended on the group working together and cooperation is much more likely if people share a desire to agree. A band of doubters, dissenters, and proud nonconformists would not do so well hunting and gathering on the plains of Africa.

Conformity is also a good way to benefit from the pooling of information. One person knows only what he knows but 30 people can draw on the knowledge and experience of 30, and so when every-one else is convinced there are lions in the tall grass it's reasonable to set aside your doubts and take another route back to camp. The group may be wrong, of course. The collective opinion may have been unduly influenced by one person's irrational opinion or by bad or irrelevant information. But still, other things being equal, it's often best to follow the herd.

It's tempting to think things have changed. The explosion of sci-entific knowledge over the last five centuries has provided a new basis for making judgments that is demonstrably superior to personal and collective experience. And the proliferation of media in the last several decades has made that knowledge available to anyone. There's no need to follow the herd. We can all be fully independent thinkers now.

Or rather, we can be fully independent thinkers if we understand the following sentence, plucked from the *New England Journal of Medicine*: "In this randomized, multicenter study involving evaluators who were unaware of treatment assignments, we compared the efficacy and safety of posaconazole with those of fluconazole or itra-conazole as prophylaxis for patients with prolonged neutropenia." And this one from a physics journal: "We evaluate the six-fold inte-gral representation for the second-order exchange contribution to the self-energy of a dense three-dimensional electron gas on the Fermi surface." And then there's this fascinating insight from a journal of cellular biology: "Prior to microtubule capture, sister centromeres resolve from one another, coming to rest on opposite surfaces of the condensing chromosome."

Clearly, today's fully independent thinker will have to have a thorough knowledge of biology, physics, medicine, chemistry, geology, and statistics. He or she will also require an enormous amount of free time. Someone who wants to independently decide how risky it is to suntan on a beach, for example, will find there are thousands of rel-evant studies. It would take months of reading and consideration in order to draw a conclusion about this one, simple risk. Thus if an independent thinker really wishes to form entirely independent judgments about the risks we face in daily life, or even just those we hear about in the news, he or she will have to obtain multiple university degrees, quit his or her job, and do absolutely nothing but read about all the ways he or she may die until he or she actually is dead.

Most people would find that somewhat impractical. For them, the only way to tap the vast pools of scientific knowledge is to rely on the advice of experts – people who are capable of synthesizing information from at least one field and making it comprehensible to a lay audience. This is preferable to getting your opinions from people who know as little as you do, naturally, but it too has limitations. For one thing, experts often disagree. Even when there's widespread agreement, there will still be dissenters who make their case with impressive statistics and bewildering scientific jargon.

Another solution is to turn to intermediaries – those who are not experts themselves but claim to understand the science. Does abortion put a woman's health at risk? There's heaps of research on the subject. Much of it is contradictory. All of it is complicated. But when I took a look at the website of Focus on the Family, a conservative lobby group that wants abortion banned, I see that the research quite clearly proves that abortion does put a woman's health at risk. Studies are cited, statistics presented, scientists quoted. But then when I look at the website of the National Abortion Rights Action League (NARAL), a staunchly pro-choice lobby group, I discover that the research indisputably shows abortion does not put a woman's health at risk. Studies are cited, statistics presented, scientists quoted.

Now, if I happened to trust NARAL or Focus on the Family, I might decide that their opinion is good enough for me. But a whole lot of people would look at this differently. NARAL and Focus on the Family are lobby groups pursuing political agendas, they would think. Why should I trust either of them to give me a disinterested assessment of the science? As Homer Simpson sagely observed in an interview with broadcaster Kent Brockman, "People can come up with statistics to prove anything, Kent. Forty per cent of all people know that."

There's something to be said for this perspective. On important public issues, we constantly encounter analyses that are outwardly impressive – lots of numbers and references to studies – that come to radically different conclusions even though they all claim to be portraying the state of the science. And these analyses have a suspicious tendency to come to exactly the conclusions that those doing the analyzing find desirable. Name an issue, any issue. Somewhere there are lobbyists, activists, and ideologically driven newspaper pundits who would be delighted to provide you with a rigorous and objective evaluation of the science that just happens to prove that the interest, agenda, or ideology they represent is absolutely right. So, yes, skepticism is warranted.

But Homer Simpson isn't merely skeptical. He is cynical. He denies the very possibility of knowing the difference between true and untrue, between the more accurate and the less. And that's just wrong. It may take a little effort to prove that the statistic Homer cites is fabricated, but it can be done. The truth is out there, to quote another staple of 1990s television.

Along with truth, cynicism endangers trust. And that can be dangerous. Researchers have found that when the people or institutions handling a risk are trusted, public concern declines: It matters a great deal whether the person telling you not to worry is your family physician or a tobacco company spokesman. Researchers have also shown, as wise people have always known, that trust is difficult to build and easily lost. So trust is vital.

But trust is disappearing fast. In most modern countries, political scientists have found a long–term decline in public trust of various authorities. The danger here is that we will collectively cross the line separating skepticism from cynicism. Where a reasonable respect for expertise is lost, people are left to search for scientific understanding in Google and Internet chat rooms and the sneer of the cynic may mutate into unreasoning, paralyzing fear. That end state can be seen in the anti-vaccination movements growing in the United States, Britain, and elsewhere. Fuelled by distrust of all authority, anti-vaccination activists rail against the dangers of vaccinating children (some imaginary, some real-but-rare) while ignoring the immense benefits of vaccination – benefits that could be lost if these movements continue to grow.

This same poisonous distrust is on display in John Weingart's *Waste Is a Terrible Thing to Mind*, an account of Weingart's agonizing work as the head of a New Jersey board given the job of finding a site for a low-level radioactive waste disposal facility. Experts agreed that such a facility is not a serious hazard, but no one wanted to hear that. "At the Siting Board's open houses," writes Weingart, who is now a political scientist at Rutgers University, "people would invent scenarios and then dare Board members and staff to say they were impossible. A person would ask, 'What would happen if a plane crashed into a concrete bunker filled with radioactive waste and exploded?' We would explain that while the plane and its contents might explode, nothing in the disposal facility could. And they would say, 'But what if explosives had been mistakenly disposed of, and the monitoring devices at the facility had malfunctioned so they weren't noticed?' We would head down the road of saying that this was an extremely unlikely set of events. And they would say, 'Well, it could happen, couldn't it?'"

Fortunately, we have not entirely abandoned trust and experts can still have great influence on public opinion, particularly when they manage to forge a consensus among themselves. Does HIV cause AIDS? For a long time, there were scientists who said it did not but the overwhelming majority said it did. The public heard and accepted the majority view. The same scenario is playing out now with climate change – most people in every Western country agree that man-made climate change is real not because they've looked into the science for themselves, but because they know that's what most scientists think.

But as Howard Margolis describes in *Dealing with Risk*, scientists can also find themselves resoundingly ignored when their views go against strong public feelings. Margolis notes that the American Physical Society – an association of physicists – easily convinced the public that cold fusion didn't work but it had no impact when it issued a positive report on the safety of high-level nuclear waste disposal.

So scientific information and the opinions of scientists can certainly play a role in how people judge risks, but – as the continued divisions between expert and lay opinion demonstrate – they aren't nearly as influential as scientists and officials might like. We remain a species powerfully influenced by the unconscious mind and its tools – particularly the Example Rule, the Good–Bad Rule, and the Rule of Typical Things. We also remain social animals who care about what other people think. And if we aren't sure whether we should worry about this risk or that, whether other people are worried makes a huge difference.

"Imagine that Alan says that abandoned hazardous waste sites are dangerous, or that Alan initiates protest action because such a site is located nearby," writes Cass Sunstein in *Risk and Reason*. "Betty, otherwise skeptical or in equipoise, may go along with Alan; Carl, otherwise an agnostic, may be convinced that if Alan and Betty share the relevant belief, the belief must be true. It will take a confident Deborah to resist the shared judgments of Alan, Betty and Carl. The result of these sets of influences can be social cascades, as hundreds, thousands or millions of people come to accept a certain belief because of what they think other people believe."

Of course it's a big leap from someone in a laboratory going along with the group answer on meaningless questions to "hundreds, thousands or millions of people" deciding that something is dangerous simply because that's what other people think. After all, people in laboratory experiments know their answers don't really matter. They won't be punished if they make mistakes and they won't be rewarded for doing well. But in the real world, our views do matter.

For one thing, we are citizens of democracies in which popular opinion influences how governments respond – or don't respond – to risks. More concretely, what we think about risks can be critical in our personal lives. Will you support the creation of a hazardous waste site in your region? If it goes ahead, it means jobs and economic growth. But it could also mean a threat to the health of your family. Will you shrug off the threat of pedophiles and hoodlums and let your kids play unsupervised in the neighbourhood park? Will you eat foods with trans-fats? Each of these questions matters far more than whether line number four is longer than line number five, so it's hard to believe that on these important matters we would so casually abandon our own judgment and follow the herd.

In fact, there is some evidence that the importance of these questions would change the rate at which we conform to the group view. It would *increase* it. Substantially.

Psychologists at the University of Iowa – Robert Baron, Joseph Vandello, and Bethany Brunsman – designed an experiment in which they told participants they were testing the accuracy of eyewitness verifications. The testing would involve slides appearing briefly and questions based on what was shown: Was the man wearing glasses? Did you see the man in the police lineup? Three people took the test each round. This was a ruse, of course. Two of the three test-takers were actually part of the real experiment, which was to see if people would go along with the false answers they gave.

Two new variables set this experiment apart from the earlier research on conformity. In some trials, the slides were shown repeatedly or they were left on the screen for a full five seconds. The researchers knew from earlier testing that people almost never make mistakes under those conditions. But in other trials, the slide would flash onscreen only briefly, making the questions much harder to answer. The researchers also gave participants different background information about the purpose of the experiment. Some were told it was merely a pilot study intended to get a general sense of how people perceive things that might be used sometime in the future "to develop a test that lets us know how accurate people are as witnesses." This was the "low importance" version of the experiment. But others were told the researchers had already developed the "Iowa Witness Identification Test" that "will soon be adopted by police departments and courtrooms in cases involving eyewitness testimony," the researchers said. "Over the next few weeks, we will be running research participants such as yourselves through the revised I.W.I.T. to establish reliable norms. As a result, we hope that you try your best on this test because establishing accurate norms is crucial. Most people do try hard on this test because they are interested in seeing how good their eyewitness accuracy is compared to others. But, to increase your interest in doing well on this test, we will be awarding prizes of $20 at the end of the experimental testing period to the participants who score the highest in accuracy." This was the "high importance" condition.

The first results were an almost exact duplicate of the original conformity experiments: When the task was easy and people thought the experiment was "low importance," one-third abandoned their own judgment and conformed to the group answer. Then came the "easy task/high importance" version. The researchers expected conformity would fall under those conditions, and it did. But it didn't disappear: Between 13 per cent and 16 per cent still followed the group.

Things got intriguing when the questions became harder to answer. Among those who thought the test was "low importance," a minority conformed to the group, just as they did when the questions were easy to answer. But when the test was "high importance," conformity actually went *up*. The researchers also found that under those conditions, people became *more* confident about the accuracy of their group-influenced answers. "Our data suggest," wrote the researchers, "that so long as the judgments are difficult or ambiguous, and the influencing agents are united and confident, increasing the importance of accuracy will heighten confidence as well as conformity – a dangerous combination."

Judgments about risk are often difficult and important. If Baron, Vandello, and Brunsman are right, those are precisely the conditions under which people are most likely to conform to the views of the group and feel confident that they are right to do so.

But surely, one might think, an opinion based on nothing more than the uninformed views of others is a fragile thing. We are exposed to new information every day. If the group view is foolish, we will soon come across evidence that will make us doubt our opinions. The blind can't go on leading the blind for long, can they?

Unfortunately, psychologists have discovered another cognitive bias that suggests that, in some circumstances, the blind can actually lead the blind indefinitely. It's called confirmation bias and its operation is both simple and powerful. Once we have formed a view, we embrace information that supports that view while ignoring, rejecting or harshly scrutinizing information that casts doubt on our view. Any belief will do. It makes no difference whether the thought is about trivia or something important. It doesn't matter if the belief is the product of long and careful consideration or something I believe simply because everybody else in the Internet chat room said so. Once a belief is established, our brains will seek to confirm it.

In one of the earliest studies on confirmation bias, psychologist Peter Wason simply showed people a sequence of three numbers – 2, 4, 6 – and told them the sequence followed a certain rule. The participants were asked to figure out what that rule was. They could do so by writing down three more numbers and asking if they were in line with the rule. Once you think you've figured out the rule, the researchers instructed, say so and we will see if you're right.

It seems so obvious that the rule the numbers are following is "even numbers increasing by two." So let's say you were to take the test. What would you say? Obviously, your first step would be to ask:

"What about 8, 10, 12? Does that follow the rule?" And you would be told, yes, that follows the rule.

Now you are really suspicious. This is far too easy. So you decide to try another set of number. Does "14, 16, 18" follow the rule? It does.

At this point, you want to shout out the answer – the rule is even numbers increasing by two! – but you know there's got to be a trick here. So you decide to ask about another three numbers: 20, 22, 24. Right, again!

Most people who take this test follow exactly this pattern. Every time they guess, they are told they are right and so, it seems, the evidence that they are right piles up. Naturally, they become absolutely convinced that their initial belief is correct. Just look at all the evidence! And so they stop the test and announce that they have the answer: It is "even numbers increasing by two."

And they are told that they are wrong. That is not the rule. The correct rule is actually "any three numbers in ascending order."

Why do people get this wrong? It is very easy to figure out that the rule is not "even numbers increasing by two." All they have to do is try to *disconfirm* that the rule is even numbers increasing by two. They could, for example, ask if "5, 7, 9" follows the rule. Do that and the answer would be, yes, it does – which would instantly disconfirm the hypothesis. But most people do not try to disconfirm. They do the opposite, trying to confirm the rule by looking for examples that fit it. That's a futile strategy. No matter how many examples are piled up, they can never prove that the belief is correct. Confirmation doesn't work.

Unfortunately, seeking to confirm our beliefs comes naturally, while it feels strange and counterintuitive to look for evidence that contradicts our beliefs. Worse still, if we happen to stumble across evidence that runs contrary to our views, we have a strong tendency to belittle or ignore it. In 1979 – when capital punishment was a top issue in the United States – American researchers brought together equal numbers of supporters and opponents of the death penalty.

The strength of their views was tested. Then they were asked to read a carefully balanced essay that presented evidence that capital punishment deters crime and evidence that it does not. The researchers then re-tested people's opinions and discovered that they had only gotten stronger. They had absorbed the evidence that confirmed their views, ignored the rest, and left the experiment even more convinced that they were right and those who disagreed were wrong.

Peter Wason coined the term *confirmation bias* and countless studies have borne out his discovery – or rather, his demonstration of a tendency thoughtful observers have long noted. Almost 400 years ago, Sir Francis Bacon wrote that "the human understanding when it has once adopted an opinion (either as being a received opinion or as being agreeable to itself) draws all things else to support and agree with it. And though there be a greater number and weight of instances to be found on the other side, yet these it either neglects and despises, or else by some distinction sets aside and rejects; in order that by this great and pernicious predetermination the authority of its former conclusions may remain inviolate. . . ." Wise words proven true every day by countless pundits and bloggers.

The power of confirmation bias should not be underestimated. During the U.S. presidential election of 2004, a team of researchers led by Drew Westen at Emory University brought together 30 committed partisans – half Democrats, half Republicans – and had them lie in magnetic resonance imaging (MRI) machines. While their brains were being scanned, they were shown a series of three statements by or about George W. Bush. The second statement contradicted the first, making Bush look bad. Participants were asked whether the statements were inconsistent and were then asked to rate how inconsistent they were. A third statement then followed that provided an excuse for the apparent contradiction between the statements. Participants were asked if perhaps the statements were not as inconsistent as they first appeared. And finally, they were again asked to rate how inconsistent the first two statements were. The experiment was repeated with John Kerry as the focus and a third time with a neutral subject.

The superficial results were hardly surprising. When Bush supporters were confronted with Bush's contradictory statements, they rated them to be less contradictory than Kerry supporters. And when the explanation was provided, Bush supporters considered it to be much more satisfactory than did Kerry supporters. When the focus was on John Kerry, the results reversed. There was no difference between Republicans and Democrats when the neutral subject was tested.

All this was predictable. Far more startling, however, was what showed up on the MRI. When people processed information that ran against their strongly held views – information that made their favoured candidate look bad – they actually used *different parts of the brain* than they did when they processed neutral or positive information. It seems confirmation bias really is hard–wired in each of us, and that has enormous consequences for how opinions survive and spread.

Someone who forms a belief based on nothing more than the fact that other people around him hold that belief nonetheless has a belief. That belief causes confirmation bias to kick in so in–coming information is screened: If it supports the belief, it is readily accepted; if it goes against the belief, it is ignored, scrutinized carefully, or flatly rejected. Thus, if the information that turns up in newspapers, televisions, and conversation is mixed – and it very often is when risk is involved – this bias will steadily strengthen a belief that originally formed only because it's what everybody else said during a coffee break.

That's on the individual level. What happens when people who share a belief get together to discuss it? Psychologists know the answer to that, and it's not pretty. They call it group polarization.

It seems reasonable to think that when like–minded people get together to discuss a proposed hazardous waste site, or the breast implants they believe are making them sick, or some other risk, their views will tend to coalesce around the average within the group. But they won't. Decades of research has proved that groups usually come to conclusions that are more extreme than the average view of the individuals who make up the group. When opponents of a hazardous waste site gather to talk about it, they will become convinced the site is more dangerous than they originally believed. When a woman who believes breast implants are a threat gets together with women who feel the same way, she and all the women in the meeting are likely to leave believing they had previously underestimated the danger. The dynamic is always the same. It doesn't matter what the subject under discussion is. It doesn't matter what the particular views are. When like-minded people get together and talk, their existing views tend to become more extreme.

In part, this strange human foible stems from our tendency to judge ourselves by comparison with others. When we get together in a group of like-minded people, what we share is an opinion that we all believe to be correct and so we compare ourselves with others in the group by asking "*How* correct am I?" Inevitably, most people in the group will discover that they do not hold the most extreme opinion, which suggests they are less correct than others. And so they become more extreme. Psychologists confirmed this theory when they put people in groups and had them state their views without providing reasons why – and polarization still followed.

A second force behind group polarization is simple numbers. Prior to going to a meeting of people who believe silicone breast implants cause disease, a woman may have read several articles and studies on the subject. But because the people at the meeting greatly outnumber her, they will likely have information she was not aware of. Maybe it's a study suggesting implants cause a disease she has never heard of, or it's an article portraying the effects of implant-caused diseases as worse than she knew. Whatever it is, it will lead her to conclude the situation is worse than she had thought. As this information is pooled, the same process happens to everyone else in the meeting, with people becoming convinced that the problem is bigger and scarier than they had thought. Of course, it's possible that people's views could be moderated by hearing new information that runs in the opposite direction – an article by a scientist denying that implants cause disease, for example. But remember confirmation bias: Every person in that meeting is prone to accepting information that supports their opinion and ignoring or rejecting information that does not. As a result, the information that is pooled at the meeting is deeply biased, making it ideal for radicalizing opinions. Psychologists have also demonstrated that because this sort of polarization is based on information-sharing alone, it does not require anything like a face-to-face conversation – a fact amply demonstrated every day on countless political blogs.

So Alan convinces Betty, which persuades Carl, which settles it for Deborah. Biased screening of information begins and opinions steadily strengthen. Organizations are formed, information exchanged. Views become more extreme. And before you know it, as Cass Sunstein wrote, there are "hundreds, thousands or millions of people" who are convinced they are threatened by some new mortal peril. Sometimes they're right. It took only a few years for almost everyone to be convinced that AIDS was a major new disease. But they can also be very wrong. As we saw, it wasn't science that transformed the popular image of silicone breast implants from banal objects to toxic killers.

Reasonable or not, waves of worry can wash over communities, regions, and nations, but they cannot roll on forever. They follow social networks and so they end where those networks end – which helps explain why the panic about silicone breast implants washed across the United States and Canada (which also banned the implants) but caused hardly a ripple in Europe.

The media obviously play a key role in getting waves started and keeping them rolling because groups make their views known through more than conversations and e-mail. Groups also speak through the media, explicitly but also implicitly. Watch any newscast, read any newspaper: Important claims about hazards – heroin is a killer drug, pollution causes cancer, the latest concern is rapidly getting worse – will simply be stated as true, without supporting evidence. Why? Because they are what "everybody knows" is true. They are, in other words, group opinions. And like all group opinions, they exert a powerful influence on the undecided.

The media also respond to rising worry by producing more reports – almost always emotional stories of suffering and loss – about the thing that has people worried. And that causes the Guts of readers and viewers to sit up and take notice. Remember the Example Rule? The easier it is to recall examples of something happening, Gut believes, the more likely it is to happen. Growing concern about silicone breast implants prompted more stories about women with implants and terrible illnesses. Those stories raised the public's intuitive estimate of how dangerous silicone breast implants are. Concern continued to grow. And that encouraged the media to produce more stories about sick women with implants. More fear, more reporting. More reporting, more fear. Like a microphone held too close to a loudspeaker, modern media and the primal human brain create a feedback loop.

"Against this background," writes Cass Sunstein, "it is unsurprising that culturally and economically similar nations display dramatically different reactions to identical risks. Whereas nuclear power enjoys widespread acceptance in France, it arouses considerable fear in the United States. Whereas genetic engineering of food causes immense concern in Europe, it has been a non-issue in the United States, at least until recently. It is also unsurprising that a public assessment of any given risk may change suddenly and dramatically even in the absence of a major change in the relevant scientific information."

So far we've identified two sources – aside from rational calculation – that can shape our judgments about risk. There's the unconscious mind – Gut – and the tools it uses, particularly the Example Rule and the Good–Bad Rule. And there are the people around us, whose opinions we naturally tend to conform to. But if that is all there were to the story, then almost everybody within the same community would have the same opinions about which risks are alarming and which are not.

But we don't. Even within any given community opinions are often sharply divided. Clearly something else is at work, and that something is culture.

This is tricky terrain. For one thing, "culture" is one of those words that mean different things to different people. Moving from psychology to culture also means stepping from one academic field to another. Risk is a major subject within sociology, and culture is the lens through which sociologists peer. But the psychologists who study risk and their colleagues in the sociology departments scarcely talk to each other. In the countless volumes on risk written by sociologists, the powerful insights provided by psychologists over the last several decades typically receive little more than a passing mention, if they are noticed at all. For sociologists, culture counts. What happens in my brain when someone mentions lying on the beach in Mexico – do I think of tequila or skin cancer? – isn't terribly interesting or important.

In effect, a line has been drawn between psychology and culture, but that line reflects the organization of universities far more than it does what's going on inside our skulls. Consider how the Good–Bad Rule functions in our judgment of risk. The thought of lying on a beach in Mexico stirs a very good feeling somewhere in the wrinkly folds of my brain. As we have seen, that feeling will shape my judgment about the risk involved in lying on a beach until I turn the colour of a coconut husk. Even if a doctor were to tell me this behaviour will materially increase my risk of getting skin cancer, the pleasant feeling that accompanies any discussion of the subject will cause me to intuitively downplay the risk: Head may listen to the doctor but Gut is putting on sunglasses.

Simple enough. But a piece of the puzzle is missing. *Why* does the thought of lying on a Mexican beach fill me with positive feelings? Biology doesn't do it. We may be wired to enjoy the feeling of sun-light – it's a good source of heat and vitamin D – but we clearly have no natural inclination to bake on a beach since humans only started doing this in relatively modern times. So where did I learn that this is a Good Thing? Experience, certainly. I did it and it was delightful. But I thought it would be delightful *before* I did it. That was why I did it. So again, I have to ask the question: Where did I get this idea from?

For one, I got it from people who had done it and who told me it's delightful. And I got it from others who hadn't done it but who had heard that it was delightful. And I got it – explicitly or implicitly – from books, magazines, television, radio, and movies. Put all this together and it's clear I got the message that it's delightful to suntan on a Mexican beach from the culture around me. I'm Canadian. Every Canadian has either gone south in the winter or dreamed of it. Tropical beaches are as much a part of Canadian culture as wool hats and hockey pucks, and that is what convinced me that lying on a beach in Mexico is delightful. Even if I had never touched toes to Mexican sand, the thought of lying on a beach in Mexico would trigger nice feelings my brain – and those nice feelings would influ-ence my judgment of the risks involved.

This is a very typical story. There are, to be sure, some emotional reactions that are mainly biological in origin, such as revulsion for corpses and feces, but our feelings are more often influenced by experience and culture. I have a Jewish friend who follows Jewish dietary laws that forbid pork. He always has. In fact, he has internal-ized those rules so deeply he literally feels nauseated by the sight of ham or bacon. But for me, glazed ham means Christmas and the smell of frying bacon conjures images of sunny Saturday mornings. Obviously, eating pork is not terribly dangerous but still there is a risk of food poisoning (trichinosis in particular). If my friend and I were asked to judge that risk, the very different feelings we have would lead our unconscious minds – using the Good–Bad Rule – to very different conclusions.

The same dynamic plays a major role in our perceptions about the relative dangers of drugs. Some drugs are forbidden. Simply to possess them is a crime. That is a profound stigma, and we feel it in our bones. These are awful, wicked substances. Sometimes we talk about them almost as if they are sentient creatures lurking in alleyways. With such strong feelings in play, it is understandable that we would see these drugs as extremely dangerous: Snort that cocaine, shoot that heroin, and you'll probably wind up addicted or dead.

There's no question drugs can do terrible harm, but there is plenty of reason to think they're not nearly as dangerous as most people feel. Consider cocaine. In 1995, the World Health Organization completed what it touted as "the largest global study on cocaine use ever undertaken." Among its findings: "Occasional cocaine use," not intensive or compulsive consumption, is "the most typical pattern of cocaine use" and occasional cocaine use does not typically lead to severe or even minor physical or social problems."

Of course it is very controversial to suggest that illicit drugs aren't as dangerous as commonly believed, but exaggerated perceptions of risk are precisely what we would expect to see given the deep hostility most people feel toward drugs. Governments not only know this, they make use of it. Drug–use prevention campaigns typically involve advertising and classroom education whose explicit goal is to increase perceived risk (the WHO's cocaine report described most drug education as "superficial, lurid, excessively negative") while drug agencies monitor popular perceptions and herald any increase in perceived risk as a positive development. Whether the perceived risks are in line with the *actual* risks is not a concern. Higher perceived risk is always better.

Then there are the licit drugs. Tobacco is slowly becoming a restricted and stigmatized substance, but alcohol remains a beloved drug in Western countries and many others. It is part of the cultural fabric, the lubricant of social events, the symbol of celebration. A 2003 survey of British television found alcohol routinely appeared in "positive, convivial, funny images." We adore alcohol and for that reason it's no surprise that public health officials often complain that people see little danger in a drug whose consumption can lead to addiction, cardiovascular disease, gastrointestinal disorders, liver cirrhosis, several types of cancer, fetal alcohol syndrome, and fatal overdose – a drug that has undoubtedly killed far more people than all the illicit drugs combined. The net effect of the radically different feelings we have for alcohol and other drugs was neatly summed up in a 2007 report of the Canadian Centre on Substance Abuse: Most people "have an exaggerated view of the harms associated with illegal drug use, but consistently underestimate the serious negative impact of alcohol on society." That's Gut, taking its cues from the culture.

The Example Rule provides another opportunity for culture to influence Gut. That's because the Example Rule – the easier it is to recall examples of something happening, the greater the likelihood of that thing happening – hinges on the strength of the memories we form. And the strength of our memories depends greatly on attention: If I focus strongly on something and recall it repeatedly, I will remember it much better than if I only glance at it and don't think about it again. And what am I most likely to focus on and recall repeatedly? Whatever confirms my existing thoughts and feelings. And what am I least likely to focus on and recall repeatedly? Whatever contradicts my thoughts and feelings. And what is a common source of the thoughts and feelings that guide my attention and recall? Culture.

The people around us are another source of cultural influence. Our social networks aren't formed randomly, after all. We are more comfortable with people who share our thoughts and values. We spend more time with them at work, make them our friends, and marry them. The Young Republican with the Ronald Reagan T-shirt waiting in an airport to catch a flight to Washington, D.C., may find himself chatting with the anti-globalization activist with a Che

Guevara beret and a one-way ticket to Amsterdam but it's not likely he will be adding her to his Christmas card list – unlike the MBA student who collides with the Young Republican at the check-in line because she was distracted by the soaring eloquence of Ronald Reagan's Third State of the Union Address playing on her iPod. So we form social networks that tend to be more like than unlike, and we trust the people in our networks. We value their opinions and we talk to them when some new threat appears in the newspaper headlines. Individually, each of these people is influenced by culture just as we are, and when culture leads them to form a group opinion, we naturally want to conform to it.

The manifestations of culture I've discussed so far – Mexican vacations, alcohol and illicit drugs, kosher food – have obvious origins, meaning, and influence. But recent research suggests cultural influences run much deeper.

In 2005, Dan Kahan of the Yale Law School, along with Paul Slovic and others, conducted a randomly selected, nationally representative survey of 1,800 Americans. After extensive background questioning, people were asked to rate the seriousness of various risks, including climate change, guns in private hands, gun control laws, marijuana, and the health consequences of abortion.

One result was entirely expected. As in many past surveys, non-whites rated risks higher than whites and women believed risks were more serious than men. Put those two effects together and you get what is often called the white male effect. White men routinely feel hazards are less serious than other people. Sociologists and political scientists might think that isn't surprising. Women and racial minorities tend to hold less political, economic, and social power than white men and have less trust in government authorities. It makes sense that they would feel more vulnerable. But researchers have found that even after statistically accounting for these feelings, the disparity between white men and everybody else remains. The white male effect also cannot be explained by different levels of scientific education – Paul

Slovic has found that female physical scientists rate the risks of nuclear power higher than male physical scientists, while female members of the British Toxicological Society were far more likely than male members to rate the risk posed by various activities and technologies as moderate or high.

It is a riddle. A hint of the answer was found in an earlier survey conducted by Paul Slovic in which he discovered that it wasn't *all* white males who perceived things to be less dangerous than everybody else. It was only a subset of about 30 per cent of white males. The remaining 70 per cent saw things much as women and minorities did. Slovic's survey also revealed that the confident minority of white men tended to be better-educated, wealthier, and more politically conservative than others.

The 2005 survey was designed in part to figure out what was happening inside the heads of white men. A key component was a series of questions that got at people's most basic cultural world views. These touched on really basic matters of how human societies should be organized. Should individuals be self-reliant? Should people be required to share good fortune? And so on. With the results from these questions, Kahan slotted people into one of four world views (developed from the Cultural Theory of Risk first advanced by the anthropologist Mary Douglas and political scientist Aaron Wildavsky). In Kahan's terms they were individualist, egalitarian, hierarchist, and communitarian.

When Kahan crunched his numbers, he found lots of correlations between risk and other factors like income and education. But the strongest correlations were between risk perception and world view. If a person were, for example, a hierarchist – someone who believes people should have defined places in society and respect authority – you could quite accurately predict what he felt about various risks. Abortion? A serious risk to a woman's health. Marijuana? A dangerous drug. Climate change? Not a big threat. Guns? Not a problem in the hands of law-abiding citizens.

Kahan also found that a disproportionate number of white men were hierarchists or individualists. When he adjusted the numbers to account for this, the white male effect disappeared. So it wasn't race and gender that mattered. It was culture. Kahan confirmed this when he found that although black men generally rated the risks of private gun ownership to be very high, black men found to be individualist rated guns a low risk – just like white men who were individualist.

Hierarchists also rated the risk posed by guns to be low. Communitarians and egalitarians, however, feel they are very dangerous. Why? The explanation lies in feelings and the cultures that create them. "People who've been raised in a relatively individualistic community or who've been exposed to certain kinds of traditional values will have a positive association with guns," Kahan says. "They'll have positive emotions because they'll associate them with individualistic virtues like self–reliance or with certain kinds of traditional roles like a protective father. Then they'll form the corresponding perception. Guns are safe. Too much gun control is dangerous. Whereas people who've been raised in more communitarian communities will develop negative feelings toward guns. They'll see them as evidence that people in the community are distrustful of each other. They'll resent the idea that the public function of protection is taken by individuals who are supposed to do it for themselves. People who have an egalitarian sensibility, instead of valuing traditional roles like protector and father and hunter, might associate them with patriarchy or stereotypes that they think treat women unfairly and they'll develop a negative affective orientation toward the gun." And once an opinion forms, information is screened to suit.

In the survey, after people were asked to rate the danger posed by guns, they were then asked to imagine that there was clear evidence that their conclusion about the safety of guns is wrong. Would they still feel the same way about guns? The overwhelming majority said yes, they would. That's pretty clear evidence that what's driving people's feelings about the risks posed by guns is more than the perceived risks posed by guns. It's the culture, and the perception of guns within it.

That culture, Kahan emphasizes, is American and so the results he got in the poll apply only to the United States. "What an American who has, say, highly egalitarian views thinks about risk may not be the same as what an egalitarian in France thinks about risk. The American egalitarian is much more worried about nuclear power, for example, than the French egalitarian." This springs from the different histories that produce different cultures. "I gave you the story about guns and that story is an American story because of the unique history of firearms in the United States, both as tools for settling the frontier and as instruments for maintaining authority in a slave economy in the South. These created resonances that have persisted over time and have made the gun a symbol that evokes emotions within these cultural groups that then generate risk perceptions. Something completely different could, and almost certainly would, happen some place else that had a different history with weapons."

In 2007, Kahan's team ran another nation-wide survey. This time the questions were about nanotechnology – technology that operates on a microscopic scale. Two results leapt out. First, the overwhelming majority of Americans admitted they knew little or nothing about this nano–whatzit. Second, when asked if they had opinions about the risks and benefits of nanotechnology, the overwhelming majority of Americans said they did, and they freely shared them.

How can people have opinions about something they may never have heard of until the moment they were asked if they had an opinion about it? It's pure affect, as psychologists would say. If they like the sound of "nanotechnology," they feel it must be low risk and high benefit. If it sounds a little creepy, it must be high risk and low benefit. As might be expected, Kahan found that the results of these uninformed opinions were all over the map, so they really weren't correlated with anything.

But at this point in the survey, respondents were asked to listen to a little information about nanotechnology. The information was deliberately crafted to be low key, simple, factual – and absolutely balanced. Here are some potential benefits. Here are some potential risks. And now, the surveyors asked again, do you have an opinion about the risks and benefits of nanotechnology?

Sure enough, the information did change many opinions. "We predicted that people would assimilate balanced information in a way biased by their cultural predispositions toward environmental risks generally," says Kahan. And they did. Hierarchists and individualists latched onto the information about benefits, and their opinions became much more bullish – their estimate of the benefits rose while the perceived risks fell. Egalitarians and communitarians did exactly the opposite. And so, as a result of this little injection of information, opinions suddenly became highly correlated to cultural world views. Kahan feels this is the strongest evidence yet that we unconsciously screen information about risk to suit our most basic beliefs about the organization of society.

Still, it is early days for this research. What is certain at this point is that we aren't the perfectly rational creatures described in outdated economics textbooks, and we don't review information about risks with cool detachment and objectivity. We screen it to make it conform to what we already believe. And what we believe is deeply influenced by the beliefs of the people around us and of the culture in which we live.

In that sense, the metaphor I used at the start of this book is wrong. The intuitive human mind is not a lonely Stone Age hunter wandering a city it can scarcely comprehend. It is a Stone Age hunter wandering a city it can scarcely comprehend in the company of millions of other confused Stone Age hunters. The tribe may be a little bigger these days, and there may be more taxis than lions, but the old ways of deciding what to worry about and how to stay alive haven't changed.

FEAR INC.

A little boy grins as he kicks a soccer ball across grass as green and trim as an Augusta fairway. Above, not a wisp of cloud troubles the azure sky. And behind, making this happy moment possible, is a seven-foot electrified fence.

It's not clear how much juice is in the fence, although I suppose it has to be the low-voltage, zap-and-get-rattled variety, or there would have to be another fence to protect the boy from the first fence. I also don't know if the boy is inside the fence or out. Just who is being contained here? It doesn't really matter, I suppose. The image appears on a banner put up by the fence manufacturer and it clearly wasn't designed to inspire questions. Its message is simple: The world is filled with lurking dangers but you can protect those you love by taking sensible precautions such as installing a reasonably priced seven-foot electrified fence. A company spokesperson would be happy to discuss the matter further.

Welcome to Security Essen, a trade show in Essen, Germany, where more than 1,000 exhibitors, spread across 75,000 square metres of exhibit space, shill for 40,000 visitors from 55 countries at the world's biggest demonstration of what happens when capitalism meets fear. Military wares aren't included at Security Essen – although that rule was stretched a bit by the Russian company exhibiting grenade launchers and a silencer-equipped sniper rifle ("for riots and more") – but there's just about anything else one could ever need to fend off the forces of darkness. There are batons, pepper sprays, uniforms, sprinkler systems and hand-held chemical analysis units that can detect everything from ecstasy to anthrax. There is a vast array of home alarms, high-tech ID badges, retina and fingerprint scanners, software to shut out hackers, shredders to keep identity thieves at bay, transponders that allow children to be tracked like FedEx packages.

But more than anything else, there are cameras. Everywhere I turn, I see my face captured and displayed on laptops and flat-screen televisions by exhibitors promising security through spying. One camera is a tiny thing that fits in a door's peephole. Another, big as a bazooka, can see for 30 kilometres. I turn a corner and my picture is being matched against a database of wanted criminals. Around another corner, an infrared camera generates a spectral image of my face highlighted by the veins pulsing beneath my skin. It can all be a little unnerving. Happily, feelings of twitchy paranoia can be eased with the purchase of a personal counter-surveillance kit that comes in a slim briefcase suitable for travel.

For the more discriminating security shopper, Jaguar is displaying a sleek new model whose features include an ivory interior, leather steering wheel, DVD player, bullet-proof windows, armoured doors. and "under-floor hand grenade protection." An on-board oxygen system is optional. Anyone that serious about security will also be interested to learn about the heavy steel road barriers on display in an adjacent hall – just the thing to stop suicide truck bombers – and the new filtration systems designed to keep chemical weapons from being slipped into a building's air-conditioning system. Not that anything like that has ever happened. But you never know.

A new addition at Security Essen this year is a hall devoted exclusively to terrorism. "Developments in the USA are already far advanced," the show's promotional literature says, but the other side of the Atlantic isn't going to miss out. "A new market segment which is devoted especially to the actions against terrorism is arising in Europe, too."

Not that the security business really needed a new market segment. Over the last 25 years, private security has expanded massively in Germany, the United States, and every other Western country. Tyco Fire and Security, an American company, has 90,000 employees and $11.5 billion in annual sales. Securitas AB, a Swedish company headquartered in London, has more than 230,000 employees and operations in over 30 countries. Group 4 Securicor, also headquartered in England, has 400,000 employees in 110 countries.

Most people know the security industry through its ubiquitous pitches for home alarms, whose essential message is usually little different than that of the banner in Essen. Some alarm ads are more visceral, however. One American TV spot depicts a pleasant suburban home bathed in warm, morning sunlight. A pretty housewife kisses her handsome husband goodbye while a jogger passes by on the sidewalk. The husband gets in the car and drives away. The wife goes back in the house, closes the door, and turns on her electronic sentry. The commercial cuts back to the jogger, who stops, flips up the hood on his sweater, runs straight at the front door, and smashes it in with a kick. The alarm blares. The man freezes, turns, and runs. Finally, we see the grateful wife, smiling and safe once again, on the phone with the alarm company.

These ads are not designed to inspire a rational appreciation of risk. If they were, they wouldn't depict such very unlikely crimes as a stranger smashing in the front door of a home in a prosperous suburban neighbourhood at eight o'clock in the morning. (The few alarm ads that do address statistics and probabilities can be just as misleading, however. One ad on my local radio station told listeners they should buy a home alarm because "break-ins are on the rise!" – which the police told me was correct only if one defined the phrase "on the rise" to mean "declining.")

What these ads do is market fear. Prosperous suburban neighbourhoods may not be where the crime is but they are the most lucrative
markets, so it makes perfect sense to threaten suburban housewives
with violence if they don't bolt their doors and buy an alarm.

If my description sounds a little extreme, consider how the
unconscious minds of suburban housewives process the information
in the ad. Gut can't blow it off as a meaningless commercial because
Gut can't tell the difference between ads, the evening news, and what
it sees out the front window. Gut simply knows it's seeing or hearing
something frightening, even terrifying. Something it can personally
identify with. So Gut experiences a wave of what psychologists would
call negative affect. Using the Good–Bad Rule, Gut concludes that the
likelihood of the portrayed crime happening is high. The emotion
may even be strong enough to cause probability blindness, so Gut
recoils as if the crime were a certainty. And that's just one way Gut can
process the ad. It could also turn to the Example Rule. The vivid and
frightening nature of the ad makes it more likely to grab our attention
and form lasting memories. When suburban housewives later ask
themselves how likely is it that they could be victims of crime, Gut
will easily recall these memories and form the unsettling conclusion:
It is very likely.

Of course, Gut doesn't work alone. Head can always intervene,
adjust or overrule the intuitive judgments made by Gut. As we have
seen, though, Head sometimes falls asleep on the job, or its involvement is half-hearted and inadequate. And even when Head does step
in, tells Gut it's wrong, and takes control of the final judgment, Gut
keeps insisting there's danger ahead. Nagging worry may be torment-
ing to those who experience it, but it is a marvellous marketing tool
for companies selling security.

Many others find it handy, too. Politicians promote fear to win
elections. Police departments and militaries do it to expand budgets
and obtain new powers. And although we tend to think of public-
service agencies and non-governmental organizations as working

entirely for the public good, they have vested interests just like every other organization – and many realize that fear is an excellent way of promoting their issue, boosting memberships and donations, and enhancing political clout.

We encounter the messages of these merchants of fear daily, at every turn. It would be impossible to come up with a complete list of the organizations and individuals who stand to profit one way or another by elevating public anxiety. There are simply too many.

It would even be impossible to list all the corporations whose self-interest is served by marketing fear. We saw how a software company spotted a marketing opportunity in the "50,000 predators" said to be trolling the Internet for children. Lighting manufacturers talk up crime before revealing the good news that lighting is an effective way to defeat the dangers lurking in shadows. Companies that sell water filters like to mention the risk of getting cancer from chlorinated drinking water. The opportunities for finding a fear, promoting it, and leveraging it to increase sales are limited only by imagination. And corporate marketers are very imaginative.

Germs were a market waiting to be exploited. Filthy, dangerous, and invisible, germs could be anywhere. And the news is filled with stories about frightening new bugs like Ebola, West Nile virus, SARS, and avian flu, which may not be relevant to the question of what lurks in kitchen sinks and bathroom stalls but that hardly changes the impression that the world is getting buggier – an impression a great many corporations are only too happy to enhance. The slogan of Purell – a hand sanitizer manufactured by Pfizer – is "Imagine a Touchable World." It's hard to miss the implication that the world in its current state is untouchable, a message underscored on Purell's website, which includes a handy list of "99 Places Where Germs Are Likely To Lurk – 99 Reasons to Use Purell Instant Hand Sanitizer." Number 6: subway seats and poles. Number 18: calculator keypads. Number 58: thermostats. Number 67: shopping cart handles. Number 83: library books. While there is solid evidence that the reasonable use of hand sanitizers in settings like classrooms and daycares is beneficial, Pfizer portrays virtually any object touched by humans as a potential threat and any contact with any such object as a crisis that calls for a squirt of Purell. Welcome to the world of Howard Hughes.

Purell was originally created for medical professionals but it was brought to the consumer market with a publicity blitz in 1997. A gold rush followed and there are now countless brands of hand sanitizers and disinfectant wipes. Commuters can hang on to subway poles with portable subway straps or anti-bacterial gloves. Shoppers can slip disposable covers onto the icky handles of shopping carts and slip disposable covers over doorknobs and toilet seats in the unfortunate event that they are forced to use a public washroom. Passengers on airplanes can relax and lean back on sterile headrest covers and they can hang "personal air purifiers" around their necks, ostensibly to reduce the risk of contaminated air slipping up their nostrils. Wholesale markets are opening up as well, as restaurants and bars seek to please germaphobic customers with sanitizer dispensers and boxes that automatically spray disinfectant on doorknobs every few minutes. There is even hope for the notorious germ vectors known as children: *Germs Are Not for Sharing* is a book for preschoolers that asks, "What are too small to see but can have the power to make us sick? Germs! They're in the air, in food and water, on our bodies, and on all the things we touch – and they're definitely not for sharing." Frequent hand washing is important, kids are told. And it's very important you don't touch anyone when you play together. No more holding hands and high fives. Have fun but stay safe!

However hyped the risk of germs may be, it is at least real. Some corporations go so far as to conjure threats where there are none. A television ad for Brita, the German manufacturer of water filtration systems, starts with a close-up of a glass of water on a kitchen table. The sound of a flushing toilet is heard. A woman opens a door, enters the kitchen, sits at the table, and drinks the water. The water in your toilet and the water in your faucet "come from the same source," the commercial concludes. Sharp-eyed viewers will also see a disclaimer at the start of the ad printed in tiny, white letters: "Municipal water is treated for consumption." This is effectively an admission that the shared origin of the water in the glass and the toilet is irrelevant and so the commercial makes no sense – at least not on a rational level. As a pitch aimed at Gut, however, it makes perfect sense. The danger of contaminated drinking water is as old as humanity, and the worst contaminant has always been feces. Our hard-wired defence against contamination is disgust, an emotion that drives us to keep our distance from the contaminant. By linking the toilet and the drinking glass, the commercial connects feces to our home's drinking water and raises an ancient fear – a fear that can be eased with the purchase of one of the company's many fine products.

Another, subtler form of fear marketing popped up in my doctor's waiting room one day. A large poster on the wall entertained bored patients with "One Hundred Ways to Live to One Hundred." Most of the 100 items listed were printed in small, pale letters and they were about as insightful and provocative as Mother's Day cards. "Number 1: Enjoy yourself." "Number 73: Soak in the tub." But seven items were printed in large, black letters that made them the visual focus of the poster. The first of these was "Number 22: Exercise regularly." Hard to object to that. But then came "Number 44: Reduce the amount of cholesterol in your diet." That's a bit odd. Cholesterol isn't inherently dangerous so you may not need to reduce your cholesterol. It's also hard to see why cholesterol would rank among the fundamentals of staying alive, along with exercise. It is not remotely as important as eating lots of fruits and vegetables, not smoking, and many other things that aren't mentioned on the poster. So why does it get top billing over them?

Hints of an explanation appeared in the items that followed. "Number 56: Take your medicine as prescribed." Then "Number 62: If you've had a heart attack or stroke and stopped taking your medication, speak to your doctor." And "Number 88: Ask your doctor about new medications." Finally, there was "Number 100: Listen to your doctor."

Taken as a whole, the poster's basic message is that pills are absolutely essential for a long life. That's not a message you will hear from disinterested medical experts, but it is what you would expect to hear from a pharmaceutical company like the Bristol-Myers Squibb Pharmaceutical Group, identified as the maker of the poster in small print at the bottom left-hand corner. Bristol-Myers Squibb is also the maker of Pravachol, a cholesterol-reducing drug. According to the U.S. Food and Drug Administration, American sales of Pravachol earned Bristol-Myers Squibb $1.3 billion in 2005 alone and that's just a sliver of the market for cholesterol pills. Worldwide, Pfizer's Lipitor racked up $12.2 billion in 2005.

This sort of camouflaged marketing is typical of the pharmaceutical industry and it's not limited to doctor's offices. Health lobby groups, professional associations, and activists are routinely funded by pharmaceutical giants. Much of this is uncontroversial but critics say Big Pharma deliberately blurs the line between disinterested advice and sales pitches. "Would the pharmaceutical companies spend billions of dollars a year if they didn't think it was valuable? Of course not," said Dr. Jerome Kassirer, a professor at the Tufts University School of Medicine and former editor-in-chief of the *New England Journal of Medicine*. That's troubling enough, but more disturbing than Big Pharma's marketing methods are its goals.

It is not in the economic interests of a corporation selling pills to unhealthy people for people to be healthy, or rather – to be more precise – for them to *perceive* themselves to be healthy. Their actual physical state is irrelevant. What matters is whether someone believes there is something wrong that can be cured with a pill. If so, the corporation has a potential customer. If not, no sale. It doesn't take an MBA to figure out what pharmaceutical companies need to do to expand their markets and boost sales.

Critics call it "disease mongering." Australians Roy Moynihan and David Henry, a journalist and a pharmacologist respectively, wrote in the April 2006 edition of the journal *Public Library of Science Medicine* that

"many of the so-called disease awareness campaigns that inform con-
temporary understanding of illness – whether as citizens, journalists,
academics or policymakers – are underwritten by the marketing
departments of large drug companies rather than by organizations
with a primary interest in public health. And it is no secret that those
same marketing departments contract advertising agencies with
expertise in 'condition branding', whose skills include 'fostering the
creation' of new medical disorders and dysfunctions."

The evidence assembled by Moynihan and Henry in their book
*Selling Sickness: How the World's Biggest Pharmaceutical Companies Are Turning
Us All Into Patients* is extensive. A good illustration of the general
pattern is a confidential plan to market GlaxoSmithKline's drug
Lotronex in Australia by transforming the perception of irritable
bowel syndrome. "IBS must be established in doctors' minds as a significant and discrete disease state," notes the plan, written by a
medical marketing company. Patients "need to be convinced that IBS
is a common and recognized medical disorder." This would be accomplished by moving on several fronts simultaneously, including the
creation of a panel of "key opinion leaders" who would advise the
corporation on opinions in gastroenterology and "opportunities for
shaping it," drafting "best practice guidelines" for dealing with irritable bowel syndrome, launching a new newsletter to convince the
"specialist market" that the condition is a "serious and credible
disease," and running ads targeting general practitioners, pharmacists,
nurses, and patients. Another component of the plan is to involve a
medical foundation that is described as having a "close relationship"
with the plan's drafters. The plan also calls for a comprehensive media
strategy because "PR [public relations] and media activities are crucial
to a well-rounded campaign – particularly in the area of consumer
awareness." It all came to naught, however. The U.S. Food and Drug
Administration received reports that Lotronex caused serious and
even fatal adverse reactions. The big push was abandoned, and the
drug is now prescribed only to women with severe symptoms.

This is much bigger than advertising. It is about nothing less than shifting the line between healthy and diseased, both in consumers' perceptions and in medical practice itself. Steven Woloshin and Lisa Schwartz, doctors and researchers at the Dartmouth Medical School, were among the first to analyze this process. In 1999, they published a paper examining proposals by various professional associations to change the thresholds for diagnosis of high blood pressure, diabetes, high cholesterol, and obesity. In every case, the new thresholds made it easier for people to be qualified as having these conditions. They then calculated that if all the new standards were put in place, 87.5 million otherwise healthy Americans would suddenly be deemed to have at least one chronic condition – and three-quarters of all Americans would be considered "diseased."

Erectile dysfunction, female sexual dysfunction, hair loss, osteo-porosis, restless leg syndrome, shyness: These are just a few of the conditions whose seriousness and prevalence have been systemati-cally inflated by drug companies seeking bigger markets. Language is one of the most basic means of medicalizing a problem, the critical first step to getting people to ask their doctors for a pill. So "impotence" becomes "erectile dysfunction," an impressively medical-y phrase that pushes away consideration of factors like stress and anxiety as causes of impotence that can be cured without a pill. Numbers are also key. People will be more likely to conclude they have a condition if they think it's common, and so drug companies push statistics like "more than half of all men over 40 have difficulties getting or maintaining an erection" – a number that is grossly misleading because it comes from a study not taken seriously by experts in the field.

"The rhetoric surrounding disease mongering suggests that it will promote health," writes Iona Heath, a British physician, in the *Public Library of Science Medicine*, "but the effect is in fact the opposite. Much disease mongering relies on the pathologizing of normal biological and social variation and on the portrayal of the presence of risk factors for disease as a disease state in itself. When pharmaceuticals are used to treat risk factors, the vicious circle is completed because anyone who takes medicine is by definition a patient."

There's no better example of this than the warning about cholesterol on my doctor's wall. High cholesterol is not a disease, merely a risk factor for cardiovascular disease. There are many such risk factors, including lack of exercise, smoking, an unbalanced diet, high blood pressure, obesity, and diabetes. Most of these can be improved with simple lifestyle changes. Cholesterol, however, can be reduced with pills. And so drug companies singled out cholesterol and promoted it as if it were a disease in itself. In 2003, Pfizer led a major "public awareness" campaign, ostensibly to raise awareness of heart disease and heart attack in France and Canada. The ads were shockingly blunt. On Canadian television, a woman with two young children weeps in a hospital waiting room. A doctor emerges and says her husband is dead. Then time reverses. We see the man wheeled down the hospital hall, in the ambulance, and collapsing at a sunny picnic. It's high cholesterol, we are told. Even if you seem healthy, it can kill you. Get tested. Then the man and his kids are shown smiling and laughing – their grim fate has been averted.

Responding to the French version of Pfizer's campaign, Jonathan Quick and colleagues in the Department of Essential Drugs and Medicines Policy of the World Health Organization wrote a stinging letter to the British medical journal *The Lancet*. "Of all the major factors accepted as cardiovascular disease risks, only cholesterol is addressed – the campaign's stated aim is not pursued. No mention is made of an actual medical product, but the campaign coincided with publication, in *The Lancet*, of [a study] showing reductions in major cardiovascular events after use of atorvastatin." Atorvastatin is the proper name of Lipitor, Pfizer's lucrative anti–cholesterol drug. "We believe the campaign could have worried patients, encouraging them to request a prescription for statins." Quick and his colleagues added that the "information used contained misleading statements and omissions likely to induce medically unjustifiable drug use or to give rise to undue risks." For that reason, Quick concluded, the ads "did not respect several of WHO's ethical criteria." Barbara Mintzes, a professor of health care and epidemiology at the University of British Columbia, was more pointed in an article in the *Public Library of Science Medicine*: Pfizer, she wrote, is using the "fear of death" to promote sales.

The subterfuge of public information campaigns is necessary in most Western countries because only New Zealand and the United States allow full, direct-to-consumer advertising of pharmaceuticals. But even in the United States, federal regulations require ads to follow public-interest guidelines, and the pharmaceutical industry insists its advertising simply provides solid information and is therefore in the public interest. Many observers think this is nonsense. Writing in the *Annals of Family Medicine*, Douglas Levy of the School of Medicine at the University of Southern California and David Kessler, the former head of the U.S. Food and Drug Administration, noted that drug company spending on TV ads in the United States "doubled from $654 million in 2001 to a staggering $1.19 billion in 2005. Nearly one-third of the 2005 spending was only one category: sleep medicines. Yet sleep disorders, however problematic and serious they may be, are almost inconsequential when compared to the major causes of death in the United States: cardiovascular disease, cancer and unintentional injuries. No matter how much the industry claims its advertising provides public health benefits, the amount spent promoting drugs for conditions of varying severity begs the question of whether the industry truly is acting for the public benefit."

In 2007, a team led by Dominick Frosch of the Department of Medicine at the University of California published (in the *Annals of Family Medicine*) the first comprehensive analysis of the content of the 30 hours of drug ads the average American sees on TV each year. "Most ads (82 per cent) made some factual claims and made rational arguments (86 per cent) for product use, but few described condition causes (26 per cent), risk factors (26 per cent), or prevalence (25 per cent)." The researchers feel these omissions have an important consequence. "By ambiguously defining who might need or benefit from the products, [direct-to-consumer-advertising] implicitly focuses on convincing people that they may be at risk for a wide array of health conditions that product consumption might ameliorate, rather than providing education about who may truly benefit from treatment."

Another matter that gets short shrift is lifestyle change. The first thing any physician will do when considering how to treat a condition is ask whether lifestyle changes – stop smoking, eat better, exercise – can do the job by themselves. In the Frosch study, 19 per cent of ads mentioned that lifestyle changes could be made in conjunction with taking pills. But not one ad mentioned that lifestyle changes were a potential alternative to popping pills. In fact, almost 19 per cent of ads went so far as to explicitly state that lifestyle changes were *not* enough. "Several ads for cholesterol-lowering drugs appeared to suggest that non-pharmacological approaches were almost futile," the researchers wrote.

What drug ads emphasize is emotion. The Frosch study found that almost all ads – 95 per cent – contained a positive emotional appeal, while 69 per cent played up negative feelings. "Most ads showed characters who lost control of their lives as a result of conditions and used medication to regain control. This loss of control extended beyond specific medical problems and often included an inability to participate in social, leisure or work activities. Characters typically regained complete control over their lives after using the product, whereupon they also received social approval from friends and family." The fundamental message, then, is little different than that of home security ads and the image of the little boy playing soccer beside an electrified fence: You are in danger but if you buy our product your life will be filled with smiles, sunshine, and pink-cheeked children at play.

"Disease mongering exploits the deepest atavistic fears of suffering and death," writes Iona Heath. It also exploits the desire for happiness and social acceptance. The result is a neat emotional symmetry. Without our product, you will experience fear, disease, rejection, death; with it, you will have joy, vitality, acceptance, life. It's hard to imagine a better way to rouse Gut and open a customer's wallet.

An obvious question is whether pharmaceutical companies, security companies, and all the others who use fear and hope to press our psychological buttons fully understand what they are doing. Did they just stumble on this by trial and error? Or have they learned from the scientific advances of the last 30 years and put them into practice? There's plenty of reason to think the latter is closer to the truth.

As far back as the 1970s, marketing researchers were discussing brands and the emotions that make them potent. At that point, a few pioneering psychologists had begun delving into the two-system – Head and Gut – model of human thought, and research on the role of emotion in decision making had begun. But it would be a decade or more before these became hot topics in psychology and at least another 10 years before they became predominant ways of thinking about thinking. And yet at least one industry was taking notes and drawing conclusions long ago.

"I was given some marketing documents from the tobacco industry going back 20 or 30 years," says Paul Slovic, who was hired in 2001 as an expert witness in a lawsuit brought by the U.S. government against Big Tobacco. "It was stunning. It was shocking. Consultants for the tobacco companies were doing studies and reporting the results, and basically they were 20 years ahead of many of the cognitive and social psychologists in understanding the importance of affect. They basically had a good understanding of this concept of System One [Gut] thinking and the importance of images to which positive feelings are attached. And that was the basis of all of their advertising."

Amos Tversky once joked that he and other scientists investigating how people make decisions were merely catching up with "advertisers and used car salesmen." He had no idea how right he was.

What Big Tobacco figured out decades ago is surely understood today by the other major industries profiting from fear, for the integration of leading-edge psychological research with corporate marketing is itself a booming industry. In marketing journals and trade publications, the breakthroughs Kahneman and Tversky revealed in their famous 1974 paper – the Example Rule, the Rule of Typical Things, and the Anchoring Rule – are common knowledge, and the expanding scientific research on the role emotion plays in decision making is followed with all the passion of a banker monitoring Wall Street.

Many business school professors with training in cognitive psychology operate private consultancies and charge corporate clients fat fees to apply the latest science to product launches and promotions. They include Gerald Zaltman, a marketing professor at the Harvard Business School, fellow at Harvard's Mind, Brain, Behavior Initiative, and author of *How Customers Think*. Corporations should treat the unconscious mind as the frontier of business, Zaltman writes. "Most influences on consumer behavior reside at this frontier; consumers encounter these influences and process them unknowingly. Firms that most effectively leverage their explorations of this frontier will gain crucial competitive advantages." The sophistication major corporations are bringing to these "explorations" is impressive. "Some companies, such as Coca-Cola, Unilever, Hallmark, Sungenta, Bank of America, Glaxo, American Century and General Motors are beginning to conduct 'deep dives' on specific emotions in order to understand their subtle nuances and operation," writes Zaltman. "For example, a study of the meaning of 'joy' conducted for one of the world's leading brands identified more than 15 elements of this basic emotion. These insights are leading the firm to a major overhaul of the brand story."

Even neuroscience is being brought to bear in the pursuit of sales, giving rise to "neuromarketing." Instead of quizzing people in traditional focus groups – a flawed process because it's never clear if answers are anything more than conscious rationalizations of unconscious judgments – marketers attach them to MRIs. When subjects are exposed to products or ads, their brains light up. Electrodes are also used to monitor heart rates, skin temperatures, and the near-invisible twinges of facial muscles that betray surges of emotion. Analysis of the results can reveal a great deal about emotional engagement and how feelings influence thoughts. This means, in effect, marketers can access both Head and Gut. Done well, neuro-marketing can give marketers an understanding of what happens inside a brain that not even the owner of that brain can match.

Here, then, is another answer to the question posed at the begin-ning of this book. We are safer and healthier than ever and yet we are more worried about injury, disease, and death than ever. Why? In part, it's because there are few opportunities to make money from convincing people they are, in fact, safer and healthier than ever – but there are huge profits to be made by promoting fear. "Unreasoning fear," as Roosevelt called it, may be bad for those who experience it and society at large, but it's wonderful for shareholders. The oppor-tunities for growth are limitless. All that's required is that fears keep rising, and those who reap the profits know which buttons to push in our Stone Age minds to ensure that happens.

H.L. Mencken once wrote that "the whole aim of practical politics is to keep the populace alarmed (and hence clamorous to be led to safety) by menacing it with an endless series of hobgoblins, all of them imaginary." Mencken penned this line in 1920, at the height of the first Red Scare. At the time, American anarchists were blowing up buildings and people at an alarming rate. The attorney general, Alexander Mitchell Palmer, twice escaped assassination attempts. In the crackdown that followed – the infamous "Palmer Raids" – gross abuses of civil liberties were committed but no Bolshevik conspiracy was uncovered. It was clear that, terrible as the violence was, it was the work of a tiny number of radicals. On balance, Mencken was right to think politicians were hyping the threat out of all proportion because it suited their interests to do so – but he was quite wrong to deny the *bona fides* of politicians who saw a Red under every bed. The beliefs were sincere, if misguided. The fact that the Red Scare was also wonderfully convenient for many politicians and officials – especially a young J. Edgar Hoover – didn't change that.

Like Mencken, we often make the mistake of thinking that politicians rattle the rubes with scary stories then laugh about it over drinks. In reality, the fact that a politician may have something to gain by promoting a threat does not mean he or she does not believe the threat is real. This goes for the pharmaceutical industry, security companies, and all the others who promote and profit from fear. In fact, I'm quite sure that in most cases those promoting fear are sincere, for the simple reason that humans are compulsive rationalizers. People like to see themselves as being basically good, and so admitting that they are promoting fear in others in order to advance their interests sets up a nasty form of cognitive dissonance: I know I'm basically a nice person; what I'm doing is awful and wrong. Those are two thoughts that do not sit comfortably in the same head and the solution is rationalization: Suburban housewives really *are* at risk if they don't buy my home alarm, and I'm doing them a service by telling them so. Self-interest and sincere belief seldom part company.

The marketing of fear for political advantage has become so ubiquitous the phrase "the politics of fear" is almost a cliché, but still many doubt the power of fearful messages to influence voters. "Despite the best of intentions, election campaigns can quickly turn into a competition about who can most effectively frighten voters," complained Dr. Rowan Williams, the Archbishop of Canterbury, in a letter sent to Britain's party leaders prior to the 2005 election. Don't let this happen, the archbishop asked. It's unethical and destructive. And besides, it doesn't work. "Like a lot of other people, I suspect that voters don't make up their minds primarily on the grounds of fear, and that this aspect of campaigning, while it certainly grabs headlines, may not be especially decisive. The technique is a bit too transparent and usually too over-the-top to be taken wholly seriously."

Academic research on this point is surprisingly limited. Even the role of emotions in campaign ads – the most explicit and quantifiable means of deploying emotion in politics – has been little studied. But still, among campaign consultants and political journalists, there is "widespread agreement about the practices of selling candidates," writes Ted Brader, a political scientist at the University of Michigan, in *Campaigning for Hearts and Minds*. "These political observers believe that emotional appeals are powerful staples of campaign advertising, embedded in music and images, that manipulate uneducated and uninformed voters." To put this in psychological terms, when an educated and informed voter sees an ad, Gut may react but Head corrects and adjusts; when an uneducated and uninformed voter sees the same ad, Gut reacts but Head does not step in, and so that person is swayed by the emotional pitch. Or so the political experts assume.

Brader first tested these assumptions by conducting a large-scale analysis of ad content. "Almost all campaign ads appealed to the emotions of viewers and yet a substantial majority, 79 per cent, also appealed to the viewers' capacity to reason by encouraging them to draw conclusions from evidence," Brader wrote. "Nevertheless, the reputation of political advertising as primarily emotional is well founded: in nearly 72 per cent of ads, the appeal to emotions dominated the appeal to logic." Only 10 per cent of ads targeted a single emotion. Three-quarters included at least one enthusiastic appeal – Fred Jones for a brighter future! – while "nearly half of all ads include some sort of appeal to fear, anger and pride." The ads Brader analyzed came from elections in 1999 and 2000, including the notably low-key presidential contest between Al Gore and George W. Bush. The 2004 presidential election was a far nastier affair and it's safe to say that fear was more widely deployed in that campaign. So were TV ads. "Americans in 2004 were collectively exposed to over a million campaign ads on television," Brader writes. "Candidates, parties and groups spent over $1 billion on advertising."

Brader found that political ads use fairly predictable sound and images to enhance emotional content. Enthusiastic appeals are drenched in bright colours, sunshine, smiling children, and soaring or sentimental music. Fear ads are often shot in black and white or very dark colours. They are "rich in visual cues associated with death, decay and desolation" such as old people and barren landscapes. Music is either tense or sombre, or it's simply discordant noise.

Although ads usually have a dominant emotional theme, one-third "contain appeals to both positive and negative emotions." Brader notes this fits with how Rutgers professor Montague Kern described political advertising in the 1980s: It is "the 'get 'em sick, get 'em well' advertising concept, in which advertisers try to create anxieties and then reassure people they have the solution." This should sound familiar. It is the same message used in those cholesterol ads, home security pitches, and the banner featuring a little boy playing soccer behind an electrified fence: You are threatened by something bad or scary but if you buy our product – also known as the "candidate" – life will be delightful.

To see precisely who is influenced by these emotional appeals, Brader devised an ingenious series of experiments. Simply having people sit down and look at pretend ads for fake candidates wouldn't do, he reasoned. People come to ads with prior beliefs and feelings. And they don't see ads in isolation – they pop up amid news stories and McDonald's commercials. Sometimes people notice them and pay attention, sometimes they don't. To simulate this and produce reliable data is a challenge, but Brader found a way: In 1998, he recruited 286 volunteers through community-service announcements and flyers in 11 communities in Massachusetts. At the time, a primary election race was underway, with two leading candidates vying to be the Democratic nominee to be governor of Massachusetts. It was an "impressively lackluster" contest, Brader writes, with no major controversies or hot issues in a time of peace and prosperity. That was perfect for Brader's purposes because it made it a "fairly demanding test case for the ability of campaign ads to elicit enthusiasm, fear or any other emotion."

As they arrived at the libraries, meeting halls, and churches where the experiments were held, people were asked to have a seat and watch a videotape of a newscast. The purpose of the experiment, they were told, was to figure out what people take away from the news. They then watched half an hour of a news show, including the commercials. One of the commercials was, of course, an ad for one of the two leading candidates for the Democratic nomination. These ads weren't real, however. They were created by Brader using scripts he wrote, along with video clips and music taken from past political ads. There were four in all. The first ad featured a voice-over that was "enthusiastic" and positive but the images and music were bland; the second ad used the same voice-over but the words were matched with soaring music and images of sunny skies and grinning children. A third ad featured a fearful script about crime and drugs, but again it used bland pictures and music, unlike the fourth ad, which had the same script but paired it with ominous music and harsh images of guns, criminals, and drugs. The idea was to separate the effects of negative and positive *information* from those of negative and positive *emotion* – since both versions of the ads had the information but only the second versions were "juiced" with emotion. When the screening ended, participants answered a series of written questions about the newscast, the commercials, and the upcoming elections. The results were startling: People who saw the "juiced" version of the enthusiastic ad were more likely to say they would volunteer for a campaign, vote in the primary election, and vote in the general election than were those who saw the bland version of the same ad. Note that this was the result of a single, casual viewing of one short ad.

Fear seemed to be much less influential, however, as there was little difference between the answers of those who saw the fear-drenched ad and those who saw the neutral version. But Brader had also asked people to answer factual questions about the election and he used that information to divide them into those who know more about politics and those who know less. That changed everything. It turned out that the effect of the emotional "enthusiasm" ad was universal – it influenced everybody, whether they knew anything about politics or not. But the effect of the fear-based ad was divided. It did not boost the rate at which those who knew less about politics said they would get involved. But it did significantly influence those who knew *more* – making them much more likely to say they would volunteer and vote.

So the assumption of political experts is wrong. It isn't the less informed who are likely to be influenced by fear-driven advertising. It is the more informed. Apparently, greater awareness and commitment make emotional messages more resonant – and being better informed is no guarantee that Head will step in and tell Gut to relax.

Still, if the political experts were wrong about who is more likely to be influenced by fear, they were dead-on about the central role played by emotion in political marketing. "The audiovisual 'packaging' may be paramount to their effectiveness," Brader writes. Remove the word "may" and replace it with "is" and you have the standard advice supplied by every political consultant. "A visual context that supports and reinforces your language will provide a multiplier effect, making your message that much stronger," advises Republican guru Frank Luntz in his book *Words That Work*. But more than that, "a striking visual context can overwhelm the intended verbal message entirely." Luntz makes his point by recounting a story Lesley Stahl relates in her autobiography, *Reporting Live*. In 1984, Stahl filed a story for the *CBS Evening News* which was so critical of the Reagan White House she feared her sources in the administration "would be angry enough to freeze me out." But after the story aired, the deputy chief of staff told her the White House loved it. Stahl asked him, "Didn't you hear what I said?" The politico responded: "Nobody heard what you said. . . . You guys in televisionland haven't figured it out yet, have you? When the pictures are powerful and emotional, they override if not completely drown out the sound. I mean it, Lesley. Nobody heard you."

Even in 1984, this was old hat. "The real question in political advertising is how to surround the voter with the proper auditory and visual stimuli to evoke the reaction you want from him," wrote Tony Schwartz, a political consultant, in 1973. Five years earlier, the campaign of Richard Nixon ran a television ad in which pictures of a serene-looking Hubert Humphrey were interspersed with rapid-fire images of riots, street fighting, and destruction in Vietnam. Not a word was spoken; it was a pitch aimed exclusively at Gut. If an ad like that were run today, psychologists might see it as proof that spin doctors were learning from their work, but the truth is that spin doctors – like Amos Tversky's "advertisers and used car salesmen" – figured it out first.

Of course, it's not hard for most people to believe spin doctors traffic in fear. Nor is it a stretch to imagine corporations boosting sales with similar techniques. They are self-interested, after all, and they advance their interests however they can.

Activists, non-governmental organizations, and charities are another matter. They have their own interests, as everyone does. And they, too, could use fear to expand memberships, boost donations, and increase their media profile and political clout. But unlike spin doctors and corporations, activists and others explicitly seek to advance the public good – it's the very reason they exist – so it seems strange that they would scare the very public they wish to serve. And yet it is precisely that high-minded motivation that so often leads activists, NGOs, and charities to market fear.

Leaving my neighbourhood grocery store one afternoon, I came across a poster featuring a sad-eyed boy wearing a T-shirt embla-zoned with the words "I'm hungry." The caption read: "One in five Canadian children lives with hunger." It was an appeal for donations to "The Grocery Foundation," an organization established by the big grocery store chains and food companies to support school breakfast programs and other programs for needy kids. The cause is irreproach-able. But I'd never heard that statistic before and I couldn't believe the situation was this dire. The wording was also odd. What does it mean that a child "lives with" hunger? Does that mean they experience it every day? Once a week? How is hunger defined and measured? I wanted to know more so I e-mailed the executive director of the foundation, John McNeil.

In his e-mailed response, McNeil directed me to other non-governmental organizations working in this field. But they didn't know the source of the number, so I contacted McNeil again. This time he sent me an excerpt from a letter written by Sue Cox, the former head of the Daily Bread Food Bank and "an acknowledged authority on hunger and poverty," according to McNeil. Cox's case for the one-in-five statistic went like this: first, "child hunger and child poverty are inextricably linked"; second, Statistics Canada says the "current rate of child poverty is one in six"; third, the real number is likely closer to one in five because the telephone survey used to come up with the one-in-six number would not catch very poor people who can't afford telephones.

What Cox didn't mention is that Statistics Canada has no data on "child poverty" or any other kind of poverty. What the agency has is something called the "Low Income Cut-off," or LICO. That's where the one-in-six number came from. But the LICO is not a "poverty" number, as Cox claimed. It is a measure of *relative* deprivation only, intended to identify "those who are substantially worse off than the average," in the words of Ivan Fellegi, the head of Statistics Canada. If the income of the top 10 per cent in the country doubled tomorrow, the number of people who fall below the LICO would soar – even though all the people who suddenly dropped below that line would have exactly the same income they had before. The statistics agency has repeatedly stated that it does not consider LICO to be a measure of poverty. "Statistics Canada does not and cannot measure the level of 'poverty' in Canada," wrote Fellegi.

So the basis for the claim that "one in five Canadian children lives with hunger" is this: A number that Statistics Canada says is not a measure of poverty was used as a measure of poverty; the word "poverty" was changed to "hunger"; and the number was arbitrarily reduced from one in six to one in five.

I e-mailed McNeil again and told him I thought his number was dubious. Would he care to respond? "It was not my analysis," he wrote. "However, I think we have sufficiently debated your concern, whether it's 1 in 4 or 1 in 6, there are a lot of Canadian children wandering around with empty bellies which we're trying to do something about."

The cause is worthy and the intentions honourable, McNeil seemed to be saying. Why worry about the accuracy of information used to advance a good cause?

A similar scenario played out in the United States in 1991, when an American activist group named the Food Research and Action Center (FRAC) released a report claiming "one out of eight American children" had gone hungry at some time in the previous year. The report garnered widespread press coverage despite being fatally flawed by an unrepresentative survey sample and questions drafted too broadly to be meaningful. On the most precise question – "Did any of your children ever go to bed hungry because there was not enough money to buy groceries?" – just one-third of those counted in the report as "hungry" said "yes." That alone should have cast doubt on the validity of the report but almost every new story about the report passed along the statistic as if it were unchallenge-able fact. (Someone at *CBS Evening News* not only accepted the study as hard fact, but misread it in almost comical fashion – which resulted in Dan Rather leading off the newscast by announcing, "A startling number of American children in danger of starving. Dan Rather reporting. Good evening. One out of eight American children is going hungry *tonight*.")

In January 2005, Canadians awoke to full-page newspaper ads that declared the country is "losing control" of cancer. "Four in 10 of us will get it. In 10 years, it'll be five in ten. It's time to start controlling cancer instead of letting cancer control us. If we don't, more of us will get cancer and more of us will die from it than ever before." The ads were placed by "The Campaign to Control Cancer," a consortium of cancer and health organizations formed to press the federal government to implement a national cancer strategy. All the statements in the ad were true. On current trends, more people *would* get cancer than ever, and more *would* die from it. But what the ad didn't mention is that this is because the population is growing – more people means more cancer – and it is aging, which means more cancer because aging is by far the biggest risk factor for cancer. The ad also failed to note that the death *rate* from cancer is falling and expected to fall further, nor did it mention that the incidence rates of most types of cancer – after taking population aging into account – are flat or falling.

.When Ian MacLeod of the *Ottawa Citizen* wrote an article laying out these facts in a straightforward, balanced news story, readers were furious. MacLeod was peppered with angry e-mails and phone calls. One man accused him of being "pro-cancer." A letter to the editor argued, "It is worth the price of a few print ads, and the shock value of some tough language, to draw attention to the patchwork [cancer-care] system we have in place right now."

Simon Sutcliffe and Barbara Whylie, two physicians with the Campaign to Control Cancer, also responded in writing. They didn't dispute any of the facts MacLeod presented. "The Campaign to Control Cancer does not deny progress is being made," they wrote, but the growing number of cancer cases would place terrible strain on the health care system and much more could be done to ease that burden with simple prevention measures and other strategies. This is true. But the balance and reasonableness the doctors presented in the letter was wholly absent from the ad their organization placed.

In the summer of 2007, the American Cancer Society ran ads in 15 women's magazines featuring a young woman holding up the photograph of a smiling blonde. "My sister accidentally killed herself," reads the headline. "She died of skin cancer." The ad goes on to say that "left unchecked, skin cancer can be fatal." It urged young women to "use sunscreen, cover up and watch for skin changes." That sounds pretty reasonable until you learn that almost all skin cancer deaths are caused by melanoma, a rare type of skin cancer, and that scientists don't fully understand the relationship between sun exposure and melanoma or what to do about it. "We do have pretty good evidence that sunscreen will reduce your risk of the less lethal forms of skin cancer," Dr. Barry Kramer, associate director for disease prevention at the National Institute of Health, told the *New York Times*, but "there's very little evidence that sunscreens protect you against melanoma, yet you often hear that as the dominant message." Dr. Leonard Lichtenfeld, deputy chief medical officer at the American Cancer Society, admitted to the *Times* that "we have taken some license in taking that message and using it the way we've used it because that's the way to get the message to our target audience." Another troubling point about those ads: Although the only logo that appears is that of the highly respected American Cancer Society, they were actually paid for by Neutrogena, a company owned by consumer-products giant Johnson & Johnson. One of Neutrogena's main product lines is sunscreen.

All this is done with the best of intentions. There really are hungry children. Sun exposure really does cause cancer. It may seem pedantic to demand accurate information in messages about such serious problems. Surely what matters is raising awareness and getting action.

That attitude is all too common and the result is a parade of half-truths, quarter-truths, and sort-of-truths. In the mail, I got a brochure from the government warning me that "car crashes are the number one cause of death for Canadian children!" That's true, as far as it goes.

But the brochure doesn't mention that the rate of fatal car crashes is steadily falling and is now far lower than a generation ago (the number of fatalities dropped 37 per cent between 1986 and 2005, despite rising numbers of people on the roads). Nor does it say that car crashes became the number one killer of children only because the toll inflicted by other causes (notably infectious diseases) declined even more rapidly. It's no mystery why this good news was omitted. The point of the brochure is to get me to install car seats for my kids, and information that puts the risk of car crashes into perspective isn't going to contribute to that goal. It's much more effective to use a misleading factoid to deliver a simple and scary message: *Your children are in danger!*

Sins of omission are far more common than active deceit in fear marketing, but out-and-out lies do occasionally come to light. Dick Pound, the crusading chairman of the World Anti-Doping Agency, caused a furor when he said one-third of the players in the National Hockey League were using illegal performance-enhancing drugs so Michael Sokolove asked Pound (for an article that appeared in the *New York Times*) how he came up with that figure. "He leaned back in his chair and chuckled," wrote Sokolove, "completely unabashed to admit that he had just invented it. 'It was pick a number,' he said. 'So it's 20 per cent. Twenty-five per cent. Call me a liar.'" A liar he may be, but Dick Pound is no fool. As Sokolove wrote, Pound is passionate about the fight against doping and he knows that "his best weapon is his brilliance as a formulator of quotes, his ability to make headlines and call attention to his cause." Pound even wrote a book called *High Impact Quotations*.

Pound's "high-impact quotations" are one solution to a problem faced by every activist, NGO, charity, and consultant with a cause. To succeed, they need the public's support. To get the public's support, people must hear their message. But people are deluged with images, words, noise, and pleas for their attention, most of which is ignored.

In that information maelstrom, how do you get people to stop, hear, and think about what you have to say?

Even multi-billion-dollar corporations struggle with this, although the dilemma is considerably less challenging for those who have huge quantities of cash and the best marketing expertise money can buy. To an extent, that includes government agencies and the major non-governmental organizations. They may not have the monetary resources of a Pfizer but they do have budgets big enough to advertise widely and they can tap into the same pool of expertise used by corporations. In the United Kingdom, the Central Office of Information, a 600-person agency that implements all the government's public information campaigns, is the nation's third-largest advertiser; its CEO is Alan Bishop, formerly the chairman of Saatchi and Saatchi, one of the biggest ad agencies in the world. In the United States, the Ad Council is a privately funded organization that arranges for ad agencies to produce public-service campaigns on behalf of government agencies and others, which it then distributes. Much of the work done in these circles is as sophisticated as anything in the corporate world. Practitioners call it social marketing.

Vivid, frightening images abound in social marketing for the same reason home alarm companies show criminals kicking in suburban doors: They get attention, stir feelings, and form lasting memories – making Gut sit up and take notice – and so they are far more likely to influence behaviour than an earnest request to "please, wear your seat belt." This thinking lay behind the American Cancer Society's ads telling young women to use sunscreen or risk death. The ACS's research found "young women as a group were oblivious to the risk and felt that skin cancer isn't a serious problem," Dr. Leonard Lichtenfeld told the *New York Times*. Women told the ACS that "to get the message through to me, you have to shock me and get my attention." So they did. Countless other groups have learned this lesson and the result is a steady escalation of what some have dubbed shockvertizing. "You have to try something new to get through," an ad exec said in defence of his workplace safety campaign, which featured graphic deaths and corpses. "It's a never-ending arms race in the advertising business."

An insidious new weapon in the arms race is the video news release, filmed and distributed by public relations companies. Raw video has always been made available to television news programs for use in newscasts but video news releases are intended to look and sound like the finished product so television stations are able to run them, in whole or in part, as news stories in their newscasts. And they do. For a 2006 report, the Center for Media and Democracy in Washington, D.C., tracked a sample of 36 video news releases and found 77 television stations ran them without telling viewers the material was not produced by reporters. In one-third of those cases, the entire video news release was aired. This practice has erupted into public controversy several times – particularly in 2004, when the Congressional Government Accountability Office revealed that several federal agencies distributed video news releases that didn't identify the source of this "news" – but still it goes on. For TV producers, it's free. For marketers, it's the ideal way to inject a message into the body politic without anyone seeing the needle.

Still, most activists, NGOs, and charities with a message they want the public to hear can only dream of deploying such sophisticated techniques. For them, there is only one option: Take it to the media. But there is a limited number of reporters, news pages, and airtime available – and vast numbers of individuals and organizations who have a message they want delivered to the public. Attracting the media's attention is a major challenge.

One technique for getting noticed is the sort of camera-friendly stunt pioneered by Greenpeace – hang a banner from a bridge or climb a nuclear plant's cooling tower. Celebrities also help. But for those who have neither the ability to scale major infrastructure nor Sean Penn on speed dial, there is really only one way to grab the attention of distracted editors and reporters: It is to dispense with earnest, thoughtful, balanced, well-researched work and turn the message into a big, scary headline.

"What Danger Lurks in the School Cafeteria?" asks a January 2007 press release from the Center for Science in the Public Interest (CSPI), a Washington, D.C., consumer advocacy group. "Conditions in America's school cafeterias could trigger potentially disastrous outbreaks of food poisoning at any time, according to the Center for Science in the Public Interest, which ranks food service operations in a new report released today." Of course it is true that "potentially disastrous outbreaks" could happen "at any time," just as it's true that a school could be crushed by an asteroid any second now. The crucial question is how likely it is. The answer is hinted at near the bottom of the press release, where CSPI says it has documented "over 11,000 cases of foodborne illnesses associated with schools between the years 1990–2004." That may sound frightening but compare it to the Centers for Disease Control's estimated number of food poisonings across the United States in a single year: 76 million. And 11,000 food poisonings in schools over 14 years works out to 786 cases a year – in a student population of more than 50 million. That means the chance of a student getting food poisoning at school is about 0.00157 per cent. It seems the accurate headline for this press release would be "School Cafeterias Reasonably Safe" – but a press release with a headline like that will never get a second look inside a newsroom.

The competing demands of being accurate and being heard can be particularly hard on scientists. Stephen Schneider – a Stanford climatologist and an early proponent of the hypothesis that human activity was changing climate – spoke about this with admirable clarity in an interview with *Discover* magazine. "On the one hand, as scientists we are ethically bound to the scientific method, in effect promising to tell the truth, the whole truth and nothing but – which means that we must include all the doubts, the caveats, the ifs, ands, and buts. On the other hand, we are not just scientists but human beings as well. And like most people we'd like to see the world a better place, which in this context translates into our working to reduce the risk of disastrous climate change. To do that we need to get some broad-based support, to capture the public's imagination. That, of course, means getting loads of media coverage. So we have to offer up scary scenarios, make simplified, dramatic statements, and make little mention of any doubts we may have. This 'double ethical bind' we frequently find ourselves in cannot be solved by any formula. Each of us has to decide what the right balance is between being effective and being honest. I hope that means being both."

Unfortunately, the language of science is the opposite of the simple, definitive statements the media want. In science, all knowledge is tentative, every fact open to challenge. Science never delivers absolute certainty. Instead, facts are said to be known with degrees of confidence. Is the earth getting warmer and is human activity the cause? In 1995, the Intergovernmental Panel on Climate Change (IPCC) answered that question with this statement: "The balance of evidence suggests a discernable human influence on global climate." In 2001, the IPCC said, "There is new and stronger evidence that most of the warming observed over the last 50 years is attributable to human activities." And in 2007, with further research pointing to the same conclusion, the IPCC reported that "most of the observed increase in globally averaged temperatures since the mid-20th century is very likely due to the observed increasing anthropogenic greenhouse gas concentrations." The phrase "very likely" is about as strong as science gets. In the 2007 IPCC report, it was defined as meaning a 95 per cent chance that it is so. That's a common scientific convention: Something is taken as established fact if there is 95 per cent confidence that it is correct.

When the national science academies of 11 leading nations got together in 2005 to issue a historic joint statement on climate change, the first sentence read: "There will always be uncertainty in understanding a system as complex as the world's climate." It goes on to say,

"There is now strong evidence that significant global warming is occurring. . . . It is likely that most of the warming in recent decades can be attributed to human activities. This warming has already led to changes in the Earth's climate." By scientific standards, that language is tough, and yet it still hinges on the phrase "it is likely." Uncertainty is so central to the nature of science that it provides a handy way of distinguishing between a scientist talking as a scientist and a scientist who is using the prestige of his white lab coat to support political activism: Look at the language. If a scientist delivers the simple, unconditional, absolutely certain statements that politicians and journalists want, he is talking as an activist, not a scientist.

In January 2007, a group of leading scientists, including astrophysicist Stephen Hawking, announced that the hands of the "Doomsday Clock" – a creation of the board of directors of the *Bulletin of Atomic Scientists* – would be moved forward. It was "five minutes to midnight," they said. A key reason for this warning was the fact that, according to the statement of the board of directors, "global warming poses a dire threat to human civilization that is second only to nuclear weapons." Thanks to the prestige of the scientists involved, this statement garnered headlines around the world. But it was politics, not science.

According to the IPCC, there are still enormous uncertainties about the consequences of climate change, and it is very possible those consequences will be nothing like the civilizational crisis claimed by Stephen Hawking and his colleagues. Even the most basic consequences – things that activists typically assume will happen – are uncertain. The report says it is "likely" that drought will increase – meaning greater than a 66 per cent chance. How great that increase will be if it happens is far less clear, and more work needs to be done before the degree of certainty improves. The report also states that it's "likely" that sea levels will rise but scientists debate how high they will go. We don't hear about this uncertainty from activists, though. In a magazine ad from the World Wildlife Fund, a boy in a baseball uniform stands with his bat ready, waiting for the pitch, paying no attention to the fact that he is submerged in water up to his shoulders. "Ignoring global warming won't make it go away," says the ad. It's an arresting image, but the IPCC estimates that, under a variety of scenarios, climate change will cause the oceans to rise somewhere between 7 and 23 inches. That is serious but it doesn't lend itself to public campaigning, because a picture of someone shin–deep in water isn't going to catch the attention of a bored woman flipping through a magazine in her dentist's waiting room. A boy oblivious to the fact he is about to drown may be misleading but it certainly gets the job done.

Some organizations certainly *try* to strike a balance between accuracy and effectiveness. A common way to do this is to prepare an informed, responsible, balanced report – and then publicize it with a simplistic and frightening press release. "Global cancer rates could increase by 50 per cent to 15 million by 2020," reads the headline of a press release announcing the publication of the World Health Organization's *World Cancer Report*. Following this is a barrage of frightening statistics and statements – "Cancer rates are set to increase at an alarming rate globally" – that goes on for six paragraphs before this little sentence appears: "The predicted sharp increase in new cases . . . will mainly be due to steadily ageing populations in both the developed and developing countries and also to current trends in smoking prevalence and the growing adoption of unhealthy lifestyles." So the biggest source of the frightening headline is population aging, and population aging is partly the result of people living longer than ever before – which is actually good news, one would think. As for smoking, those of us living in the developed world can be heartened by the fact that smoking rates are declining and cancers caused by smoking are falling as a result. Put all this together and you get a sense of what the report actually shows: The truth about cancer is a mix of good news, bad news, and uncertainties that does not lend itself to a scary headline and shocking one–line summary. But the WHO's publicists know a scary headline and some "alarming" facts are essential to getting media coverage and so they portrayed their report as the frightening wake-up call it is not.

If press-release hype stayed in press releases, none of this would matter. But it doesn't, and this does matter. Reporters are increasingly asked to do more in less time and, as a result, they commonly do not read the studies they write about. What they read is the press release. It is the basis of the story, not the report. Savvy organizations know this, which is why press releases are written in a format that mirrors the standard news story: headline, lead sentence framing the issue, details, key numbers, quotations from officials and experts. Reporters pressed for time can whip out a superficially satisfying story in no time if they follow the press release's structure and use the facts and quotations provided. Sometimes they do. More often, they'll frame the story as the press release has framed it but add some comments from other experts or, perhaps, some facts and figures gleaned from a quick scan of the report. What the reporter is very unlikely to do, however, is read the study, think about the issue, and decide for herself what's important and how the story should be framed. The press release settles that, particularly the press release's headline and lead sentence – and since the headlines and lead sentences of press releases are so often sensationalized, so is the story.

The reader will have noticed how references to "the media" sprouted throughout this chapter. That's because for every organization marketing fear – from corporations to charities – the media play an essential role. And so it's to the newsrooms and television studios we go next.

8

ALL THE FEAR THAT'S FIT TO PRINT

The toddler grins madly and leans toward the camera, one bare foot forward, as if she is about to rush ahead and wrap her arms around the photographer's knees. She is so young. Baby fat bulges at her wrist. It is an image suffused with joy – a gorgeous, glowing, black–and–white portrait a mother would place on a bedside table, or perhaps in the front hall to be shown to anyone who comes through the door. But it is instead on the front page of a newspaper, which can only mean tragedy.

The little girl's name is Shelby Gagne. The tragedy is hinted at in a detail easily missed: Her hair is short and wispy, like a newborn's, or a toddler undergoing radiation treatment and chemotherapy.

When Shelby was 22 months old, an inexplicable lump appeared in her shoulder. "She had stage 4 Ewing's carcinoma, a kind of bone–and–soft–tissue cancer that affects boys more often than girls, usually teenagers. Shelby was a one–in–a–million case. And her cancer was running like mad: In three days between CT scans, the spots on her lungs grew from pepper–like flecks to recognizable nodules of cancer," wrote Erin Anderssen. A barrage of surgeries and radical treatments followed. Her mother, Rebecca, "immediately quit her job, splitting

24-hour shifts at the hospital with her mother, Carol McHugh. Her husband, Steve, a car salesman, had to continue pitching options and warranties knowing that his child was dying. Someone had to cover the mortgage."

The little girl descended into agony. "She had high fevers. She suffered third-degree radiation burns. Her mouth became so raw with sores she couldn't swallow her own saliva. She threw up five to ten times a day." It was all futile. Shelby was moved into palliative care. "Even drugged," Anderssen writes, "Shelby coughs and vomits and shivers. It does not stop. It is more than any human should bear, let alone a little, brown-eyed girl just turned three. People still write Rebecca to say they are hoping for a miracle. But she knows Shelby is beyond the kind of miracle they're hoping for. Holding her, here in the soft shadows of the hospital room, Rebecca Gagne does not pray for her daughter to live. She prays, with the selfless love of a mother, for Shelby to die." And she did, not long after.

Under the headline "Cancer: A Day in the Life," Shelby Gagne's portrait covered almost the entire front page of the *Globe and Mail* on Saturday, November 18, 2006. The *Globe* was launching an ambitious series of articles about cancer and Shelby was its star: As the articles rolled out in the days and weeks that followed, the little girl's pain-fully beautiful portrait appeared at the start of each one. In effect, the newspaper made Shelby the face of cancer.

And that was odd because the face of cancer looks nothing like Shelby's. "Cancer is primarily a disease of the elderly," the Canadian Cancer Society says in its compilation of cancer statistics. In 2006, the society notes, 60 per cent of all those who lost their lives to cancer were 70 or older. A further 21 per cent were in their sixties. "In contrast, less than one per cent of new cases and of deaths occur prior to age 20." The precise figures vary from country to country and year to year but everywhere the basic story is the same: The risk of cancer falls heavily on older people and a story like Shelby's is vanishingly rare.

The *Globe*'s profile of Shelby, especially that stunning photograph, is journalism at its best. It is urgent and moving. But the decision to put the little girl at the centre of a series about cancer is journalism at its worst. It was obvious that this "one-in-a-million case" was fantastically unrepresentative but the newspaper chose story over statistics, emotion over accuracy, and in doing so it risked giving readers a very false impression about a very important issue.

This sort of mismatch between tragic tale and cold numbers is routine in the media, particularly in stories about cancer. In 2001, researchers led by Wylie Burke of the University of Washington published an analysis of articles about breast cancer that appeared in major U.S. magazines between 1993 and 1997. Among the women that appeared in these stories, 84 per cent were younger than 50 years old when they were first diagnosed with breast cancer; almost half were under 40. But as the researchers noted, the statistics tell a very different story: Only 16 per cent of women diagnosed with breast cancer were younger than 50 at the time of diagnosis, and 3.6 per cent were under 40. As for the older women who are most at risk of breast cancer, they were almost invisible in the articles: Only 2.3 per cent of the profiles featured women in their sixties and not one article out of 172 profiled a woman in her seventies – even though *two-thirds* of women diagnosed with breast cancer are 60 or older. In effect, the media turned the reality of breast cancer on its head. Surveys in Australia and the United Kingdom made the same discovery.

This is troubling because it has a predictable effect on women's perceptions of the risk of breast cancer. Profiles of victims are personal, vivid, and emotional – precisely the qualities that produce strong memories – so when a woman exposed to them later thinks about the risk of breast cancer she will quickly and easily recall examples of young women with breast cancer, while finding it a struggle (assuming she does not have personal experience) to come up with examples of old women with breast cancer. The woman's Gut will use the Example Rule to conclude that the risk of breast cancer is slight for old women and substantial for young women. Even if she reads the statistics that reveal the truth – the older a woman is, the greater the risk – these numbers may not make a difference because statistics do not sway Gut, and Gut often has the final word in people's judgments.

And that is precisely what research has found in several countries. A 2007 survey of British women by Oxford University researchers, for example, asked at what age a woman is "most likely to get breast cancer": 56.2 per cent said, "Age doesn't matter;" 9.3 per cent said the risk was greatest in the forties; 21.3 per cent said it was in the fifties; 6.9 said the sixties; 1.3 per cent said the risk was highest in the seventies. The correct answer – "80 or older" – was chosen by a minuscule 0.7 per cent.

"Exaggerated and inaccurate perceptions of breast cancer risk could have a variety of adverse effects on patients," noted Wylie Burke. Older women may not bother getting screened if they believe breast cancer is a disease of the young, while younger women may worry unreasonably, "which in itself might be considered a morbid condition."

These distortions can result from words alone but on television and in print, words are rarely alone. In the news, we are presented with words and images together, and researchers have found that our memories tend to blend the two – so if the sentence "A bird was perched atop the tree" is accompanied with a photograph of an eagle in a tree, it will likely be remembered that "an eagle was perched atop the tree." Rhonda Gibson, a professor of journalism at Texas Tech University, and Dolf Zillman, a communications professor at the University of Alabama, took this research one step further and applied it to risk perception.

To ensure they were starting with a clean slate, Gibson and Zillman used a fictitious threat – "Blowing Rock Disease" – which was said to be a newly identified illness spread by ticks in the American southeast. Children were deemed particularly vulnerable to this new danger.

Gibson and Zillman asked 135 people, mainly university students, to read two articles – the first about wetlands and another about Blowing Rock Disease – taken from national news magazines, with questions about facts and opinions asked after each. The first article really did come from a national news magazine. The second was fictitious, but made to look like a typical piece from the magazine *U.S. News and World Report* with a headline that read, "Ticks Cutting a Mean Path: Areas in the Southeast Hardest Hit by Deadly New Disease." Participants were presented with one of several versions of the article. One was text only. The second also had photos of ticks, seen in creepy close-up. The third had the ticks plus photos of children who were said to be infected. The text of the article was the same in every case – it informed the reader that children were at more risk than adults, and it had profiles of children who had contracted the disease.

If factual information and logic were all there were to risk perception, the estimates of the danger posed by "Blowing Rock Disease" would have been the same no matter which version of the article they read. But those who read the version that had no pictures gave a lower estimate of the risk than all the others. Those who got the second version of the story – with photos of ticks – believed the risk was significantly higher, while those who saw photos of ticks and children pegged the risk higher still. This is the Good–Bad Rule in action. No picture means no charged emotion and no reason for Gut to inflate its hunch about the risk; a close-up of a diseased tick is disturbing and Gut uses that emotion to conclude the risk is higher; images of ticks and sad children are even worse, and so Gut again ratchets up its estimate. The result is a series of risk estimates that have nothing to do with factual information and everything to do with how images make people feel.

The power of images to drive risk perceptions is particularly important in light of the media's proven bias in covering causes of death. As Paul Slovic was among the first to demonstrate, the media give disproportionate coverage to dramatic, violent, and catastrophic causes of death – precisely the sort of risks that lend themselves to vivid, disturbing images – while paying far less attention to slow, quiet killers like diabetes. A 1997 study in the *American Journal of Public Health* that examined how leading American magazines covered a list of killers found "impressively disproportionate" attention given to murder, car crashes, and illicit drugs while tobacco, stroke, and heart disease got nowhere near the coverage proportionate to their death toll. A 2001 study by David McArthur and other researchers at the University of California that compared local television news in Los Angeles County with the reality of injuries and deaths from traumatic causes got much the same results: Deaths caused by fire, murder, car crash, and police shooting were widely reported; deaths caused by falls, poisonings, or other accidents got little notice. Injuries were also much less likely to be reported, although injuries caused by fires or assaults were actually better represented than accidental deaths. Overall, the picture of traumatic injury and death presented by the news is "grossly" distorted, the authors concluded, with too much attention paid to "events with high visual intrigue" and too little for those that didn't offer striking images. The other consistent factor, they noted, was crime – the news heavily tilted toward injuries or deaths caused by one person hurting another at the expense of injuries and deaths where no one was to blame.

The information explosion has only worsened the media's biases by making information and images instantly available around the world. The video clip of a helicopter hovering above flood waters as a man is plucked from the roof of a house or a tree is a staple of evening news broadcasts. The flood may be in New Zealand and the broadcast in Missouri, or the other way around, but the relevance of the event to the people watching is of little concern to the broad-caster. It's exciting and that's enough. Watching the evening news recently, I was shown video of a riot in Athens. Apparently, students were protesting changes in "how universities are governed." That tells me nothing but it doesn't matter because the words aren't the point.

The images are. Clouds of tear gas billowing, masked men hurling Molotovs, riot cops charging: It's pure drama and so it's being shown to people for whom it is completely meaningless.

If this were unusual, it wouldn't matter much. But it's not unusual because there is always another flood, riot, car crash, house fire, or murder. That's not because the societies we live in are awash in disaster. It's that the societies we live in have a lot of people. The population of the United States is 300 million, the European Union 450 million, and Japan 127 million. These numbers alone ensure that rare events – even one-in-a-million events – will occur many times every day, making the wildly improbable perfectly routine. That's true even in countries with relatively small populations, such as Canada (32 million people), Australia (20 million), the Netherlands (17 million), and New Zealand (4 million). It's even true within the borders of cities like New York (8 million people), London (7.5 million), Toronto (4.6 million), and Chicago (2.8 million). As a result, editors and producers who put together the news have a bottomless supply of rare–but–dramatic deaths from which to choose. And that's if they stick with the regional or national supply. Go international and every newspaper and broadcast can be turned into a parade of improbable tragedy. Remove all professional restraints – that is, the desire to portray reality as it actually is – and you get the freak show that has taken over much of the media: "The man who was tied up, stabbed several times during sex, and watched as the woman he was with drank his blood is speaking only to ABC15!" announced the KNXV anchorman in Phoenix, Arizona. "You wouldn't expect this type of thing is going to happen during sex," the victim said with considerable understatement.

The skewed images of mortality presented by the media have two effects. As we saw earlier, it fills our memories with examples of dramatic causes of death while providing few examples of mundane killers – and so when Gut uses the Example Rule, it will tend to overestimate the risk of dramatic causes of death while underestimating others. It also showers the audience with emotional images that drive risk perceptions via the Good–Bad Rule – pushing Gut further in the same direction. As a result, it's entirely predictable that people would tend to overestimate the risk of dramatic deaths like murder, fire, and car crashes while underestimating such undramatic killers as asthma, diabetes, and heart disease. And that's what researchers consistently find.

But distorted coverage of causes of death is far from the sole failure in the media's handling of risk. Another is failing to ask the question that is essential to understanding any risk: How *likely* is it?

"The cholesterol–lowering statin Crestor can cause dangerous muscle problems," my morning newspaper told me in an article that rounded up revelations about prescription–drug health risks in 2005. "The birth control method Depo–Provera is linked to bone loss. The attention–deficit/hyperactivity disorder drug Strattera might make children want to hurt themselves. It's enough to make you clear out your medicine cabinet." The writer feels these drugs pose a significant risk and she is inviting me to share that conclusion. But this is all she wrote about these drugs and telling me that something *could* happen actually tells me very little. As I sit at my desk typing this sentence, it is possible that a passenger jet will lose power in all four engines, plummet from the sky, and interrupt my work in spectacular fashion. It *could* happen. What matters far more is that the chance of it happening is so tiny I'd need a microscope to see it. I know that. It's what allows me to conclude that I can safely ignore the risk and concentrate instead on finishing this paragraph. And yet news stories routinely say there is a possibility of something bad happening without providing a meaningful sense of how *likely* that bad thing is.

John Roche and Marc Muskavitch, biologists at Boston College, surveyed articles about West Nile virus that appeared in major North American newspapers in 2000. The year was significant. This exotic new threat first surfaced in New York City in the summer of 1999, and its rapid spread through the eastern states, and later across the border into Canada, pushed the needle of public concern into the red zone. A 2002 survey by the Pew Research Center of Washington, D.C., found that 70 per cent of Americans said they followed the West Nile virus story "very" or "fairly" closely – only a little less than the 77 per cent who said they were following preparations for the invasion of Iraq – even though this was a virus that had still not appeared in most of the United States.

Making this attention all the more remarkable is the fact that West Nile isn't a particularly deadly virus. According to the Centers for Disease Control, 80 per cent of those infected with the virus never experience even the slightest symptoms, while almost all the rest suffer nothing worse than a fever, nausea, and vomiting that will last somewhere between a few days and a few weeks. One in 150 infected with the virus develops severe symptoms, including high fever, disorientation, and paralysis, and most of these very unlucky people fully recover after several weeks – only about 3 to 15 per cent die. But these basic facts were rarely put at the centre of the news about West Nile. Instead, the focus was on a family struggling with the loss of a beloved mother or a victim whose pleasant walk in the woods ended in a wheelchair.

There were statistics to go with these sad stories, of course. Roche and Muskavitch found that almost 60 per cent of articles cited the number of people sickened by the virus and 81 per cent had data on deaths. But what do these sorts of numbers actually tell us about the risk? If I read that the virus has killed 18 people (as it had by 2001), should I worry? It depends. If it is 18 dead in a village of 100, I definitely should. But if it is 18 in a city of one million people, the risk is slim. And if it is 18 in a nation of 300 million – the population of the United States – it is almost non-existent. After all, 875 Americans choked to death on the food they were eating in 2003 but people don't break into a cold sweat before each meal. But Roche and Muskavitch's survey found that 89 per cent of the articles about West Nile virus had "no information whatsoever" about the population on which the statistics were based. So readers were informed that West Nile virus had killed some people and, in many articles, they were also introduced to a victim suffering horribly or to the family of someone killed by the disease, but there was nothing else. With only that information, Head is unable to figure out how great the risk is and whether it's worth worrying about. But not Gut. It has all the evidence it needs to conclude that the risk is high.

Not surprisingly, a poll taken by the Harvard School of Public Health in 2002 found that Americans grossly overestimated the danger of the virus. "Of people who get sick from the West Nile virus," the survey asked, "about how many do you think die of the disease?" There were five possible answers: Almost None, About One in 10, About One in 4, More Than Half, and Don't Know. Fourteen per cent answered "Almost None." The same number said more than half, while 18 per cent chose one in four and 45 per cent said one in ten.

Call it "denominator blindness." The media routinely tell people "X people were killed" but they rarely say "out of Y population." The "X" is the numerator, "Y" is the denominator. To get a basic sense of the risk, we have to divide the numerator by the denominator – so being blind to the denominator means we are blind to the real risk. An editorial in *The Times* of London is a case in point. The newspaper had found that the number of Britons murdered by strangers had "increased by a third in eight years." That meant, it noted in the fourth paragraph, that the total had increased from 99 to 130. Most people would find that at least a little scary. Certainly the editorial writers did. But what the editorial did not say is that there are roughly 60 million Britons and so the chance of being murdered by a stranger rose from 99 in 60 million to 130 in 60 million. Do the math and the risk is revealed to have risen from an almost invisible 0.0001 per cent to an almost invisible 0.00015 per cent.

An even simpler way to put a risk in perspective is to compare it to other risks, as I did earlier by putting the death toll of West Nile virus alongside that of choking on food. But Roche and Muskavitch found that a mere 3 per cent of newspaper articles that cited the death toll of West Nile gave a similar figure for other risks. That's typical of reporting on all sorts of risks. A joint survey of British and Swedish newspapers published in the journal *Public Understanding of Science* found a small minority of Swedish articles did compare risks but "in the U.K. there were almost no comparisons of this nature" – even though the survey covered a two-month period that included the tenth anniversary of the Chernobyl disaster and the peak of the panic over BSE ("mad cow disease"). Readers needed perspective but journalists did not provide it.

Another common failure was illustrated in the stories reporting on a September 2006 announcement by the U.S. Food and Drug Administration that it was requiring the product information sheet for the Ortho Evra birth-control patch to be updated with a new warning to include the results of a study that found – in the words of one newspaper article – "women who use the patch were twice as likely to have blood clots in their legs or lungs than those who used oral contraceptives." In newspapers across North America, even in the *New York Times*, that was the only information readers got. "Twice the risk" sounds big, but what does it actually mean? If the chance of something horrible happening is one in eight, a doubling of the risk makes it one in four: Red alert! But if the risk of a jet crashing onto my desk were to double, I still wouldn't be concerned because two times almost zero is still almost zero. An Associated Press story included the information readers needed to make sense of this story: "The risk of clots in women using either the patch or pill is small," the article noted. "Even if it doubled for those on the patch, perhaps just six women out of 10,000 would develop clots in any given year, said Daniel Shames, of the FDA's Center for Drug Evaluation and Research." The AP story was carried widely across North America but many newspapers that ran it, including the *New York Times*, actually cut that crucial sentence.

Risks can be described in either of two ways. One is "relative risk," which is simply how much bigger or smaller a risk is relative to something else. In the birth–control patch story, "twice the risk" – women who use the patch have twice the risk of those who don't – is the relative risk. Then there's "absolute risk," which is simply the probability of something happening. In the patch story, six in 10,000 is the absolute risk. Both ways of thinking about risk have their uses, but the media routinely give readers the relative risk alone. And that can be extremely misleading.

When the medical journal *The Lancet* published a paper that surveyed the research on cannabis and mental illness, newspapers in Britain – where the issue has a much higher profile than elsewhere – ran frightening headlines such as this one from the *Daily Mail*: "Smoking just one cannabis joint raises danger of mental illness by 40 per cent." Although over–dramatized with the "just one cannabis joint" phrasing, this was indeed what the researchers had found. Light users of cannabis had a 40 per cent greater risk of psychosis than those who had never smoked the drug, while regular users were found to be at 50 to 200 per cent greater risk. But there were two problems here. The first – which the *Daily Mail* and other newspapers noted in a few sentences buried in the depths of their stories – is that the research did not show cannabis use *causes* mental illness, only that cannabis use and mental illness are statistically associated, which means cannabis *may* cause mental illness or the association may be the result of something else entirely. The second is that the "40 per cent" figure is the relative risk. To really understand the danger, people needed to know the absolute risk – but no newspaper provided that. An Agence–France Press report came closest to providing that crucial information: "The report stresses that the risk of schizophrenia and other chronic psychotic disorders, even in people who use cannabis regularly, is statistically low, with a less than one–in–33 possibility in the course of a lifetime." That's enough to work out the basic figures: Someone who never uses cannabis faces a lifetime risk of around 1 per cent; a light user's risk is about 1.4 per cent; and a regular user's risk is between 1.5 and 3 per cent. These are significant numbers but they're not nearly as scary as those that appeared in the media.

Why do journalists so often provide information about risks that is misleading and unduly frightening? The standard explanation for media hype is plain old self-interest. Like corporations, politicians, and activists, the media profit from fear. Fear means more newspapers sold and higher ratings, so the dramatic, the frightening, the emotional, and the worst-case are brought to the fore while anything that would suggest the truth is not so exciting and alarming is played down or ignored entirely.

The reality varies by place, time, medium, and institution, but in general there is obviously something to this charge. And there's reason to worry that sensationalism will get worse as the proliferation of information sources continues to fracture the media audience into smaller and smaller segments. Evening news broadcasts in the United States fell from more than 50 million viewers in 1980 to 27 million in 2005, with the audience departing first to cable TV then the Internet. Cable news audiences have started to slip. Newspapers are in the most trouble – particularly in the United States, where readership has fallen from 70 per cent of Americans in 1972 to one-third in 2006. Things aren't so grim in other countries but everywhere the trend to fewer readers and smaller audiences is the same. The business of news is suffering badly and it's not clear how, or even if, it will recover. As the ships sink, it is to be expected that ethical qualms will be pitched overboard.

But still it is wrong to say, as many do, that the drive for readers and ratings is the *sole* cause of the exaggeration and hysteria so often seen in the news.

For one thing, that overlooks a subtler effect of the media's business woes, one that is – again – particularly advanced in the United States. "In some cities, the numbers alone tell the story," wrote the authors of *The State of the News Media 2006*, published by the Project for Excellence in Journalism. "There are roughly half as many reporters covering metropolitan Philadelphia, for instance, as in 1980. . . . As recently as 1990, the *Philadelphia Inquirer* had 46 reporters covering the city. Today it has 24." At the same time that the number of reporters is declining, the channels of communication are multiplying and the sheer volume of information being pumped out by the media is growing rapidly. How is this possible? In one sense, fewer people are doing more: The reporter who puts a story on the website at 11 a.m. also does a video spot at 3 p.m, and files a story for the next day's newspaper at 6 p.m. But reporters are also doing much less – less time out of the office, less investigation, less verification of numbers, less reading of reports. In this environment, there is a growing temptation to simply take a scary press release at face value, rewrite it, and move on. With countless corporate marketers, politicians, officials, and activists seeking to use the media to market fear, that has profound implications. Reporters are a filter between the public and those who would manipulate them, and that filter is wearing thin.

In 2003, the pharmaceutical company GlaxoSmithKline launched a "public awareness" campaign on behalf of restless legs syndrome, an uncomfortable urge to move the legs that worsens when the legs are at rest, particularly at night. First came a study that showed one of GlaxoSmithKline's existing drugs also worked on restless legs. This was immediately followed by a press release announcing a survey that was said to reveal that a "common yet under-recognized disor- der – restless legs syndrome – is keeping Americans awake at night." Then came the ad blitz. In 2006, Steven Woloshin and Lisa Schwartz of the Dartmouth Medical School examined 33 articles about the syn- drome published in major American newspapers between 2003 and 2005. What they found was "disturbing," they wrote.

There are four standard criteria for diagnosing restless legs syn- drome but almost every article the researchers found cited a survey that asked for only one symptom – and came up with the amazing conclusion that one in ten Americans was afflicted by the syndrome. The likelier prevalence of the syndrome, the authors wrote, is less than 3 per cent. Worse, almost half the articles illustrated the syndrome with only an anecdote or two and almost all of those involved people with unusually severe symptoms, including suicidal thoughts. Not one story provided an anecdote of someone who experienced the symptoms but didn't find them terribly troubling – which is actually common. Half the stories mentioned GlaxoSmithKline's drug by name (ropinirole) and about half of those illustrated the drug's curative powers by telling the story of someone who took the drug and got better. Only one story actually quantified the benefits of the drug, which Woloshin and Schwartz rightly describe as "modest" (in a clinical trial, 73 per cent of those who took the drug got at least some relief from their symptoms compared to 57 per cent who were given a placebo). Two-thirds of the articles that discussed ropinirole did not mention the drug's potential side effects and only one quantified that risk. One-fifth of the articles referred readers to the "non-profit" Restless Legs Foundation but none reported that the foundation's biggest donor by far is GlaxoSmithKline. "The media seemed to have been co-opted," Woloshin and Schwartz concluded.

But there is another, more fundamental problem with blaming the if-it-bleeds-it-leads mentality entirely on the pursuit of profit. The reader got a sense of it reading the awful story of Shelby Gagne at the start of this chapter. As painful as it was, the reporter's description of the family's struggle and the little girl's suffering was absorbing and moving. Anyone with a heart and a conscience would be affected – and that includes reporters.

For the most part, reporters, editors, and producers do not misrepresent and exaggerate risks because they calculate that this is the best way to boost revenues and please their corporate masters. They do it because information that grabs and holds readers grabs and holds reporters. They do it because they are human.

"Human beings have an innate desire to be told and to tell dramatic stories," wrote Sean Collins, a senior producer with National Public Radio News in a letter to the *Western Journal of Medicine*. Collins was responding to the study of television news in Los Angeles

County, which included some tough criticism by David McArthur and his colleagues. "I am at a loss to name a single operatic work that treats coronary artery disease as its subject but I can name several where murder, incest, and assassination play a key part in the story. Check your own instinct for storytelling by asking yourself this: If, driving home from work, you passed a burning building, would you wait to tell your spouse about it until you first explained the number of people who died that day from some form of neoplastic disease?"

Pamphlets peddled on the streets of Elizabethan England were filled with tales of murder, witchcraft, and sexual misbehaviour of the most appalling sort. By the early 19th century, recognizably modern newspapers were flourishing in London, and in 1820 came the first example of what a later age would call a media circus. The story that occasioned this momentous event was not a war, revolution, or scientific triumph. It was the unpopular King George IV's attempt to divorce his wife by having her tried for adultery – which turned the queen's sex life into a matter of public record and a source of endless fascination for every Englishman who could read or knew someone who could. In journalism schools today, students are told there is a list of qualities that make a story newsworthy, a list that varies from teacher to teacher, but always includes novelty, conflict, impact, and that beguiling and amorphous stuff known as human interest. A royal sex scandal scores on all counts, then and now. "Journalism is not run by a scientific formula," wrote Collins. "Decisions about a story being newsworthy come from the head, the heart and the gut."

From this perspective, it makes perfect sense that stories about breast cancer routinely feature young women even though most women with breast cancer are old. It's a simple reflection of our feelings: It may be sad when an 85-year-old woman loses her life to cancer, but it is tragic when the same happens to a young woman. Whether these contrasting valuations are philosophically defensible is irrelevant. This is how we feel, all of us. That includes the reporters who find themselves moved by the mother of young children dying of breast cancer, or the man consigned to a wheelchair by West Nile virus, and are convinced by what they feel that this is a great story that should be the focus of the report. The statistics may say these cases are wildly unrepresentative but given a choice between a powerful personal story and some numbers on a chart, reporters will go with the story. They're only human.

So much of what appears in the media – and what doesn't – can be explained by the instinct for storytelling. Conflict draws reporters because it is essential to a good story; *Othello* wouldn't be much of a play if Iago didn't spread that nasty rumour. Novelty is also in demand – "three-quarters of news is 'new,'" as an editor once instructed me. The attraction to both qualities – and the lack of interest in stories that fail to provide them – was evident in the results of a 2003 study by The King's Fund, a British think-tank, of reporting on health issues. "In all the news outlets studied," the researchers concluded, "there was a preponderance of stories in two categories. One was the National Health Service – mostly stories about crises besetting the service nationally or locally, such as growing waiting times or an increased incidence of negligence. The other was health 'scares' – that is, risks to public health that were widely reported but which often involved little empirical impact on illness and premature death." That second category includes so-called mad-cow disease, SARS, and avian flu – all of which offered an abundance of novelty. What was ignored? The slow, routine, and massive toll taken by smoking, alcohol, and obesity. By comparing the number of stories a cause of death garnered with the number of deaths it inflicted, the researchers produced a "death-per-news-story" ratio that "measures the number of people who have to die from a given condition to merit a story in the news. It shows, for example, that 8,571 people died from smoking for each story about smoking on the BBC news programs studied. By contrast, it took only 0.33 deaths from vCJD (mad-cow disease) to merit a story on BBC news."

An on-going narrative is also highly valued because a story that fits an existing storyline is strengthened by that larger story. Celebrity news – to take the most extreme example – is pure narrative. Once the Anna Nicole Smith narrative was established, each wacky new story about Anna Nicole Smith was made more compelling by the larger storyline of Anna Nicole Smith's wacky life and so we got more and more stories about Anna Nicole Smith even after Anna Nicole Smith was no longer providing fresh material. Even the smallest story could be reported – I actually got a CNN news alert in my e-mail when a judge issued an injunction temporarily stopping the burial of the body – because it didn't have to stand on its own strengths. It was part of the larger narrative. And if the big narrative is considered important or compelling, no story is too small to run. Conversely, if a story isn't part of a larger narrative – or worse, if it contradicts the narrative – it is far less likely to see the light of day. This applies to matters considerably more important than celebrity news.

In the early 1990s, the AIDS epidemic in the developed world was showing the first signs of being more manageable than had been feared. But the storyline it had inspired – exotic new virus emerges from the fetid jungles of Africa and threatens the world – didn't fade, thanks mainly to the release of Richard Preston's *The Hot Zone* in 1994. Billed as "a terrifying true story," *The Hot Zone* was about a shipment of monkeys sent to Virginia, where they were discovered to be infected with Ebola. There was no outbreak in Virginia, and if there had been it wouldn't have amounted to much because the particular strain of the virus the monkeys had was not lethal to humans, but that didn't stop *The Hot Zone* from becoming an international best-seller. The media started churning out endless stories about "emerging viral threats" and the following year a Hollywood movie inspired by *The Hot Zone* – *Outbreak* – was released. More books were commissioned. Documentaries were filmed. And when Ebola actually did break out in the Congo (then known as Zaire), reporters rushed to a part of the world that is generally ignored. The coverage was massive, but the 1995 Ebola outbreak didn't lead to chaos and disaster. It just ran the usual sad course, killing about 255 people in all.

For the people of Congo and central Africa, however, chaos and disaster really were coming. In 1998, a coup led to civil war that sparked fighting across the whole region and civil authority collapsed. It's hard to know precisely how many lives were lost, whether to bullet, bomb, or disease, but many authorities suggest three million or more died over the first several years. The developed world scarcely noticed. The war fit no existing narrative, and without any obvious relevance to the rich world it couldn't start one, so the media gave it a tiny fraction of the attention they lavished on the 1995 Ebola outbreak – even though the war killed roughly 11,700 people for every one lost to Ebola.

Even compelling stories that fit narratives can disappear if the narrative isn't operational when they happen. In 2006, a Tennessee school district sent home 1,800 students following reports that radioactive cooling water was leaking at a nearby nuclear plant. It was the first nuclear-related evacuation in the United States since the Three Mile Island accident of 1979. If it had occurred at a time when the "nuclear accident" narrative had been in place – as it was for years after Three Mile Island and again after Chernobyl – it would have been major news. But in 2006, that narrative was gathering dust and so the incident was treated as a minor local story and ignored.

Terrorism is obviously a major narrative today, as it has been for some time, but a decade ago it was quite different. The 1995 Oklahoma City bombing made terrorism the story of men like the bomber, Timothy McVeigh, a white, paranoid, anti-government radical. Following that storyline, journalists churned out countless articles about tiny groups of cranky gun enthusiasts who grandly styled themselves "militias." There wasn't much evidence that the militias were a serious threat to public safety but McVeigh had briefly belonged to one and so reporters flocked to cover their every word and deed. The

September 11 attacks scrapped this storyline and replaced it with the story of Islamist terrorism that is still going strong today – which is why, when a suicide bomber detonated himself outside a packed stadium at the University of Oklahoma on October 1, 2005, the media scarcely reported the incident. The bomber, Joel Henry Hinrichs III, wasn't Muslim. He was a disturbed white guy with a thing for explosives whose initial plan was apparently to detonate a bomb identical to that used by Timothy McVeigh. If he had carried out his attack at the University of Oklahoma in the late 1990s, it would have been major news around the world, but in 2005 it didn't fit the narrative so it, too, was treated as a minor local story and ignored.

This happened again in April 2007, when six white men belonging to the "Alabama Free Militia" were arrested in Collinsville, Alabama. Police seized a machine gun, a rifle, a sawed-off shotgun, two silencers, 2,500 rounds of ammunition, and various homemade explosives, including 130 hand grenades and 70 improvised explosive devices (IEDs) similar to those used by Iraqi insurgents. The leader of the group was a wanted fugitive living under an alias who often expressed a deep hatred of the government and illegal immigrants. At a bail hearing, a federal agent testified that the group had been planning a machine-gun attack on Hispanics living in a small nearby town. The media weren't interested and the story was essentially ignored. But one week later, when a group of six Muslims was arrested for conspiring to attack Fort Dix, it was major international news – even though these men were no more sophisticated or connected to terrorist networks than the "Alabama Free Militia" and they had nothing like the arsenal of the militiamen.

Another element essential to good storytelling is vividness, in words or images, and good journalists constantly seek to inject it into their work. This has profound consequences for perceptions of risk.

"Mad cow disease" is the sort of short, vivid, punchy language that newspapers love, and not surprisingly the term was coined by a newspaperman. David Brown of the *Daily Telegraph* realized the scientific name – bovine spongiform encephalopathy (BSE) – is dry and abstract and, as he later recalled in an interview, he wanted people to pay attention and demand something be done about the problem. "The title of the disease summed it up. It actually did a service. I have no conscience about calling it mad cow disease." The label was indeed potent. A 2005 paper examining how the BSE crisis played out in France found that beef consumption dropped sharply when the French media used the "mad cow" label rather than BSE. To bolster those results, Marwan Sinaceur, Chip Heath, and Steve Cole – the first two professors at Stanford University, the last with University of California at Los Angeles – conducted a lab study that asked people to imagine they had just eaten beef and heard a news item about the disease. They found that those who heard the disease described as mad cow disease expressed more worry and a greater inclination to cut back on beef than those who were asked about bovine spongiform encephalopathy. This is the Good–Bad Rule at work. "The Mad Cow label caused them to rely more on their emotional reactions than they did when scientific labels were used," the researchers wrote. "The results are consistent with dual–system theories in that although scientific labels did not eliminate the effect of emotion, they caused people to think more deliberatively." Gut jumped at the mention of mad cow disease, in other words, while bovine spongiform encephalopathy got Head to pay attention.

Even more than emotional language, the media adore bad news and so journalists often – contrary to the advice of the old song – accentuate the negative and eliminate the positive. In October 2007, Britain's *Independent* ran a banner headline – *Not An Environment Scare Story* – above a grim article about the latest report from the United Nations Environment Program. The tone was justified, as the report contained documentation of worsening environmental trends. But as the UN's own summary of the report noted in its first paragraph, the report also "salutes the real progress made in tackling some of the world's most pressing environmental problems." There wasn't a word about progress in the *Independent*'s account.

The same newspaper was even more tendentious when it reported on a 2006 survey of illicit drug prices in the United Kingdom conducted by the DrugScope charity. DrugScope's own report opens with this sentence: "Despite a wealth of dubious media stories about cocaine flooding playgrounds, crack and heroin being easier to buy than take away pizzas and an explosion of cannabis smoking sparked by reclassification, a snapshot of average illicit drug prices in 20 towns and cities undertaken in July and August reveals prices have remained relatively stable in the last year." The lead sentence of the *Independent*'s report on the survey was somewhat different: "The cost of drugs in many parts of Britain has plummeted in the past year, an authoritative study on the country's booming industry in illegal substances has revealed." DrugScope also reported that "the forecasted crystal meth epidemic has failed to materialize and it was not considered a significant part of any of the 20 drug markets." Predictably, this was not mentioned in the *Independent* article.

When the American Cancer Society released 2006 statistics showing overall cancer rates had declined in New York City and across the United States, the *New York Post* managed to turn this good news bad in a story headlined "Cancer Alarm." "About 88,230 Big Apple residents were diagnosed with cancer this year," read the first sentence, "and 35,600 died – many from preventable lung and prostate cancers, a new study shows." Only in a single sentence of the third paragraph did the *Post* acknowledge, grudgingly, that the cancer *rate* – the statistic that really matters – had declined. It took similar creativity for the *Toronto Star* to find bad news in the Statistics Canada announcement that the lifespan of the average Canadian male had reached 80 years. After devoting a single sentence to this historic development, the reporter rushed on to the thrust of the rest of the article: "The bad news is these booming ranks of elderly Canadians could crash our health system."

Scientists, particularly medical researchers, have long complained that the media favour studies that find a threat over those that don't. Eager to test this observation empirically, doctors at the Hospital for Sick Children in Toronto noticed that the March 20, 1991, edition of the *Journal of the American Medical Association* had back-to-back studies on the question of childhood cancers caused by radiation. The first study was positive – it showed a hazard existed. The second study was negative – it found no danger. Since the media routinely report on studies in JAMA, this was a perfect test of bias. In all, the researchers found 19 articles related to the studies in newspapers. Nine only mentioned the study that found there is a danger. None reported only the study that found there isn't a threat. Ten articles reported both – but in these, significantly more attention was given to the study that said there is a danger than to the one that said there isn't.

As unfortunate as this bias may be, it is just as understandable as the tendency to prefer emotional stories over accurate data. "We don't like bad news," observes a character in a Margaret Atwood short story. "But we need it. We need to know about it in case it's coming our way. Herd of deer in the meadow, heads down, grazing peacefully. Then *woof woof* – wild dogs in the woods. Heads up, ears forward. Prepare to flee!" It's a primitive instinct. Our ancestors didn't jump up and scan the horizon when someone said there were no lions in the vicinity but a shout of "lion!" got everyone's attention. It's the way we are wired, reporter and reader alike. A study by psychologists Michael Siegrist and George Cvetkovich found that when students at the University of Zurich were given new research on a health risk (a food colouring, electromagnetic fields), they considered the research more credible when it indicated there is a hazard than when it found no danger. "People have more confidence in studies with negative outcomes than in studies showing no risks," the researchers concluded.

For the reporter, the natural bias for bad news is compounded by the difficulty of relating good news in the form of personal stories. How do you tell the story of a woman who doesn't get breast cancer?

The ex-con who obeys the law? The plane that makes a smooth landing right on schedule? "Postal Worker Satisfied with Life" isn't much of a headline – unlike "Postal Worker Kills Eight," which is bound for the front page.

It can even be a challenge to turn statistically representative examples of bad news into stories. Stories about serial killers may be fascinating but the average criminal is a 17-year-old shoplifter and stories about 17-year-old shoplifters will never be as interesting as stories about serial killers. As for the statistically representative victim of West Nile virus – no symptoms, no consequences – the writer has not been born who could make this story interesting to anyone but a statistician.

And this is just to speak of the *news* media. The bias in favour of sensational storytelling is all the more true of the *entertainment* media because in show business there is no ethic of accuracy pushing back. Novels, television, and movies are filled with risk-related stories that deploy the crowd-pleasing elements known to every storyteller from Homer to Quentin Tarantino – narrative, conflict, surprise, drama, tragedy, and lots of big emotions – and bear no resemblance to the real dangers in our lives. Evening television is a particularly freakish place. One episode of *CSI* featured the murder of a ruthless million-aire casino owner – a case solved when diaper rash on the body led investigators to discover the victim had a sexual fetish that involved being stripped down and treated like a baby. Meanwhile, on the medical drama *Grey's Anatomy*, a beautiful young woman presents herself for a routine checkup, is told she has advanced cervical cancer, and is dead by the end of the show – just another day in a hospital where rare disorders like Rasmussen's encephalitis turn up with amazing frequency and no one ever gets diabetes or any of the boring diseases that kill more people than all the rare disorders combined.

It's the information equivalent of junk food, and, like junk food, consuming it in large quantities may have consequences. When we watch this stuff, Head knows it's just a show – that cops don't spend their time investigating the murders of millionaires in diapers and hospitals aren't filled with beautiful young women dying of cancer. But Gut doesn't know any of that. Gut only knows it is seeing vivid incidents and feeling strong emotions and these things satisfy the Example Rule and the Good–Bad Rule. So while it's undoubtedly true that the news media contribute to the fact that people often get risk wrong, it is likely the *entertainment* media must share some of that blame.

An indication of how influential the media can be comes from the most unlikely place. Burkina Faso is a small country in West Africa. It was once a French colony, and French is the dominant language. The French media are widely available, and the local media echo the French media. But Burkina Faso is one of the poorest countries on earth, and threats to life and limb there are very different than in France. So when researchers Daboula Kone and Etienne Mullet got 51 residents of the capital city to rate the risk posed by 90 activities and technologies – on a scale from zero to 100 – it would be reasonable to expect the results would be very different than in similar French surveys. They weren't. "Despite extreme differences in the real risk structure between Burkina Faso and France," the researchers wrote, "the Burkina Faso inhabitants in this sample responded on the questionnaire in a way which illustrates approximately the same pre-occupations as the French respondents and to the same degree."

That said, people often exaggerate the influence the media have on society in part because they see the media as something quite apart from society, as if it were an alien occupying force pumping out information from underground bunkers. But the reporters, editors, and producers who are "the media" have houses in the suburbs, kids in school, and a cubicle in an office building just like everybody else. And they, too, read newspapers, watch TV, and surf the Internet.

In the 1997 study that found the media paid "impressively dis-proportionate" attention to dramatic causes of death, cancer was found to be among the causes of death given coverage greater than the proportion of deaths it causes. The authors ignored that finding but it's actually crucial. Cancer isn't spectacular like a house fire or homicide and it's only dramatic in the sense that any potentially deadly disease is dramatic – including lots of deadly diseases that get very little media attention. What cancer does have, however, is a powerful presence in popular culture. The very word is black and frightening. It stirs the bleak feelings psychologists call negative affect, and reporters experience those feelings and their perceptions are shaped by them. So when the media give disproportionate coverage to cancer, it's clear they are reflecting what society thinks, not directing it. But at the same time, the disproportionate attention to cancer in the media can lead people to exaggerate the risk – making cancer all the more frightening.

Back and forth it goes. The media reflect society's fear, but in doing so, the media generate more fear, and that gets reflected back again. This process goes on all the time but sometimes – particularly when other cultural concerns are involved – it gathers force and pro- duces the strange eruption sociologists call a moral panic.

In 1998, *Time* magazine declared, "It's high noon on the country's streets and highways. This is road recklessness, auto anarchy, an epi- demic of wanton carmanship." Road rage. In 1994, the term scarcely existed and the issue was nowhere to be seen. In 1995, the phrase started to multiply in the media, and by 1996 the issue had become a serious public concern. Americans were increasingly rude, nasty, and violent behind the wheel; berserk drivers were injuring and killing in growing numbers; it was an "epidemic." Everyone knew that, and, by 1997, everyone was talking about it. Then it stopped. Just like that. The term *road rage* still appears now and then in the media – it's too catchy to let go – but the issue vanished about the time Monica Lewinsky became the most famous White House intern in history and today it is as dated as references to Monica Lewinsky.

When panics pass, they are simply forgotten and where they came from and why they disappeared are rarely discussed in the media that featured them so prominently. If the road rage panic were to be subjected to such an examination, it might reasonably be suggested that its rise and fall simply reflected the reality on American roads. But the evidence doesn't support that. "Headlines notwithstanding, there was not – there is not – the least statistical or other scientific evidence of more-aggressive driving on our nation's roads," concluded journalist Michael Fumento in a detailed examination of the alleged epidemic published in *The Atlantic Monthly* in August 1998. "Indeed, accident, fatality and injury rates have been edging down. There is no evidence that 'road rage' or an aggressive-driving 'epidemic' is anything but a media invention, inspired primarily by something as simple as alliteration: road rage."

Of course the media didn't invent the road rage panic in the same sense that marketers hope to generate new fads for their products. There was no master plan, no conspiracy. Nor was there fabrication. The incidents were all true. "On Virginia's George Washington Parkway, a dispute over a lane change was settled with a high-speed duel that ended when both drivers lost control and crossed the center line, killing two innocent motorists," reported *U.S. News and World Report* in 1997. That really happened. It was widely reported because it was dramatic, tragic, and frightening. And there were other, equally serious incidents that were reported. A new narrative of danger was established: Drivers are behaving worse on the roads, putting themselves and others at risk. That meant incidents didn't have to be interesting or important enough to stand up as stories on their own. They could be part of the larger narrative, and so incidents that would not previously have been reported were. The same article also reported "the case in Salt Lake City where 75-year-old J.C. King – peeved that 41-year-old Larry Remm Jr. honked at him for blocking traffic – followed Remm when he pulled off the road, hurled his prescription bottle at him, and then, in a display of geriatric resolve, smashed Remm's knees with his '92 Mercury. In tony Potomac, Md., Robin Flicker – an attorney and ex-state legislator – knocked the glasses off a pregnant woman after she had the temerity to ask him why he bumped her jeep with his." Today, these minor incidents would never make it into national news, but they fit an established narrative at the time and so they were reported.

More reporting puts more examples and more emotions into more brains. Public concern rises, and reporters respond with more reporting. More reporting, more fear; more fear, more reporting. The feedback loop is established and fear steadily grows.

It takes more than the media and the public to create that loop, however. It also takes people and institutions with an interest in pumping up the fear, and there were plenty of those involved in the manufacture of the road rage crisis, as Fumento amply documented. The term *road rage* and the alleged epidemic "were quickly popularized by lobbying groups, politicians, opportunistic therapists, publicity-seeking safety agencies and the U.S. Department of Transportation." Others saw a good thing and tried to appropriate it – spawning "air rage," "office rage," and "black rage." In the United Kingdom, therapists even promoted the term *trolley rage* to describe allegedly growing numbers of consumers who flew into a fury behind the handle of a shopping cart just as drivers lost it behind the wheel of a car.

With road rage established as something "everyone knows" is real, the media applied little or no scrutiny to frightening numbers spouted by self-interested parties. "Temper Cited as Cause of 28,000 Road Deaths a Year," read a headline in the *New York Times* after the head of the National Highway Transportation Safety Administration (NHTSA) – a political appointee whose profile grew in lockstep with the prominence of the issue – claimed that two-thirds of fatalities "can be attributed to behavior associated with aggressive driving." This became the terrifying factoid that gave the imprimatur of statistics to all the scary anecdotes. But when Fumento asked an NHTSA spokesperson to explain the number, she said, "We don't have hard numbers but aggressive driving is almost everything. It includes weaving in and out of traffic, driving too closely, flashing your headlights – all kinds of stuff. Drinking, speeding, almost everything you can think of, can be boiled down to aggressive driving behaviors."

With such a tenuous link to reality, the road rage scare was not likely to survive the arrival of a major new story, and a presidential sex scandal and impeachment was certainly that. Bill Clinton's troubles distracted reporters and public alike, and so the feedback loop was broken and the road rage crisis vanished. In 2004, a report commissioned by the NHSTA belatedly concluded, "It is reasonable to question the claims of dramatic increases in aggressive driving and road rage. . . . The crash data suggest that road rage is a relatively small traffic safety problem, despite the volume of news accounts and the general salience of the issue. It is important to consider the issues objectively because programmatic and enforcement efforts designed to reduce the incidence of road rage might detract attention and divert resources from other, objectively more serious traffic safety problems." A wise note of caution, seven years too late.

In 2001, the same dynamic generated what the North American media famously dubbed the Summer of the Shark. On July 6, 2001, off the coast of Pensacola, Florida, an eight-year-old boy named Jessie Arbogast was splashing in shallow water when he was savaged by a bull shark. He lost an arm but survived, barely, and the bizarre and tragic story with a happy ending became headline news across the continent. It established a new narrative and "suddenly, reports of shark attacks – or what people thought were shark attacks – came in from all around the U.S.," noted the cover story of the July 30, 2001, edition of *Time* magazine. "On July 15, a surfer was apparently bitten on the leg a few miles from the site of Jessie's attack. The next day, another surfer was attacked off San Diego. Then a life guard on Long Island, N.Y., was bitten by what some thought was a thresher shark. Last Wednesday, a 12-foot tiger shark chased spear fishers in Hawaii." Of course, these reports didn't just "come in." Incidents like these happen all the time but no one thinks they're important enough to make national news. The narrative changed that, elevating trivia to news.

The *Time* article was careful to note that "for all the terror they stir, the numbers remain minuscule. Worldwide, there were 79 unprovoked attacks last year, compared with 58 in 1999 and 54 the year before. . . . You are 30 times as likely to be killed by lightning. Poorly wired Christmas trees claim more victims than sharks, according to Australian researchers." But this nod to reason came in the midst of an article featuring graphic descriptions of shark attacks and colour photos of sharks tearing apart raw meat. And this was the cover story in one of the most important news magazines in the world. The numbers may have said there was no reason for alarm but to Gut, everything about the story shouted: Be afraid!

In early September, a shark killed a 10-year-old boy in Virginia. The day after, another took the life of a man swimming in the ocean off North Carolina. The evening newscasts of all three national networks made shark attacks the top item of the week. This was what the United States was talking about at the beginning of September 2001.

On the morning of Tuesday, September 11, predators of another kind boarded four planes and murdered almost 3,000 people. Instantly, the feedback loop was broken. Reports of sharks chasing spear fishers vanished from the news and the risk of shark attack reverted to what it had been all along – a tragedy for the very few touched by it, statistical trivia for everyone else. Today, the Summer of the Shark is a warning of how easily the public – media and audience together – can be distracted by dramatic stories of no real consequence.

Storytelling may be natural. It may also be enlightening. But there are many ways in which it is a lousy tool for understanding the world we live in and what really threatens us. Anecdotes aren't data, as scientists say, no matter how moving they may be or how they pile up.

Criticisms like this bother journalists. It is absurd that the news "should parallel morbidity and mortality statistics," wrote Sean Collins, the producer who took exception to criticisms of media coverage by public health experts. "Sometimes we have to tell stories that resonate some place other than the epidemiologists' spreadsheet."

He's right, of course. The stories of a young woman with breast cancer, a man paralyzed by West Nile virus, and a boy killed by a shark should all be told. And it is wonderful that the short life of Shelby Gagne was remembered in a newspaper photograph of a toddler grinning madly. But these stories of lives threatened and lost to statistically rare causes are not what the media present "sometimes." They are standard fare. It is stories in line with the epidemiologists' spreadsheet that are told only sometimes – and that is a major reason that Gut so often gives us terrible advice.

CRIME AND PERCEPTION

"Pedophiles watch our children from the shadows,"
warned U.S. Attorney General Alberto Gonzales. "They
lie in wait, studying, planning to ensnare and violate
the innocent."

The attorney general's audience that day in February 2007 was
trainees at the Project Safe Childhood Training Program, hosted by
the National Center for Missing and Exploited Children. They had a
mission, Gonzales told them. "It is our responsibility, in law enforcement and as adults, to find the predators first. To bring them to justice
before they catch their prey: our kids. . . . At this training program,
you will learn how best to pursue them, to interrupt their sadistic
hunt. Together, we can make these hunters feel like they are the
hunted. Because we all pray for, and work for, a day when children in
this country are safe from the leering eyes, the insidious stalking, and
the unthinkable cruelty that pedophiles inflict upon them."

There is probably no figure more reviled in modern Western
culture than the man – he's always a man – who hunts, sexually
abuses, and even kills children. In the tabloid press, he's a "monster,"
a "pervert," or a "paedo." A headline in the *Lancashire Evening Post* blares,

"Sex Beast Caged." The British tabloid *Daily Star* warns, "Pervs Now Rife in Our Schools." The revulsion is so profound and universal that even quality American newspapers, which are normally scrupulous about avoiding prejudicial language, have taken to calling sex offenders "predators." Politicians have reflected the shift by making promises to crack down on lurking pedophiles a staple of election campaigns.

He is worse than the drug dealer, the murderer, even the terrorist. He is the embodiment of evil, the stuff of nightmares. "It is every parent's fear, having your child taken," intoned Anderson Cooper, the popular host of CNN's *Anderson Cooper 360*, using the standard journalistic formulation to introduce a special, hour-long edition of his show in January 2007. "No child, of course, is immune."

The focus of Cooper's show was the story of Ben Ownby and Shawn Hornbeck, two Missouri boys. When Hornbeck was 11, he was abducted while riding his bicycle. Four years later, Ownby, 13, was snatched at his school bus stop. Acting on a tip, police found Ownby shortly after he was taken. They were also startled to discover a now 15-year-old Shawn Hornbeck. Both boys had been kidnapped by Michael Devlin, a seemingly ordinary man who is "a chilling reminder that the co-worker and neighbour you think you know so well may be a monster," Cooper said.

CNN is not tabloid TV and this show – entitled "Taken: Children Lost and Found" – was relatively restrained in its presentation of what is an inherently terrifying issue. There were interviews with Hornbeck's parents, Devlin's former employer, and a psychiatrist who discussed why a kidnapped child may not run at the first opportunity. There was also a look at how forensic artists "age" photos of young children. But mostly, there were agonizing stories of lost children and shattered parents. "Four o'clock, the bus came and we heard it. And she just never came up the driveway," said one mother who lost her daughter 20 years ago. "We were at home," recalled another. "He decided he wanted to go out and ride his bicycle. I guess it was about 2:30, somewhere around there. . . . And I stood at the door and watched him get on his bike and ride down the street. And that was the last I saw of my son."

"These are the kind of stories that keep parents awake at night worrying," Cooper observed. "Coming up, teaching your child to fight back if they come face to face with a kidnapper. Tips from an expert that could save a child's life."

The tips from "family safety expert Bob Stuber" included telling children that if someone is following them in a car, they should run in the opposite direction to buy time as he turns the car around. Stuber also suggested teaching children that if someone tries to snatch them off a bicycle – "a common scenario" – they should hang on to the bike in order to "make yourself too big and too bulky to be put into a car."

"For a lot of parents, it's a nightmare thinking about their child being thrown into the trunk of a car," Cooper said. "If a kid is in the trunk of a car, is there anything they can do then?"

"You know, there's not a lot you can do in the trunk of a car," Stuber replied. "You can kick and scream. Nobody is going to hear you, nobody's going to see you. But here's something that will work. Disconnect the brake or tail-light wires. Now, you can teach a three-year-old, four-year-old how to do this. You pull them real tight, the wires at the rear of the trunk. It takes the brake or tail lights out. Now, the police may pull that – in fact, there's a 50 per cent chance that the cops will pull that car over, not because you're in the trunk but because it has no brake or tail lights. Then they're going to be able to hear you and come rescue you."

Cooper thanks his guest and closes out the interview with the observation that "we all hope your children never have to use these tips, but better [to] be prepared than not."

And with that, one hour of parental terror ends. Not a word about probability has been spoken.

Of course Cooper was right when he said at the start of the show that "no child is immune." But saying that something could happen is close to meaningless. What matters is how *likely* something is to happen. On that score, Gut will definitely have a strong opinion: Having just seen a string of horrifying examples, Gut will use the Example Rule to conclude that the chances of this crime happening are high. What's more, these crimes are so hideous that anyone watching the show will feel intense sorrow and revulsion – which will also lead Gut to conclude, using the Good–Bad Rule, that the likelihood of this sort of attack is high. It's also possible – perhaps even likely – that the emotions will be so intense that they will drive out any thought of probability: *This is so horrible! I have to protect my kids!* As for Head, it has no reason to step in and adjust Gut's conclusion because it has been given no information that would allow it to rationally assess the risk.

Or rather, almost no information. As these sorts of television shows often do, a few statistics appeared on-screen briefly as the show faded to commercial breaks. Cooper didn't read them aloud and they were very easy to miss. Viewers who did happen to see them, however, read this, once: "Of an estimated 115 'stereotypical kidnappings' of children per year . . ." 40 per cent are killed, 60 per cent are recovered, 4 per cent are not found.

Why these numbers add up to more than 100 per cent wasn't explained. Neither is the strange term *stereotypical kidnapping*. Even if this had been cleared up, however, it would have made little difference to what the audience got out of the show. These numbers are far too incomplete to get a real sense of the probabilities involved. And whatever the statistics presented, they were up against a litany of graphic, horrifying stories about children stolen and murdered. Toss a handful of statistical fragments into that emotional storm and they'll be blown away like so much dust.

So what are the real numbers? In the 1980s, when one of the first waves of what has become a recurring panic over child abductions swept across the United States, there were no accurate data. Officials, activists, and reporters repeatedly said 50,000 or 75,000 children were stolen from their parents' arms each year but no one knew where those figures came from. Like the 50,000 pedophiles said to be prowling the Internet today, they seem to have been someone's guess that was believed and repeated as fact until its origins were lost. Finally, with fears for the safety of children rising, Congress asked a federal agency to do proper research and produce reports on the number of missing kids. The first such report – known by the acronym NISMART (National Incidence Studies of Missing, Abducted, Runaway, and Thrownaway Children) – covered cases in 1988. The second looked at 1999.

That second report found that an estimated 797,500 people under the age of 18 went missing for any reason. The study then broke that number down and showed the largest category by far was runaways. Another large portion involved more than 200,000 cases of "family abductions" – which typically meant a divorced parent keeping a child longer than legally permitted. There were also 58,200 "non-family abductions." That may sound like strangers stealing children but it's not. It is in fact a very broad category that can include, for example, a 17-year-old girl whose ex-boyfriend won't let her get out of his parked car.

In order to get a number that matches the sort of pedophile-in-the-shadow attacks that terrify parents, NISMART created a category called stereotypical kidnappings: A stranger or slight acquaintance takes or detains a child overnight, transports the child more than 50 miles, holds the child for ransom or with the intention of keeping him or her, or kills the child. NISMART estimated that in one year the total number of stereotypical kidnappings in the United States is 115. If that number is adjusted to include only children younger than 14 when they were kidnapped – kids like Ben Ownby and Shawn Hornbeck – it is 90.

To look at these statistics rationally, we have to remember that there are roughly 70 million American children. With just 115 cases of kids under 18 being stolen by strangers, the risk to any one American minor is about 0.00016 per cent, or 1 in 608,696. For kids 14 and under, the numbers are only slightly different. There are roughly 59 million Americans aged 14 and under, so the risk is 0.00015 per cent. That's 1 in 655,555.

To put that in perspective, consider the swimming pool. In 2003, the total number of American children 14 and younger who drowned in a swimming pool was 285. Thus the chance of a child drowning in a swimming pool is 1 in 210,526 – or more than 3 times greater than the chance of a child being abducted by a stranger. Also in 2003, 2,408 children 14 and younger were killed in car crashes. That makes the probability of such a death 1 in 24,502. Thus, a child is *26 times* more likely to die in a car crash than to be abducted by a stranger.

The numbers vary from country to country, but everywhere the likelihood of a child being snatched by a stranger is almost indescribably tiny. In the United Kingdom, a Home Office report states, "There were 59 cases involving a stranger successfully abducting a child or children, resulting in 68 victims." With 11.4 million children under 16, that works out to a risk of 1 in 167,647. (Note that the British and American numbers are based on different definitions and calculation methods; they aren't directly comparable and we shouldn't make much of the differences between them.)

In Canada, Marlene Dalley of the RCMP's National Missing Children Services carefully combed police data banks for the years 2000 and 2001 and discovered the total number of cases in which a child was abducted by a "stranger" – using a definition that included "neighbour" or "friend of the father" – was five. As for abductions by true strangers, there was precisely one in two years. There are roughly 2.9 million children aged 14 or younger in Canada. Thus the annual risk to one of those children is 1 in 5.8 million.

As to how these terrible cases end, the statistics flashed briefly by CNN were almost accurate. According to NISMART's rounded numbers (hence they don't quite add up to 100 per cent), 57 per cent of children abducted by strangers in a stereotypical kidnapping were returned alive, while 40 per cent were killed. Four per cent were not located.

One critical fact not mentioned in the show is that nine out of ten stranger abductions are resolved within 24 hours.

Having a child abducted by a stranger and returned later is awful but the ultimate nightmare is having a child stolen by a stranger and murdered – or simply vanishing from the face of the earth. According to NISMART, that nightmare scenario happens to about 50 teens and children a year in the United States. That's 50 out of 70 million Americans under 18. Thus the annual risk of a teen or child being abducted by a stranger and killed or not returned is 0.00007 per cent, or one in 1.4 million.

Risk regulators use a term called *de minimis* to describe a risk so small it can be treated as if it were zero. What qualifies as a *de minimis* risk varies, with the threshold sometimes as big as one in 10,000, but a one-in-a-million risk is definitely *de minimis*.

All these numbers boil down to something quite simple. First, the overwhelming majority of minors are not abducted. Second, the overwhelming majority of minors who are abducted are not taken by strangers. Third, the overwhelming majority of minors abducted by strangers are not taken in circumstances resembling the stereo-typical kidnapping that so terrifies parents. Fourth, the number of stereotypical kidnappings is so small that the chance of that happen-ing to a child is almost indescribably tiny. And finally, in the incredibly unlikely event that a child is snatched by a lurking pedophile, there is a good chance the child will survive and return home in less than a day.

This is not what Anderson Cooper told his audience. In effect, it is the *opposite* of what Cooper told them. There was no mention of the key facts, but the show did present case after case of children snatched by strangers under the most frightening circumstances. And in almost every case on the show, the child was held for months or years, or vanished forever.

The problem here is not Anderson Cooper. The total reversal of reality portrayed on "Taken: Children Lost and Found" is actually typical of how news media cover child abductions. A child *not* abducted is not news. And parental abductions are generally ignored unless there's a strange twist, such as a particularly violent ending. But pedophiles snatching children are always a big story. Uwe Kolbig, a 42-year-old German with a history of sexually abusing children, made the news around the world when he kidnapped, raped, and murdered a nine-year-old boy in February 2007. "Monster and His Prey," read an Australian headline. What made the crime particularly sensational was videotape taken by a security camera on a Leipzig tram that showed Kolbig chatting and joking with the little boy. Still pictures from the video appeared alongside every newspaper article, and Kolbig's grin was shown on national TV broadcasts in the United States, Canada, Ireland, Britain, and Europe.

It doesn't take a particularly sophisticated knowledge of psychology to understand how people who saw the Kolbig story were affected. They felt horror and anger – emotions Gut would use to conclude that this is a serious danger. Rationally, of course, a single crime in Germany says absolutely nothing about the safety of children in other countries and continents – or in Germany, for that matter – but that rational conclusion is likely to be blown away in the storm of emotions whipped up by such horrific images.

It's understandable, then, that stranger abductions have been the source of some of the biggest media frenzies in recent years. When Holly Wells and Jessica Chapman disappeared in August 2002, the British media talked about little else until the girls' killer, Ian Huntley, was arrested three weeks later. In that short time, the ten national newspapers published 598 articles on the case. An even bigger storm followed the June 2002 abduction of Elizabeth Smart from her parents' upper-middle-class Utah home. Day after day for weeks, and then months, television shows like CNN's *Larry King Live* talked about the case from every conceivable angle. With concern for abductions high, the media gave greater prominence to reports that even vaguely resembled the Smart case, which inevitably created the appearance of a rise in such incidents – a classic feedback loop. On Fox News, Bill O'Reilly declared 2002 "a summer of hell for America's kids." The kidnappings edged out the looming invasion of Iraq as the fourth-most-followed story of 2002, according to the Pew Research Center's surveys, with four out of five Americans saying they followed "very closely" (49 per cent) or "fairly closely" (30 per cent). In May 2007, the disappearance of three-year-old Madeleine McCann, who was with her vacationing British parents in Portugal, resulted in massive media coverage not only in the United Kingdom but all across the Western world – a snapshot of the little girl made the cover of the May 28 edition of *People* magazine.

Entertainment media are not limited to actual incidents, of course, and that freedom has allowed books, TV, and movies to make stranger abductions a dramatic staple in works ranging from tawdry thrillers to high art. The best-selling novel *The Lovely Bones* opens with a girl telling the reader she was murdered on December 6, 1973, "before kids of all races and genders started appearing on milk cartons . . . when people believed things like that didn't happen."

Politicians, newspapers, the evening news, novels, movies: They are all portraying the fantastically rare as typical, while what truly is typical goes all but unmentioned. And that's true not only of child abductions. It applies to *all* crime.

Researchers have found – to no one's surprise – that crime makes up a large and growing portion of the stories told by the news media. The numbers vary depending on the country, but most surveys show crime makes up about 10 to 30 per cent of newspaper content, with quality newspapers at the low end of that range and tabloids at the top. National television news tends to carry more crime, and local TV more still. A survey of local television news in the United States by the Center for Media and Public Affairs found one story in five involved crime, making it by far the most popular subject.

Another consistent finding in the research is that the media focus heavily on individual acts and say little about broader contexts and issues. Reporters tell us about the little old lady held up at gunpoint. They don't tell us how many little old ladies are held up at gun-point, whether more or fewer are being held up than in the past, who is holding them up and why, or what policies might protect little old ladies. So we should be careful with our terms. The media actually pay very little attention to "crime." It is "crimes" they can't get enough of.

This has enormous consequences, one of which is a bias in favour of bad news that runs even deeper than the media's usual bias in favour of bad news. Rising crime means more crimes are committed. It's easy to reflect that: Simply run more stories of people assaulted and murdered. But falling crime means fewer crimes are being com-mitted, a trend that cannot be captured by stories of individual crimes because a crime that is not committed is not a story. And so simply because the media focus heavily on *crimes* while ignoring *crime*, rising crime will always get far more attention than falling crime.

To see how profound this bias is, imagine that a government agency releases a report on violence against intimate partners that reveals domestic assault has soared by nearly two-thirds over the past decade and is now at a record high. And now try to imagine the media completely ignoring this report. No news stories. No angry opinion columns. No feature stories examining the frightening trend. Of course, that would never happen. And yet, in December 2006, the U.S. Bureau of Justice Statistics released a report that showed domes-tic assaults in the United States had *declined* by nearly two-thirds in the previous decade and were now at record lows. This astonishingly good news went almost completely unreported.

An even more dramatic example occurred in Toronto, in December 2005. The day after Christmas, with bargain-seeking shoppers crowd-ing the streets, rival gang members crossed paths. Guns flashed, bullets raced, and a beautiful 15-year-old girl named Jane Creba was killed. The murder would have been a shock under any circum-stances, but gang-related murders committed with handguns had been surging for months, and Canada was in the midst of a federal election. Inevitably – and not unreasonably – guns, gangs, and murder dominated public debate. Politicians pounded podiums and newspaper columnists raged. But the wave of gang killings had actually peaked prior to this awful crime and, with the election over and the gunfire lessening, the issue quickly and quietly faded. Still, the violence kept ebbing. By the end of 2006, gun murders had declined 46 per cent. But this went almost unmentioned in the media. There were a few stories, of course, but they referred to the decline in passing, sometimes burying it in stories about other police issues, as if it were a statistical quirk of the sort that only policy wonks would care about. And so a surge in crime that inspired a deluge of emotional stories and an impassioned national debate declined and disappeared virtually unnoticed.

The media's skewed picture of crime also extends to *which* crimes get ink and airtime. Murder is always the favourite. Some studies find it accounts for as much as one-half of all crime reporting in some media. The Center for Media and Public Affairs' study of local TV news in the United States found 29 per cent of all crime stories were about murders, with "non-fatal shootings" coming a distant second at 7 per cent. This pattern has been found in study after study, in many countries, for decades. Even in 1950s-era Britain – when the homicide rate was vanishingly small – "homicide was by far the most common type of crime reported" in newspapers, wrote criminologist Robert Reiner.

Violence that isn't as dramatic as murder gets less attention. Still less is given to property crime. The result is a very clear pattern in reporting. The more heinous the crime, the more attention the media give it. Of course any crime may still be reported if a politician is making an issue of it or if the victims are old people, children, or pets. Similarly, the involvement of royalty or celebrities – as either victim or culprit – will draw reporters. But generally, non-violent crimes lose to violent, and less bloody violence loses to more bloody. Hence, in the media, murder is king.

This may seem like a perfectly reasonable way of reporting crime because it means the more serious a crime is, the more likely it will be reported, and it's the more serious crimes people need to hear about. This is indisputably true. And it wouldn't be such a problem if the media balanced these stories of crimes with a lot of good analysis of crime that provided the broad picture, but they don't. So the media tell stories of one atrocity after another – a pedophile abducts and kills a boy, a disgruntled employee kills five – that eventually come together to create an image of crime that bears little resemblance to reality.

In the United States in 2005, the FBI recorded 1,390,695 violent crimes. In the same year, the FBI counted 10,166,159 property crimes. So property crimes outnumbered violent crimes by more than *seven times*. Or to put it differently, violent crime accounted for just 12 per cent of all crime.

Think of crime as an Egyptian pyramid. Most of it is made up of incidents involving no violence, with only a little chunk on top being violent crime. Within that little chunk, there were 417,122 robberies, which is 3.6 per cent of all crime. There were 93,934 rapes, or 0.8 per cent of all crime. And murder, with 16,692 cases, accounted for just 0.14 per cent of all recorded offences in the United States. In the pyramid of crime, murder is only the tip of the point on top.

So the media image of crime is upside down. The crimes that are by far the most common are ignored, while the rarest crimes get by far the most attention. Gallup polls consistently find about 20 per cent of Americans say they "frequently" or "occasionally" worry about getting murdered despite the fact that only 0.0056 per cent of Americans actually *are* murdered annually. The average American is three times as likely to be killed in a car crash. And bear in mind that this is in the country with by far the highest homicide rate in the Western world.

The habit of reporting the rare routinely and the routine rarely can be seen even within the category of murders. The media do not report every murder – even in a country like Australia, which had just 294 homicides in 2004–05 – nor do they give equal attention to the murders they do report. "There's an upside–down logic of press coverage in homicide where the nature of the news is to cover the man-bites–dog story," Jill Leovy, a crime reporter with the *Los Angeles Times* told NPR News. "And what you end up doing is covering the statistical fringe of homicide. You cover the very unlikely cases that don't represent what's really happening in Los Angeles County." In practice, that means that if a poor young, black, or Hispanic man murders a poor young, black, or Hispanic man – a common scenario in Los Angeles – the newspaper is likely to give it only a tiny mention, or none at all. But if a poor young black or Hispanic man kills a rich, old white woman – a very rare event – there's a good chance that story will not only be reported, it will land on the front page.

The misrepresentation of crime victims is universal. "The most common victims of violence according to official crime statistics and victim surveys are poor, young black males," notes Robert Reiner. "However, they figure in news reporting predominantly as perpetrators." The media pay far more attention to incidents in which the victims are children, women, and old people, a tendency that is particularly misleading in the case of the elderly because they are by far the *least* likely to be victims of crime. Statistics Canada's surveys have found that Canadians aged 15 to 24 are *20 times* more likely to be victims of any sort of crime than those 65 and older. Even 55- to 64-year–olds were four times more likely to be victims of crime than senior citizens. In the United States, the Bureau of Justice Statistics found that Americans aged 55 to 64 were five times more likely to be victims of a violent crime than seniors while teens aged 16 to 19 were *22 times* more likely to suffer violence. These figures are essential to understand the risk and yet I have never seen any of these statistics in news stories.

If the news media turn the reality of crime upside down, the entertainment media turn it upside down and shake it till coins drop from its pockets. "In most years, around 20 per cent of all films are crime movies, and around half of all films have significant crime content," writes Reiner. Of course not all crimes are the stuff of entertainment. Aside from daring jewel heists perpetrated by dashing thieves, property crime scarcely exists in fictional worlds. Murder is the alpha and omega of the fiction writer's imagination, and it always has been. The authors of *Prime Time: How TV Portrays American Culture* conducted a content analysis of American television in the 1950s and found there were seven murders shown for every 100 characters, which resulted in a homicide rate roughly 1,400 times higher than the actual homicide rate at the time. And these are not the boring murders of reality, which typically involve a poor, young man impulsively lashing out at another poor, young man without the slightest "malice aforethought." No, these murders are the products of the creative genius of writers. Prime-time television is an endless Darwinian contest to create novel scenarios of human life abused and extinguished, with each killing a little more exotic, explicit, and divorced from reality. A decade ago, it would have been satirical to imagine a show about a killer who kills killers but the remorseless logic of televisual homicide actually made it inevitable that such a thing would come to pass. It's called *Dexter* and it premiered to critical acclaim in 2006.

Ordinarily, we speak of *news* and *entertainment* as the two separate categories that make up the media. But in the case of crime, there is the third category of true crime, in which the cases are real but the ethos of quality journalism does not apply. Some true crime is unabashedly about amusing the audience, like *Cops*, the long-running television show that started in the United States but has spawned copies in many other countries. Nominally, it gives us insight into what a beat cop sees. In reality, it exists in order to deliver the thrilling sight of shirtless young men – always shirtless, for reasons no one has been able to explain – chased, taken down, and handcuffed. It is little more than a gentler, televised version of gladiatorial games.

The other stream of true crime takes itself much more seriously. In bookstores, it consists of biographies of serial killers and gangsters written by low-rent Mickey Spillanes. On television, it takes the form of Court TV and shows like *The O'Reilly Factor, Nancy Grace,* and *America's Most Wanted.* The attitude that energizes the genre is summed up in the titles of the three books written by John Walsh, the host of *America's Most Wanted: Tears of Rage, No Mercy,* and *Public Enemies.* Walsh, like Nancy Grace, is the victim of a horrific crime – in his case, the 1981 abduction and murder of his six-year-old son, Adam. Following his son's murder, Walsh became an activist and promoted the idea, so widespread in the 1980s, that child abductions were epidemic. "Fifty thousand children disappear annually and are abducted by strangers for reasons of foul play," he told Congress in the 1980s. "This country is littered with mutilated, decapitated, raped, and strangled children." Walsh was instrumental in getting major federal legislation passed in 1982 and 1984. In 2006, on the 25th anniversary of the disappearance of Walsh's son, President Bush signed the Adam Walsh Child Protection and Safety Act, which set up a national sex offender registry. In the universe of "true crime," virtually all crime is abduction, rape, or murder, all criminals are sociopathic beasts, and all children are in danger. Sad and horrible tales are the stock in trade. Accurate statistics are rarely or never mentioned.

With the media relentlessly misrepresenting the reality of crime, it is not surprising to find that people have some funny ideas about the issue. Julian Roberts, a criminologist at Oxford University, reviewed many of the studies on public perceptions and found that – in country after country – most people think "violent crime accounts for approximately half of all crime recorded by the police." Research in Ohio, Roberts noted, found that only one person in five could provide an estimate of the violent crime rate that was anywhere near accurate, and "one-third of the respondents provided an estimate of the violent crime rate that was at least six times higher than the actual rate."

Another consistent finding is pessimism. Crime is getting worse. Always. "Whenever polls have asked people about changes in crime rates, most people respond that crime rates have been increasing rapidly," Roberts writes.

The authors of crime surveys often sound a little bemused when they write about this. "Despite the number of crimes estimated by the [British Crime Survey] falling in recent years," notes the 2005–06 BCS, "63 per cent of people thought that crime in the country as a whole had increased." This is a startling contrast with reality: Between 1995 and 2005, the British Crime Survey recorded a 44 per cent *decline* in crime.

The United States experienced an even more spectacular crime drop in the 1990s. It was so huge, so unprecedented, the media even noticed it. And yet, after seven straight years of plummeting crime, a Gallup poll taken in 2000 found 47 per cent of Americans still said crime was rising.

Still, in all the surveys there is a minority that has a rough grasp of the facts. And many people's views do change in tandem with major rises or falls in crime. During the great crime drop of the 1990s, for example, Gallup found the percentage of Americans who said crime was declining went from 4 per cent in 1993 to 43 per cent in 2001. Media analysis of crime – there is a little – probably had a hand in that. But so did what people saw with their own eyes and heard from their friends and neighbours. Personal experience is a major influence, and we must not forget the innate desire we have to conform to the opinions of those around us. It's easy to forget this when discussing the bedazzling power of the media, but it's always true.

The relative influence of the media and what we recognize in our own lives can be seen in a curious fact about crime surveys. When researchers ask people if crime is increasing or decreasing *in the nation*, they get one answer. When they ask if it's increasing or decreasing *in your area*, they get quite a different answer – almost always a more positive answer. In the British Crime Survey that found 63 per cent said crime was rising in Britain, 42 per cent said it was rising in their local area. The annual Gallup poll on crime in the United States finds the same gap year after year, always with opinions about local crime being rosier than the national situation. In 2000, when 47 per cent said crime was rising in the United States, only 26 per cent of Americans said the same of their own area. In part, this gap is the result of the fact that when people judge the local situation, they have more resources to rely on. They have their own experience and that of their family, and they have what they hear in conversations. But in judging what's happening across the nation, they have to rely on what the media tell them, and what the media tell them is that murder and mayhem are rampant.

The big question is whether the excessively grim and frightening image of crime so many people have courtesy of the media translates into fear of crime. Sociologists have wrestled with this for decades. For the most part, they have proved there is an important correlation: The more you read and watch, the more you fear. That's what psychology would predict. A steady diet of vivid, violent images allows Gut – using the Example Rule – to conclude the danger is high. And crime stories are drenched with powerful, awful emotions that will – thanks to the Good–Bad Rule – strengthen Gut's sense that this is a serious threat.

But social science can be tricky stuff. The simple fact that people who read and watch more fear more does not prove that reading and watching *cause* fear. It could be that being fearful causes people to read and watch more. So far, no one's really been able to untangle this and show what causes what. Most experts have come to the sensible conclusion that it goes both ways: If you read and watch more, you fear more; and if you fear more, you read and watch more. "They reinforce each other," in the words of Aaron Doyle, a sociologist at Carleton University.

This is actually more disturbing than a model in which the media simply scare the bejeezus out of people. If people who fear crime turn to the media, they will get more images and feelings that amplify their fears. Those amplified fears would, in turn, lead them to read and watch more. This has the potential to create a spiral of anxiety. And the effect of fear-saturated media may not be limited to our feelings about crime. Recall the experiment conducted by psychologists Amos Tversky and Eric Johnson in which they asked Stanford University students to read a tragic story of a death caused by leukemia, fire, or murder and then asked them to rate a list of 12 risks. In that experiment, reading the tragic story had the unsurprising effect of raising people's perceptions of the danger posed by the cause of death in the story, but Tversky and Johnson also discovered that reading the tragic story caused people to raise their estimates for *all* risks, not only the one portrayed in the story. The fire story caused an overall increase in perceived risk of 14 per cent. The leukemia story raised it by 73 per cent. And the murder story drove it up 144 per cent.

We live in an environment saturated with media offering stories of abduction, rape, and murder, of cruelty and innocence savaged, of loss and lingering sorrow. Head may understand that these stories – some fictional, some from far away, few from the communities I live and work in – tell me little about the risks faced by me and my family. But that's not what Gut thinks when it watches television.

Humans have been telling each other stories about crime since Cain slew Abel, and for good reason. "We are social mammals whose brains are highly specialized for thinking about others," wrote Daniel Gilbert, a Harvard psychologist, in the *Los Angeles Times*. "Understanding what others are up to – what they know and want, what they are doing and planning – has been so crucial to the survival of our species that our brains have developed an obsession with all things human. We think about people and their intentions; talk about them; look for and remember them." It's not a coincidence that one of the most popular magazines in the world is called *People*.

Nor is it a coincidence that *People*'s endless stories about celebrities are interspersed with stories about crimes. Celebrities and murders go together not because movie stars are especially likely to kill or be killed but because our interest in celebrity tattle and bloody crimes are both manifestations of the same human instinct to observe people and think about why they do what they do. Crimes are particularly intriguing for us because, from the perspective of survival, they're especially important. Living in little bands of 30 wandering the plains of Africa, our ancestors depended on cooperation to stay alive. Cooperation required rules, so understanding how and why people broke rules was crucial to survival. It was also vital to instill the message that rule-breakers are identified and held responsible for their transgressions, which is why stories about crime routinely come to that audience-pleasing conclusion.

The instinct to gossip about crime is a powerful thing. In the same interview in which *L.A. Times* crime reporter Jill Leovy complained about the excessive coverage given to wildly unusual murders, she described how she attended an immersion project with an inner-city homicide unit. "They had around 70 murders that year, just running on homicides all the time." At the time, Scott Peterson – a wealthy, handsome, young white California man – was being tried for the murder of his pregnant wife, Laci. The Peterson trial was a frenzy, dominating cable news and talk shows. There were books about it and endless articles in newspapers and magazines. It was precisely the sort of binge coverage of an extremely unusual case that Leovy loathes. "And in the morning in the [homicide] unit," she recalled, "we would drink coffee and talk about what was new with the Laci Peterson case. And then move on to dozens of other homicides. It was a little bit surreal."

What's particularly intriguing about our interest in crime stories is how most such stories are obviously lacking in any objective importance, and how little that matters to those who follow them.

When Madeleine McCann vanished in Portugal, endless commentators tried to extract some meaning from the tragedy but in reality the tragedy said little or nothing about parenting, safety or anything else that might be relevant to the tens of millions of people who followed the story all across the Western world. It was pure drama. The shocking nature of the crime gave the story its initial prominence but then it became an established narrative sustained by a steady stream of relatively trivial information and speculation. Month after month, people followed it, and the cast of the drama became as familiar as that of the characters in a soap opera – which is essentially what the crime had become.

As with all stories of loss, emotions are essential to crime stories but the emotions crime stirs are often more potent and of a different quality. That's because they stir not only sorrow, but anger. If a little boy in a German city falls in front of a tram and is killed, it is a tragedy and any feeling person will experience a tinge of sorrow on hearing of it. The newspapers in that city may briefly mention the death, but that is the only notice it will receive and the family will grieve alone. But if that same little boy gets on the tram, meets a pedophile and is raped and murdered, it is not merely a tragedy. It is an outrage, and it may become news all over the world.

It is anger that distinguishes our feelings about crime. The burning sense that someone who hurts someone else must be punished and order restored is, remember, hard-wired by evolution. It doesn't matter if the offender will be a danger in the future or not. He must be punished and the scales balanced. It's not about safety. It's about justice.

Justice and safety are two separate issues. Looking at the video of the German pedophile luring a boy to his death, it is perfectly logical to say that this criminal must be caught and severely punished – while also acknowledging that this incident tells us nothing about the safety of the average child in Germany or elsewhere. But the unconscious mind isn't so fine-tuned. Gut only knows it is experiencing the intensely negative feelings of sorrow and anger, and when it runs those feelings through the Good–Bad Rule, it concludes that the risk of an attack like this is high, or that this threat is so awful probability is irrelevant. In either case, Gut sounds the alarm. In this way, the line between justice and safety is erased and the feelings we have about justice dominate our conclusions about safety.

This effect was demonstrated by Joseph Arvai and Robyn Wilson, researchers at Ohio State University, in an unlikely experiment. Participants were told that they were in charge of a state park that had a fund of $100,000 set aside to deal with unexpected problems. Now, they were told, a problem has come up. Bearing in mind that any money spent on this problem won't be available for future contingencies, how much of the fund should be spent?

One group was told the problem in question was deer overpopulation. Deer were eating so much they were destroying plant life. Worse, they were a menace on the roads, causing collisions with visitors' cars that damaged the cars and, occasionally, the people inside. On a ten–point scale, the estimated risk posed by deer to human safety is four, the risk to property five, and the risk to environmental health four. So how much of the $100,000 would they spend to deal with this? A second group was told the problem was crime – specifically, theft from cars, vandalism that damages property and plant life, and purse snatchings that sometimes caused minor injuries to the victims. In this case, the risk posed to human safety was rated to be three, the risk to property four, and the risk to environmental health four. Finally, a third group was told both problems – deer overpopulation and crime – had come up. They were also told the precise risk assessments above, which showed the crime problem was a little less serious than the deer problem.

The researchers expected – and they confirmed in questions during the experiment – that deer overpopulation is not something that has a lot of emotional meaning for people. But crime is another matter. Vandalism and property crime may be not be rape and murder but they do press emotional buttons. This meant there were two forms of information available in this experiment, emotions and numbers. Ordinarily, we might expect emotion to have the edge but the participants – ordinary people from the town of Eugene, Oregon – were hardly in circumstances that encouraged them to follow their feelings. They were sitting in a quiet room, taking part in scientific research that involved imagining themselves to be bureaucrats managing a budget. If any environment could steer people to the numbers, this was it.

Participants answered individually and the results were averaged. The group that dealt with deer overpopulation said they would spend $41,828. The group that handled the crime problem said they would spend $43,469. This made sense. Both groups had nothing to compare their judgments to so they both chose a number that provided a good chunk of cash but left more than that for future problems.

The surprise came with the group that was asked to deal with both problems. They said they would spend $30,380 on deer overpopulation and $43,567 on crime. The numbers said the deer problem was slightly worse than the crime problem but they spent far more money on crime than deer. So Gut won, hands down.

Still, in this version of the experiment the numbers for the two problems weren't all that different. What if the numbers for the crime problem were very small and the deer numbers very big? Would that be enough to overcome the influence of crime's emotional edge? Arvai and Wilson did the whole experiment again with different people, but this time the three numerical ratings for the deer problem were nine, ten, and ten. Crime, however, was rated a mere three, four, and four. The message told by the numbers was unmistakable: The deer overpopulation was practically a crisis, while the crime was annoying but not all that serious.

Once again, the groups that evaluated the two problems separately chose to spend roughly the same amounts of money. But the group that dealt with both problems did things a little differently than the first time around: They essentially provided *equal* amounts of money to the deer and crime problems. That's quite an amazing result. The numbers for the deer problem were 2.5 to 3 times higher than for the crime problem and yet people still gave the two problems equal funding.

This result is a textbook example of Head and Gut having a conversation and coming up with an answer that doesn't quite make sense. It starts with the phrase "deer overpopulation." People hear it and they feel nothing. Gut shrugs. "It's up to you," Gut says to Head. Head looks at the numbers, thinks about it, and comes to a rational conclusion. But then people hear "crime" and "purse snatching" and "vandalism." They see some young punk breaking into parked cars or knocking old ladies to the ground. They feel something and it's not pleasant. This time, Gut doesn't shrug. Using the Good–Bad Rule, Gut concludes the risk is high. Forget Bambi, Gut says, deal with this. But Head intervenes. The numbers show deer overpopulation is a far more serious problem, so Head takes Gut's conclusion and adjusts it. But, as usual, the adjustment is not enough to bring the conclusion in line with what strict logic says it should be and so equal amounts of money are spent on problems the numbers say are very unequal.

The crimes involved in this experiment were quite minor, and so are the emotions they stir up. Each step up the hierarchy of crime, emotions get stronger. A young man's stereo is stolen, he is punched, he is beaten to death. At each step, emotions swell like storm clouds.

The media are often accused of "man bites dog" coverage, always seeking the novel and bizarre, and there's much to that charge, of course. Humans are wired to notice the unusual and reporters are human. Sensation and sales also play a role. But the scale of emotion is a more critical factor in the media's distorted portrait of crime. On the evening news recently, I saw video from a security camera that showed a 101-year-old woman being punched and having her purse stolen. I felt a wave of disgust and anger, as anyone would, but it is doubtful this broadcast was a calculated attempt to make the audience feel disgust and anger. Instead, the people who put the news together felt the same disgust and anger as everyone else and those feelings convinced them this was important. If the victim had been a young man, neither the reporters nor the audience would have reacted as strongly – which is why the robbery of young men rarely makes the news but attacks on centenarians do.

We feel more in response to violent crime than property crime. We feel more in response to murder than a punch in the nose. We feel more in response to the murder of a little girl than a young man. And truth be told, we feel more for those we can personally relate to than those on the far side of racial and class lines. The media's image of crime may turn reality upside-down but it is a very accurate reflection of our feelings.

So that's the tango. The media influence people's thoughts and feelings. People's thoughts and feelings influence the media. But then politics cuts in.

As hard as it may be to imagine today, crime has not always been a staple of high-level democratic politics, even in the United States. In 1964, Republican Barry Goldwater was the first candidate to make crime and punishment part of a campaign for the presidency. In 1968, Richard Nixon made it central to his successful run for the White House, and the prominence of crime in electoral campaigns – at all levels – grew steadily in the decades that followed.

In 1988, crime played a central role in getting George H.W. Bush elected president. In fact, one crime did it: In 1986, Willie Horton, a Massachusetts convict serving life but out of prison on a brief furlough, broke into a home, tied up a man, and raped his wife. The governor of Massachusetts, Michael Dukakis, supported the revocation of furloughs for lifers but it made no difference when, in 1988, he was the Democratic nominee for the presidency. Republican spinmeister Roger Ailes (now president of Fox News) designed an ad showing a revolving door at the entrance of a Massachusetts prison, suggesting the Horton case was typical. The fact that Horton was black also helped. An ad appeared showing Horton's glowering mug shot. It was denounced as racist, and the Bush campaign claimed it had nothing to do with it but the damage was done, and a single crime, skilfully manipulated, had made a major contribution to deciding who would hold the most powerful office on earth.

That much of the story is infamous. Less well known is that it was not a Republican who first spotted the political value of Willie Horton's crime and used it against Dukakis. It was Dukakis's rival for the Democratic nomination, a senator from Tennessee by the name of Al Gore. No party or ideology has a monopoly on the use of crime as a political weapon.

A key moment in Bill Clinton's bid for the presidency was his decision to break off his campaign and return to Arkansas and his role of governor in order to personally preside over the execution of a man so mentally retarded that after he ate what he was told would be his last meal, he asked guards to set aside a slice of pecan pie "for later." After the execution, Clinton observed that "I can be nicked on a lot but nobody can say I'm soft on crime." He was right, and as president he stuck to a tough line, signing into law a long list of punitive bills and presiding over such spectacular growth in the prison population that the United States passed Russia as the nation with the world's highest incarceration rate. He may have regretted it, though. Mandatory minimum sentences are "unconscionable" and "we really need an examination of our entire prison policy," Clinton told a reporter from *Rolling Stone* magazine – two weeks before he left office.

The basic technique of the politics of crime is little different than that used by security companies selling home alarms or pharmaceutical companies peddling cholesterol pills: Raise fear in the public, or amplify existing fears, then offer to protect the public against that which they fear. Naturally, the crime–fighting policies offered must be attuned to the primal feelings involved. Intervention in the lives of troubled children and families may be a proven method of reducing crime years later – when the children become teenagers – but it neither delivers results now nor satisfies the craving for retribution. Better to go with the old standards: more cops and tougher sentences.

Perhaps not surprisingly, University of Chicago economist Steven Levitt discovered that American police officers tend to be disproportionately hired in years when there is a campaign for the mayor's office or governor's mansion. And tougher sentences became such a fixture of American politicking in the 1980s and 1990s that the prison population soared from 400,000 in 1980 to 2.1 million by 2000.

The latest flavour in American crime politics is the sex offender, a special breed of criminal said to – as Alberto Gonzales put it – "lie in wait, studying, planning to ensnare and violate the innocent." Bravely denouncing the evil lurking in the shadows, politicians promise to intervene and defend all that is good and pure – to "protect our children," as they inevitably put it. This genre of political marketing was elegantly summed up in an Internet ad produced for New York State senator Caesar Trunzo: Newspaper headlines flash one after the other – *Accused of Making Girl His Sex Slave, Perv Just Can't Stop: Judge* – until bold letters appear, asking "Who's Protecting Your Children?" As we've seen, the vast majority of abductions are committed by parents and other relatives, not strangers, and the same is true of all forms of sexual abuse. A massive Department of Justice study of offenders serving time for sex offences against children found "88 per cent had a prior relationship with their victims." The numbers are similar in other countries. But politicians focus on the 12 per cent, not the 88 per cent, because winning the votes of parents requires a threat "out there" which the politician can promise to fend off.

Press conferences in which politicians are flanked by grieving parents are a standard feature in this brand of political marketing. And legislation named for children who died under circumstances that are both exceptionally awful and exceptionally rare – something that would have been considered unspeakably distasteful in another era – has become routine. One of the latest to sweep the United States is "Jessica's Law," named after Jessica Lunsford, a nine-year-old girl whose abduction and murder in 2005 by convicted sex offender John Couey was national news. The first "Jessica's Law" was passed in Florida in 2005 but because it was then the toughest in the country – it mandated an automatic minimum of 25 years in prison for first-time sex offenders – it set a new standard and spread rapidly. The thinking behind Jessica's Law is that any sex offender – a term that covers everything from violent pedophiles to an 18-year-old who has consensual sex with his 15-year-old girlfriend – is an irredeemable creature whose crimes will inevitably escalate to raping and murdering children if he isn't taken out of circulation. This belief is popular but wrong: Many studies, including those of the U.S. Department of Justice, show sex offenders are actually *less* likely to commit another crime after release than other sorts of criminals. John Couey is hardly typical of sex offenders.

Numbers are another important part of political rhetoric. We have already seen the "50,000 predators on the Internet" statistic. A similar figure puts the number of children solicited for sex at one in five. "If you're a parent and your child is using the Internet, it is very likely that your child has been solicited for activity of a sexual manner. That's a startling piece of information for parents," said Republican senator Judd Gregg, the chairman of a congressional subcommittee. But notice what's missing: *Who* is doing this soliciting? And what does "soliciting" mean? Those who repeat this statistic routinely omit this key information, leaving people to fill in the blanks with scary images of children in chat rooms with middle-aged pedophiles.

The source of this number is a survey by University of New Hampshire researchers and what it actually found is considerably less frightening than that unadorned number. First, the number is actually falling. When the survey was first conducted in 2000, it came up with the one in five figure. But when it was repeated in 2006, it had declined to a little less than one in seven. More importantly, the survey, which covered 10- to 17-year olds, found that 81 per cent of all solicitations involved teens 14 and older. In fact, "no ten-year-olds and only three per cent of 11-year-olds were solicited." It's impossible to know the actual ages of those doing the soliciting, but the definition used by the researchers included any sexually themed communication – a lewd remark would do – from an adult or an unwanted sexual communication from a fellow teenager. Fourteen per cent of solicitations even came from "offline acquaintances, mostly peers." Solicited teens were also asked to rate how they felt after the incident: Two-thirds said it didn't bother them.

The researchers attempted to separate the more serious incidents by creating the category of "aggressive solicitation," which involved at least an invitation to meet or to communicate by telephone or mail. Only 4 per cent of teens said that had happened to them – and remember that teenagers, not balding perverts, may be behind these incidents as well. As for actual luring – the stuff of parental nightmares – the two versions of the survey uncovered a total of two cases in which youths met with someone who solicited them on-line and were sexually assaulted. That's two out of 3,001 interviews. Clearly, these surveys show on-line safety is a serious issue but they are not nearly as frightening as hearing a politician say "one in five" children has been "solicited."

Having warned of a threat, politicians must also come up with new ways to deal with it. In one month in 2006, the Louisiana state legislature passed 14 laws targeting sex offenders (an output one state senator justified on the grounds that "every time you turn on the news, some kid is getting abducted, raped, and murdered"). But after giving first offenders an automatic 25-year minimum sentence; after passing laws that allow for offenders who have served their sentence to be imprisoned indefinitely if they are deemed dangerous; after ordering released offenders to register and making their names, faces, addresses, and places of employment available on the Internet; after barring offenders from many forms of work; after banning them from living within 1,000 feet of schools, parks, and so many other places that they are often rendered homeless and driven out of town; after requiring released offenders to wear satellite tracking devices for the rest of their lives – after all that, what's left? It's a dilemma. The latest rage is for measures dealing with Internet luring but those opportunities won't last long and anyone aspiring to high office had better have something more to offer. In the 2006 gubernatorial race in Georgia, one candidate – the lieutenant-governor – called for a crackdown on Internet luring. That put his opponent – the governor – in a bind. He couldn't simply second the proposal. So the following day, the governor announced that if he were re-elected he would authorize juries to sentence child molesters to death.

Few of these policies are inspired by criminological research and even fewer actually contribute to public safety. Sex offender registries, for example, may be wildly popular but there's simply no reliable evidence that they work. When a task force convened by Canada's federal government reviewed all available evidence in 2000, it concluded a registry "would not significantly improve" public safety, and the money spent on a registry would do more good elsewhere. The government went ahead anyway, and the minister in charge privately apologized to the civil servants handling the file. "It's politics," he told them.

The politicization of crime, and the "get tough" spirit that goes along with it, is far more advanced in the United States than elsewhere but as British sociologist David Garland and others have shown, it is showing up elsewhere in the Western world. Many of the new American crime policies – three strikes laws, mandatory minimum sentences, supermax prisons, sex offender registries – have been introduced or discussed everywhere from Australia to the Netherlands. In the French presidential election of 2007, the Socialist candidate tried to diminish the appeal of Nicolas Sarkozy's tough talk on law and order by promising to build boot camps for young punks. In Canada, American tough-on-crime policies and language – "zero tolerance," "truth in sentencing," "adult time for adult crime" – are popping up in the media and political platforms with increasing

frequency while the reform agenda of the current Conservative government reads like an American campaign brochure from the 1990s.
In the British election of 2005, Conservative leader Michael Howard
pushed the fear of crime so fiercely that the Association of Chief
Police Officers took the unprecedented step of rebuking him for misleading the public about the level of crime. Tony Blair's Labour
government followed the American lead in creating a sex offender
registry and, in 2007, toyed with making the information in it available to the public, as it is in the United States; they even planned to
name the legislation "Sarah's Law" in honour of a murdered girl.

Politicians are far from alone in marketing crime, however. As we
have seen, feelings of insecurity are essential to the growth prospects
of the security industry. Police also know on which emotion their
budgets depend.

"Violent crime is accelerating at an alarming pace," concluded a
2006 report entitled *A Gathering Storm* from the Police Executive
Research Forum (PERF). PERF bills itself as a Washington, D.C., think-
tank, but with a board composed entirely of big-city police chiefs it
is effectively the chiefs' Washington lobby. "In 2005, there were 30,607
more violent crimes committed compared to 2004. This is the largest
single-year increase for violent crime in 14 years." That may sound
frightening but the truth is the increase in 2004 was – by PERF's own
numbers – only 2.3 per cent over the previous year. The reason it was
"the largest single-year increase" in 14 years is simply that violent
crime had fallen or been flat for 14 years. "If left unchecked," the report
continues, "violent crime may once again reach the heights of the early
1990s, which at their peak in 1991 left more than 24,500 dead and thousands more injured." Thus, a small increase in violent crime following
the longest, most sustained drop in crime in modern history means we
absolutely must act now or tens of thousands will die. And since the
inadequate funding of police departments is one of the key reasons
that crime is soaring, according to the chiefs, it is essential that police
budgets be increased. Incidentally, *A Gathering Storm* was funded by

Motorola – manufacturers of radios and many other products purchased by police departments when budgets permit.

American police are certainly not unique in making use of crime.
Julian Fantino, chief of police in Toronto between 2000 and 2005, and
currently commissioner of the Ontario Provincial Police, is notorious
for deploying rhetorical truncheons in support of his calls for longer
sentences and tougher prisons. "The criminal justice system is broken.
It does not work. We have the victims to prove it." As Toronto's police
chief, that was Fantino's mantra, repeated at every opportunity. When
critics responded that crime was not out of control, that it was in fact
dropping, Fantino was dismissive. "For all those people talking about
crime [being] down," he said in November 2003, "well, it may be down
in the numbers, but violent crime, it's been up, it's been going up for
years." Actually, violent crime had been falling for years but that
wasn't helpful to a police chief who wanted laws changed.

Agencies are another source of hype. Whether inside or outside
government, agencies very often have a direct interest in seeing the
profile of their particular issue raised, whether it is a sincere commitment to advancing a cause or simply a pitch for bigger budgets. The
U.S. Justice Department, for example, often quotes the statistics on
Internet sexual solicitation of minors mentioned earlier. So does the
National Center for Missing and Exploited Children (a private non-
profit group co-founded by *America's Most Wanted* host John Walsh and
created by an act of the U.S. Congress). But these organizations don't
say that the research does not mean what people naturally assume it
means – that one in five children on the Internet have been contacted
by pedophiles. In a February 2007 press release, UNICEF, the United
Nations' child welfare agency, went one step further: "One in five children who use computer chat rooms has been approached over the
Internet by a pedophile," the agency stated.

For prison guards, job security comes from rising crime and
tougher laws – or at least the perception of it, which is enough to get
those tougher laws. In California, the guards' union is a legendary

political machine. In the 1980s, it provided most of the funding to create the new victims' rights organizations that became key players in the push for longer sentences. The union funded the victorious "yes" side when the state's ferocious three-strikes law – the one that has locked away petty thieves for life – was put to a state-wide vote in 1994, and it funded the victorious "no" side when there was a vote to narrow the law modestly a decade later. California's prisons have been at double maximum capacity for years, even though the state built new prisons at a feverish pace. For guards, overcrowding means overtime, and in California, overtime typically means $37 an hour. According to Daniel Macallair of the Center on Juvenile and Criminal Justice in San Francisco, a liberal NGO in San Francisco that tracks the union's activities, "It is not uncommon for California prison guards to earn over $100,000 a year, including their overtime."

California's prison guards are also generous to politicians. One beneficiary was Gray Davis, the Democratic governor of California. In 2002, Davis responded to a grave fiscal crisis by cutting budgets in education, health care, and many other areas. At the same time, he agreed to a new contract giving prison guards a 37.7 per cent increase in pay and more vacation. The governor stoutly denied that he was influenced in any way by the $3 million he received in campaign contributions from the guards' union.

A unique place among those marketing fear is held by security consultants. They don't campaign like politicians, lobby like police chiefs, or advertise like security companies. Instead, they speak to reporters who present them as disinterested experts, although they are anything but disinterested.

Bob Stuber, the "family safety expert" interviewed on Anderson Cooper's show, is a former California police officer whose main line of work is presenting what his website calls "the *Safe Escape* show – a live multimedia program that empowers children and parents to make split-second, life-saving decisions when suddenly confronted with unexpected danger." A video disc – *Safe Escape: 50 Ways to Prevent*

Abduction – is also available for $25, plus $4.99 shipping and handling.

Stuber is all over television. He has appeared on *The O'Reilly Factor*, *America's Most Wanted*, and the *Today* show. He has been on *Oprah*. And as a consultant for ABC, he helped produce a series of *Primetime Live* specials about child abduction, rape, and school shootings. "The possibility of a school shooting has become a serious concern at schools across the United States," correspondent Chris Cuomo says to open *Primetime*'s November 10, 2005, show. "The issue of safety's a big issue," the principal of a high school in Shawnee, Oklahoma, tells the reporter. "I mean, it's one of the primary issues of our school and every school that I know of." The school has an armed police officer on duty at all times, and it conducts regular lockdown drills. So *Primetime* put that security to the test, with the help of Bob Stuber.

"The school staff and students were asked to behave just as they would if there were an armed intruder in the school," Cuomo tells viewers as teens rush through the halls during a lockdown drill. It all goes well and everyone's satisfied. They then prepare to do the drill a second time except the students aren't told that Stuber and an assistant will play the part of killers stalking the halls. "You're dead!" Stuber shouts at bewildered teens. "You're dead!" Cuomo finds the results realistic. "Even though they knew it was only a drill, a sense of panic replaced the smiles that came with the first drill."

The program then shifted to Stuber explaining what teens can do to save themselves from armed maniacs. Never go in a room without windows, he said. Pour liquid soap on the floor. "You get to do what nobody else ever gets to do in this situation," Stuber tells the kids. "You get to do it again." So the kids do the lockdown once more, they follow Stuber's advice, and everyone feels America's kids are safer than before.

Are they really? In the 1997–98 school year, 34 students were killed in the United States. In 2004–05 – the latest year for which data are available – there were 22 homicides. Each homicide represents a tragedy, but these murders should be kept firmly in perspective. For one thing, vastly more young people are killed *outside* school. In 1997–98, for every one young person killed in a school, 53 were killed elsewhere. Six years later, for every one killing inside, there were 75 outside. The enormous size of America's school population must also be considered. In 1997–98, there were about 52 million kids in school and with a number that large it is inevitable that even the most fantastically rare danger will strike somewhere. The simple fact is, the average American student had a 0.00006 per cent chance of being murdered at school in 1997–98. That's 1 in 1,529,412. And the risk has shrunk since then.

These numbers come from an annual report called *Indicators of School Crime and Safety*, which Congress demanded after the 1997 "Jonesboro massacre" first brought the issue of school shootings to national prominence. *Indicators of School Crime and Safety* also tracks what it calls "serious violent crime" – meaning rape, sexual assault, robbery, and assault with a weapon. In 1994, the rate of such crimes in schools was 13 per 1,000 students. That number is a bit misleading, of course, because it is the average across all American schools and there are big differences between poor, inner-city schools and those in wealthy suburbs or rural regions. Regardless, that rate didn't last. It fell steadily through the 1990s and by 2004 it was four per 1,000 students – less than one-third the level of a decade earlier. In 1993, 12 per cent of kids told surveyors they had carried a weapon of some kind onto school property within the last 30 days; a decade later, that had fallen to 6 per cent.

So the story inside America's schools was clear when *Indicators of School Crime and Safety* was first issued in 1998, and it remains clear today: Murders in schools are so rare that the risk to any one student is effectively zero, and the rate of serious violence has dropped steadily and dramatically.

Of course this isn't people's sense of reality – thanks mainly to the fact that on April 20, 1999, two heavily armed teenagers walked into Columbine High School in Littleton, Colorado. They murdered 1 teacher and 12 students, wounded 24, and stunned hundreds of millions of people around the world. The Columbine massacre got massive news coverage. The Pew Research Center found that almost 7 out of 10 Americans said they followed the event "very closely," making it by far the biggest story of 1999 and the third-biggest story of the entire decade. The biggest story the previous year was the Jonesboro massacre.

These back-to-back horrors created a feedback loop of monstrous proportions. The media turned even trivial school safety incidents into national and international news, usually accompanied with the comments of "security experts" who talked as if civil war had broken out inside every school. "Zero tolerance" policies – ordering students suspended or expelled for even the slightest violation of anti-violence rules – were expanded and fiercely enforced. The term *lockdown* moved from prison jargon to standard English as it became routine to conduct drills in which students imagined armed maniacs in the halls. Money shifted from books and maintenance to metal detectors, cameras, and guards.

For parents, it was a frightening time. The media and the people around them were all but unanimous that the threat was serious, and Gut – following the Example Rule and the Good-Bad Rule – emphatically agreed. Head would have struggled to correct that feeling under any circumstances but with the media failing to provide the statistics that put the risk in perspective, it had little reason to intervene.

The result of this one-sided mental debate showed in opinion polls. Shortly after the Jonesboro massacre, an NBC/*Wall Street Journal* poll found that 71 per cent of Americans said it was likely or very likely that a school shooting would happen in their community, while a *USA Today* poll taken following the Columbine massacre got almost the same result. One month after Columbine, a Gallup poll found that 52 per cent of parents feared for their children's safety at school; five months later, that number was almost unchanged at 47 per cent.

As hideous as the Columbine massacre was, it didn't change the fact that most schools, and most students in them, were perfectly safe – a fact politicians could have hammered home but did not. Instead, there were endless speeches blaming bad parenting, violent movies, or Goth music for leading youth astray. In part, that's because of a calculation every political adviser makes in crises like these: The politician who says the event is tragic but doesn't change the fact that we remain safe will be hit by his opponents with the accusation that he does not understand how serious the situation is, or worse, that he does not care. It's a huge political risk, with no reward for those who take it. Few do. And so politicians do not struggle to quell the "unreasoning fear" Roosevelt warned against. They embrace and amplify it.

The furor after Columbine faded eventually, but in the fall of 2006, the whole terrible scenario – from tragedy to panic – was revisited. On September 13, a former student entered Dawson College in Montreal with a rifle. One student was killed, 19 injured. On September 27, a 53–year–old man entered a high school in Colorado, took six girls hostage, and killed one. Two days later, a ninth grader in Wisconsin shot his principal to death. And on October 2, a 32–year–old man entered a primary school in Pennsylvania and shot to death five girls. "This week's school shootings in Amish country, in which five children died, are just the latest in a seemingly never–ending string of spectacular mass murders to hit the headlines of the United States," a breathless correspondent reported in Britain's *The Independent*.

The feedback loop cranked up, and once again it looked as if American schools were under siege. The Bush administration responded by convening a high–profile conference to discuss school safety on October 10, which may have been an effective political move but it only added to the sense of crisis. Schools across the United States reviewed emergency response plans, barred their doors, and ran lockdown drills.

On December 4, the latest version of the government's report on school crime and safety was released. It was no different than all the earlier reports. Kids are far safer inside school walls than outside, it showed. Violence was 50 per cent lower than a decade earlier and the rate of serious violent crime was down by more than two-thirds. The report also showed yet again that a student's risk of being murdered in school was *de minimis* – so tiny it was effectively zero. This report, like those that preceded it, went virtually unreported.

In the 2006 version of Gallup's annual survey of American opinions about crime, "fear for school-aged children's physical safety at school" was found to be the top crime concern. One in five Americans said they "frequently" worry their school-aged children will be physically harmed at school. Another one in five said they worry "occasionally."

When we succumb to wildly improbable fears, there are consequences. Lock all the doors and treat every visitor as a potential homicidal maniac and a school's connections to the community are cut, a tangible loss because, as research shows, schools function best when their community connections are strong. Spend money on metal detectors, guards, and consultants who tell kids how to flee gunmen and that money can't be spent on books, teachers, and everything else kids really do need.

There are less obvious costs as well. In August 2006 – a month before school shootings returned to the headlines and the whole panic cranked up again – the American Psychological Association adopted a resolution calling for schools to modify "zero tolerance" discipline because research showed this approach "can actually increase bad behavior and also lead to higher drop-out rates." In March 2007, the American Civil Liberties Union issued a report that described the police presence in New York City's public schools as "massive and aggressive." Every morning, the report noted, students line up and wait to go through metal detectors. "It used to take me an extra hour and a half to wait in line for the scans, so I would have to leave my home really early in the morning and then wait forever on the sidewalk outside of school," says an 18-year-old student. "The scans make you feel like an animal, like less of a person. You even start to become suspicious of yourself because the officers treat you like a criminal."

The better-safe-than-sorry attitude – driven as it is by unreasoning fear – can even result in a reduction of the very thing it values above all else. On October 20, 2006, in the midst of the nation-wide panic over school shootings, an 18-year-old was shot and critically injured a block away from a middle school in Asbury Park, New Jersey. It was clear from the beginning that the shooting had nothing to do with the school, and yet city officials ordered five public schools closed for two days. "Our schools are not equipped with metal detectors," an official told the *New York Times*. "If we kept them open, we risk having another Columbine." One councilman spotted the flaw in this thinking. "I think it would be safer for the kids to be in school," he said. He was indisputably right.

Whether the phantom fear is school shooters or strangers lurking in bushes, the damage is all too real. Kidscape, a child safety NGO, found in a 1993 survey that British parents' greatest fear was the abduction of their children by strangers. A poll by the NOP research firm in October 2004, found that three-quarters of British parents believe the risks of children playing outside are growing, and two-thirds say they are anxious whenever their children leave the house. One-third of children *never* go out alone. Inevitably, more children spend time doing nothing – almost half of British children, according to the survey, spent three hours or more sitting and staring at a television or computer. They are being raised like "battery chickens," the director of one child-welfare agency said.

We can only speculate about the consequences of raising children this way but many experts are alarmed. In 2007, a group of 270 child psychologists and therapists from the United Kingdom, the United States, Canada, and Australia insisted in an open letter to the British newspaper the *Daily Telegraph* that "outdoor, unstructured, loosely supervised play" was essential to child development and its loss – due in part to "parental anxiety about 'stranger danger'" – may be behind "an explosion in children's diagnosable mental health problems."

Admittedly, this is largely speculation, but it is still a more substantial concern than stranger abductions and other popular fears. And with boys and girls continuing to be taught that every stranger is a threat, with entire generations being told that danger lurks around every corner, it's only a matter of time before we have more evidence about what this is doing to the children who become men and women, and to the societies they form.

It is particularly unfortunate that corrosive fears of violence are spreading at this moment because they obscure a fact of immense significance: Modern developed countries have become some of the most peaceful societies in human history. Of course, this is the opposite of what most people believe, and not without reason. Most people know that crime started rising rapidly in the 1960s, got worse in the 1970s, and peaked in the 1980s. In the mid-1990s, crime trends in most countries either flattened or dropped substantially (even dramatically, in Canada and the United States) but there is still more crime now than in the 1950s. In the United States, the homicide rate was 5.6 per 100,000 population in 2005, compared to 4.1 in 1955. In England and Wales, the rate was 1.4 in 2005, more than double the 0.63 of 1955.

But this is only the record over five decades, which is less than one human lifespan. The long term is measured in centuries, not decades, and it is when we take that view that we can see what peaceful times we live in.

Here's a story that might have made headlines in 1278 if there had been newspapers in 13th century London: "Symonet Spinelli, Agnes his mistress and Geoffrey Bereman were together in Geoffrey's house when a quarrel broke out among them; Symonet left the house and returned later the same day with Richard Russel his Servant to the house of Geoffrey le Gorger, where he found Geoffrey; a quarrel arose and Richard and Symonet killed Geoffrey." Historian James Buchanan Given unearthed this story while sifting through the records of London's "eyre court" – records that are so meticulous Given was able to calculate London's homicide rate in 1278. It was 15 per 100,000 population. That is almost 11 *times higher* than the current rate.

Since Given completed his study, many other historians have done similar work in England and other Western European countries and the results are always the same. In the late Middle Ages, there "may have been about 20 homicides per 100,000 population," writes Manuel Eisner, a criminologist at the University of Cambridge. That's 14 times higher than the current homicide rate in England, and close to four times higher than the homicide rate in the United States, even though the modern American tally is greatly assisted by an abundance of cheap firepower unavailable to murderous medievals.

If this were true only of late medieval Western Europe, it wouldn't be terribly relevant to today. But historians and criminologists have been digging in archives all across Western Europe, and they have discovered a startling pattern: The extreme homicide rates of the Middle Ages dropped slowly but steadily as the decades and centuries passed until they bottomed out in the early 20th century. They wobbled up and down until the 1960s, climbed modestly until the 1980s or 1990s, then drifted down again. And so, despite the crime rises in recent decades, the homicide rates today are among the lowest in eight centuries.

They may even be among the lowest ever. As Lawrence Keeley demonstrates in *War Before Civilization: The Myth of the Peaceful Savage*, archeologists and anthropologists are rapidly accumulating evidence that levels of violence among ancient humans and isolated tribes in the modern world were, and are, terrifyingly high. For decades, the Kung San of the Kalahari Desert were considered gentle by visiting Europeans. A book about them was even entitled *The Harmless People.* But when researchers took a closer look, writes Keeley, they discovered the homicide rate was "20 to 80 times that of major industrial nations during the 1950s and 1960s." When an isolated band of 15 Copper Eskimo families was first contacted early in the 20th century, *"every adult male had been involved in a homicide."* In the late 19th century, the Yaghan, an isolated tribe of nomads living at the southern tip of South America, was estimated to have a homicide rate ten times higher than that of the United States.

Some researchers have said it's misleading to call these sorts of killings "homicides" because some of the violence is more akin to warfare than domestic crime. Taking that argument at face value, Keeley cites the example of the Gebusi, a tribe in New Guinea. "Calculations show that the United States military would have had to kill nearly the whole population of South Vietnam during its nine-year involvement there, in addition to its internal homicide rate, to equal the homicide rate of the Gebusi."

Taken together, this evidence, plus much more like it, suggests that the levels of violence in developed countries today are far lower than is normal in human affairs. In fact, they are very likely among the lowest in all of human history.

And it's not just disorganized violence that has declined. In recent decades, even war has been on the wane. "War between countries is much less likely than ever and civil war is less likely than at any time since 1960," Monty Marshall of George Mason University told the *New York Times* in 2005. A major study released later that year by the Human Security Centre at the University of British Columbia came to the same conclusion. "Over the past dozen years, the global security climate has changed in dramatic, positive, but largely unheralded ways," the report states. "Civil wars, genocides and international crises have all declined sharply. International wars, now only a small minority of conflicts, have been in steady decline for a much longer period, as have military coups and the average number of people killed per conflict." Since the early 1990s alone, the report found, there was a 40 per cent decline in all forms of armed conflict. Most people think the opposite is true, Andrew Mack, the director of the Human Security Centre, told me. That's because "whenever a war starts or there's an act of gross political terrorism or whatever, it gets lots of coverage [in the news] if there's lots of blood. When wars quietly come to an end, they sort of peter out. If it does get reported at all, it will be on page 16 of the *New York Times* in one paragraph. And so the impression people come away with is that we have a constant increase in the number of wars and they don't understand that in fact a lot more wars have come to an end than have started."

Crime is way down. War is declining. And that's far from the end of the good news. "Cruelty as entertainment, human sacrifice to indulge superstition, slavery as a labor-saving device, conquest as the mission statement of government, genocide as a means of acquiring real estate, torture and mutilation as routine punishment, the death penalty for misdemeanors and differences of opinion, assassination as the mechanism of political succession, rape as the spoils of war, pogroms as outlets of frustration, homicide as the major form of con- flict resolution – all were unexceptionable features of life for most of human history," writes Steven Pinker. "But, today, they are rare to nonexistent in the West, far less common elsewhere than they used to be, concealed when they do occur, and widely condemned when they are brought to light."

We are, in a phrase, more civilized. This is very good news, indeed. Just don't expect to hear about it on CNN.

10

THE CHEMISTRY OF FEAR

"Our bodies have become repositories for dozens of toxic chemicals," begins a report from Greenpeace. "It is thought that every person on Earth is now contaminated and our bodies may now contain up to 200 synthetic chemicals."

"Toxic Chemicals Are Invading Our Bodies," warns a headline on the website of the World Wildlife Fund. When the WWF analyzed the blood of 13 families in Europe, it discovered 73 man-made chemicals, while testing in the United Kingdom "found evidence of DDT and PCBs, two dangerous chemicals banned years ago," in almost everyone. "Hazardous chemicals are found in the tissue of nearly every person on earth and exposure to them has been linked to several cancers and to a range of reproductive problems, including birth defects," WWF says in a website article illustrated with a bag of blood stamped "CONTAMINATED."

Some see a connection between this pollution and trends in health. In a 2006 Canadian Broadcasting Corporation (CBC) documentary, journalist Wendy Mesley recounted how she was shocked to learn, after being diagnosed with breast cancer, that a baby born today has a one in two chance of getting cancer in its lifetime. "I set out to figure out what on earth is causing that." Smoking and sun exposure obviously contribute to cancer, she reported, as does the aging of the population. But those factors don't explain why "child-hood cancers have increased over 25 per cent in the last 30 years." Mesley had her blood tested and discovered it was contaminated with 44 chemicals and heavy metals, including PCBs. "I'm full of car-cinogens and apparently that's normal," she commented. Mesley interviewed Sam Epstein, a University of Illinois scientist. Cancer is "epidemic," Epstein declared.

Messages like these are reflected in popular opinion surveys Paul Slovic and colleagues conducted in the United States, Canada, and France. In each country, the results were roughly the same: Three-quarters of those surveyed said they "try hard to avoid contact with chemicals and chemical products in my daily life"; the same propor-tion said that "if even a tiny amount of a cancer-producing substance were found in my tap water, I wouldn't drink it"; seven in ten believed that "if a person is exposed to a chemical that can cause cancer, then that person will probably get cancer some day"; and six in ten agreed that "it can never be too expensive to reduce the risk from chemicals."

We really don't like chemicals. We don't even like the word. In surveys of the American public, Slovic asked people to say what comes to mind when they hear the word *chemical*. The results were "domi-nated by negative imagery," he says. "Death." "Toxic." "Dangerous." In Canadian surveys carried out by Daniel Krewski, an epidemiologist at the University of Ottawa, people were asked what thought pops into their minds when they hear the word *risk*. One common answer was "chemical."

Water is a chemical, and so is mother's milk. But that's not how people use the word today. Chemicals are invented in laboratories and manufactured in giant industrial plants. And they are inherently dangerous, something to be avoided whenever possible. It is this cultural re-definition of "chemical" that has transformed organic produce from a niche market into a booming, multi-billion-dollar industry, and why the word *natural* has become the preferred adjective of corporate marketers, no matter what they're selling. "The tobacco in most cigarettes contains additives drawn from a list of 409 chemicals commonly used in tobacco products," reads an ad that appeared in American magazines in 2006. "Natural American Spirit is the only brand that features both cigarettes made with 100 per cent organic tobacco as well as cigarettes made with 100 per cent additive-free natural tobacco."

This is new. Prior to the 1960s, "chemical" was associated with the bounty of science. It meant progress and prosperity, an image the DuPont corporation sought to capitalize on in 1935 with the help of a new slogan: "Better things for better living . . . through chemistry." New products came to market with little or no testing and were used in massive quantities with scarcely a thought for safety. It was an era in which children caught in the mist of a crop duster had their faces washed by mothers who had no idea it would take more than a damp facecloth to make their children clean again.

The end of that era came in 1962, when Rachel Carson, a marine biologist with the U.S. Fish and Wildlife Service, published a book called *Silent Spring*. "For the first time in the history of the world," Carson wrote, "every human being is now subjected to contact with dangerous chemicals, from the moment of conception until death."

Carson's primary concern in *Silent Spring* was the damage being inflicted on the natural world by the indiscriminate use of synthetic chemicals, particularly DDT, a pesticide she believed was annihilating bird populations and threatening to usher in a springtime made silent by the absence of bird song. But the book likely would not have come to much if it had stopped at that. Carson further argued that the chemical stew that was crippling the natural world was also doing terrible harm to *Homo sapiens*. In a chapter entitled "One in Every Four," Carson noted that the proliferation of synthetic chemicals that started in the late 19th century was paralleled by a rise in cancer. In the United States, Carson wrote, cancer "accounted for 15 per cent of the deaths in 1958 compared with only four per cent in 1900." The lifetime risk of getting cancer would soon be a terrifying one in four and "the situation with respect to children is even more deeply disturbing. A quarter century ago, cancer in children was considered a medical rarity. *Today, more American school children die of cancer than from any other disease.* . . . Twelve per cent of all deaths in children between the ages of one and 14 are caused by cancer." (Emphasis in the original.)

It would be difficult to exaggerate the impact of *Silent Spring*. The book influenced a whole generation of policy-makers and thought-ful citizens, including Supreme Court justice William O. Douglas and President John F. Kennedy. The chemical industry launched a cam-paign of nasty attacks on Carson – that "hysterical woman" – but that only raised the book's profile and damaged the industry's image. Commissions were launched to investigate Carson's claims and citi-zens' groups formed to press for a ban on DDT and other chemicals. It was the beginning of the modern environmental movement.

In 1970, the first Earth Day was celebrated. In 1972, DDT was banned in the United States. In 1982, DuPont dropped the "through chemistry" part of its famous slogan. At the end of the century, *Silent Spring* routinely appeared on lists of the most influential books of all time and *Time* named Carson one of the "100 People of the Century."

Carson didn't live to see her words change the world. She died in 1964 – killed by breast cancer.

Cancer is the key to understanding why *Silent Spring* set off the explosion it did. It wasn't just any disease Carson warned of. The very word *cancer* is "unclean," wrote a survivor in a 1959 memoir. "It is a crab-like scavenger reaching its greedy tentacles into the life of the soul as well as the body. It destroys the will as it gnaws away the flesh." Cancer has a unique image in modern culture. It is not merely a disease – it's a creeping killer and we fear it like no other. Paul Slovic's surveys show cancer is the only major disease whose death toll is actually overestimated by the public. It also has a presence in the media even bigger than its substantial toll.

And yet, despite its enormous presence in our culture, cancer wasn't always the stuff of nightmares. "In 1896," writes Joanna Bourke in *Fear: A Cultural History*, "the *American Journal of Psychology* reported that when people were asked which diseases they feared, only five per cent named cancer, while between a quarter and a third drew attention to the scary nature of each of the following ailments: smallpox, lockjaw, consumption and hydrophobia [rabies]. In the fear-stakes, being crushed in a rail accident or during an earthquake, drowning, being burned alive, hit by lightning, or contracting diphtheria, leprosy or pneumonia all ranked higher than cancer."

That changed after the Second World War. By 1957, cancer was such a terror that an oncologist quoted by Bourke complained that the disease had been transformed into "a devil" and the fear of cancer – "cancerophobia," as he called it – had become a plague in its own right. "It is possible that today cancerophobia causes more suffering than cancer itself," he wrote. With *Silent Spring*, Carson told people that this new spectre wasn't just in their nightmares. It was all around them, in the air they breathe, the soil they walk on, and the food they eat. It was even in their blood. Small wonder people paid attention.

Carson's numbers suggested fear of cancer was rising rapidly simply because cancer was rising rapidly. But her numbers were misleading.

Carson's statement that cancer "accounted for 15 per cent of the deaths in 1958 compared with only four per cent in 1900" makes the common mistake of simply assuming that the disease's larger share of the total is the result of rising rates of the disease. But according to U.S. Census Bureau data, cancer was the number seven killer in the period 1900 to 1904. Number one was tuberculosis. Number four was diarrhea and enteritis. Number ten was typhoid fever followed by diphtheria at number 11. Scarlet fever, whooping cough, and measles ranked lower but still took a significant toll. By the time Carson was writing in the late 1950s, vaccines, antibiotics, and public sanitation had dramatically reduced or even eliminated every one of these causes of death. (In 1958, tuberculosis had fallen from the number one spot to number 15. Enteritis was number 19. Deaths due to diphtheria, scarlet fever, and the rest had all but vanished.) With the toll of other causes dropping rapidly, cancer's *share* of all deaths would have grown greatly even if the rate of cancer deaths hadn't changed in the slightest.

The same facts take the sting out of the statement Carson thought was so important she put it in italics: *"Today, more American school children die of cancer than from any other disease."* By 1962, traditional child killers such as diphtheria had been wiped out. More children were dying of cancer than any other disease not because huge numbers of children were dying of cancer but because huge numbers of children were *not* dying of other diseases.

As for the title of Carson's chapter on cancer – "one in every four" – it comes from a 1955 report by the American Cancer Society (ACS) predicting that the then–current estimate of cancer striking one person in five would rise to one in four. But as age is the primary risk factor for cancer, the fact that far more people were surviving childhood and living to old age would inevitably mean more people would get cancer – mostly when they were old – and so the "lifetime risk" would rise. However, the ACS noted that wasn't the whole story. Data on cancer were still sketchy in that era but in the previous two decades there was an apparent 200 per cent rise in the incidence of cancer among women and a 600 per cent rise among men, which was mostly the result of a rise in only one type of cancer. Lung cancer "is the only form of cancer which shows so definite a tendency," the report noted.

Lung cancer started to soar in the 1920s, 20 years after the habit of smoking cigarettes took off among men in the United States and other Western countries. Women didn't start smoking in large numbers until the 1920s and 1930s – and 20 years after that, cancer among women took off as well. When smoking rates started to decline in the 1960s and 1970s – again, first among men – so did many cancers 20 years later. This pattern mainly involves lung cancer, but other forms of cancer are also promoted by smoking: cancers of the larynx, pancreas, kidney, cervix, bladder, mouth, and esophagus.

But Carson didn't write a word about smoking in *Silent Spring*. In fact, the only mention of tobacco is a reference (again italicized for emphasis) to arsenic-bearing insecticides sprayed on tobacco crops: *"The arsenic content of cigarettes made from American-grown tobacco increased more than 300 per cent between the years 1932 and 1952."* Carson was nodding toward a popular theory of the day. It isn't inhaling tobacco smoke that kills. Tobacco is natural and safe. It's the *chemicals* added to tobacco that kill. This theory was advocated by Wilhelm Hueper of the National Cancer Institute, who was a major influence on Carson's views and is repeatedly quoted in *Silent Spring*.

At the time, that hypothesis was not unreasonable. The research linking smoking to cancer was fairly new and very little was known about synthetic chemicals and human health. And while the rise in cancer may not have been as enormous as Carson made it out to be, it was real, and the possibility that all these new wonder chemicals were the source was truly scary.

Adding to the reasons to worry was a study conducted by a scientist named John Higginson – who later founded the World Health Organization's agency for research on cancer – that compared cancerous tumours among Africans with those of African-Americans. Higginson discovered there was far more cancer in the second group. This indicated heredity was not among the bigger factors driving cancer. Based on this study and others, Higginson estimated that about two-thirds of all cancers had what he called an environmental cause. He didn't mean environmental in the way that word came to be understood after *Silent Spring*, however. To Higginson, environmental simply meant anything that isn't genetic. Even smoking was included. "Environment is what surrounds people and impinges on them," he said in an interview with *Science* in 1979. "The air you breathe, the culture you live in, the agricultural habits of your community, the social cultural habits, the social pressures, the physical chemicals with which you come in contact, the diet, and so on." As the science advanced, Higginson's theory was vindicated and it became routine for cancer specialists to say that most cancers have environmental causes, but that only deepened the misunderstanding. "A lot of confusion has arisen in later days because most people have not gone back to the early literature, but have used the word 'environment' to mean chemicals," Higginson said.

That mistaken belief is still widespread among environmental activists. "Cancer has been identified as an environmental disease – that is to say, it is unleashed in our cells by the absorption of toxic chemicals from our air, our water, our food," wrote Bob Hunter, the co-founder of Greenpeace, in 2002 (who was battling prostate cancer at the time and would be killed by it three years later).

Higginson cited several reasons that his theory was misunderstood. One was the chemical industry's blithe indifference to safety in the era prior to *Silent Spring*, which made it easy to see it as the villain of the cancer drama. And "Rachel Carson's book was a watershed, as suddenly we became aware of the vast quantities of new chemicals, pollutants, pesticides, fibers and so forth in the environment." Higginson also said environmentalists "found the extreme view convenient because of the fear of cancer. If they could possibly make people believe that cancer was going to result from pollution, this would enable them to facilitate the clean-up of water, of the air, or whatever it was. Now I'm all for cleaning up the air, and all for cleaning up trout streams, and all for preventing Love Canals, but I don't think we should use the wrong argument for doing it. To make cancer the whipping boy for every environmental evil may prevent effective action when it does matter, as with cigarettes."

Higginson was careful not to accuse environmentalists of deliberate dishonesty. It was more a case of excessive zeal. "People would love

to be able to prove that cancer is due to pollution or the general environment. It would be so easy to say 'let us regulate everything to zero
exposure and we have no more cancer.' The concept is so beautiful that
it will overwhelm a mass of facts to the contrary." That "mass of facts"
included the observation that "there are few differences in cancer patterns between the polluted cities and the clean cities," Higginson said.
"You can't explain why Geneva, a non-industrial city, has more cancer
than Birmingham in the polluted central valleys of England."

That was 1979. Since then, the "mass of facts" has grown steadily
and today there is a consensus among leading cancer researchers that
traces of synthetic chemicals in the environment – the stuff that turns
up in blood tests of ordinary people – are not a major cause of cancer.
"Exposure to pollutants in occupational, community, and other settings is thought to account for a relatively small percentage of cancer
deaths," says the American Cancer Society in *Cancer Facts and Figures,
2006*. Of those, occupational exposures – workers in aluminum
smelters, miners who dug asbestos under the unsafe conditions of the
past – are by far the biggest category, responsible for perhaps 4 per
cent of all cancer. The ACS estimates that only 2 per cent of all cancers
are the result of exposure to "man-made and naturally occurring"
environmental pollutants – a massive category that includes everything from naturally occurring radon gas to industrial emissions to
car exhaust.

It's critical to understand that not all carcinogenic chemicals in
the environment are man-made. Far from it. To take just one example,
countless plants produce carcinogenic chemicals as defences against
insects and other predators and so our food is positively riddled with
natural carcinogens. They are in coffee, carrots, celery, nuts, and a
long, long list of other produce. Bruce Ames, a leading cancer scientist at the University of California at Berkeley, estimates that "of all
dietary pesticides people eat, 99.99 per cent are natural" and half of
all chemicals tested – synthetic and natural – cause cancer in high-
dose lab animal experiments. So it's highly likely that synthetic

chemicals are responsible for only a small fraction of the 2 per cent of cancers believed to be caused by environmental pollution; Ames believes the precise figure is much less than 1 per cent.

Major health organizations agree that traces of synthetic chemicals in the environment are not a large risk factor. What is hugely important is lifestyle. Smoking, drinking, diet, obesity, and exercise: These things make an enormous difference – by most estimates, accounting for roughly 65 per cent of all cancers. As early as the 1930s, researchers found that cancer rates were higher in the rich world than the poor, a division that continues to this day thanks to differences in lifestyle. "The total cancer burden is highest in affluent societies, mainly due to a high incidence of tumors associated with smoking and Western lifestyle," the World Health Organization noted in its *World Cancer Report*. There's an obvious paradox here. Those of us living in wealthy societies are enormously lucky, but it is precisely that wealth that supports a lifestyle which, in many ways, promotes cancer.

None of this has persuaded the legion of environmentalists, activists, and concerned citizens campaigning against chemicals they believe are a major cause – some would say *the* major cause – of cancer. The interesting question is why. When there is such widespread scientific agreement, why do people persist in believing the opposite? There are several answers, but the most profound was hinted at by John Higginson in that 1979 interview. "I think that many people had a gut feeling that pollution ought to cause cancer," he said.

Paul Slovic's surveys revealed how true that is. Large majorities in the United States, Canada, and France said they avoided chemicals as much as possible, they wouldn't drink tap water that had even a tiny amount of a cancer-causing substance, and they believed that someone exposed to a chemical that can cause cancer "will probably get cancer some day." For these people, it would seem obvious that having carcinogenic chemicals floating in our bodies is a major threat.

But that's not how toxicologists see it. "All substances are poisons; there is none that is not a poison," wrote Paracelsus in the 16th century. "The right dose differentiates a poison from a remedy." That is the first principle of toxicology. Drink enough water and the body's sodium and potassium levels can be thrown out of balance, inducing seizures, coma, and even death. Consume even very lethal substances in a sufficiently tiny portion and no harm will come of it – like the trillions of radioactive uranium atoms that are present in our bodies as a result of eating plants and drinking water that absorb naturally occurring uranium from the soil. What matters isn't whether a substance is in us or not. It's *how much* is in us. "It's important for people to know that the amounts to which they're exposed is the first thing they should think about," says Lois Swirsky Gold, senior scientist at the U.S. Department of Energy's Lawrence Berkeley National Laboratory and director of the Carcinogenic Potency Project at the University of California at Berkeley.

That perspective changes everything. When Paul Slovic surveyed toxicologists in the United States, the United Kingdom, and Canada, he found large majorities said they do *not* try to avoid chemicals in their daily lives, they are *not* bothered by the presence of trace contaminants, and they do *not* agree that any exposure to a carcinogen means that the person exposed is likely to get cancer. The quantities of synthetic chemicals turned up in blood analysis are almost always incredibly tiny. They are measured in parts per billion, sometimes even parts per trillion. To most toxicologists, they are simply too tiny to worry about.

But that doesn't make intuitive sense. Humans instinctively recoil from contamination without the slightest regard for the amounts involved. Paul Slovic calls this "intuitive toxicology." It can be traced back to our ancient ancestors. Every time they found drinking water, they had to decide if the water was safe. Every time they picked a berry off a bush, or cut up a carcass, they had to judge whether they could eat what was in their hands. Every time someone was taken with fever, they had to think about how to help without becoming sick themselves, and when death came, they had to safely dispose of the corpse and the unlucky person's possessions. We've been dealing with dangerous substances for a very long time.

Consider one of the most threatening contaminants our ancestors faced – human waste. Disease loves it. The entire life cycle of cholera, for example, hinges on feces: Someone who drinks water infected with the bacterium will expel huge quantities of watery diarrhea that can spread the disease to any water sources it touches. And so, throughout history, avoiding all contact with feces, or anything that had contact with feces, has been absolutely essential for survival. There could be no exceptions. Any contact with any quantity was dangerous and must be avoided: Those who followed this rule tended to survive better than those who didn't, and so it became hard-wired instinct.

We can understand the toxicological principle that "the poison is in the dose" rationally. But Gut doesn't get, it doesn't make intuitive sense, and that can lead to some very odd conclusions. In *The Varieties of Scientific Experience*, the late astronomer Carl Sagan tells how, when it appeared that the Earth would pass through the long tail of Halley's comet in 1910, "there were national panics in Japan, in Russia, in much of the southern and mid-western United States." An astronomer had found that comet tails include, among other ingredients, cyanide. Cyanide is a deadly poison. So people concluded that if the Earth were to pass through a comet tail, everyone would be poisoned. "Astronomers tried to re-assure people," Sagan recounted. "They said it wasn't clear that the Earth would pass through the tail, and even if the Earth did pass through the tail, the density of [cyanide] molecules was so low that it would be perfectly all right. But nobody believed the astronomers. . . . A hundred thousand people in their pajamas emerged onto the roofs of Constantinople. The pope issued a statement condemning the hoarding of cylinders of oxygen in Rome. And there were people all over the world who committed suicide."

Our ancestors could only analyze the world with their eyes, nose, tongue, and fingers, and intuitive toxicology makes sense for humans limited to such tools. But science revealed what was in a comet's tail.

It also discovered contamination of earth, water, and air in quantities smaller than the senses can detect. In fact, today, we have technology that can dissect the components of drinking water to the level of one part per billion – equivalent to a single grain of sugar in an Olympic-size swimming pool – while even finer tests can drill down to the level of parts per *trillion*. Gut hasn't a clue what numbers like that mean. They're even a stretch for a fully numerate Head – which is why, to even begin to understand them, we have to use images like a grain of sugar in a swimming pool.

The synthetic chemicals in our bodies that disturb people are typically found only in these almost indescribably minute quantities. They are traces, mere whispers, like the radioactive uranium we consume all our lives in blissful ignorance of its benign presence. It's true that many of those chemicals *can* cause cancer and other horrible effects but the science on which those conclusions are based almost never involves these sorts of traces. Quite the contrary.

The first step in testing for a carcinogenic effect is to stuff rats and mice with so much of the suspect substance that they die. This tells researchers that the given quantity is above what is called the "Maximum Tolerated Dose" (MTD). So it's reduced a little and injected into some more animals. If they live, the researchers then know the MTD. In the next step, 50 mice are injected with the MTD of the chemical. Another batch of 50 is injected with one-tenth or one-half the MTD. Finally, 50 very lucky mice are put in a third group that isn't injected with anything. This routine is followed day after day for the entire natural life of the animals – usually about two years. Then scientists cut all the mice open and look for cancerous tumours or other damage. In parallel with this project, the whole procedure is done with other groups of mice and at least one other species, usually rats.

These tests find lots of cancer. Almost a third of rodents develop tumours even if they aren't injected with anything. So to identify the chemical as a carcinogen, the animals injected with it must have cancer at even higher rates. And they very often do. "Half of everything tested

is a carcinogen in high–dose tests," says Lois Swirsky Gold. But the relevance of these findings to trace contamination is doubtful because
the quantities involved are so spectacularly different. "With pesticide
residues, the amounts [found in the body] are a hundred thousand or
a million or more times below the doses they gave to rodents in the
cancer tests," Swirsky Gold. There's also the question of whether
bodies of rats and mice react the same way to the presence of a substance as the body of a human. Lab tests showed, for example, that
gasoline causes cancer in male rats, but when scientists did further
research to figure out exactly how gasoline was causing cancer, they
discovered that the key mechanism involved the binding of a chemical in the gasoline to a protein found in the kidneys of male rats – a
protein that doesn't exist in humans. Unfortunately, rigorous analysis to determine precisely how a chemical causes cancer in lab
animals hasn't been done for most chemicals deemed carcinogens so
there's a very long list of chemicals that has been shown to cause
cancer in mice and rats, but it's not clear how many of the chemicals
on the list actually cause cancer in humans.

A second tool scientists use in deciding if a chemical is carcinogenic are studies that look at broad populations to see if people
exposed to the chemical are more likely to get cancer. This is the field
of epidemiology, which has made huge contributions to health over
the last century and a half. Unfortunately, when epidemiology finds
that one thing is associated with another, it is often not because the
first thing causes the second. Criminals and tattoos, for example, are
highly correlated but tattoos do not cause crime. And so when epidemiologists showed shipyard workers who handled asbestos had
higher rates of cancer, it was a strong clue that asbestos causes cancer
but it was not proof. That came with later work. "Epidemiology is fantastically difficult," Bruce Ames says. "You're talking about studying
humans and there are a million confounders. A study will say this
and another will say the opposite." The steady proliferation of studies
saying one thing is "linked" to another – that there is a correlation,

but nothing more – invites abuse. "You can easily hype it up. Our local paper has a scare story every couple of weeks. They like those scare stories. But I don't believe any of them." Ames cites the example of a controversy in California's Contra Costa county. "There are a lot of refineries and there is more lung cancer. Ah, the refineries are causing the lung cancer. But who lives around refineries? Poor people. And who smokes more? Poor people. And when you correct for smoking, there's no extra risk in the county."

The limitations of animal testing, epidemiology, and other forms of evidence are why regulatory agencies have classification systems for carcinogens. The terms vary, but they typically label a substance a "potential," "likely," or "known" carcinogen. These levels indicate degrees of certainty, based on what the evidence looks like when it is all assembled. Scientists today place much less weight on any one piece of evidence, and high–dose tests on lab animals have particularly fallen out of favour. They're still treated as valid evidence, but they don't carry nearly as much weight as laypeople think they do.

Aside from Gut's ancient aversion to contamination, culture also drives the perception that exposure to traces of synthetic chemicals is dangerous. Corporate marketers love to label products "natural" because they understand that natural is equated with wholesome and nurturing – and safe. "People have this impression that if it's natural, it can't be harmful, and that's a bit naïve," says Bruce Ames. "The other night in Berkeley, I noticed they were selling a bag of charcoal briquettes and it said 'no artificial additives, all natural.' And it's pure carcinogen!"

In Daniel Krewski's 2004 survey, "natural health products" were deemed by far the safest of the 30 presented – safer even than X–rays and tap water. Prescription drugs were seen to be riskier, while pesticides were judged to be more dangerous than street crime and nuclear power plants. It's not hard to guess at the thinking behind this, or to see how dominated it is by Gut. Natural and healthy are very good things so natural health products must be safe. Prescription drugs save lives, so while they may not be as safe as "natural health products" – everyone knows prescription drugs can have adverse effects – they are still good and therefore relatively safe. But "pesticides" are "man-made" and "chemical" – and therefore dangerous. The irony here is that few of the "natural health products" that millions of people happily pop in their mouths and swallow have been rigorously tested to see if they work and the safety regulations they have to satisfy are generally quite weak – unlike the laws and regulations governing prescription drugs and pesticides.

Many companies – and whole industries, in the case of organic foods – actively promote the idea that chemicals are dangerous. "What you don't know about chlorine could hurt you," warns the website of a Florida company selling water purification systems that remove by-products of chlorine treatment that may raise the risk of cancer by some infinitesimal degree. On occasion, politicians also find it convenient to hype the risk of chemical contamination. "Arsenic is a killer," declared U.S. congressman Henry Waxman. "If there is one thing we all seem to agree on it is that we do not want arsenic in our drinking water." Arsenic happens to be common in the natural environment, and tiny levels of it are often found in drinking water – but in the spring of 2001, Waxman suddenly found that fact intolerable after the Bush administration suspended the existing regulation on permissible levels of arsenic in water and ordered more study. This was a dispute over how much arsenic content was safe, not whether there should be any at all, but the congressman and his Democratic colleagues saw obvious advantage in framing it as Bush-wants-to-put-poison-in-the-water.

The media, in pursuit of the dramatic story, are another contributor to prevailing fears about chemicals. Robert Lichter and Stanley Rothman scoured stories about cancer appearing in the American media between 1972 and 1992 and found that tobacco was only the second-most mentioned cause of cancer – and it was a distant second. Man-made chemicals came first. Third was food additives. Number 6 was pollution, 7 radiation, 9 pesticides, and 12 was dietary choices. Natural chemicals came 16th. Dead last on the list of 25 – mentioned in only nine stories – was the most important factor: aging. Lichter and Rothman also found that of the stories that expressed a view on whether the United States was facing a cancer epidemic, 85 per cent said it was.

This has a predictable effect on public opinion. In November 2007, the American Institute of Cancer Research (AICR) released the results of a survey in which Americans were asked about the causes of cancer. The institute noted with regret that only 49 per cent of Americans identified a diet low in fruits and vegetables as a cause of cancer; 46 per cent said the same of obesity; 37 per cent, alcohol; and 36 per cent, diets high in red meat. But 71 per cent said pesticide residues on food cause cancer. "There's a disconnect between public fears and scientific fact," said an AICR spokesperson.

Lichter and Rothman argue that the media's picture of cancer is the result of paying too little attention to cancer researchers and far too much to environmentalists. As John Higginson noted almost 30 years ago, the idea that synthetic chemicals cause cancer is "convenient" for activists opposed to chemical pollution. If DDT had threatened only birds, Rachel Carson would probably never have created the stir she did with *Silent Spring*. It's the connection between pollution and human health that makes the environment a personal concern, and connecting synthetic chemicals to health is easy because the chemicals are everywhere and Gut tells us they must be dangerous no matter how tiny the amounts may be. Add the explosive word *cancer* and you have a very effective way to generate support for environmental action.

However laudable the ultimate goal, many experts are not pleased with what environmentalists have been telling the public about chemicals and health. "This is irresponsible, hysterical scaremongering," said Alan Boobis, a toxicologist with the faculty of medicine of Imperial College, London, in 2005. Boobis and other leading British scientists were furious that several environmental organizations, particularly the World Wildlife Fund, were massively publicizing the presence of "hazardous chemicals" in blood, food, and even babies' umbilical cords. "Most chemicals were found at a fraction of a part per billion. There is no evidence such concentrations pose any threat to people's health," Boobis told *The Guardian.* "The message they are putting across is misleading, and deliberately so," David Coggon, a specialist in occupational and environmental causes of cancer and other diseases at the University of Southampton, told the BBC. "By and large, I think people shouldn't be worried. Most chemicals will not do any great harm at these very low levels," added Richard Sharpe, an expert on endocrine disrupters at the Medical Research Council's Human Reproductive Unit in Edinburgh. "You have to put this in perspective."

Campaigns like the WWF's are common in many countries. "Pollutants Contaminate Blood of Federal Politicians" read the headline of a 2007 press release from Canada's Environmental Defence announcing that testing had found dozens of "harmful pollutants" in the blood and urine of several leading Canadian politicians. Enormous media coverage followed, most of it focused heavily on the scary nature of the chemicals and giving little mention, if any, to the quantities involved. It was another success for a campaign Environmental Defence calls "Toxic Nation," whose slogan is "Pollution. It's In You." There is extensive information on the "Toxic Nation" website about the abundance of synthetic chemicals in our bodies but there's almost no mention that the presence in the body of tiny quantities of "dangerous" chemicals may not actually be dangerous. Only in a glossary of technical terms, under the definition of *toxic,* does the website let slip that while chemicals *may* cause harm "the quantities and exposures necessary to cause these effects can vary widely."

Such sins of omission are common. "Many pesticides that have been shown to cause cancer in laboratory animals are still being used," says the website of Natural Resources Defense Council, a leading

American organization. There is, of course, no concern expressed at the one-half of natural chemicals that have also been shown to cause cancer in laboratory animals. Similarly, the Environmental Working Group (EWG), a Washington, D.C., organization, says on its website that "there is growing consensus in the scientific community that small doses of pesticides and chemicals can adversely affect people, especially during vulnerable periods of fetal development and childhood when exposures can have long-lasting effects." It's true that scientists agree these chemicals *can* do harm, and there is no definition of "small doses" in this statement so in a very narrow sense this statement isn't wrong. But EWG has widely publicized – always with a tone of alarm – the fact that traces of these chemicals exist in our bodies, and so it is making it easy for people to conclude that there is "a growing consensus in the scientific community" that the tiny amounts of these chemicals in our bodies "can adversely affect people." And that's false.

There's also an essay on the website of the Worldwatch Institute that warns readers that "the 450 million kilograms of pesticides that U.S. farmers use every year have now contaminated almost all of the nation's streams and rivers, and the fish living in them, with chemicals that cause cancer and birth defects." Left unmentioned is the fact that the level of contamination in most places is believed by most scientists to be far too low to actually cause these harms to humans, which would explain why the United States is not experiencing massive increases in cancers and birth defects despite this massive contamination.

But then, the existence of an "epidemic of cancer" is often taken by environmentalists to be such an obvious fact that its existence hardly needs to be demonstrated. In a 2005 newspaper column, Canada's David Suzuki – a biologist and renowned environmentalist – blamed chemical contamination for the "epidemic of cancer afflicting us." His proof consisted of a story about catching a flounder that had cancerous tumours and the fact that "this year, for the first time, cancer has surpassed heart disease as our number one killer." But it is not true, as Suzuki seems to assume, that cancer's rise to leading killer means cancer is killing more people. It is possible that heart disease is killing *fewer* people. And that turns out to be the correct explanation. Statistics Canada reported that the death rates of both cardiovascular disease and cancer are falling but "much more so for cardiovascular disease."

The Cancer Prevention Coalition (CPC), an activist group headed by Sam Epstein, made a more determined effort in a 2007 press release. "The incidence of cancer has escalated to epidemic proportions, striking most American families," the release says. "Cancer now impacts about 1.3 million Americans annually and kills 550,000; 44 percent of men and 39 percent of women develop cancer in their lifetimes. While smoking-related cancers have decreased in men, there have been major increases in non-smoking cancers in adults as well as childhood cancers." Elsewhere, the CPC puts it a little more colourfully: "Cancer strikes nearly one in every two men and more than one in every three women."

What's left out here is the simple fact that cancer is primarily a disease of aging, a fact which has a profound effect on cancer statistics. The rate of cancer deaths in Florida, for example, is almost three times higher than in Alaska, which looks extremely important until you factor in Florida's much older population. "When the cancer death rates for Florida and Alaska are age-adjusted," notes a report from the American Cancer Society, "they are almost identical."

Lifetime risk figures – like "one in every two men" or Rachel Carson's famous "one in every four" – ignore the role of aging and don't take into account our steadily lengthening lifespans. To see how deceptive that is, consider that if every person lived to 100, the lifetime risk of cancer would likely rise to almost 100 per cent. Would we say, in shocked tones, that "cancer will strike nearly every person"? Probably not. I suspect we'd consider it cause for celebration.

Conversely, if some new plague ensured that we all died at 35, the life-time risk of getting cancer would fall spectacularly but no one would be dancing in the streets.

In the 1990s, as worries about breast cancer rose, activists often said that "one in eight" American women would get breast cancer in their lifetimes. That was true, in a sense. But what wasn't mentioned was that to face that full one-in-eight risk, a woman has to live to 95. The numbers look very different at younger ages: The chance of getting breast cancer by age 70 is 1 in 14 (or 7 per cent); by age 50, it is 1 in 50 (2 per cent); by age 40, 1 in 217 (0.4 per cent); by age 30, 1 in 2,525 (0.03 per cent). "To emphasize only the highest risk is a tactic meant to scare rather than inform," Russell Harris, a cancer researcher at the University of North Carolina, told *U.S. News and World Report*.

Aging shouldn't affect data on *childhood* cancers, however, and those who claim chemical contamination is a serious threat say child-hood cancers are soaring. They are up "25 per cent in the last 30 years," journalist Wendy Mesley said in her CBC documentary. That statistic is true, to a degree, but it is also a classic example of how badly pre-sented information about risk can mislead.

Mesley is right that the rate of cancer among Canadian children is roughly 25 per cent higher now than it was 30 years ago. But what she didn't say is that the increase occurred between 1970 and 1985 and then stopped. "The overall incidence of childhood cancer has remained relatively stable since 1985," says the 2004 *Progress Report on Cancer Control* from the Public Health Agency of Canada.

It is also misleading to note the *relative* increase in risk – 25 per cent – but not the actual size of the risk. In 1970, there were a little more than 13 cases of cancer for every 100,000 children. It then rose to a peak of 16.8 cases per 100,000 children – meaning the annual risk of a child getting cancer was 0.0168 per cent. Now, put all this information together and it sounds like this: In 1970, the risk of childhood cancer was very small. It increased until 1985 but has remained stable ever since. Despite the increase, the risk continues to be very small. "Cancer in children is rare, accounting for only about one per cent of cases," notes the *Progress Report*. That is hardly the description of an epidemic. In addition, the rate of childhood cancer *deaths* has fallen steadily over the last three decades. In 1970, about 7 children per 100,000 were killed by cancer; 30 years later, the rate had dropped to 3.

American figures are almost identical. According to a 1999 publication of the U.S. National Cancer Institute, childhood cancers rose from 1975 until 1991 and then declined slightly. In 1975, there were about 13 cases per 100,000 children. In 1990, that had risen to 16. The death rate dropped steadily, from 5 per 100,000 children in 1975 to 2.6 two decades later.

British statistics show the same trend. From 1962 until 1971, the rate of childhood cancer cases was flat. It then rose steadily until 1995 but appears to have stabilized. In 1971, there were 10.1 cases per 100,000 children. In 1995, there were 13.6. The death rate fell steadily throughout this period, from 7.8 per 100,000 children to 3.2. Medicine is steadily breaking cancer's grip on children.

Still, the increased risk of children getting cancer may have stopped rising but it did rise. What could have caused that rise if not chemical contamination? Here, it's very important to remember that numbers are only as good as the methods used to calculate them. All statistics have strengths and weaknesses. Cancer data are a perfect demonstration of that universal truth.

There are two ways to measure how much cancer there is in society. One is simply to count deaths caused by cancer. Most such deaths are unmistakable and they're carefully recorded, which makes death stats a reliable way to track the disease's prevalence. Or at least they were in the past. Treatments have improved dramatically in recent decades and so, increasingly, victims survive who would not have in the past. As a result, cancer death rates may decline even if the actual cancer rate doesn't and so death statistics tend to underestimate the reality.

The other way of tracking cancer is to use what are called incidence rates. These are based simply on the number of people diagnosed with cancer and they would seem to more accurately reflect the real level of cancer in society. But incidence rates can be tricky, too. If physicians get better at diagnosing a cancer, the number of diagnosed cases will rise even if the actual prevalence of cancer doesn't. Even changes in how bureaucrats file paperwork and collect numbers can artificially push up incidence numbers. What really throws the numbers off, however, are screening programs. Many forms of cancer – including breast, prostate, thyroid, and skin – are known to produce cancers that just sit there. They don't do any damage, don't progress, and don't cause any symptoms. Those who have them may live out their lives without ever knowing of their existence. But screening programs – such as blood tests for prostate cancer and mammograms for breast cancer – can detect both the aggressive and the irrelevant cancers and so when they are introduced, or improved, incidence rates soar. When that happens, it doesn't mean more people are getting cancer, only that more cancer is being uncovered.

So to get a sense of what's really happening, experts look at both death and incidence statistics. If they rise together, cancer probably is on the rise. They're also reliable indicators if they go down together. But they often point in opposite directions – as they did with child-hood cancers in the 1970s and 1980s. To sort things out when that happens, experts have to investigate from every angle and consider the relative weight of the many factors that may be pushing the numbers one way or another. And even then there are likely to be some uncertainties because that's the best science can do.

And that conclusion seems to be the answer to the rise in child-hood cancers that ended in the mid–1980s. "Improvements in the efficiency of systems for the diagnosis and registration of cancer may have contributed to the increase in registration rates," noted Cancer Research UK. "It has also probably become easier to track and record the diagnosis of new patients as treatment has become more

centralized. The amount of real change, if any, in the underlying incidence rates is not clear."

Variations between sexes, populations, and countries make it difficult to generalize about cancer in adults. Even more importantly,
cancer isn't really one disease, it is many. But still, the broad outlines
are clear.

The age-adjusted rates of deaths caused by most types of cancer
have been falling for many years in developed countries. (An important exception is smoking-related cancers among those groups in
which smoking rates have yet to fall.) As for incidence rates, they rose
in the 1970s, rose more rapidly in the 1980s, but then levelled off in the
last 10 or 15 years. It is not a coincidence that the period that saw the
most rapid increases – the 1980s – also saw the introduction of major
screening programs. There is a consensus among researchers that a big
chunk of the rise in incidence rates over the last three decades was the
result of better screening, diagnosis, and collection of statistics.

And, in any event, the rise in incidence rates has generally
stopped. In the United States, the numbers for the last several years –
both incidence and death rates – have been remarkably encouraging.
Even the total number of deaths caused by cancer has fallen, which
is pretty amazing considering that the American population is
growing and aging. Summing up the trends, Bruce Ames says, "If you
take away the cancer due to smoking and the extra cancer due to the
fact that we're living longer, then there's no increase in cancer."

Advocates of the chemicals-are-killing-us claim respond with
one final sally. We don't know, they say. "The worrying reality is that
no one really knows what effects these chemicals have on humans,"
reads a Greenpeace report. "We are all unwittingly taking part in an
unregulated global experiment that needs to be stopped," says the
World Wildlife Fund.

There has been an enormous amount of scientific study of chemicals over the last half century but still it's true that a great many synthetic chemicals have not been rigorously analyzed, either separately

or in their combined effects with other chemicals. There really is lots we don't know. That's particularly true in case of the raging controversy over the endocrine disruptor hypothesis – the idea that trace amounts of synthetic chemicals such as bisphenol A can throw the body's hormones off balance, lowering sperm counts, causing cancer and maybe much more. The hypothesis first got widespread attention in the mid–1990s and scores of scientists have been studying the issue for more than a decade but still the science remains contradictory and unsettled. Regulatory agencies in Europe, the United States, and Japan, have reviewed the evidence on bisphenol A and decided there is no reason to ban the chemical, but the investigation goes on. Slow and complicated: That's science at work.

Fine, many people say. But until more is known, the sensible thing to do is err on the side of caution by banning or restricting suspected chemicals. Better safe than sorry, after all.

This attitude has been enshrined in various laws and regulations as the precautionary principle. There are many definitions of that principle but one of the most influential comes from Principle 15 of the Rio Declaration on Environment and Development: "Where there are threats of serious or irreversible damage, lack of full scientific certainty shall not be used as a reason for postponing cost–effective measures to prevent environmental degradation." Like many international resolutions, this is full of ambiguity. What qualifies as "serious" damage? What are "cost–effective measures"? And while it may be clear that we don't need "full scientific certainty," how much evidence should we have before we act? And this is only one of more than 20 definitions of the precautionary principle floating about in regulations and laws. Many are quite different and some are contradictory on certain points. As a result, there is a vast and growing academic literature grappling with what exactly "precaution" means and how it should be implemented. Politicians and activists like to talk about the precautionary principle as if it were a simple and sensible direction to err on the side of caution. But there's nothing simple about it.

Nor is it all that sensible. As law professor Cass Sunstein argues in *Laws of Fear*, the precautionary principle is more a feel-good sentiment than a principle that offers real guidance about regulating risks. Risks are everywhere, he notes, and so we often face a risk in acting and a risk in *not* acting – and in these situations, the precautionary principle is no help.

Consider chlorine. Treat drinking water with it and it creates by-products that have been shown to cause cancer in lab animals in high doses and may increase the cancer risk of people who drink the water. There's even some epidemiological evidence that suggests the risk is more than hypothetical. So the precautionary principle would suggest we stop putting chlorine in drinking water. But what happens if we do that? "If you take the chlorine out of the drinking water, as was done in South America, you end up with an epidemic of 2,000 cases of cholera," says Daniel Krewski. And cholera is far from the only threat. There are many water-borne diseases, including typhoid fever, a common killer until the addition of chlorine to drinking water all but wiped it out in the developed world early in the 20th century. So, presumably, the precautionary principle would say we *must* treat drinking water with chlorine. "Because risks are on all sides, the Precautionary Principle forbids action, inaction, and everything in between," writes Sunstein. It is "paralyzing; it forbids the very steps that it requires."

So should we ban or restrict synthetic chemicals until we have a full understanding of their effects? This attractively simple idea is a lot more complicated than it appears. If pesticides were banned, agricultural yields would decline. Fruits and vegetables would get more expensive and people would buy and eat fewer of them. But cancer scientists believe that fruits and vegetables can reduce the risk of cancer if we eat enough of them, which most people do not do even now. And so banning pesticides in order to reduce exposure to carcinogens could potentially result in *more* people getting cancer.

Consider also that scientists are at least as ignorant of *natural* chemicals as they are of the man–made variety. And since there is no reason to assume – contrary to what our culture tells us – that natural is safe and man–made dangerous, that suggests we should worry as much about natural chemicals, or perhaps even more because natural chemicals vastly outnumber their man–made cousins. "The number of naturally occurring chemicals present in the food supply – or generated during the processes of growing, harvesting, storage and preparation – is enormous, probably exceeding one million different chemicals," notes a 1996 report by the U.S. National Academy of Sciences. Everyone who digs into a delicious meal of all–natural, organically grown produce is swallowing thousands of chemicals whose effects on the human body aren't fully understood and whose interaction with other chemicals is mysterious. And remember that of the natural chemicals that have been tested, one–half have been shown to cause cancer in lab animals. If we were to strictly apply the banned–until–proven–safe approach to chemicals, there would be little left to eat.

Partisans – both enviros and industry – prefer to ignore dilemmas like these and cast issues in much simpler terms. In an article entitled "Lessons of History," the World Wildlife Fund tells readers that when the pesticide DDT "was discovered by Swiss chemist Paul Muller in 1939, it was hailed as a miracle. It could kill a wide range of insect pests but seemed to be harmless to mammals. Crop yields increased and it was also used to control malaria by killing mosquitoes. Muller was awarded the Nobel Prize in 1944. However, in 1962, scientist Rachel Carson noticed that insect and worm–eating birds were dying in areas where DDT had been sprayed. In her book *Silent Spring*, she issued grave warnings about pesticides and predicted massive destruction of the planet's ecosystems unless the 'rain of chemicals' was halted." This hardly looks like a dilemma. On the one hand, DDT was used to increase crop yields and control malaria, which is nice but hardly dramatic stuff. On the other hand, it threatened "massive destruction." It's not hard to see what the right response is.

Unfortunately, there's quite a bit wrong with the WWF's tale (the least of which is saying DDT was discovered in 1939, when it was first synthesized in 1874 and its value as an insecticide revealed in 1935). It doesn't mention, for example, that the first large-scale use of DDT occurred in October 1943, when typhus – a disease spread by infected mites, fleas, and lice – broke out in newly liberated Naples. Traditional health measures didn't work so 1.3 million people were sprayed with the pesticide. At a stroke, the epidemic was wiped out – the first time in history that a typhus outbreak had been stopped in winter. At the end of the war, DDT was widely used to prevent typhus epidemics among haggard prisoners, refugees, and concentration camp inmates. It's rather sobering to think that countless Holocaust survivors owe their lives to an insecticide that is reviled today.

As for malaria, DDT did more than "control" it. "DDT was the main product used in global efforts, supported by the [World Health Organization], to eradicate malaria in the 1950s and 1960s," says a 2005 WHO report. "This campaign resulted in a significant reduction in malaria transmission in many parts of the world, and was probably instrumental in eradicating the disease from Europe and North America." Estimates vary as to how many lives DDT helped save, but it's certainly in the millions and probably in the tens of millions.

In recent years, however, anti-environmentalists have constructed an elaborate mythology around the chemical: DDT is perfectly harmless and absolutely effective; DDT single-handedly wiped out malaria in Europe and North America; DDT could do the same in Africa if only eco-imperialists would let Africans use the chemical to save their children. For the most part, this mythology unfairly belittles the proven harms DDT inflicted on non-human species, particularly birds, and it ignores the abundant evidence – which started to appear as early as 1951 – that mosquitoes rapidly develop resistance to the insecticide. In fact, the indiscriminate spraying of DDT on farm

fields during the 1950s contributed to the development of mosquitoes' resistance and so the banning of the pesticide for agricultural
use actually helped preserve its value as a malaria-fighting tool.

The truth about DDT is that the questions about how to deal with
it were, and are, complex. So what does the precautionary principle
tell us about this most reviled of chemicals? Well, once typhus and
malaria have been removed from the equation, it would probably
come down on the side of a ban. But what does "precaution" mean
when insect-borne disease is still very much present? The WHO estimates that malaria kills one million people a year, and contributes to
another two million deaths. Most of the dead are children, and most
of those children are African. If DDT is used to fight malaria in Africa,
it carries certain risks. And there are risks to not using it. So how do
we decide? The precautionary principle is no help.

"Why, then, is the Precautionary Principle widely thought to give
guidance?" asks Cass Sunstein. The answer is simple: We pay close
attention to some risks while ignoring others, which very often causes
the dilemma of choosing *between* risks to vanish. If we ignore malaria,
it only seems prudent to ban DDT. Ignore the potential risks of natural
chemicals, or the economic costs, and it becomes much easier to
demand bans on synthetic chemicals. Ignore the threat of fire and it
seems obvious that the flame-retarding chemicals polluting our
blood must be eliminated. And if we don't know anything about
typhoid or cholera, it's easy to conclude that we should stop treating
water with a chemical that produces a known carcinogen. "Many
people who are described as risk averse are, in reality, no such thing.
They are averse to particular risks, not risks in general," Sunstein
writes. And it's not just individuals who have blind spots. "Human
beings, cultures and nations often single out one or a few social risks
as 'salient', and ignore the others."

But how do people choose which risks to worry about and which
to ignore? Our friends, neighbours, and co-workers constantly supply
us with judgments that are a major influence. The media provide us

with examples – or not – that Gut feeds into the Example Rule to estimate the likelihood of a bad thing happening. Experience and culture
colour hazards with emotions that Gut runs through the Good–Bad
Rule. The mechanism known as habituation causes us to play down
the risks of familiar things and play up the novel and unknown. If we
connect with others who share our views about risks, group polarization can be expected – causing our views to become still more
entrenched and extreme.

And of course, for risks involving chemicals and contamination,
there is "intuitive toxicology." We are hard–wired to avoid contamination, no matter how small the amounts involved. With the culture
having defined *chemical* to mean man–made chemical, and *man-made
chemical* as dangerous, it is all but inevitable that our worries about
chemical pollution will be out of all proportion to the real risks
involved. Confirmation bias is also at work. Once we have the feeling
that chemical contamination is a serious threat, we will tend to latch
onto information that confirms that hunch – while dismissing or ignoring anything that suggests otherwise. This is where the complexity of
science comes into play. For controversial chemicals, relevant studies
may number in the dozens or the hundreds or the thousands, and they
will contradict each other. For anyone with a bias – whether a corporate spokesman, an environmentalist, or simply a layperson with a
hunch – there will almost always be evidence to support that bias.

The first step in correcting our mistakes of intuition has to be a
healthy respect for the scientific process. Scientists have their biases,
too, but the whole point of science is that as evidence accumulates,
scientists argue among themselves based on the whole body of evidence, not just bits and pieces. Eventually, the majority tentatively
decides in one direction or the other. It's not a perfect process, by
any means; it's frustratingly slow and it can make mistakes. But it's
vastly better than any other method humans have used to understand reality.

The next step in dealing with risk rationally is to accept that risk is inevitable. In Daniel Krewski's surveys, he found that about half the Canadian public agreed that a risk-free world is possible. "A majority of the population expects the government or other regulatory agencies to protect them completely from all risk in their daily lives," he says with more than a hint of amazement in his voice. "Many of us who work in risk management have been trying to get the message out that you cannot guarantee zero risk. It's an impossible goal." We often describe something as "unsafe" and we say we want it to be made "safe." Most often, it's fine to use that language as shorthand but bear in mind that it's not fully accurate. In the risk business, there are only degrees of safety. It is often possible to make something *safer*, but *safe* is usually out of the question.

We must also accept that regulating risk is a complicated business. It almost always involves trade-offs – swapping typhoid for carcinogenic traces in our drinking water, for example. And it requires careful consideration of the risks and costs that may not be so obvious as the things we worry about – like more expensive fruits and vegetables leading to an increase in cancer. It also requires evidence. We may not want to wait for conclusive scientific proof – as the precautionary principle suggests – but we must demand much more than speculation.

Rational risk regulation is a slow, careful, and thoughtful examination of the dangers and costs in particular cases. If banning certain synthetic pesticides can be shown to reduce a risk materially at no more cost than a modest proliferation of dandelions, say, it probably makes sense. If there are inexpensive techniques to reduce the amount of chlorine required to treat drinking water effectively, that may be a change that's called for. Admittedly, this is not exciting stuff. There's not a lot of passion and drama in it. And while there are always questions of justice and fairness involved – Who bears the risk? Who will shoulder the cost of reducing the risk? –

there is not a lot of room for ideology and inflammatory rhetoric.

Unfortunately, there are lots of activists, politicians, and corporations who are not nearly as interested in pursuing rational risk regulation as they are in scaring people. After all, there are donations, votes, and sales to be had. Even more unfortunately, Gut will often side with the alarmists. That's particularly true in the case of chemicals, thanks to a combination of Gut's intuitive toxicology and the negative reputation chemicals have in the culture. Lois Swirsky Gold says, "It's almost an immutable perception. I hear it from people all the time. 'Yes, I understand that 50 per cent of the natural chemicals tested are positive, half the chemicals that are in [the Carcinogenic Potency Project] data base are positive, 70 per cent of the chemicals that are naturally occurring in coffee are carcinogens in rodent tests. Yes, I understand all that but still I'm not going to eat that stuff if I don't have to.'"

All this talk of tiny risks adds up to one big distraction, says Bruce Ames. "There are really important things to worry about and it gets lost in the noise of this constant scare about unimportant things." By most estimates, more than one-half of all cancers in the developed world could be prevented with nothing more than lifestyle changes ranging from exercise to weight control and, of course, not smoking. Whatever the precise risk of cancer posed by synthetic chemicals in the environment, it is a housefly next to that elephant.

But lifestyle is a much harder message to get across, says Swirsky Gold. "You tell people you need lifestyle change, you need to exercise more, you need to eat more fruits and vegetables and consume fewer calories, they just look at you and walk into McDonald's." The problem is that only part of the mind hears and understands the message about lifestyle and health. Head gets it. But Gut doesn't understand statistics. Gut only knows that lying on the couch watching television is a lot more enjoyable than sweating on a treadmill, that the cigarettes you smoke make you feel good and have never done you any harm, and the Golden Arches call up happy memories of childhood and that clown with the red hair. Nothing to worry about in any of that, Gut concludes. Relax and watch some more TV.

And so we do, until a story on the news reports that a carcinogenic chemical has been detected in the blood of ordinary people. *We are contaminated.* Now that's frightening, Gut says. Sit up and pay close attention.

11

TERRIFIED OF TERRORISM

"**T**he deliberate and deadly attacks which were carried out yesterday against our country were more than acts of terror. They were acts of war. This will require our country to unite in steadfast determination and resolve. Freedom and democracy are under attack."

When U.S. president George W. Bush spoke these words the morning of September 12, 2001, smoke still curled upward from the rubble that had been the World Trade Center, and the numbing shock had just begun to thaw. With every photograph of the missing, every story of loss, sorrow surged like a flooding river. Every scrap of information about the terrorists was pure oxygen hissing over the red coals of rage. And in the quiet moments, when the television was turned off, the mind marvelled at this unholy new world, struggled to imagine what horrors were to come, and felt cold fear.

Seen with the sort of detachment that the passage of years can provide, the dread of terrorism that raced across the United States and the rest of the Western world that fall is understandable.

What happened on September 11, 2001, was – for most of us – as startling and incomprehensible as the appearance of a second moon in the night sky. Who is this bin Laden? How did he do this? Why? Our ignorance was almost total. This was radical unfamiliarity – the alarming opposite of the comforting routine that allows villagers to sleep soundly on the slopes of a volcano in the Canary Islands. The only thing we knew is that the threat seemed to be as big as the towers we watched crumble. Signal value is the term risk researchers use to describe the extent to which an event seems to inform us of future dangers – and 9/11's signal value was off the meter.

It also made an enormous difference that we had seen televised images so clear, immediate, and graphic it was as if we had watched everything through the living–room window. Many even saw the catastrophe live. That magnified the shock. What was happening was so perfectly unanticipated and so horrific we balked at comprehension even as the images burned into our memories like acid etching steel.

For Gut, these memories remain as a permanent reference. Simply mention the word *terrorism* and they roar back to consciousness. Gut, using the Example Rule, comes to an urgent conclusion: This will probably happen again.

Then there were the feelings: sorrow, rage, fear. Even for those who had no personal stake in the events of September 11, the emotions of that day, and those that followed, were among the most intense and dreadful we will ever experience. To an unconscious mind so sensitive to feelings that even minor changes in language can influence its perception of a threat, these emotions were the wail of an air raid siren.

And that was before the anthrax. One week after the attacks, five letters bearing a Trenton, New Jersey, postmark – they were probably dropped in a mailbox just outside Princeton University – entered the U.S. postal system. Four went to New York–based media – ABC, NBC, CBS, and the *New York Post* – while one went to the Boca Raton, Florida, office of the *National Enquirer*. Inside each was a granular brown powder containing *Bacillus anthracis*, anthrax, a deadly organism that occurs naturally in soil. Three weeks later, two more letters were mailed, this time to two Democratic senators. In all, 22 people were infected, 11 seriously.

Five died. "Death to America. Death to Israel," the letters proclaimed. "Allah is great."

One bolt from the blue had been followed by another. Terrorism became a universal obsession. Like ancient hunters watching lions emerge from the long grass, we could see, hear, and smell nothing else.

A Gallup poll taken in mid-October found 40 per cent of Americans said it was "very likely" there would be more terrorism "over the next several weeks." Another 45 per cent said it was "somewhat likely." Only a fringe of optimists thought it "not too likely" (10 per cent) or "not at all likely" (3 per cent).

The danger was also intimate. Gallup asked, "How worried are you that you or someone in your family will become a victim of terrorism?" In October, one-quarter of Americans said they were "very worried." A further 35 per cent said they were "somewhat worried."

These are startling results. One of the many psychological biases we have is what's called optimism bias or the better-than-average effect – the tendency to see ourselves in a more positive light than the rest of the population. This bias appears in risk perceptions as well, except with risk it drives the perception downward. Ask a young woman how dangerous it is for a young woman to take a late-night walk in a park and she will give one answer; ask a young woman how dangerous it is for *her* to take a late-night walk in a park and she will give a different estimate – a *lower* estimate. So when Gallup asked Americans about the risk to "you and your family," the results were certain to be skewed downward by optimism bias. Despite that, more than half of Americans felt there was a realistic chance they and their families could be injured or killed by terrorists. If the purpose of terrorism is to terrify, the terrorists had succeeded.

Humans adapt, though. November came and went without another attack on American soil. And December. By the following spring, the sense of raw fear had ebbed. In an April 2002 poll, only a little more than one-third of Americans said they worried that terrorists might strike them or their families. A March poll found 52 per cent said that over the next several weeks, it was "very" or "somewhat" likely there would be terrorist attacks in the United States – a steep drop from the 85 per cent five months earlier.

In psychological terms, this decline in concern was as understandable as the surge had been. Eight months after the attacks, not only had the feared chaos failed to materialize, we knew a great deal about Osama bin Laden and terrorism was no longer a bewildering novelty. The memories were there to drive the Example Rule, and thoughts of terrorism still stirred black clouds, so Gut still sensed that the risk was high. But it was no longer what it had been that awful autumn.

Then the polls registered something surprising. The decline stopped.

When the fifth anniversary of 9/11 was marked on September 11, 2006, there had not been another terrorist attack in the United States. Five years earlier, almost no one would have predicted that. It was an astonishing and wonderful turn of events. And yet, when Gallup asked Americans how likely it is that there would be acts of terrorism in the United States "over the next several weeks," 9 per cent said it was "very likely" and another 41 per cent said "somewhat likely." That 50 per cent total is essentially identical to the 52 per cent who said the same thing four and a half years earlier, in March 2002.

Gallup's question about personal danger was even more revealing. In August 2006, 44 per cent of Americans said they were very or somewhat worried that they or their families would be victims of terrorism. That was actually *up* from 35 per cent in the spring of 2002.

These numbers did not play out in smooth lines over the years. They bounced up and down considerably between 2002 and 2006, but the basic trend is unmistakable: Worry about terrorism did not decline as time passed and the threatened onslaught failed to materialize; instead, it slowly rose.

It's not only the trend that makes these results strange. It's that so many people think there is a real possibility – a worryingly high chance – that they could be killed by terrorists.

Almost 3,000 people were killed in the September 11 attacks. At the time, the population of the United States was around 281 million. Thus, the chance of any one American dying in the attacks that day was 0.00106 per cent, or 1 in 93,000. Compare that to the 1 in 48,548 annual risk a pedestrian has of being struck and killed by a car, or the 1 in 87,976 annual risk of drowning.

Of course, nobody knew at the time that September 11, 2001, would be a horribly unique day. There could have been other, equally destructive attacks in the months that followed. Presuming that there had been one attack each month for one full year – with each attack inflicting a death toll equal to that of 9/11 – the total number of dead would have been 36,000. This would be horrific but it would still not be a mortal threat to the average American. The chance of being killed in this carnage would be about 0.0127 per cent. That's roughly one in 7,750. By comparison, the annual risk of dying in a motor-vehicle accident is one in 6,498.

The slaughter of civilians by non–state actors to advance political goals is not new. It's not even new to New York City. On September 16, 1920, anarchists drove a horse–drawn wagon down Wall Street containing 100 pounds of dynamite and 500 pounds of cast–iron slugs. In the midst of noon–hour crowds, the bomb was detonated. Thirty-eight people died. More than 400 were injured. Almost nine decades have passed since that dreadful day, and in all that time the deadliest terror attack in the world, aside from 9/11, was the bombing of Air India Flight 182 in 1985, which took 329 lives.

According to the RAND–MIPT terrorism database – the most comprehensive available – there were 10,119 international terrorist incidents worldwide between 1968 and April 2007. Those attacks took the lives of 14,790 people, an average annual worldwide death toll of 379. Clearly, what the world saw that September morning was completely out of line with everything that went before or since. Terrorism is hideous, and every death it inflicts is a tragedy and a crime. But still, 379 deaths worldwide annually is a very small number. In 2003, in the

United States alone, 497 people accidentally suffocated in bed; 396 were unintentionally electrocuted; 515 drowned in swimming pools; 347 were killed by police officers. And 16,503 Americans were murdered by garden-variety criminals.

And that 379 figure actually overstates the toll inflicted on Americans, Britons, and other residents of the Western world because most deaths caused by international terrorism happen in distant, tumultuous regions like Kashmir. In North America, between 1968 and 2007, all international terrorist incidents combined – including 9/11 – killed 3,765 people. That is only slightly more than the number of Americans killed while riding a motorcycle in the single year of 2003. In Western Europe, the death toll due to international terrorism between 1968 and April 2007 was 1,233. That is 6 per cent of the number of lives believed lost *every year* in Europe to the naturally occurring radon gas that few people pay the slightest attention to.

In 2005, K.T. Bogen and E.D. Jones of the Lawrence Livermore National Laboratory were asked by the U.S. government to conduct a comprehensive statistical analysis of the terrorism figures in the RAND–MIPT database. The researchers concluded that for the purposes of understanding the risk of terrorism, the world should be divided in two: Israel and everywhere else. In Israel, terrorism is a serious threat. The chance of being injured or killed over a lifetime (70 years) ranged between 1 in 100 and 1 in 1,000, which is high enough that most people will at least know someone who has been a casualty of a terrorist attack. But in the rest of the world, the lifetime risk of injury or death falls between 1 in 10,000 and 1 in a million.

Compare that to an American's lifetime risk of being killed by lightning: 1 in 79,746; or being killed by a venomous plant or animal: 1 in 39,873; or drowning in a bathtub: 1 in 11,289; or committing suicide: 1 in 119; or dying in a car crash: 1 in 84. Bogen and Jones noted that if the risk posed by terrorism were considered in a public health context, it would certainly fall within the range that regulators called *de minimis*: too small for concern.

The enormity of 9/11 in our consciousness also obscures an important trend. From the 1960s until the early 1990s, the number of international terrorist incidents steadily increased, but when the Soviet Union collapsed, so did terrorism. The peak was reached in 1991, when there were 450 incidents recorded in the RAND–MIPT terrorism database. By 2000, that number had plummeted to 100.

In 2000, the trend reversed. By 2004, incidents had soared to 400 a year. But Andrew Mack, the director of the Human Security Centre at the University of British Columbia, which tracks international violence, notes that if you take the Middle East out of the equation, the trend is flat. If South Asia is also taken out, the decline in international terrorism that started at the end of the Cold War actually continued. "That suggests there has been a net decline in terrorism in all regions of the world except the Middle East and South Asia from the early 1990s," Mack concludes.

Terrorist attacks are not the only measure of the terrorist threat, of course. We also have to look at foiled plots. Among Western countries, the United Kingdom has struggled most with terrorism since 9/11 but even in the United Kingdom only five plots were uncovered in the two years after the suicide bombings of July 7, 2005. In November 2006, the head of MI5 claimed her service knew of 30 more plots on the go. If we assume all these numbers represent actual attacks that would have been carried out if law enforcement hadn't acted – a huge assumption – they still wouldn't even come close to making terrorism a significant and rising threat to the safety of the average Briton.

The picture is more startling in the United States, where years of feverish intelligence work has uncovered astonishingly little. In March 2005, *ABC News* reported it had obtained a secret 32–page FBI report that suggested there was a simple reason that networks of Osama bin Laden's operatives hadn't been uncovered in the United States: There may be nothing to uncover. The terrorists' "intention to attack the United States is not in question," ABC quoted the report saying. "However, their capability to do so is unclear, particularly in regard to 'spectacular' operations. We believe that al-Qa'ida's capability to launch attacks within the United States is dependent on its ability to infiltrate and maintain operatives in the United States. . . . Limited reporting since March indicates al-Qa'ida has sought to recruit and train individuals to conduct attacks in the United States, but is inconclusive as to whether they have succeeded in placing operatives in this country. . . . U.S. Government efforts to date also have not revealed evidence of concealed cells or networks acting in the homeland as sleepers."

It's also important to realize that a 9/11-style attack is probably impossible now. We all know that the old rule of hijackings – stay calm and cooperate – is out, and without that small numbers of lightly armed terrorists cannot commandeer passenger jets. Many experts even doubt the capacity of terrorists to mount assaults of this scale by *any* means. "While another attack on the scale of 9/11 cannot be ruled out entirely," writes the dean of terrorism analysts, Brian Michael Jenkins, in *Unconquerable Nation*, "there is growing consensus among analysts that such an attack on the United States is not likely."

The standard response to all these points is that they miss the real danger. The statistics that show terrorism isn't a major killer are irrelevant. The decline in terrorist attacks in most of the world is irrelevant. The fact that 9/11 was unlikely to succeed and almost certainly wouldn't if it were attempted again is irrelevant. All that matters is that if terrorists get their hands on weapons of mass destruction (WMDs), they could inflict the sort of devastation it took armies to accomplish in the past. This is new, and it makes terrorism a risk that vastly exceeds all others. "Inexorably, terrorism, like war itself, is moving beyond the conventional to the apocalyptic," wrote Michael Ignatieff, then a professor at Harvard, now deputy leader of Canada's Liberal Party.

We have only to look at Israel to doubt this line. International terrorism in modern form essentially dates from the late 1960s and in all that time Israel has suffered most. For the world's worst terrorists

– those who do not hesitate to strap explosives to children – Israel is an object of obsessive, burning hate. Their keenest desire is to wipe the tiny country off the map, and these terrorists have often enjoyed the sponsorship of Middle Eastern states that share the dream of destroying the "Zionist entity" but don't dare attack directly. And yet Israel has never suffered an attack by terrorists armed with weapons of mass destruction. This is a pretty strong indication that getting and using such weapons isn't quite as easy as some would have us think.

In theory, terrorists could obtain viruses, nukes, and the like from black markets but these seem to be found mainly in James Bond movies and newspaper articles trafficking in rumour and speculation. They could also obtain weapons of mass destruction from one of the very few states that have such weapons and would like to see Israel or the United States suffer, but any leader pondering such a move has to consider that if his role in an attack were uncovered, his country would quickly be reduced to rubble. That's a significant deterrent: Osama bin Laden and his followers may desire martyrdom but Kim Jong Il and other dictators do not. States also have to consider that they may not be able to control when or how terrorists use the weapons they provide. And they have to worry that "the surrogate cannot be trusted, even to the point of using the weapon against its sponsor," noted the 1999 report of the Gilmore Committee, a congressional advisory committee named for its chair, Jim Gilmore, the former Republican governor of Virginia. These considerations have kept states from supplying terrorists with nuclear, chemical, or biological weapons for decades. There's no reason to think they will not continue to be persuasive.

That leaves DIY. Many media reports make it sound as if weapons of mass destruction can be manufactured with nothing more than an Internet recipe and some test tubes. Fortunately, "the hurdles faced by terrorists seeking to develop true weapons of mass casualties and mass destruction are more formidable than is often imagined," the Gilmore Committee wrote. "This report does not argue that terrorists cannot produce and disseminate biological or chemical agents capable of injuring or indeed killing relatively small numbers of persons . . . or perhaps inflicting serious casualties even in the hundreds. The point is that creating truly mass-casualty weapons – capable of killing in tens of thousands, much less in the thousands – requires advanced university training in appropriate scientific and technical disciplines, significant financial resources, obtainable but nonetheless sophisticated equipment and facilities, the ability to carry out rigorous testing to ensure a weapon's effectiveness, and the development and employment of effective means of dissemination." The demands are so high that they "appear, at least for now, to be beyond the reach not only of the vast majority of existent terrorist organizations but also of many established nation-states." A Library of Congress report issued the same year similarly concluded, "Weapons of mass destruction are significantly harder to produce or obtain than what is commonly depicted in the press and today they probably remain beyond the reach of most terrorist groups."

It's also important to remember that despite Osama bin Laden's wealth, his bases in Afghanistan, and the relatively free hand he had in the 1990s when the United States paid little attention to the man who grandiosely "declared war" in 1996, he failed. "While there can be little doubt that some members of al-Qaeda displayed a keen interest in acquiring chemical weapons," writes Louise Richardson, the dean of the Radcliffe Institute of Advanced Studies at Harvard and a leading expert on terrorism, "there is no evidence that they succeeded in doing so." Desire and capability are not interchangeable.

Bin Laden was not the first to learn that lesson. Focused as the world is on murderous Islamists, it's easy to forget that the first religious zealots to obtain and deploy weapons of mass destruction in terrorism belonged to the Japanese cult of Aum Shinrikyo. Led by Shoko Asahara, Aum was fixated on the idea of inflicting mass-casualty terrorist attacks in hopes of sparking an apocalyptic war. Aum's resources were formidable. At its peak, the cult had a membership of around

60,000. Outside Japan, it had offices in Australia, Germany, Russia, and even New York City. It had at least several hundred million dollars in cash and perhaps as much as $1 billion. And it had highly skilled members. Aum went to the best universities in Japan and aggressively courted graduate students in biology, chemistry, physics, and engineering, giving them the finest equipment and facilities money could by. One Aum scientist later confessed he joined simply because Aum's laboratories were so superior to those of his university. At one point, Aum had 20 scientists working on biological weapons. Another 80 investigated chemical weapons.

Naturally, Aum also sought nuclear weapons, going so far as to purchase a 500,000-acre sheep station in a remote part of Australia with plans to mine uranium and ship it to Japan "where scientists using laser enrichment technology would convert it into weapons-grade nuclear material," according to the Gilmore Committee. Aum also tried very hard to buy off-the-shelf. In Russia, the group bought large quantities of small arms "and is known to have been in the market for advanced weaponry, such as tanks, jet fighters, surface-to-surface rocket launchers and even a tactical nuclear weapon."

No opportunity was overlooked. When Ebola broke out in central Africa in October 1992, Shoko Asahara personally led 40 of his followers to the region on what was billed as a humanitarian mission. Officials now believe Aum was attempting to collect samples of the virus so it could be mass-produced in Japan. They failed.

That was far from Aum's only failure. The cult's first known bio-terror attack involved the spraying of botulinum toxin – the extremely deadly substance that causes botulism – from three trucks at targets that included American naval bases, an airport, Japan's parliament, and the Imperial Palace. No one got sick. No one even knew there had been attacks – the truth was discovered three years later. Another botulinum attack failed in June 1993. The same month, the cult's first anthrax attack failed. In all, Aum made nine attempts to inflict mass death with two of the most feared bio-terrorism weapons.

They killed no one. It seems that not even Aum, with all its resources, could overcome the many practical barriers to isolating virulent forms of the deadly pathogens and disseminating them broadly.

So the cult switched its focus to chemical weapons and nerve agents. Here, Aum met with considerable success, producing substantial quantities of mustard gas, sodium cyanide, vx, and sarin – the latter two being among the deadliest nerve gases. When police finally raided Aum's facilities in 1995, the cult had enough sarin to kill an estimated 4.2 million people.

As terrifying as that is, it's also strangely reassuring. After all, here was a cult that wanted to kill millions and it had cleared the many barriers between it and possession of weapons that were at least theoretically capable of doing just that. And yet, Aum *still* failed to cause mass death.

On June 27, 1994, Aum members drove a converted refrigerator truck into a residential neighbourhood of Matsumoto, Japan. Inside, terrorists activated a computer–controlled system that heated liquid sarin to a vapour and blew it into the air with a fan. The wind conditions were perfect, slowly nudging the deadly cloud toward windows left open to the warm night air. Seven people died, and over 140 suffered serious injuries.

On March 20, 1995, Aum tried another delivery method. Five members dressed in business suits and carrying umbrellas stepped aboard five different trains in the heart of Tokyo's notoriously crowded subway system. In all, they carried 11 plastic bags filled with sarin. Placing the bags on the floor, the terrorists poked holes in them with their umbrellas and fled the trains. Three of the 11 bags failed to rupture. The other eight spilled roughly 159 ounces of sarin. As the liquid fanned out, it evaporated and vapours rose. Twelve people died. Five more were critically injured but survived. Another 37 were deemed severely injured, while 984 suffered modest symptoms.

Japanese authorities raided Aum properties all over the country and were astonished at what they discovered. Despite the scale of

Aum's murderous operations, despite the cult's many efforts to acquire the means of slaughter, despite the repeated attacks, the police had little idea what was happening in their midst. It's hard to imagine a worse scenario: A fanatical cult with a burning desire to inflict mass slaughter has heaps of money, international connections, excellent equipment and laboratories, scientists trained at top–flight universities, and years of near–total freedom to pursue its operations. And yet Aum's 17 attacks with chemical or biological weapons killed far fewer lives than the 168 people who died in Oklahoma City when Timothy McVeigh detonated a single bomb made of fertilizer and motor–racing fuel.

"Aum's experience suggests – however counter–intuitively or contrary to popular belief – the significant technological difficulties faced by any non–state entity in attempting to weaponize and disseminate chemical and biological weapons effectively," concluded the Gilmore Committee. Crucial to this failure, the committee noted, is the atmosphere within a conspiracy fuelled by religious mania. "Aum scientists, socially and physically isolated and ruled by an increasingly paranoid leader, became divorced from reality and unable to make sound judgment."

For terrorists with dreams of apocalypse, this is discouraging. Al–Qaeda and other Islamist terrorists have few of the advantages Aum had. They do not have the money, infrastructure or equipment, or the freedom from scrutiny, or the ability to travel openly. Most importantly, they do not have the scientists – al–Qaeda has tried to recruit trained minds but consistently failed, which is the main reason they have never shown even a fraction of the technical sophistication of Aum. The one factor they share with the Japanese cult is the hothouse atmosphere that crippled Aum's efforts.

As the Aum experience showed, mass–casualty terrorist attacks using chemical or biological weapons are certainly possible, but terrorists quickly discover many serious obstacles if they start down this path. There's a reason that even the most sophisticated and ruthless terrorists have stuck almost exclusively to bombs and bullets – or, in the case of the worst terrorist attack in history, box-cutters and airplane tickets.

Of course, the calculations change when weapons go nuclear. "Perhaps the only certain way for terrorists to achieve bona fide mass destruction would be to use a nuclear weapon," wrote the Gilmore Committee. A nuclear attack would undoubtedly be an almost unimaginable horror and the contemplation of that horror inevitably stirs emotions strong enough to drive out any thought of probabilities. And that's a mistake. Probability is always important in dealing with risks, even catastrophic risks – *especially* catastrophic risks. The biggest risk humanity faces is, after all, not nuclear terrorism. It is a collision with an asteroid or comet of planet-killing size. If we considered only the potential destruction of such an event and ignored its probability, we would pour trillions of dollars into the construction of vast, impenetrable, globe-girdling defence systems. But pretty much everybody – including the astronomers who wish we would spend just a little more money to detect asteroids – would say that's a foolish waste of resources because the probability of mass extinction by collision is incredibly tiny and that money could do a lot more good down here on earth. We shouldn't ignore the threat – refusing to pay a modest amount of money to detect major asteroids and calculate pending collisions is ridiculous – but we also shouldn't go crazy about it. The same cool head has to be brought to bear on nuclear terrorism.

What is the probability of an American city going up in a mushroom cloud? It's not possible to calculate that in the way that we calculate, say, the chance that a child sitting in a properly installed car seat may die in a crash because it has never happened so there are no numbers to crunch. In the absence of data, all we can do is look at the complex facts about the construction and availability of nuclear weapons and make a judgment call.

The Gilmore Committee did that. It started by noting that the collapse of the Soviet Union did not result in Soviet nukes popping up in black markets, despite widespread fears during the 1990s. In particular, reports that Russia's notorious "suitcase nukes" went missing did not hold up and, in any event, the devices require regular maintenance in order to function properly. Even if some disgruntled Russian officer did manage to sell a bomb, the buyers would still have the difficult job of smuggling and detonating it – the latter being particularly difficult because nuclear devices typically have tamper-proof seals and other security measures designed to prevent precisely this scenario.

As for DIY, it's not something that can be done in the average suburban garage. "Building a nuclear device capable of producing mass destruction presents Herculean challenges for terrorists and indeed even for states with well-funded and sophisticated programs," the Gilmore Committee wrote. In the 1980s, Saddam Hussein poured Iraq's vast oil-funded resources into a nuclear program but failed to produce even a single weapon before the first Gulf War, and subsequent sanctions, scuttled his ambitions. Apartheid South Africa did succeed in building a small nuclear arsenal but "it took scientists and engineers – who were endowed with a large and sophisticated infrastructure – four years to build their first gun-type system (the crudest form of nuclear bomb)."

And yet, however unlikely it may be, it could happen. "We have learned that it is not beyond the realm of possibility for a terrorist group to obtain a nuclear weapon," former CIA director George Tenet wrote in his memoirs. "Such an event would place Al Qaeda on a par with the superpowers and make good bin Laden's threat to destroy our economy and bring death into every American household." "Were a nuclear terrorist attack to occur," said former UN secretary general Kofi Annan, "it would cause not only widespread death and destruction, but would stagger the world economy and thrust tens of millions of people into dire poverty."

By most accounts, a successful nuclear detonation in an urban centre would kill in the order of 100,000 people. With a death toll of

100,000, the chance of any one American being killed in the explosion would be 0.033 per cent, or 1 in 3,000. As for the collective risk, a death toll of 100,000 is not much more than the number of Americans killed each year by diabetes – 75,000 – and it is roughly equal to the number of American lives lost annually to accidents or to infections contracted in hospital. So simply in terms of numbers of lives lost, a nuclear terrorist attack would hardly be the apocalypse.

It is often assumed, however, that such a strike would also unleash panic that would multiply the destruction and might even collapse the civil order. The problem with this assumption is that it's based on a long-discredited myth: Decades of extensive research on how people behave in emergencies has consistently found that panic is quite rare. "Even when people confront what they consider to be the worst case, they organize themselves to provide succor and salvation to their friends, and even to complete strangers," writes Lee Clarke, a sociologist at Rutgers University. Even people caught in the flaming wreckage of downed airplanes routinely look to the needs of others rather than pushing and screaming their way to safety. We should have learned this lesson on September 11, 2001, when New Yorkers responded to a bewildering disaster with dignity, compassion, cooperation, and generosity.

A nuclear terrorist attack would certainly do massive economic damage but George Tenet's claim that it would "destroy" the American economy is ridiculously inflated. Again, the best proof of this is 9/11 itself. The attack wasn't on the scale of a nuclear detonation, of course, but the terrorists did destroy two vital cogs in the machinery of American capitalism, paralyze the most important city in the United States, halt all air travel, and bring American commerce and society to a shuddering halt. As expected, stock markets around the world plunged. But it took just 40 days for the Dow Jones Industrial Average to bounce back to the level it had closed at on September 10, 2001. "If you look closely at the trend lines since 9/11," William Dobson wrote in *Foreign Policy* magazine on the fifth anniversary of the attacks, "what is remarkable is how little the world has changed." The value of American exports continued to rise steadily, and while the value of global trade dipped slightly in 2001 from $8 trillion to $7.8 trillion – it was a bad year even prior to the attacks – it "came racing back, increasing every subsequent year to $12 trillion in 2005." The American economy was not devastated, nor was globalization set back. Instead, the United States picked itself up, brushed off the dust, and carried on. Even New York City proved to be so resilient that it was soon enjoying a new Golden Age.

Another demonstration of the fundamental strength of American society came on August 29, 2005, when Hurricane Katrina roared ashore and breached the levees protecting New Orleans. More than 1,500 people died, while most of the rest fled. The parallel with a nuclear strike is far from exact but here we saw a great American city suddenly smashed and abandoned. The experience was wrenching and the costs – estimated to be around $80 billion in direct damage alone – were huge. But America was not crippled. Far from it. The economy scarcely hiccupped, and the loss of one of the most storied cities in the nation did essentially no damage whatsoever to American military, political, or cultural power.

So let's add this all up. First, 9/11 was a dramatic deviation from what terrorism usually entails. Second, even including the toll of 9/11, international terrorism poses an infinitesimal risk to the life of any individual American or any other resident of a Western country. Third, even if there were a long series of attacks in the United States, each on the scale of 9/11, the risk to any one American would still be much smaller than other risks people routinely shrug off. Fourth, outside the Middle East and South Asia, the rate of international terrorist attacks has been falling for about a decade and a half. Fifth, it is very hard for terrorists to get their hands on, much less deploy, chemical, biological, or – especially – nuclear weapons, and even if they did overcome the many barriers between them and a successful attack the toll would very likely be a small fraction of what we see in our nightmares. Sixth, even if terrorists succeeded in launching a truly catastrophic attack with a death toll many times that of 9/11 – such as by detonating a nuclear bomb – the risk to any one person would still be small and the United States would remain the most prosperous and powerful nation in history.

And finally, number seven: Almost one-half of Americans are worried that they or their families could be killed by terrorists – a level of concern that is actually higher than it was four years earlier, even though there have been no terrorist attacks on American soil.

No, this does not add up. The fact that people had wildly unrealistic worries in November 2001 made sense. Psychology can explain that. On a smaller scale, the same thing happened after the Oklahoma City bombing of 1995. It also makes sense that the worry slowly declined as time passed and nightmares did not materialize. That, too, happened after Oklahoma City. But psychology alone cannot explain why the decline stopped, or why it crept back up as the United States enjoyed one terrorism-free year after another.

To understand that, we have to go back to September 12, 2001, and George W. Bush's declaration that the events of the previous day were "more than acts of terror. They were acts of war. . . . Freedom and democracy are under attack." British prime minister Tony Blair added his own rhetorical escalation four days later when he warned, "We know that they would, if they could, go further and use chemical or biological or even nuclear weapons of mass destruction." This theme re-cast the destruction wrought by 9/11. Instead of it being the result of 19 fanatics armed with nothing more than box-cutters and good luck, it was definitive proof of the fantastic power, reach, and sophistication of the enemy. Instead of it being seen as a horrible deviation from the terrorist norm, it was both the new normal – expect more attacks on the same scale – and a sign that much worse was to come.

The media picked up this language and it became routine to say that "everything had changed." We had entered the "Age of Terror." Some conservatives dubbed it the "Third World War" – or fourth, for those who thought the Cold War should be included in the list. The president himself endorsed this view on May 6, 2006, when he referred to the passenger revolt on Flight 93 as "the first counter-attack to World War Three." Another popular phrase was "existential struggle," which suggested the very existence of the United States was in jeopardy. Others went further. "This conflict is a fight to save the civilized world," Bush declared in October 2001. The logical end of this rhetorical expansion was reached by Irwin Cotler, Canada's Liberal justice minister and a renowned human rights activist, who often referred to terrorism as "an existential threat to the whole of the human family."

The events of 9/11 and what followed could have been framed any number of ways but the president chose to call it a "war on terrorism" – a global clash between mighty forces that can end only in victory or destruction – and his administration has stuck with that frame ever since. "The civilized world faces unprecedented dangers," he declared in the January 2002 State of the Union address. "Unless we act to prevent it, a new wave of terrorism, potentially involving the world's most destructive weapons, looms in America's future," the president's National Strategy for Homeland Security warned in 2002. "It is a challenge as formidable as any ever faced by our Nation. . . . Today's terrorists can strike at any place, at any time, and with virtually any weapon."

In the 2003 State of the Union address, the president said the fight against terrorism was the latest in a succession of struggles against "Hitlerism, militarism, and communism" and that, "once again, this nation and all our friends are all that stand between a world at peace, and a world of chaos and constant alarm."

In 2006, Homeland Security chief Michael Chertoff said in a speech commemorating the fifth anniversary of 9/11 that the United States had emerged "from the Cold War and the struggles of World War Two" only to "face a new challenge that has every bit as much danger as the challenges we have faced in prior decades."

In 2007, the White House website called the 9/11 attacks "acts of war against the United States, peaceful people throughout the world, and the very principles of liberty and human dignity."

The Bush administration hammered these themes month after month, year after year. Tens of millions of Americans had a powerful, psychologically grounded sense that terrorism was a grave personal threat. That's what Gut told them. Head could have intervened, but it didn't. Why would it? The administration said Gut was right. The nation – even civilization – was in jeopardy.

The failure of the administration to put the risk in perspective was total. The president never said that, as serious as terrorism is, it does not pose a significant risk to any one person. He never said, "Calm down." He never said, "You've got a better chance of being killed by lightning." Neither did any other major politician, Republican or Democrat. In June 2007, New York mayor Michael Bloomberg came close. "There are a lot of threats to you in the world," he told the *New York Times*. He rattled off a few, including heart attacks and lightning strikes. "You can't sit there and worry about everything. Get a life!" The sentiment is noble but Bloomberg essentially ignored probability by lumping together heart attacks – a significant risk for most people – with the extreme improbability of death by lightning strike and terrorist attack. Only John McCain specifically instructed Americans to pay attention to probability: "Get on the damn elevator! Fly on the damn plane! Calculate the odds of being harmed by a terrorist! It's still about as likely as being swept out to sea by a tidal wave." Unfortunately, McCain made this daring statement only in a 2004 book. His public statements, before and after, stuck to the standard script of American politics: We are at war against a mighty enemy.

The United States was in a literal war within a year and a half of 9/11 but the enemy in that war was Saddam Hussein, not Osama bin Laden. There is no credible evidence that the Iraqi dictator had anything to do with 9/11, but there are indications that top figures in the Bush administration were looking for an opportunity to depose the Iraqi dictator when they entered the White House in January 2001, and it is well-established – not least by Richard Clarke, the White House's terrorism chief – that the administration launched efforts to pin 9/11 on Hussein even before the smoke had cleared at Ground Zero. The key to accomplishing both those objectives was the threat of terrorists getting hold of weapons of mass destruction.

The narrative was already clear by the time the president delivered his first State of the Union address, on January 29, 2002. "As we gather tonight, our nation is at war. Our economy is in recession, and the civilized world faces unprecedented dangers," Bush began. "Iraq continues to flaunt its hostility toward America and to support terror. The Iraqi regime has plotted to develop anthrax, and nerve gas, and nuclear weapons for over a decade." Bush also singled out Iran and North Korea. "States like these, and their terrorist allies, constitute an axis of evil, arming to threaten the peace of the world. By seeking weapons of mass destruction, these regimes pose a grave and growing danger. They could provide these arms to terrorists, giving them the means to match their hatred. They could attack our allies or attempt to blackmail the United States. In any of these cases, the price of indifference would be catastrophic."

The same theme appeared in the infamous "Downing Street Memo," a secret British document prepared in July 2002 that was leaked after the war. In the memo, the head of MI6, Britain's external intelligence service, reported on his discussions in Washington: "There was a perceptible shift in attitude," he noted. "Military action was now seen as inevitable. Bush wanted to remove Saddam, through military action, justified by the conjunction of terrorism and WMD. But the intelligence and facts were being fixed around the policy."

By the time of the next State of the Union address, in January 2003, the administration was preparing to invade Iraq and the president's tone was as intense as a Tom Clancy novel. "Saddam Hussein aids and protects terrorists, including members of al Qaeda. Secretly, and without fingerprints, he could provide one of his hidden weapons to terrorists, or help them develop their own. Before September 11, many in the world believed that Saddam Hussein could be contained. But chemical agents, lethal viruses, and shadowy terrorist networks are not easily contained. Imagine those 19 hijackers with other weapons and other plans – this time armed by Saddam Hussein. It would take one vial, one canister, one crate slipped into this country to bring a day of horror like none we have ever known. . . . We will do everything in our power to make sure that day never comes."

For Gut, the scenario sketched by the White House was frightening on two levels. First, there was the complexity of the story. Saddam Hussein *could* develop weapons of mass destruction; he *could* give them to terrorists; they *could* use them to attack the United States. As we saw earlier, every link in a chain of events has to happen for the final disaster to occur and for that reason the more complex a scenario is the less likely it is to come to pass. But that's not how Gut judges stories like these. If one of the links in the chain strikes us as typical – in the sense that an earthquake is typical of California or an invasion of Poland is typical of the Soviet Union – it will trigger the Rule of Typical Things and Gut will conclude that the whole scenario is more likely to happen than logic would suggest. The "typical" element in the story told by the administration was obvious. "Can anyone doubt that had Osama bin Laden's al Qaeda possessed weapons of mass destruction, they would have been used on September 11 instead of hijacked airliners?" wrote Richard Lessner, the executive director of the American Conservative Union, in *Weekly Standard*, a conservative magazine. Yes, Gut would say, that fits. And so the scenario felt more plausible than it should: Gut is always a sucker for a good story.

Of course the other possibility is that Gut would never even get around to considering the probability of the scenario. The administration's warnings were frightening, its language vivid – "We don't want the smoking gun to be a mushroom cloud" – and the emotions it evoked may have been enough to overwhelm any intuitive

consideration of the odds. As Lessner put it, "I, for one, am more concerned about a smoking ruin in an American city than a smoking gun
pointing to Saddam." To hell with probability.

"Some have said we must not act until the threat is imminent,"
Bush continued in his 2003 State of the Union address. "Since when
have terrorists and tyrants announced their intentions, politely
putting us on notice before they strike? If this threat is permitted to
fully and suddenly emerge, all actions, all words, and all recrimina-
tions would come too late."

This theme – we must act now if there is a chance of this happening in future – appeared repeatedly in White House statements
leading up to the Iraq war. In *The One Per Cent Doctrine*, a book by Ron
Suskind, a Washington journalist with remarkable access to the
capital's back rooms, it is traced to Vice-President Dick Cheney.
Immediately after 9/11, writes Suskind, Cheney directed that "if there
was even a one per cent chance of terrorists getting a weapon of mass
destruction – and there has been a small probability of such an
occurrence for some time – the United States must now act as if it
were a certainty." In effect, if not in name, Cheney was invoking the
precautionary principle.

This is a contradiction that goes to the heart of the politics of risk.
On the left, the precautionary principle is revered. It is enshrined in
European Union law. Environmentalists are always talking about it.
But the right loathes it. In fact, the Bush administration is openly
hostile to the European Union's attempts to apply the precautionary
principle in health and environmental regulations. In May 2003,
shortly after the United States had invaded Iraq on better-safe-than-
sorry grounds, John Graham, the White House's top official in charge
of vetting regulations, told the *New York Times* that the Bush administration considers the precautionary principle "to be a mythical
concept, perhaps like a unicorn." At the same time, the left – especially
the left in Europe – scoffed when George W. Bush argued in favour of
invading Iraq on the grounds that "if we wait for threats to fully

materialize, we will have waited too long." The left demanded stronger evidence that Saddam Hussein had WMDs, doubted claims that Hussein was linked to al-Qaeda, insisted there were less drastic measures that would achieve the same goal, and argued that the risk of not invading had to be carefully weighed against the risks that would be created by an invasion – exactly the same sort of arguments the Bush administration and other conservatives level when environmentalists or Europeans cite the precautionary principle as grounds for, say, banning chemicals or taking action on climate change. How selective people can be about "precaution" has never been so starkly illustrated as in the months leading up to the Iraq war.

The Bush administration's appeals carried the day. Support approached 75 per cent in the days before the tanks rolled. Saddam Hussein was so successfully connected to 9/11 in the public mind that a *New York Times* poll taken in September 2006 – long after the administration had officially admitted Hussein had nothing to do with the attacks – found that one-third of Americans still thought the Iraqi dictator had been "personally involved." The connection between terrorism and "weapons of mass destruction" was even tighter. In a 2004 Hart-Teeter poll that asked Americans to name the two types of terrorism that worried them the most, 48 per cent cited bio-terrorism, 37 per cent chemical weapons, and 23 per cent nuclear weapons. Only 13 per cent of respondents said airplane hijackings were one of the two most worrying forms of terrorism – even though that's how the whole crisis started. A 2006 Gallup poll found almost half of Americans said it is likely that within the next five years terrorists will "set off a bomb that contains nuclear or biological material."

As for the linkage of Iraq with the broader "war on terrorism," that, too, was accomplished. The percentage of Americans who told Gallup they were very or somewhat worried that they or their families would be victims of terrorism shot up from 35 per cent in April 2002 to 48 per cent by February 2003. Iraq is the "central front in the War on Terror," the president liked to say, and when victory on that front came swiftly, fear of terrorism at home fell. By July 2003, it hit a new low of 30 per cent. But as the situation in Iraq slowly swung from euphoria to despair – and images of destruction and carnage once again filled evening news broadcasts – fear of terrorism slowly inched back up, reaching 45 per cent in August 2006.

In 1933, it was in Franklin Roosevelt's political interest to tell Americans the greatest danger was "fear itself." Seventy years later, it was in George W. Bush's political interest to do the opposite: The White House got the support it needed for invading Iraq by stoking public fears of terrorism and connecting those fears to Iraq.

And Iraq was far from the only benefit the administration reaped. Until 9/11, George W. Bush was a weak leader with a flimsy mandate – he had lost the popular vote, after all – and mediocre approval ratings. After, he was a hero. Any president would have seen his support soar in the immediate aftermath of the attacks but by casting the terrorist threat as a world war of uncertain duration, the president was transformed into a defiant Churchill, and this image, instead of fading with the autumn, would last as long as the war itself – which is to say, it was permanent. "The nation is at war," the president liked to say and the most tangible reminder of this was the periodic announcement of new terror alerts. Perhaps not surprisingly, a statistical analysis by Robb Willer, a graduate student at Cornell University, found a "consistent, positive relationship" between new terror alerts and the president's approval rating. In another 2004 paper, a team of nine psychologists reported on experiments that showed that reminders of death or 9/11 increased support for the president.

Political operatives didn't need psychologists to tell them that. Even long after the Iraq venture turned sour, Bush earned his highest ratings on his handling of terrorism. The same is true of Republicans in general. When danger looms, Americans want a strong figure in charge and so Republicans worked hard to make sure Americans sensed danger looming. In the 2002 congressional elections, even moderate Republicans played almost exclusively to the theme of terrorism, war, danger, and security while the Democrats focused on the weak economy and domestic issues. The Democrats were crushed.

The Republicans followed the same template in 2004 and 2006. If there was any change, it was only to make the message even blunter and scarier. In the campaign of 2006, Vice-President Dick Cheney repeatedly warned of "mass death in the United States." One Republican television ad used the primal imagery of hungry wolves gathering in a dark forest. Another featured the sound of ticking along with real quotations from an al-Qaeda leader – "we purchased some suitcase bombs" and 9/11 was "nothing compared to what you will see next" – followed by what looks like a close-up of a nuclear fireball. An ad from the pro-Republican "Progress For America" showed images of huge crowds chanting "Death to America!" while the narrator intoned, "These people want to kill us." The point of this marketing was to collect votes, not dollars, but the basic technique is no different than that of corporations selling home alarms or choles- terol pills: Scare people, then offer to protect them.

Democrats faced a dilemma. Say that the threat isn't so grave and Republicans could savage them for not taking it seriously and thus being unfit to lead in a time of grave danger. Accept that terrorism is this serious and elections will be decided on the opposition's pre- ferred battleground. In terms of political tactics, that leaves only one option: Be just as shrill about the danger and accuse Republicans of not doing enough to protect Americans.

The terrorist threat did not win the 2006 elections for Republicans as it had the previous two rounds. In part, the responsibility for that lies with other circumstances – notably the bungled response to the Hurricane Katrina disaster. The deepening chaos in Iraq – the "central front in the war on terror" – also cast doubt on Republicans' pre- sumed superior handling of security matters. But another key is the simple difficulty of running a campaign based on fear after control- ling both the White House and Congress for so long. If Americans are in such terrible danger, doesn't that mean the Republicans have failed to deliver security? That awkward question explains the Republicans' equally awkward theme of the 2006 elections: "Safer but still not safe." It was a tricky line to walk and they stumbled.

Other Republicans, unburdened by incumbency, were able to go back to the original script. The Democrats "do not understand the full nature and scope of the terrorist war against us," Rudy Giuliani declared in April 2007. As the lauded mayor of New York City at the time of the 9/11 attacks, Giuliani had the aura of a strong leader who can weather a storm and so, as he sought the Republican candidacy for the presidential election of 2008, he naturally tried to convince Americans that they actually were in the midst of a storm. The war on terrorism is "the defining conflict of our time," Giuliani proclaimed, while warning darkly that if a Democrat entered the White House in 2008, the United States would suffer "more losses." Democrats were furious. "This administration has done little to protect our ports, make our mass transit safer and protect our cities," said Senator Hillary Clinton. "They have isolated us in the world and let al-Qaeda regroup." Giuliani fired back in a radio interview: "They do not seem to get the fact that there are people, terrorists in this world, really dangerous people, that want to come here and kill us. That in fact they did come here and kill us twice and they got away with it because we were on defence because we weren't alert enough to the dangers and the risks."

And so, more than half a decade after four jets were hijacked, the same basic messages – even some of the same lines – echoed over and over in American politics. Terrorists want to kill us, one side says. The threat is high. The other side responds that yes, the threat is high, but don't vote for them because they haven't done enough to protect you. For all the accusations and acrimony in political circles, the political establishment is essentially unanimous in saying that terrorists are a serious threat to each and every American.

Politicians are not the only guilty parties, of course. Government agencies have always understood that the most effective way to protect themselves is to err on the side of threat inflation. Few people will blame the agency that says a risk is high when it does not come to pass, but downplay a risk that later hits the evening news and you can expect a trial by inquisition. The more politically sensitive the risk, the truer this is – and in the United States, nothing is as politically sensitive as terrorism. This explains statements like that of Porter Goss, the CIA chief: "It may be only a matter of time before al-Qaeda or some other group attempts to use chemical, biological, radiological, and nuclear weapons." This is frightening but meaningless. All sorts of bad things *may* happen. This isn't substantive information, it's insurance. In the unlikely event that an attack happens, it can be pointed to as proof that the CIA was on the ball, and if it never happens, it can be forgotten. The possibility that ordinary Americans may take Goss's statement to mean the CIA has substantial reasons to believe it is *likely* that this awful event will happen is incidental.

FBI director Robert Mueller took caution to even more absurd lengths. When he testified to a congressional committee in February 2005, Mueller did not emphasize the absence of terrorist strikes, the failure to find al-Qaeda cells within the United States, or the report his agency had prepared suggesting that, perhaps, al-Qaeda simply doesn't have the horsepower to pull off serious attacks in the United States. Instead, he worried. "I remain very concerned about what we are not seeing," he said. As political scientist John Mueller acerbically noted in his book *Overblown*, "For the bureau's director, absence of evidence apparently is evidence of existence."

Other government agencies had different reasons to hype terrorism. Some did it to protect budgets. Finding that its mission had suddenly plummeted down the list of the administration's priorities, the Drug Enforcement Administration created a travelling exhibit explaining how profits from the illicit drug trade funded terrorism, while the Office of National Drug Control Policy spent millions on an ad campaign that fingered teen pot users as terrorism's financiers.

Others saw opportunity in the new environment. "After 9/11, lobbyists and politicians quickly recognized that the best way to secure legislative approval for a spending proposal is to package the idea as a 'homeland security' measure even if the expenditure had nothing to do with national defense," wrote Timothy Lynch of the Cato Institute, a Washington, D.C., think-tank. Lynch cited a few examples of this new species of security spending: $250,000 for air-conditioned garbage trucks in Newark, New Jersey; $557,400 for communications equipment in the town of North Pole, Alaska; $900,000 for the ferries operating out of Martha's Vineyard – where the harbourmaster admitted, "I don't know what we're going to do, but you don't turn down grant money." In towns and backwaters across America, officials saw federal money and became convinced that a terrorist strike was a serious possibility and it would be irresponsible of them not to take the cash.

High-end security has always been big business but after 9/11, it was the industry of the future. According to the Center for Public Integrity, a Washington watchdog group, the number of companies lobbying Homeland Security officials went from 15 in 2001 to 861 in 2004. Just as makers of police equipment have no interest in seeing the perception of crime do anything but rise, so these companies had no reason to suggest the threat of terrorism was anything less than dire. And with a spokesman of the calibre of John Ashcroft – George W. Bush's first attorney general, who, after leaving office, founded a lobbying firm that specializes in homeland security – those corporations don't have any difficulty in making their views known.

Ambitious prosecutors also discovered that talking up terrorism was an excellent way to get attention. It was "one of the most chilling plots imaginable," U.S. Attorney Roslynn Mauskopf said at a June 2007 press conference announcing the arrest of four men for plotting to bomb New York's JFK airport. "The devastation that would have been caused had this plot succeeded is unthinkable." This was particularly strong language in the city that had experienced 9/11, and yet there was nothing about the case that supported it. The four men had allegedly talked about blowing up jet fuel tanks at the airport, which they believed would devastate JFK and, apparently, cripple the entire economy of the United States. They had no connections, money, or explosives. They also had no plan, only the vague outlines of a scheme built on ignorance and daydreams. "They were foolish," the spokesman for the company that operates the fuel system at JFK told *Time* immediately after the charges were announced. Blowing up a tank would be extremely difficult, he said, and even if that were accomplished, the explosion could not travel through the connecting pipes to other tanks, as the plotters assumed, so even if the plot went off exactly as they imagined, it would have been a decidedly modest affair. No matter, though. Mauskopf's description of an attack that would have inflicted "unfathomable damage, deaths and destruction" got headlines around the world.

Non-governmental organizations also found terrorism could be used to expand the audience for their views. Greenpeace and other long-time foes of nuclear energy turned terrorism into a central theme, warning that existing nuclear reactors could be attacked by terrorists while the construction of new plants would increase the risk of nuclear materials being diverted to nefarious purposes. The Worldwatch Institute did the same with its campaign against industrialized agriculture by arguing that centralized food production could be infiltrated by terrorists and used to spread mass death ("The Bioterror in Your Burger," as one press release memorably put it). It didn't seem to matter what the issue was. Foreign aid for Africa. Climate change. Somehow it was connected to terrorism. Individually, these linkages made little difference. Collectively, they implied terrorism is a monstrous crisis that overshadowed all other concerns.

Then there's the "terrorism industry," as John Mueller calls it. Following 9/11, the ranks of terrorism experts and security analysts rapidly swelled, with predictable results. "Some of the many books that have filled the terrorism bookshelf since 9/11 are diatribes of shrill polemics and fear-mongering," wrote Brian Michael Jenkins, one of the first experts on international terrorism.

Richard Clarke, the top anti-terrorism official under Bill Clinton and George W. Bush, has spent his time since leaving the White House penning one horrific tale of terrorist savagery after another. Some are thriller novels in the style of Tom Clancy, while others purport to be realistic analyses. It's sometimes difficult to tell the fiction from the non-fiction. "The woman never hesitated. She walked to the roulette table, 50 feet from the front door, and pushed the detonator, blowing herself up. The explosion killed 38 people who were sitting and standing at nearby tables. The nails and ball bearings that flew out of the woman's vest and belt wounded more than a hundred others, even though the slot machines absorbed many of the miniature missiles. Eighteen of the hundreds of elderly gamblers in the casino suffered heart attacks that proved fatal when they could not be treated fast enough amid the rubble." No, that's not from one of Clarke's novels. It's from a January 2005 essay Clarke published in the high-brow magazine *The Atlantic Monthly*, which imagines a "second wave" of al-Qaeda attacks that starts in 2005, kicking off a complex chain of events that results in thousands dead, Muslim-Americans sent to prison camps, a coup in Saudi Arabia, worldwide economic depression, and martial law in America.

This scenario – and many others like it – was produced for public consumption, but there are plenty more like them contained within government documents. The shock of 9/11 made officials much more willing to imagine the unimaginable, a tendency that was bolstered when the 9/11 Commission said the government's chief failure prior to the attacks was a "lack of imagination." Everyone from academics to thriller authors, "futurists," and Hollywood screenwriters has been summoned to Washington and asked to dream up ways things could go horribly wrong. These exercises tend not to result in typical terrorism scenarios such as "bomb in mailbox: two dead." In the realm of imagination, terrorism tilts heavily to the exotic and catastrophic.

Imagining "what if" allows officials to spot vulnerabilities and consider responses, making it a useful exercise. But it may not end there. "These scenarios are often transformed into real threats," writes Brian Michael Jenkins. "What begins as hypothetically possible evolves into a scenario that is probable, which then somehow becomes inevitable, and, by the bottom of the page, is imminent." For psychologists, this is to be expected. Experts and officials are not immune to probability blindness. And, like everyone else, their unconscious minds use the Rule of Typical Things to analyze the likelihood of detailed scenarios – using the plausibility of some element of the scenario to judge the likelihood of the whole scenario. "This effect contributes to the appeal of scenarios and the illusory insight that they often provide," Daniel Kahneman and Amos Tversky wrote more than 30 years ago.

"A political analyst can improve scenarios by adding plausible causes and representative consequences," Kahneman and Tversky added. And so can a security analyst. "Eight years [prior to 9/11], aides to Osama bin Laden met with Sala Abdel al-Mobruk, a Sudanese military officer and former government minister who offered to sell weapons-grade uranium to the terrorists for $1.5 million," begins a 2006 article in *Foreign Policy* magazine by security experts Peter Zimmerman and Jeffrey Lewis. "He proffered up a 3-foot-long cylinder. The al Qaeda representatives agreed to the purchase, because after all, as one of them later said, 'it's easy to kill more people with uranium.' The cylinder turned out to be a dud. But had it actually contained highly enriched uranium, and if bin Laden's deputies had managed to use it to assemble, then transport and detonate a nuclear bomb, history would have looked very different. September 11 would be remembered as the day when hundreds of thousands of people had been killed."

There are many links in this chain. First, the scenario requires the Sudanese officer to actually get enriched uranium somehow, which he rather unsurprisingly did not because it is not so easy to lay one's hands on enriched uranium. Then al-Qaeda would have had to transport the uranium to a facility and begun construction of a bomb before transporting it to the target and detonating this home-made device, which may or may not work. And they would have to complete this entire chain without being detected at any point. If each of these steps is more likely to fail than not – and in several cases, the odds are tilted heavily against success – that makes the final moment of horror extremely unlikely.

Unfortunately, that's not how Gut reacts to Zimmerman and Lewis's story. If bin Laden had a nuclear weapon, would he try to bomb New York? Well, yes. That feels right. It sounds like "typical" behaviour, just as a Soviet invasion of Poland was plausible to experts two and a half decades ago. Gut would use that feeling to judge the likelihood of the whole scenario and the result would be a sense – a hunch, an intuition – that this terrible threat is far more likely to happen than logic suggests.

For this reason alone, we should be suspicious of the frightening stories so often told about possible terrorist attacks. They are almost certain to feel more likely to happen than they actually are. But beyond psychology, we should question the tales experts and pundits tell because they so often include elements that simply have not been borne out by experience. One of the staples of terrorism scenarios is a massive, violent anti-Muslim backlash following an attack – but aside from a tiny number of minor incidents, there was no anti-Muslim violence in the United States following 9/11, none in Australia after the Bali nightclub bombing, none in Spain after the Madrid train bombings, and none in the United Kingdom after the London subway bombings. Similarly, terrorism scenarios routinely involve dire economic consequences following attacks on a much smaller scale than 9/11 – even though nothing like that followed 9/11 itself.

More tall tales came from the media. After 9/11 and the anthrax attacks, terrorism was the only story for months, as if nothing else were happening on the planet, although the chief suspect was fingered almost immediately and there were no subsequent attacks to cover. There was the war in Afghanistan, of course, but preparations were slow and undramatic and when the clash itself came, there were few American soldiers on the ground and it was all over quickly. So in an all-terrorism-all-the-time atmosphere, how would the media fill vast quantities of paper and airtime? They turned to speculation. "In a large industrial country, vulnerabilities are virtually unlimited," wrote Brian Michael Jenkins, and that means media conjecture about possible terrorist attacks is effectively limited only by the imagination of reporters. Inevitably, a particularly rich source of inspiration for journalists were the tales of viral nightmares that were so popular in the 1990s. In this, they were encouraged by the Bush administration's increasingly vivid warnings about weapons of mass destruction – warnings that included serious consideration of mass inoculation against a long-defeated enemy, smallpox.

The fact that smallpox became a top worry in the wake of terrorist attacks involving box-cutters is a phenomenon future historians will puzzle over. The virus was declared globally eradicated in 1980 and today it exists only in secure government facilities in the United States and Russia. The last American case was seen in 1949, and even then smallpox was essentially a relic from another era. But still, newspapers and television were awash with stories portraying the virus as a near-unstoppable plague.

Exposed to endless scary stories and denied basic facts, Americans could be forgiven for thinking smallpox was on its way. Surveys by the Harvard School of Public Health conducted in November 2001 found slightly more than half of Americans were worried that terrorists would unleash the virus. When asked how likely it is that "you or someone in your immediate family" would contract smallpox – a question that engages "optimism bias" by making the issue personal – one in ten Americans said it was very or somewhat likely that they would contract a disease declared globally eradicated more than two decades earlier. Not that Americans knew the disease *was* eradicated: Three in ten believed there had been cases in the United States within the previous five years, while 63 per cent thought there had been infections somewhere in the world during that time.

The hyperbole and near-total absence of skepticism in the media's handling of smallpox is typical of reporting on terrorism since 9/11. The Bush administration's decision to frame the attacks and their aftermath as a clash of titans that would settle the fate of the world was unthinkingly accepted and replicated by the media. Along with the frame and the language, the media accepted the administration's facts. It is now well known that prior to the invasion of Iraq the media were shamefully gullible on the crucial issues of Saddam Hussein's alleged weapons of mass destruction and links to al-Qaeda, but many commentators have claimed that embarrassment at having been so blatantly and effectively used by the White House made a difference in the years that followed. "In many ways, the media has definitely improved," wrote Gary Kamiya in *Slate*.

Perhaps in some ways, but not in covering terrorism. In January 2003, police raided a London apartment occupied by nine Algerians. One police officer was murdered in the raid, but it was the discovery of a makeshift lab for the production of ricin – a deadly poison made from the castor bean – that made headlines all over the world. Tony Blair and then-Secretary of State Colin Powell even pointed to the discovery as further evidence bolstering the case for war with Saddam Hussein. But more than two years later, charges against four of the Algerians were dropped and another four were acquitted at trial. Only the man who murdered the police officer was convicted. The prosecutions failed because the police had, in fact, found neither ricin nor a lab for making it – only a few recipes for making ricin downloaded from the Internet. This revelation dramatically changed the nature and scale of the threat, and it raised serious questions about governments manipulating criminal cases to suit political ends. Despite this, the truth about the raid got a tiny fraction of the initial, misleading coverage.

Occasionally, journalists not only accepted official statements at face value, they inflated them. In November 2006, a frightening headline appeared on CNN.com: "U.K. Spy Chief Fears Nuclear Attack." A *New York Times* report on the same story was more precise and alarming: "Dame Eliza Manningham–Buller, the director of MI5, spoke of around 30 conspiracies that might include 'the use of chemicals, bacteriological agents, radioactive materials and even nuclear technology.'" The Canadian Broadcasting Corporation's flagship TV news program summarized it this way: "A dire warning from the usually secretive head of Britain's MI5. The spy chief says her agency knows of active terrorist plots against her country, not just one or two, but 30. Some of them involve chemical and nuclear devices."

None of this is even close to true. In a public speech, Eliza Manningham–Buller had outlined Britain's security situation as she saw it. She gave precise numbers of suspected plotters and then said this about the nature of the danger: "Today, we see the use of home-made improvised explosive devices; tomorrow's threat may include the use of chemicals, bacteriological agents, radioactive materials and even nuclear technology." Implicit in that sentence is the fact that, currently, MI5 only has evidence of terrorists using "home–made improvised explosive devices." The rest is speculation. But the media took that empty statement and turned it into an imminent threat.

The collapse of critical reasoning in media coverage of terrorism was near–total. Consider the basic question of why there were no al–Qaeda attacks in the United States in the years following 9/11. Logically, there are at least three possible answers. One, al–Qaeda was thwarted by increased law enforcement and stricter security precautions. Two, al–Qaeda chose not to attack for nefarious reasons known only to Osama bin Laden. Three, al–Qaeda wished to attack but lacked the capacity to do so inside the United States. Answer one appeared often in the media. Answer two, much less often. Answer three was almost never mentioned, not even as the remotest possibility. "The United States has escaped attack these past six years because it is harder to hit," wrote Roger Cohen of the *International Herald Tribune* in the *New York Times*, "not because the bomb-us-back-to-the-Caliphate boys took a time-out." In Cohen's mind, there simply is no Door Number Three.

Certainly the administration had skeptical critics in the media but as time passed those critics found it increasingly congenial to see the terrorist threat as great and growing. After all, the president was a Republican, and Congress was, until late in 2006, controlled by Republicans, and Republicans got the war in Iraq they claimed was the key to defeating terrorism. Thus, if terrorism were a growing menace, it would be the Republicans' fault. "We're more vulnerable to terrorists than ever," wrote *New York Times* columnist Maureen Dowd in July 2007. After all the president's "dead or alive" bluster, "we may be the ones who end up dead."

Dowd's colleague at the *Times*, Frank Rich, warned in February 2007, that the situation had become so dire that experts were going public in a desperate bid to get the attention of a White House that didn't want to listen. "Michael Scheuer, the former head of the CIA bin Laden unit, told MSNBC's Keith Olbermann last week that the Taliban and al-Qaeda, having regrouped in Afghanistan and Pakistan, 'are going to detonate a nuclear device inside the United States,'" Rich wrote. But Michael Scheuer, far from being a secretive expert reluctantly stepping out of the shadows, is the author of several polemical books and a frequent media commentator. And his statement was merely a passing comment tossed into the end of the interview. "We don't treat the – this Islamist enemy as seriously as we should," Scheuer had said. "We think that we're going to arrest them, one man at a time. These people are going to detonate a nuclear device inside the United States, and we're going to have absolutely nothing to respond against. It's going to be a unique situation for a great power, and we're going to have no one to blame but ourselves." The show's host then thanked Scheuer and that was the end of it. Scheuer presented no evidence to support his brief comment, and yet Rich presented the comment as credible evidence of a horrific threat – with nothing but the fact that Scheuer once worked at the CIA to support it. The irony is that in 2002 and 2003, when the administration was making the case that Saddam Hussein had weapons of mass destruction that posed a serious threat to the United States – with evidence provided by the CIA – Frank Rich rigorously examined that evidence, found it lacking, and denounced what he felt was a ruthless attempt to scare the public into supporting the invasion. But in 2007, the politics had changed and so had Rich's standards about what constituted reliable proof.

Still, however important these factors may be, they lay at the surface. It is underneath, moving like tectonic plates, that we find the real force driving the media's hyperbolic coverage of terrorism.

People were afraid. Their intuitive minds told them to be afraid, the Bush administration told them to be afraid, and being afraid, they wanted to know more. Reporters, editors, and producers shared these feelings. After all, they lived in the same communities as everyone else, listened to the same presidential statements, and processed it all with the same intuitive minds. And so, in living rooms and news-rooms alike, there was virtual unanimity that terrorism was a grave and growing menace.

With that belief in place, confirmation bias kicked in. Information that contradicted what everyone believed – attack statistics, mortality odds, risk comparisons, the failures of Aum Shinrikyo, the spectacu-lar plots that turned out to be much less than they appeared – got little or no attention. But reporters seized on absolutely anything that confirmed what everyone believed and fed it into the media machine – which then poured out vast volumes of biased information.

Inevitably, this strengthened the popular perception of terrorism. A mammoth feedback loop was created. To the media, actual attacks and foiled plots – of any scale or sophistication – proved that terror-ism was a grave and growing menace. So did the absence of attacks and plots. Even imaginary attacks would do. What was never consid-ered was the possibility that terrorism is *not* a grave or growing threat.

It was a grand and disturbing demonstration of the profound influence confirmation bias can have on human affairs.

With the news media, politicians, and the public locked in a feedback loop that steadily amplified the fear, the entertainment media added their contribution. It is hard to imagine a threat better suited to drama than terrorism, and for that reason it has been used in novels, movies, and TV shows for decades. Post–9/11, with fears of terrorism soaring, the image of outnumbered government agents struggling mightily to stop scowling plotters from nuking Los Angeles – most notably on the popular television show 24 – became a dramatic staple.

The most disturbing aspect of much of this entertainment was the deliberate blurring of the line between fiction and reality. "Five years ago, Sept. 11 was seared into America's memory," begins a fairly typical commercial for the Showtime series *Sleeper Cell: American Terror*. The speaker is the real President Bush delivering a speech marking the anniversary of 9/11. "Today we are safer," he says, "but we are not yet safe." Ominous drums pound. Images of flags and cities appear and go black. Then comes a furious burst of images and sounds – a man firing a gun, someone being tortured, another urgently whispering, "A nuclear attack. . . ." And finally a warning flashes on-screen: "The next attack could be anywhere."

Everything we know about risk perception suggests this stuff is poisonous to both Head and Gut. For Head, there is factual misinformation. The Centers for Disease Control actually felt compelled to issue a fact sheet explaining that smallpox isn't nearly as communicable, uncontrollable, or deadly as it was portrayed in made-for-TV movies. For Gut, there is a barrage of violent images and potent emotions that can drive its intuitive judgments. As we saw earlier, people's perceptions of the risks posed by climate change were significantly boosted by watching *The Day After Tomorrow*. If an implausible movie about a relatively abstract threat can do that, it's reasonable to assume that gritty, pulse-quickening stories about a far more visceral and emotional threat can do much more.

What's the average American to make of all this? She starts with the strong feeling that terrorism is a serious threat because that's what the memories and feelings of 9/11 lead her Gut to conclude. This sense is repeatedly confirmed by the statements of the administration and the rest of the political establishment. It's also strengthened every day by government agencies, police departments, security experts, security companies, NGOs, the media, pundits, and the entertainment industry. And this average American is surrounded by others who have the same memories and feelings, who get the same information from the government and the media, and who agree that the threat of terrorism is high. In the face of such a consensus, it's only natural to go with the group, particularly because, as we have seen, our tendency to conform to the group's opinion rises as the issue becomes more important – and this is about as important as issues come.

Strongly believing the threat of terrorism to be high, the average American then becomes subject to confirmation bias, latching on to whatever information she comes across that seems to support her belief while ignoring or dismissing whatever does not. In effect, she filters information through a screen of bias – information that has already been filtered the same way by the media and others. The result is bias squared.

It's perfectly understandable, then, that Americans' fear of terrorism actually rose during four years in which there were no terrorist attacks, or that almost one-half of Americans are worried that they or their families could be killed by terrorists. It's hard to imagine a more powerful array of factors pressing on the unconscious mind. And the influence of Gut on our conscious judgments should never be underestimated, not even when those making the judgment have spent their lives rationally analyzing information. In July 2007, Homeland Security director Michael Chertoff told the *Chicago Tribune* that he had a "gut feeling that we are in a period of vulnerability." George Tenet, the former director of the CIA, used almost exactly the same phrase in his 2007 memoirs. "I do not know why attacks didn't occur" in the years after 9/11, he wrote. "But I do know one thing in my gut: al-Qai'ida is here and waiting."

And that's just what terrorists want the gut of George Tenet and every other American to think. "America is full of fear from its north to its south, from its west to its east," Osama bin Laden said in a 2004 video. "Thank God for that."

"Terrorism," writes Brian Michael Jenkins, "is actual or threatened violence calculated to create an atmosphere of fear and alarm, which will in turn cause people to exaggerate the strength of the terrorists and the threat they pose." Terrorists are not formidable foes. If they were, they would fight using other means. It is precisely their weakness that leads them to carry out the slaughter of innocents – the one form of attack available to even the feeblest combatant. In itself, such slaughter is unlikely to deliver a serious blow to the enemy. But it does generate fear, and fear can inspire reactions that terrorists hope will advance their cause.

Louise Richardson notes that terrorists always have two sets of goals, one political, the other tactical and immediate. They almost never achieve their political goals. But they often manage to advance their tactical goals and "it is this success that appeals to disaffected youths seeking a means of rapid redress." These tactical goals can be summed up in three words: revenge, renown, and reaction.

Revenge is the only one of the three goals that the terrorists can deliver for themselves. The enemy wronged them – as they see it – so they kill the enemy's people as retribution.

"Renown" refers to the terrorists' image among potential sympathizers. They want to be seen as a major force – an army of honourable soldiers – with a realistic chance of hurting and defeating the enemy. They can do this in part by executing bold attacks – the "propaganda of the deed," as terrorism was called by 19th century anarchists. But that only goes so far. How damaging are the attacks? How powerful are the terrorists? Is the enemy seriously threatened? The terrorists don't get to answer these questions. Enemy governments and media do, and so renown depends mainly on how they describe the threat.

"Reaction" is entirely up to the enemy, of course, and terrorists' plans often hinge on it. A common hope is that terrorist attacks will provoke a violent overreaction. In the 1970s, Germany's Red Brigades thought West Germany was a fascist state that disguised its true character behind a veil of democracy and consumerism. Terrorism, they hoped, would cause the government to tear off the veil and resort to its "true" character, which would push the non-violent left to revolution. From what we can gather, Osama bin Laden seems to have anticipated that the 9/11 attacks would either lead to an American withdrawal from the Muslim world or an American invasion. For bin Laden, either result was desirable. If the United States abandoned the Middle East, the secular dictatorships supported by the White House – which were always bin Laden's chief object of hatred – would be fatally weakened. If, however, the United States invaded the Muslim world, it would confirm bin Laden's claim that the Islamic world was under attack by "the Jews and Crusaders" and bring recruits to the banner of jihad.

Seen from this perspective, the Bush administration's response to 9/11 was emotionally satisfying but utterly wrongheaded. Define the attacks as war and the terrorists become soldiers and their organization an army. Define the war as a cataclysmic fight to the death – nothing less than the Third World War – and you effectively declare to the world that al-Qaeda is so powerful it could conceivably defeat the United States of America. Insisting that America would not be defeated – as Bush did over and over throughout his presidency – did not erase this implication. It entrenched it.

This was the greatest gift Osama bin Laden has ever received. Before Bush gave it to him, he was an outlaw forced to shift his band of followers from country to country until they wound up in the deserts of Afghanistan. He grandiosely "declared war" on the United States and was ignored. He bombed American embassies in East

Africa and attacked an American ship on the Arabian coast and his profile rose a little but he still had nothing like the renown he needed to become the voice of fanatical Muslims who wished to sweep away their corrupt governments and create a new caliphate. He got that when Bush declared him an existential threat to the United States. "To be elevated to the status of public enemy number one is just what a terrorist group wants," wrote Richardson. "It gives the group stature among its potential recruits, which in turn wins it more followers. Declaring war on terrorists, in effect, hands it the renown it seeks." Osama bin Laden clearly understands this and revels in his status as the great enemy of the United States. "It is easy for us to provoke and bait," bin Laden gloated in a 2004 videotape. "All that we have to do is to send two mujahedeen . . . to raise a piece of cloth on which is written al-Qaeda in order to make the generals race there. . . ."

The framing of the attack as global war also ensured bin Laden would get the reaction he sought. The invasion of Afghanistan was supported worldwide, and if the administration had stopped there bin Laden would have been disappointed. But a modest intervention in a backwater like Afghanistan hardly seemed fitting for the Third World War. And so it was on to Iraq – an invasion that seemed to confirm the Islamists' portrayal of America as a crusader nation bent on destroying Islam. In the 1970s, the West German government refused to be goaded into overreacting by the Red Brigades; George W. Bush delivered over-reaction on a scale that is the stuff of terrorist fantasies.

"By declaring a war on terror," concluded Richardson, "far from denying [al-Qaeda] its objectives, we are conceding its objectives, and this is why the war on terror can never be won."

"Fear is the biggest danger we face," wrote Brian Michael Jenkins. Many of those who hype the threat of terrorism would agree with this point, knowing that fear can be corrosive and prompts us to react in destructive ways. But they take fear and fearful reactions as something terrorism inevitably elicits, as if we have no control over our responses. That assumption is what lies behind the remark of General

Richard Myers, the former chairman of the joint chiefs of staff, that a terrorist attack that killed 10,000 people would "do away with our way of life." Why? Four times as many Americans are killed in car crashes every year but no one worries that car crashes are a threat to the American way of life. What the general meant, of course, is that a terrorist attack of that magnitude would so terrify Americans that they would demand a police state in response. The terrorists wouldn't destroy America; the terror would.

To some extent, it's true that terrorism generates disproportionate fear and there's nothing that can be done about that beyond stopping attacks in the first place. Terrorism is vivid, violent, unjust, and potentially catastrophic. It presses all Gut's buttons. It is inevitable that we will feel it is a bigger threat than a Head–based analysis would conclude. But people are not slaves of their unconscious minds. They also have conscious minds that can overrule or at least modify their feelings. If, after the September 11 attacks, President Bush had loudly and repeatedly insisted that flying is safer than driving, even factoring in the risk of terrorism, and underscored the point by getting on a commercial jet himself, it probably wouldn't have convinced everyone to ignore their jitters and return to the airports. But it would have got the media talking about risk and statistics, and a significant proportion of those who had switched from flying to driving would have realized it was foolish to do so and switched back. Lives would have been saved.

In fighting terrorism, we have to recognize that terrorism is a psychological tactic. Terrorists seek to terrify. Controlling fear should play as large a role in the struggle against terrorists as do the prevention of attacks and the arrest of plotters. We must, as Brian Michael Jenkins put it, "attack the terror, not just the terrorists."

Attacking the terror means, first, avoiding statements that paint the threat as something greater than it is. In 2006, when German police stopped a plot to bomb two trains, former Bush speechwriter David Frum wrote a newspaper column that began with an arresting sentence. "Attention nervous flyers: don't think you can escape the terrorists by taking the train." This effectively says the risk of being killed by terrorists while travelling by plane or train is significant. That's not remotely true, but it is something terrorists would very much like us to believe.

Attacking the terror also means putting the risk of terrorism in perspective by supplying the statistics that politicians and the media have ignored. And it would mean dropping the talk of fighting a Third World War. Nazi Germany came terrifyingly close to perma-nently conquering much of the civilized world, wiping out whole peoples, and developing the first nuclear weapons. The Soviet Union, even in 1989, had six million soldiers equipped with vast quantities of tanks, jets, ships, and more than enough strategic nuclear weapons to reduce every major city in the United States and Europe to smoke and cinders in under half an hour. At its peak, al-Qaeda was a band of fanatics in possession of small arms and a network of camps in the Afghan desert. Today, they're just a band of fanatics in possession of small arms – and they should be discussed as such.

The same approach should be taken with weapons of mass destruction and worst-case scenarios, particularly a nuclear terrorist attack. We should certainly not dismiss dangers because they are improbable, but neither should we ignore their improbability – or the ability of modern countries to endure them and come out stronger than before.

There is a model for how a democratic government should talk about terrorism if it seeks to "attack the terror, not just the terrorists." Oddly enough, it was provided by Tony Blair. After years of repeating the hyperbolic rhetoric of the Bush administration's "war on terror-ism," Blair faced his own crisis on the morning of July 7, 2005, when the G8 summit he was hosting was interrupted by news that suicide bombers had struck London's subway trains and a bus, killing 56 people. Blair was steady and stoical. "It is through terrorism that the people who committed this terrible act express their values and it is right at this moment that we demonstrate ours," he said. "They are trying to use the slaughter of innocent people to cow us, to frighten us out of doing the things that we want to do, of trying to stop us going about our business as normal, as we are entitled to do. They should not and must not succeed."

"Far from elevating the rhetoric and engaging in the language of warfare or revenge," notes Louise Richardson, Blair "spoke calmly of crime scenes and police work and of Britain's quiet determination to defend its values and way of life." Ken Livingstone, the mayor of London, struck the same note in the dark hours after the attacks. "They seek to turn Londoners against each other," he said. "London will not be divided by this." The next day, Livingstone advised "those who planned this dreadful attack, whether they are still here in hiding or somewhere abroad, [to] watch next week as we bury our dead and mourn them, but see also in those same days new people coming to this city to make it their home, to call themselves Londoners, and doing it because of that freedom to be themselves." Livingstone also announced he would take the subway to work, as always. And he did.

"London is not a battlefield," declared Sir Ken Macdonald, the United Kingdom's director of prosecutions, in a January 2007 speech. "Those innocents who were murdered on July 7, 2005, were not victims of war. And the men who killed them were not, as in their vanity they claimed in their ludicrous videos, 'soldiers.' They were deluded, narcissistic inadequates. They were criminals. They were fantasists. We need to be very clear about this." That perspective is crucial, Macdonald warned, because terrorists aim to portray them-selves as a greater threat than they are and "tempt us to abandon our values. . . . We must protect ourselves from these atrocious crimes without abandoning our traditions of freedom."

How we talk about terrorism is, of course, just the beginning of a response. Governments also have to act. And actions are measured in dollars and cents.

Between 1995 and 2001, counter-terrorism spending by the U.S. federal government rose 60 per cent. Between 2001 (prior to the 9/11 attacks) and 2007, it rose another 150 per cent to $58.3 billion. These figures are for homeland security (defined as "a concerted national effort to prevent terrorist attacks within the United States, reduce America's vulnerability to terrorism and minimize the damage and recover from attacks that do occur"). They don't include military operations in Afghanistan or Iraq. If Iraq were included under the rubric of "fighting terrorism" – as the White House has always insisted it should be – total counter-terrorist spending would soar. Estimates of the anticipated total cost of the Iraq war alone fall between $500 billion and $2 trillion.

There are also hidden costs. For example, security screening added since 9/11 has slowed passage through airports, border crossings, and ports, and anything that hinders the transfer of people, goods, and service hurts economies. Roger Congleton, an economist at George Mason University, has calculated that an extra half-hour delay at American airports costs the economy $15 billion a year.

Costs are not limited to the United States, of course. The 9/11 attacks shook up priorities across the developed world. So did pressure applied by the American government – changes in American port security standards, for example, effectively became international standards because ships coming from ports that didn't meet the standards were barred from American ports. Globally, the hidden costs of counter-terrorism efforts are unknown but undoubtedly immense, while direct spending on counter-terrorism also surged to substantial levels in the post-9/11 era. "We have had a huge influx of resources in the last five years," the national security adviser to Canadian prime minister Stephen Harper told a Senate committee in 2006. "We probably have as much as we are able to absorb in the short term."

So how much is the developed world spending to reduce the risk of terrorism? No one can be sure but the direct costs alone may top

$100 billion a year, with a total bill considerably greater than that.

Does this make sense? Is this spending in proportion with the gravity of the terrorist threat? The only way to rationally answer that question is with a "cost–benefit analysis" – which simply means checking whether the benefits of a policy outweigh its costs, and giving priority to those measures that have the highest benefit-to-cost ratio. That sounds cold and technical, particularly when lives are at stake. But there's a finite amount of money and an infinite number of threats to human life: To ensure money is doing the greatest good possible, cost–benefit analysis is essential.

Unfortunately, terrorism spending has never been subjected to a cost–benefit analysis and we can only imagine what the results of such an analysis would look like. The risk of terrorism is certainly real. And while the risk of catastrophic terrorism is much lower than it is commonly portrayed, it, too, is real. We can also safely assume that if governments did nothing to fight terrorism, there would be a lot more terrorism and a lot more lives lost. So there's no question that substantial spending would be justified under a cost–benefit analysis. But it's much harder to believe that the *scale* of current spending would stand up.

Within the United States alone, there's a long list of comparisons that could be made. Here's one: Roughly 14 per cent of Americans do not have health insurance. That's 41 million people. Nine per cent of American kids – 6.5 million – have no insurance. In 2004, the Institute of Medicine – one of the National Academies of Science – issued a report that found the lack of health insurance "causes 18,000 unnecessary deaths every year in the United States." That's six 9/11s. As for the monetary costs, a committee of the Institute of Medicine concluded that the lack of health insurance costs the United States between $60 billion and $130 billion annually.

Here's another comparison: According to the Centers for Disease Control and Prevention, "hundreds of thousands" of deaths happen in the United States each year because "fewer than half of all Americans receive some of the most valuable preventive health services available."

The costs of extending health insurance to all Americans, and expanding access to prevention services, vary widely depending on the complex details involved. It would certainly be very expensive – a cost measured in the tens of billions of dollars annually. But given the number of lives that could be saved and the economic costs that could be recouped, it's probably safe to assume that either of these policies would do much better in a cost–benefit analysis than counter-terrorism. And yet neither Republicans nor Democrats have dared to compare the value of expanded health insurance or more prevention services with that of counter–terrorism spending – and they keep losing out. In the administration's 2008 budget, which again boosted counter–terrorism spending, the budget of the CDC was cut – forcing the agency to scrap a $100-million preventive health program.

Globally, there's an even longer list of comparisons that cast doubt on the wisdom of current counter–terrorism spending. Measles kills almost 300,000 children a year even though the measles vaccine costs 16 cents a dose. More than 1.6 million children are killed by easily treatable and preventable diarrhea. In 1988, polio was paralyzing 1,000 children a day but a $3-billion campaign pushed the virus to the brink of extinction by 2003 – when the money ran out and polio surged back to life in 27 countries.

In 2004, Danish political scientist Bjorn Lomborg brought together an array of experts from all over the world to discuss which of the world's many woes could be tackled most cost–effectively. Terrorism wasn't examined, unfortunately, but many other major issues were and a ranked list of priorities was produced. At the top came controlling HIV/AIDS. "At a cost of $27 billion, around 28 million cases of the illness could be prevented by 2010," Lomborg wrote in *How to Spend $50 Billion to Make the World a Better Place*. "The benefit–cost figure is predicted to be 40 times that figure."

Malaria also ranked highly in the Copenhagen Consensus. The disease kills roughly one million people a year, most of them African children, and drains $12 billion a year from African economies. Jeffrey Sachs, a renowned economist and development guru, estimates malaria could be controlled at a cost of between $2 billion and $3 billion a year, so here is a case where millions of lives could be saved and billions of dollars saved for an annual cost equivalent to about 5 per cent of the money the United States budgeted for counter-terrorism in 2007. But the money's not there. The UN spent just $220 million for malaria in Africa in 2007, while the World Bank has promised between $500 million and $1 billion over five years. In 2005, President Bush was applauded for creating the "President's Malaria Initiative" but it provides only $240 million a year for five years. And so malaria will likely continue to kill 67 times more people *each year* than the almost 15,000 killed by international terrorism over the last four decades.

None of this makes sense. It is all the product of the "unreasoning fear" that Franklin Roosevelt warned against in 1933, at a time when the economic order was collapsing, and the political order looked set to go along with it. Fascism and communism were ascendant and the shadow of war grew. It was a time so much bleaker than our own, and yet Roosevelt was calm. "This great Nation will endure as it has endured, will revive and will prosper," he said in his inaugural address – if we do not allow our thoughts and actions to be guided by "nameless, unreasoning, unjustified fear."

By word and deed, Roosevelt steadied the United States and led it away from destructive fear. He left the country stronger and more confident. By word and deed, Roosevelt's successor in the Oval Office did the opposite and he will leave the nation weakened and afraid.

12

CONCLUSION:
THERE'S NEVER BEEN A BETTER TIME TO BE ALIVE

In central Ontario, near where my parents live, there is a tiny cemetery filled with rusted ironwork and headstones heaved to odd angles by decades of winter frost and spring thaws. This was farm country once. Pioneers arrived at the end of the 19th century, cut the trees, pulled up the stumps, and discovered, after so much crushing labour, that their new fields amounted to little more than a thin layer of soil stretched across the bare granite of the Canadian Shield. Most farms lasted a generation or two before the fields were surrendered to the forests. Today, only the cemeteries remain.

The pioneers were not wealthy people but they always bought the biggest headstones they could afford. They wanted something that declared who they were, something that would last. They knew how easily their own existence could end. Headstones had to endure. "Children of James and Janey Morden," announces one obelisk in the cemetery. It's almost six feet tall. The stone says the first to die was Charles W. Morden. He was four years and nine months old.

It was the winter of 1902. The little boy would have complained that he had a sore throat. He was tired and his forehead felt a little warm to his mother's hand. A day or two passed and as Charles lay in bed he grew pale. His heart raced. His skin burned and he started to vomit. His throat swelled so that each breath was a struggle and his head was immobilized on the sweat-soaked pillow. His mother, Janey, would have known what was torturing her little boy but with no treatment she likely wouldn't have dared speak its name.

Then Charles's little brother, Earl, started to cry. His throat was sore, he moaned. And he was so hot. Albert, the oldest of the boys, said he, too, was tired. And yes, his throat hurt.

Charles W. Morden died on Tuesday, January 14, 1902. His father would have had to wrap the little boy's body in a blanket and carry him out through the deepening snow to the barn. The cold would seep into the corpse and freeze it solid until spring, when rising temperatures would thaw the ground and the father could dig his son's grave.

The next day, both Earl and Albert died. Earl was two years and ten months old. Albert was six years and four months. Their father would have gotten out two more blankets, wrapped his sons, and taken them out to the barn to freeze.

Then the girls started to get sick. On January 18, 1902, the eldest died. Minnie Morden was ten years old. Her seven-year-old sister, Ellamanda, died the same day.

On Sunday, January 19, 1902, the fever took little Dorcas, barely 18 months old. For the final time, James Morden bundled a child in a blanket, walked through the snow, and laid her down in the cold and dark of the barn, where she and her brothers and sisters would wait through the long winter to be buried.

The same fever that swept away the Morden children in the winter of 1902 leapt from homestead to homestead – the obelisk next to the Mordens' is dedicated to the two children Elias and Laura Ashton lost within weeks of their neighbours'. The Ashtons already knew what it felt like to lose children. Their 15-year-old son had died in 1900, and a five-year-old boy had been taken from them eight years before that.

It's hard to find a family that did *not* suffer losses like these in generations past. Cotton Mather, the Puritan minister in late 17th-century New England, named one of his daughters Abigail. She died. So he gave the same name to the next daughter to be born. She too died. So he named a third daughter Abigail. She survived to adulthood but died giving birth. In all, Cotton Mather – a well-to-do man in a prosperous society – lost 13 children to worms, diarrhea, measles, smallpox, accidents, and other causes. "A dead child is a sign no more surprising than a broken pitcher or blasted flower," he said in a sermon, and yet, familiar as it was, death never lost its power to make the living suffer. "The dying of a child is like the tearing of a limb from us," wrote Increase Mather, Cotton's father.

Children were especially vulnerable, but not uniquely so. The plague that swept through the homes of the Mordens and Ashtons and so many others is typical in this regard. It was diphtheria, a disease that is particularly deadly to children but can also kill adults. In 1878, the four-year-old granddaughter of Queen Victoria contracted diphtheria and passed it on to her mother, the queen's daughter. Queen Victoria was wealthy and powerful beyond compare and yet she could do nothing. Both daughter and granddaughter died.

That world is not ours. We still know tragedy and sorrow, of course, but in neither the quantity nor the quality of those who came before us. A century ago, most people would have recognized the disease afflicting Charles Morden (the enlarged neck was particularly notorious). Today, we may have heard the word "diphtheria" once or twice – it comes up when we take our babies into the doctor's office to get their shots – but few of us know anything about it. Why would we? A vaccine created in 1923 all but eradicated the disease across the developed world and drastically reduced its toll elsewhere.

The triumph over diphtheria is only one of a long line of victories that created the world we live in. Some are dramatic – the extinction of smallpox is a greater monument to civilization than the construction of the pyramids. Others are considerably less exciting –

fortifying foods with vitamins may lack glamour but it eliminated diseases, made children stronger, and contributed greatly to increased lifespans. And some are downright distasteful to talk about – we wrinkle our noses at the mere mention of human waste but the development of sewage disposal systems may have saved more lives than any other invention in history.

In 1725, the average baby born in what was to become the United States had a life expectancy of 50 years. The American colonies were blessed with land and resources and American longevity was actually quite high relative to England – where it was a miserable 32 years – and most other places and times. And it was creeping up. By 1800, it had reached 56 years. But then it slipped back, thanks in part to the growth in urban slums. By 1850, it was a mere 43 years. Once again, however, it started inching up. In 1900, it stood at 48 years.

This is the story of life expectancy throughout human history: A little growth is followed by a little decline and the centuries roll on without much progress.

But then everything changed. By 1950, American life expectancy had soared to 68. And by the end of the 20th century, it stood at 78 years. The news was as good or better in other developed countries, where life expectancy approached or exceeded 80 years at the turn of the century. In the second half of the century, similarly dramatic gains were seen throughout most of the developing world.

The biggest factor in this spectacular change was the decline in deaths among children. In 1900, almost 20 per cent of all children born in the United States – one in five – died before they were five years old; by 1960, that had fallen to 3 per cent; by 2002, it was 0.8 per cent. There have been huge improvements in the developing world, too. Fifty years ago in Latin America, more than 15 per cent of all children died before their fifth birthday; today, that figure is roughly 2 per cent. Between 1990 and 2006 alone, the child mortality rate fell 47 per cent in China and 34 per cent in India.

It is in our nature to become habituated to changes in our environment and so we think it is perfectly commonplace for the average person to be hail and hearty for more than seven or eight decades and that a baby born today will live an even healthier and longer life. But if we raise our eyes from this moment and look to the history of our species, it is clear this is not commonplace. It is a miracle.

And the miracle continues to unfold. "There are some people, including me, who believe that the increase in life expectancy in the coming century will be about as large as it was in the past century," says Robert Fogel, the economic historian and Nobel laureate who has spent decades studying health, mortality, and longevity. If Fogel is right, the change will be even more dramatic than it sounds. That's because massive reductions in child mortality – the largest source of 20th-century gains – are no longer possible simply because child mortality has already been driven so low. So for equivalent improvements in lifespan to be made in the 21st century, there will have be huge declines in adult mortality. And Fogel feels there will be. "I believe that college–age students today, half of them will live to be 100."

Other researchers are not so bullish, but there is a consensus that the progress of the 20th century will continue in the 21st. A 2006 World Health Organization study of global health trends to 2030 concluded that in each of three different scenarios – baseline, optimistic, and pessimistic – child mortality will fall and life expectancy will rise in every region of the world.

There are clouds on humanity's horizons, of course. If, for example, obesity turns out to be as damaging as many researchers believe it to be, and if obesity rates keep rising in rich countries, it could undermine a great deal of progress. But potential problems like this have to be kept in perspective. "You can only start worrying about over-eating when you stop worrying about under-eating, and for most of our history we worried about under-eating," Fogel wryly observes. Whatever challenges we face, it remains indisputably true that those living in the developed world are the safest, healthiest, and richest humans who ever lived. We are still mortal and there are many things that can kill us. Sometimes we should worry. Sometimes we should even be afraid. But always we should remember how very lucky we are to be alive *now*.

In an interview for a PBS documentary, Linda Birnbaum, a leading research scientist with the U.S. Environmental Protection Agency, struck exactly the right balance between taking potential threats seriously and keeping those threats in perspective. "I think as parents, we all worry about our children," said Birnbaum, who, at the time, led a team investigating the hypothesis that endocrine disruptor chemicals in the environment were taking a hidden toll on human health. "But I think that we have to look at the world our children are living in and realize that they have tremendous access to food, to education, to all the necessities of life plus much more. That their lifespan is likely to be greater than ours is, which is certainly greater than our parents' was and much greater than our grandparents or great-grandparents."

Anyone who has spent an afternoon in a Victorian cemetery knows that gratitude, not fear, should be the defining feeling of our age. And yet it is fear that defines us. We worry. We cringe. It seems the less we have to fear, the more we fear.

One obvious source of this paradox is simple ignorance. "Most people don't know the history," says Fogel. "They just know their own experience and what's happening around them. So they take all of the great advances for granted."

But there's much more to the explanation of why history's safest humans are increasingly hiding under their beds. There's the omnipresent marketing of fear, for one. Politicians, corporations, activists, and non-governmental organizations want votes, sales, donations, support, and memberships and they know that making people worry about injury, disease, and death is often the most effective way of obtaining their goals. And so we are bombarded daily with messages carefully crafted to make us worry. Whether that worry is reasonable or not – whether it is based on due consideration of accurate and complete facts – is not a central concern of those pumping out the messages. What matters is the goal. Fear is merely a tactic. And if twisted numbers, misleading language, emotional images, and unreasonable conclusions can more effectively deliver that goal – and they often can – so be it.

The media are among those that profit by marketing fear – nothing gives a boost to circulation and ratings like a good panic – but the media also promote unreasonable fears for subtler and more compelling reasons. The most profound is the simple human love of stories and storytelling. For the media, the most essential ingredient of a good story is the same as that of a good movie, play, or tale told by the campfire: It has to be about people and emotions, not numbers and reason. Thus the particularly tragic death of a single child will be reported around the world while a massive and continuing decline in child mortality rates is hardly noticed.

This isn't a failing of the media so much as it is a reflection of the hard-wiring of a human brain that was shaped by environments that bore little resemblance to the world we inhabit. We listen to iPods, read the newspaper, watch television, work on computers, and fly around the world using brains beautifully adapted to picking berries and stalking antelope. The wonder is not that we sometimes make mistakes about risks. The wonder is that we sometimes get it right.

So why is it that so many of the safest humans in history are scared of their own shadows? There are three basic components at work: the brain, the media, and the many individuals and organizations with an interest in stoking fears. Wire these three components together in a loop and we have the circuitry of fear. One of the three raises an alarm; the signal is picked up and repeated by the next component and then another; the alarm returns to the original component and a louder alarm goes out. Fear amplifies. Other alarms are raised about other risks, more feedback loops are created, and the "unreasoning fear" Roosevelt warned against becomes a fixture of daily life.

In part, this is an inevitable condition of modernity. Our Stone Age brains can't change, we won't abandon information technology, and the incentives for marketing fear are growing.

But while we may not be able to cut the circuitry of fear, we can at least turn down the volume. The first step is simply recognizing that there are countless individuals and organizations that have their own reasons for inflating risks, and that most journalists not only fail to catch and correct these exaggerations, they add their own. We need to be skeptical, to gather information, to think carefully about it and draw conclusions for ourselves.

We also have to recognize that the brain that is doing this careful thinking is subject to the foibles of psychology. This is actually more difficult than it sounds. Psychologists have found that people not only accept the idea that *other* people's thinking may be biased, they tend to overestimate the extent of that bias. But almost everyone resists the notion that their own thinking may also be biased. One survey of medical residents, for example, found that 61 per cent said they were not influenced by gifts from drug company salespeople but only 16 per cent said the same of other physicians. It's as if each of us recognizes that to err is human, but, happily for us, we are not human.

But even if we accept that we, too, are human, coping with the brain's biases is not easy. Researchers have tried to "debias" thinking by explaining to people what biases are and how they influence us, but that doesn't work. Consider the Anchoring Rule. The reader now knows that when we have to guess a number, we unconsciously grab onto the number we came across most recently and adjust up or down from it. But if I were to mention that Mozart died at the age of 34 and then ask you to guess how many countries have a name beginning with the letter "A," your unconscious mind would still deploy the Anchoring Rule and the number 34 would still influence your guess. Not even a conscious decision to ignore the number 34 will make a difference because the directive to ignore it comes from

Head and Head does not control Gut. We simply cannot switch off the unconscious mind.

What we can do is understand how Gut works and how it sometimes makes mistakes. "People are not accustomed to thinking hard," Daniel Kahneman wrote, "and are often content to trust a plausible judgment that quickly comes to mind." That is the most important change that has to be made. Gut is good, but it's not perfect, and when it gets risk wrong people can come to foolish conclusions such as believing that young women are at serious risk of breast cancer while older women are free and clear, or that abandoning airplanes for cars is a good way to stay safe. To protect ourselves against unreasoning fear, we must wake up Head and tell it do its job. We must learn to *think hard*.

Very often, Head and Gut will agree. When that happens, we can be confident in our judgments. But sometimes Head will say one thing, Gut another. Then there's reason to be cautious. A quick and final judgment isn't necessary to deal with most of the risks we face today so when Head and Gut can't agree, we should hold off. Gather more information. Think some more. And if Head and Gut still don't match up, swallow hard and go with Head.

After the September 11 attacks, millions of Americans did the opposite and chose to abandon planes for cars. This mistake cost the lives of more than 1,500 people. Putting Head before Gut is not easily done, but for the fears it can ease, and the lives it can save, it is worth the effort.

So maybe we really are the safest, healthiest, and wealthiest humans who ever lived. And maybe we can significantly reduce the remaining risks we face simply by eating a sensible diet, exercising, not smoking, and obeying all traffic regulations. And maybe we can expect more of this good fortune to extend into the future if current trends persist.

But, the determined worrier may ask, what if current trends don't persist? What if catastrophe strikes?

Judging by what's on offer in bookstores and newspaper commentary pages, it *will* strike. Energy depletion, climate chaos, and mass starvation are popular themes. So are nuclear terrorism and annihilating plagues. Catastrophist writing is very much in vogue and it can be terribly depressing. "Even after the terrorist attacks of September 11, 2001," wrote James Howard Kunstler, author of *The Long Emergency*, "America is still sleepwalking into the future. We have walked out of our burning house and we are now heading off the edge of a cliff." Perhaps this will be – to use the title of a book by British astronomer and president of the Royal Society Martin Rees – *Our Final Hour*.

Armageddon is in the air. Cormac McCarthy's *The Road* – a novel about a father and son wandering through a future America devastated by an unknown catastrophe – was released in 2006. A year later came Jim Crace's *The Pesthouse*, a novel about two people wandering through a future America slightly less devastated by an unknown catastrophe. When two renowned authors working in isolation come up with near-identical plots, they are tapping into the zeitgeist, and it is grim, indeed.

Even Thomas Friedman – the *New York Times* columnist who made his name as a techno-optimist – occasionally slips into fearful pessimism. In September 2003, Friedman wrote, he took his daughter to college with the sense that "I was dropping my daughter off into a world that was so much more dangerous than the world she was born into. I felt like I could still promise my daughter her bedroom back, but I could not promise her the world, not in the carefree way that I had explored it when I was her age."

Friedman's story neatly captures a common belief. The past wasn't perfect, but at least we knew where we stood. Now when we look into the future, all we see is a black void of uncertainty in which so many ways things could go horribly wrong. This world we live in really is a more dangerous place.

Oddly, though, when we look into the past that we think was not so frightening, we find a lot of people who felt about their time as we do about ours. It "was like the end of the world," wrote the German poet Heinrich Heine in 1832. Heine was in Paris and cholera was sweeping across France. In a matter of hours, perfectly healthy people would collapse, shrivel like raisins in the sun, and die. Refugees fled their homes only to be attacked by terrified strangers desperate to keep the plague away. Cholera was new to Europe and no one knew how it was spread or how to treat the victims. The terror they felt as it swept the land is unimaginable. Literally so: We know, looking back, that this was not the end of the world – when we imagine 19th-century Paris, we tend to think of the Moulin Rouge, not plague – and that knowledge removes the uncertainty that was the defining feature of the experience for Heine and the others who lived through it.

Simply put, history is an optical illusion: The past always appears more certain than it was, and that makes the future feel more uncertain – and therefore frightening – than ever. The roots of this illusion lie in what psychologists call "hindsight bias."

In a classic series of studies in the early 1970s, Baruch Fischhoff gave Israeli university students detailed descriptions of events leading up to an 1814 war between Great Britain and the Gurkas of Nepal. The description also included military factors that weighed on the outcome of the conflict, such as the small number of Gurka soldiers and the rough terrain the British weren't used to. One thing missing was the war's outcome. Instead, one group of students was told there were four possible results – British victory, Gurka victory, stalemate with no peace settlement, and stalemate with settlement. Now, they were asked, how likely was it that the war would end in each of these outcomes?

A second group of students was divided into four sections. Each section was given the same list of four outcomes. But the first section was told that the war actually did end in a British victory (which it did, incidentally). The second section was told it concluded in a Gurka victory. The third section was told it ended in a stalemate with no settlement, and the fourth was told it was a stalemate with a settlement. Now, they were asked, how likely were each of the four outcomes?

Knowing what happened – or at least believing you know – changed everything. Students who weren't told how the war ended gave an average rating of 33.8 per cent to the probability of a British victory. Among students who were told the war ended in a British victory, the chance of that happening was judged to be 57.2 per cent. So knowing how the war ended caused people's estimate of the probability to jump from one-third to better than one-half.

Fischhoff ran three other versions of the experiment and consistently got the same results. Then he did the whole thing over again, but with one change: Those who were told the war's outcome were also asked not to let their knowledge of the outcome influence their judgment. It still did.

Fischhoff came up with an ingenious twist on his research in 1972, after Richard Nixon announced he would make a historic trip to China and the U.S.S.R. Prior to the trip, students were told that certain things could happen during Nixon's travels: He may meet personally with Mao; he may visit Lenin's tomb; and so on. They were asked how likely each of those events was. Fischhoff filed that information away and waited. Months after Nixon's trip, he went back to each student and asked them about each event. Do you think it occurred? And do you recall how likely you thought it was to occur? "Results showed that subjects remembered having given higher probabilities than they actually had to events believed to have occurred," Fischhoff wrote, "and lower probabilities to events that hadn't occurred."

The effect of hindsight bias is to drain the uncertainty out of history. Not only do we know what happened in the past, we feel that what happened was *likely* to happen. What's more, we think it was *predictable*. In fact, we knew it all along.

So here we are, standing in the present, peering into the frighteningly uncertain future and imagining all the awful things that could possibly happen. And when we look back? It looks so much more settled, so much more predictable. It doesn't look anything like *this*. Oh yes, these are very scary times.

This is all an illusion. Consider the daughter that Thomas Friedman dropped off at college in 2003 – into a world "so much more dangerous than the world she was born into." That daughter was born in 1985. Was the world of 2003 "so much more dangerous" than the world of 1985? Thanks to the foibles of the human mind, it can easily seem that way.

But in 1985, the Soviet Union and the United States possessed sufficient nuclear weaponry to kill half the human race and reduce the rest to scavengers scuttling amid the ruins. These weapons were pointed at each other. They could be launched at any moment. Annihilation would come with nothing more than a few minutes' notice and, in 1985, it increasingly looked like it would. The Cold War had been getting hotter since the 1979 Soviet invasion of Afghanistan and the 1980 election of Ronald Reagan. Mikhail Gorbachev became leader of the Soviet Union in 1985, and we know now that Gorbachev and Reagan later met and steadily reduced tensions, that the Cold War ended peacefully, and the Soviet Union dissolved within a few years. But in 1985, that was all in the black void of the future. In 1985, what actually happened would have seemed wildly improbable – which is why almost no one predicted anything like it. But nuclear war? That looked terrifyingly likely.

In 1983, *The Day After*, a nightmarish look at life in small town America before and after nuclear attack, became the most talked-about TV drama of the era. In 1984, no fewer than seven novels featuring nuclear war were published. The fear was real and intense. It filled the streets of Europe and America with millions of protestors and countless heads with nightmares. "Suppose I survive," wrote British novelist Martin Amis. "Suppose my eyes aren't pouring down my face, suppose I am untouched by the hurricane of secondary missiles that all mortar, metal, and glass has abruptly become: suppose all this. I shall be obliged (and it's the last thing I feel like doing) to retrace that long

mile home, through the firestorm, the remains of the thousand-mile-
an-hour winds, the warped atoms, the groveling dead. Then – God
willing, if I still have the strength, and, of course, if they are still alive
– I must find my wife and children and I must kill them."

And if global incineration weren't enough to worry about, 1985
also saw explosive awareness about the rapid spread of a deadly new
virus. There was no treatment for AIDS. Get it and you were certain to
die a slow, wasting death. And there was a good chance you would
get it because a breakthrough into the heterosexual population was
inevitable. "AIDS has both sexes running scared," Oprah Winfrey told
her audience in 1987. "Research studies now project that one in five
heterosexuals could be dead from AIDS at the end of the next three
years. That's by 1990. One in five." Surgeon General C. Everett Koop
called it "the biggest threat to health this nation has ever faced." A
member of the president's commission on AIDS went one further,
declaring the disease to be "the greatest threat to society, as we
know it, ever faced by civilization – more serious than the plagues
of past centuries." We know now that it didn't work out that way, but
at the time there were good reasons to think it would. And to be
very, very afraid.

So was the world of 1985 so much safer? Thomas Friedman thought
so in 2003 but I think he was the victim of a cognitive illusion. He knew
the Cold War ended peacefully and AIDS did not sweep through the
United States like the Black Death. That knowledge made those outcomes appear far more likely than they did at the time. And it made
him feel that the Thomas Friedman of 1985 was much more confident
of those outcomes than the Thomas Friedman of 1985 really was.

I don't mean to knock Friedman. The point is simply that even a
renowned commentator on global affairs is vulnerable to this illusion.
And he's not alone. In a 2005 book called *Expert Political Judgment*,
Philip Tetlock, a University of California psychologist, presented the
results of a 20-year project that involved Tetlock tracking the predictions of 284 political scientists, economists, journalists, and others

whose work involved "commenting or offering advice on political or economic trends." In all, Tetlock checked the accuracy of 82,361 predictions and found the experts' record was so poor they would have been beaten by random guesses. Tetlock also found, just as Baruch Fischhoff had earlier, that when experts were asked after the fact to recall their predictions and how confident they were, they remembered themselves being more accurate and more certain than they actually were. (Unlike the Israeli students Fischhoff surveyed, however, experts often got defensive when they were told this.)

I certainly don't want to suggest all scary prognostications are wrong. Horrible things do happen, and it's sometimes possible – very difficult but possible – for smart, informed people to foresee them. Each scary prognostication has to be taken on its merits. But anyone rattled by catastrophist writing should also know that many of the horrible (and wonderful) things that come to pass are not predicted and there is a very long history of smart, informed people foreseeing disasters – they tend to focus on the negative side of things, for some reason – that never come to pass.

In 1967 – a year we remember for the Summer of Love and *Sergeant Pepper's Lonely Hearts Club Band* – Americans got a remarkably precise warning of pending catastrophe. It would strike in 1975, they were told, and the world would never be the same. *Famine – 1975!* by brothers William and Paul Paddock may be thoroughly forgotten today but it was a best-seller in 1967. The brothers had solid credentials. One was an agronomist, the other an experienced foreign service officer. The book is loaded with scientific research, studies, and data from around the world – everything from post-war Mexican wheat production to Russian economic output. And the Paddocks came to a brutal conclusion: As a result of soaring populations, the world was rapidly running out of food. Massive, worldwide starvation was coming and there was nothing anyone could do to stop it. "Catastrophe is foredoomed," they wrote. "The famines are inevitable."

The Paddocks were not cranks. There were countless experts who agreed with them. Harvard biologist George Wald predicted that absent emergency measures "civilization will end within 15 or 30 years." The loudest alarm was raised by Stanford University biologist Paul Ehrlich. "The battle to feed all of humanity is over," Ehrlich wrote in *The Population Bomb*, published in 1968. "In the 1970s and 1980s, hundreds of millions of people will starve to death in spite of any crash programs embarked upon now."

Like the Paddocks, Ehrlich loaded his book with research, studies, and statistics. He also wrote three different scenarios for the unfolding of future events in heavily dramatic style – a technique that would become common in the catastrophist genre and one which, as we have seen, is very likely to trigger the Rule of Typical Things and lead Gut to believe the predicted events are more likely than reason would suggest. "Even with rationing, a lot of Americans are going to starve unless this climate change reverses," a frustrated scientist says to his wife in the first scenario. "We've seen the trends clearly since the early 1970s, but nobody believed it would happen here, even after the 1976 Latin American famine and the Indian Dissolution. Almost a billion human beings starved to death in the last decade, and we managed to keep the lid on by a combination of good luck and brute force." That scenario ends with the United States launching a pre-emptive nuclear strike on the U.S.S.R. In the second scenario, poverty, starvation, and crowded populations allow a virus to emerge from Africa and sweep the world – one-third of the planet's population dies. In the third scenario, the United States realizes the error of its ways and supports the creation of world bodies that tax rich countries to pay for radical population control measures – one billion people still die of starvation in the 1980s but population growth slows and humanity survives. Ehrlich writes that this last scenario is probably far too optimistic because "it involves a maturity of outlook and behavior in the United States that seems unlikely to develop in the near future."

In 1970, Ehrlich celebrated the first Earth Day with an essay that narrowed the range of possibilities considerably: Between 1980 and 1989, roughly four billion people, including 65 million Americans, would starve in what he dubbed the "Great Die-Off."

The Population Bomb was a huge best-seller. Ehrlich became a celebrity, making countless appearances in the media, including *The Tonight Show* with Johnny Carson. Awareness of the threat spread and mass starvation became a standard theme in popular culture. In the 1973 movie *Soylent Green*, the swollen populations of the future are fed rations of a mysterious processed food called "Soylent Green" – and as we learn in the memorable final line, "Soylent Green is people!"

Governments did not embark on the emergency measures to control population advocated by Ehrlich and many others. And yet mass starvation never came, for two reasons. First, fertility rates declined and the population did not grow as rapidly as predicted. Second, food production soared. Many experts had said these outcomes were not only unlikely, they were impossible. But they both happened and 40 years after the publication of *Famine – 1975!*, the world's population was better fed and longer lived than ever.

One would think catastrophists would learn to be humble about their ability to predict the future but there is a noticeable absence of humility in the genre. In 1999, James Howard Kunstler wrote at great length about the disasters – including an economic recession as bad as the Great Depression of the 1930s – that would follow the breakdown of computers afflicted by the Y2K bug. Five years later, he published *The Long Emergency*, which is filled with great certainty about all manner of horrors to come. As for Paul Ehrlich, he has been repeating essentially the same arguments he made in *The Population Bomb* for 40 years. On the dust jacket of *The Upside of Down*, a 2006 book by University of Toronto professor Thomas Homer-Dixon that follows similar themes, there is a blurb from Ehrlich. The book is highly recommended, he writes, for its "insightful ideas about how to make society more resilient in the face of near-inevitable environmental

·and social catastrophes." Apparently the only thing Ehrlich has learned from the past 40 years is to put the word "near" in front of the word "inevitable."

To be fair to Homer–Dixon, his book is nowhere near as alarmist as Ehrlich's writing, or some of the others in the catastrophist genre, although that's how the marketing makes it look. In books, as in so much else, fear sells. Anyone stocking up on canned goods and shotgun shells because they've read some prediction of pending doom should keep that in mind. When Martin Rees wrote a book on threats emerging from scientific advances, he entitled it *Our Final Century?* But Rees's British publishers didn't find that quite frightening enough, so they dropped the question mark. Rees's American publishers still weren't satisfied and they changed "century" to "hour."

In an interview, Rees is much less gloomy than his marketing. He says we should worry more about nuclear weapons than we do and work harder for disarmament; given that these weapons are actually designed to cause catastrophe, it's hard not to agree. But Rees also thinks it important to acknowledge the astonishing bounty science has heaped upon us. "We are safer than ever before," he says. We worry far too much about "very small risks like carcinogens in food, the risk of train accidents and things like that. We are unduly risk averse and public policy is very risk averse for those minor matters."

A balanced perspective is vital, Rees says. There are real threats that should concern us – threats like nuclear weapons – but we also have to appreciate that "for most people in the world, there's never been a better time to be alive."

Proof of this fundamental truth can be found in countless statistics and reports. Or we can simply spend an afternoon reading the monuments to our good fortune erected in every Victorian cemetery.

AFTERWORD

I t's not easily recalled now, but in June 2008 the big news story in the United States was not terrorism, war, or economic crisis. It was tomatoes. Killer tomatoes. Or to be more precise, *potentially* killer tomatoes.

An outbreak of salmonella food poisoning that started in April had spread across most of the U.S. by June, and hundreds of people had taken sick. Tainted tomatoes were suspected. Salmonella can kill, even if it hadn't in this outbreak, so it was a serious concern. Whether it was as serious as journalists and the public believed it to be is another matter.

The media were flooded with stories about the outbreak, and food safety in general, and the public paid close attention. In a survey conducted by the Pew Research Center for the People & the Press, 66 per cent of Americans said they had heard "a lot" about the salmonella outbreak while another 28 per cent said they had heard "a little." A mere 6 per cent said they had heard nothing. Those are impressive numbers. By comparison, only 34 per cent of Americans said they had heard "a lot" about an ominously steep drop in car sales announced by Ford and General Motors.

As it turns out, tomatoes were unjustly accused. In July, the culprit was discovered to be Mexican jalapenos. The outbreak ceased. The Killer Tomato Scare of 2008 was soon forgotten.

There was another risk-related story in June 2008, but this one hasn't been forgotten because it was never noticed in the first place.

"U.S. Deaths Down Sharply in 2006" reads the June 11 press release announcing the latest statistics from the Centers for Disease Control. "The 2006 age-adjusted death rate fell to 776.4 deaths per 100,000 population from 799 deaths per 100,000 in 2005," the release says. "In addition, death rates for eight of the 10 leading causes of death in the United States all dropped significantly in 2006."

Influenza and pneumonia deaths – down 13 per cent. Stroke deaths – down 6 per cent. Heart disease deaths – down 6 per cent. Diabetes deaths – down 5 per cent. AIDS deaths – down 5 per cent. Cancer deaths – down 2 per cent. Even infant mortality was down 3 per cent. In a single year. This was important and wonderful news.

And yet, a scan of the media finds the CDC's good news was essentially ignored by television broadcasters, while newspapers relegated it to a paragraph or two on page A15. It was what we in the trade call filler. Of course, the CDC didn't help matters by writing a press release with all the colour and excitement of an accountant's spreadsheet, but that isn't why this story got so little notice. It was overlooked for reasons found in this book – the same reasons that explain why the relatively minor story of the (potentially) killer tomatoes became such a sensation.

It is inevitable that a book based largely on current events, as this one is, will be overtaken by events to some extent. The best one can hope is that the book illuminates, and is confirmed by, what happens after the final manuscript is handed over. That's certainly what happened with the two big risk stories of June 2008. In fact, I couldn't have asked for a better illustration of what the book is all about.

But the next big risk story – the story that became the monster of 2008 – is something else entirely.

Early on in the writing of this book, I decided there would be nothing about financial risks, only those risks that can sicken, injure, and kill. It's about hits to the head, I told friends, not to the bank account. This was an arbitrary decision, made in order to keep the book from bloating. It had nothing to do with the subject matter. The brain we use to grapple with financial risks is the same brain we use to decide which threats to life and limb are worth worrying about and which we should ignore. The psychology is the same. So is the critical role of the media in our decisions. And it goes without saying that there are plenty of individuals and organizations whose self-interest lies in manipulating the decisions of home buyers, consumers, and investors. From the perspective of risk perception, a risk is a risk, whether it's your skull or your retirement savings that will suffer if you make a mistake.

That decision turned out to be as unfortunate as it was arbitrary because, of course, the great risk-related story of 2008 was all about dollars and cents. The bursting of the U.S. housing bubble was followed by a credit crunch on Wall Street. Pillars of international finance wobbled and fell. Stock markets plummeted worldwide. Every economic indicator turned red, and now, at the time of writing in late 2008, we are mired in an economic crisis that has, in all likelihood, only just begun. And it all started with risk perception.

There are many places and moments we could look at to try to understand what went so catastrophically wrong. One place is San Francisco. One moment is 2005.

Home values were soaring, as they had been for years, in San Francisco and across much of the United States. So economists Robert Shiller and Karl Case decided to survey new home buyers in San Francisco and ask them a question that was on the minds of everyone buying property that year: Will home values continue to rise? If so, by how much?

Laypeople may not explicitly think of these sorts of financial questions as decisions about risk, but that's what they are. Always, in money matters, there is the prospect of gain or loss. Stuff your money under the mattress and you may avoid losing your savings in the collapse of a bank – that's a gain – but you may instead miss out on the interest earned by putting it in the bank. That's a loss. Or your house may go up in flames, along with your mattress and your cash. That's a big loss. There's no escaping it: Every financial decision is a decision about risk.

Those who decided to buy a home in San Francisco in 2005 didn't see much risk in it. What they saw was profit. The homebuyers surveyed by Shiller and Case not only expected home values to continue rising, they expected them to soar: The average expected increase was 14 per cent a year for a decade. "About a third of the respondents reported truly extravagant expectations," Shiller recounts in his book *The Subprime Solution*. Some actually anticipated increases of over 50 per cent a year.

It didn't quite turn out that way. Not long after Shiller and Case conducted their survey, the dizzying rise of American home values stopped, and then, like a rocket that's run out of fuel, prices turned and started falling back to earth. This reversal sparked the credit crisis. The credit crisis shook the stock markets. Then things got really bad. This sequence is important to bear in mind. Although many factors lay behind the economic crisis that got rolling in 2008, it simply would not have happened without the spectacular rise and catastrophic fall in American home values.

Ask most economists about what went wrong with home values and they'll talk about interest rates, sub-prime loans, predatory lending, derivatives and credit swaps, leverage, incentives, and regulations. This is the stuff of conventional economics. It is also the stuff of conventional media coverage and conventional public policies.

But there are dissident economists who think the conventional explanation, although valid in many ways, misses the core component. Robert Shiller is one of them. "The ultimate cause of the global financial crisis," he writes, "is the psychology of the real estate bubble."

More than his impressive title – the "Arthur M. Okin Professor of Economics at Yale University" – Robert Shiller's credibility rests on being right when so many others were wrong. In March 2000, at precisely the moment that Standard and Poor's 500 Index hit what would turn out to be the peak of the tech bubble, Shiller published a book – *Irrational Exuberance* – that argued there was no good reason why stocks had soared. It was a speculative bubble, he wrote, a bubble every bit as irrational and unsustainable as the very first such bubble, the Dutch tulip mania of 1637. Most analysts scoffed. The markets were headed nowhere but up, they said. (Dow 36,000!) Then the bubble burst. Shiller's book became a best-seller.

In a revised edition of *Irrational Exuberance*, released in 2005, Shiller blew the whistle on real estate. It's another bubble, he insisted. Once again, he was widely dismissed, and once again he was proven right in catastrophic fashion.

How did Shiller do it? Nothing fancy. Mostly, he looked at basic facts. A chart of the price–earnings ratio of American stocks since the 19th century showed a line rising rapidly from 1982 to 1996 and then – even though it was already far higher than the historical norm – taking off like a rocket. It wasn't hard to see this was out-of-control speculation that had very little to do with economic fundamentals. The hard part was *not* seeing it.

The same was true of the housing bubble. A chart of American home values from the late 19th century onward showed that, with the exception of a collapse during the Great Depression, they sometimes bobbled up and down but mostly stayed flat until the end of the 1990s. Then they went near-vertical. Lines charting interest rates, building costs, and population growth gave not the slightest explanation for this unprecedented explosion.

In hindsight, these bubbles are embarrassingly obvious. So why, at the time, did so few people see them for what they were?

Conventional economics struggles to answer that question because, as I noted in chapter three, it views humans not as *Homo sapiens* but as *Homo economicus*. This "economic man" is consistently rational. When making decisions, he observes facts and calculates options. He then chooses whichever course of action best advances his self-interest. What *Homo economicus* does not do is buy a house at a grossly inflated price and expect its value to keep rising rapidly.

Conventional economics is also fond of a related idea called "efficient markets theory." This is the notion that markets take all publicly available information into account at all times and so prices are always reasonable and correct. Sometimes prices may look out of line. But that's an illusion. The market is never wrong. Needless to say, the bursting of the housing bubble and subsequent disaster left "efficient markets theory" wobbling like a drunk on a one-legged stool.

It was all too much for conventional economists, including Alan Greenspan, the renowned former chairman of the U.S. Federal Reserve System. "Those of us who have looked to the self-interest of lending institutions to protect shareholders' equity, myself especially, are in a state of shocked disbelief," Greenspan told a Congressional committee in October 2008. Banks aren't run by fools, Greenspan had always believed. They would never lend large amounts of money to large numbers of homebuyers who might be unable to pay it back. And if they did do something so foolish, the sophisticated players of the financial markets would never pay good money for such bad debt. It would be contrary to their self-interest. It would be irrational.

And yet, it happened.

The 2008 meltdown was an I-told-you-so moment for the dissidents. Along with Robert Shiller, they include Dan Ariely, the MIT economist and author of *Predictably Irrational*, Cass Sunstein, the Harvard legal scholar and public policy expert quoted often in this book, and Richard Thaler, the University of Chicago economist. They are among the leading thinkers in the new and burgeoning field of "behavioural economics," which seeks to bring the insights of cognitive and social psychology to economics. That effort begins by correcting a fundamental mistake conventional economics makes – a mistake with enormous consequences. "Why did Mr. Greenspan, along with the rest of the world's regulators, fail to foresee that this could happen?" Sunstein and Thaler wrote in the *Financial Times*. "We think their mistake was to neglect the role of human nature."

People are not the rational actors of conventional economic theory, the behaviouralists say. We are only "boundedly rational" – rational within limits. The fact that we are often rational is the reason why conventional economics often works; the fact that there are limits to our rationality is the reason why conventional economics occasionally falls on its face.

An important example of bounded rationality is "loss aversion." If people were strictly rational, they would consider a gain of $100 to be the same value as a loss of $100. But they don't. As Amos Tversky and Daniel Kahneman showed, people feel much more strongly about avoiding losses than they do about acquiring gains. So a $100 loss counts for much more in their thinking than a $100 gain.

The psychology the behaviouralists bring to economics is not, please note, the "psychology" that's often mentioned by journalists and pundits on days when the markets plummet and Wall Street is said to be in a "panic" – as if wide-eyed traders are leaping around stock exchange floors like gazelles chased by lions. For one thing, extreme emotional states such as panic are rare even at the site of bombings and other catastrophes. In boardrooms and stock market floors, they are essentially non-existent.

More importantly, the fate of markets and economies is not decided on the extraordinary days when stocks soar or collapse and everyone on Wall Street goes home exhausted. After all, the housing bubble took at least half a decade to develop, while the credit crisis played out for more than a year before Wall Street was brought to its knees.

The psychology that matters is something else entirely. It's the psychology that led people to believe housing prices would keep going up and up and it was therefore a good idea to take on new and bigger mortgages and spend home equity on vacations and giant-screen televisions. It's the psychology that led banks to offer mortgages at ever easier terms to people who couldn't possibly repay the money if home values stopped inflating. It's the psychology that led financial markets to think these dangerous debts, packaged and sold as derivatives and other exotic financial instruments, were low risk – were, in fact, such a good investment that it was wise to borrow huge sums to buy them.

It shouldn't be hard for anyone who has read this book to imagine many ways in which the Anchoring Rule, the Rule of Typical Things, and the other cognitive mechanisms of the unconscious mind might have influenced the thought processes that lay behind these conclusions. Consider the Example Rule. Why did American regulators not seriously consider the possibility that there may be a major, nationwide decline in home prices? Such a thing had not happened since the Great Depression, they said; it's so unlikely it's not worth worrying about. But the run-up in prices the country was experiencing had never happened before, so simple logic would suggest this was new territory and regulatory responses should not be dictated by past experience. That's not hard to understand. And yet, regulatory responses *were* dictated by past experiences – as we would expect if the Example Rule were making itself felt in the intuitive judgments of regulators. As I quoted Robert Kates complaining in chapter three, "men on flood plains appear to be very much prisoners of their experience." Men in boardrooms, too.

At the core of the catastrophe, however, is the housing bubble, and it is best explained with the social psychology discussed in chapter six. "What started this whole thing going was a speculative bubble in which people were taking close account of the information signals of others leading to a situation in which 'everybody knew' that home prices always go up in the US, which actually isn't true," Cass Sunstein says.

The growing complexity of financial instruments – from personal mortgages to the arcane derivatives traded on financial markets – contributed to the tendency to follow the pack. "The credit markets have gotten more and more difficult to navigate in the past 20 years," Sunstein notes, "and when you have all this fine print and confusing terms, people tend to say 'yeah, whatever.'"

How does this mortgage work? Will I be able to pay it off? What exactly *is* this derivative? Is it a sound investment? For laypeople and Wall Street wizards alike, these were tough questions. They were also important questions, with serious consequences for those who answered incorrectly. And it is precisely under those conditions – as Robert Baron, Joseph Vandello, and Bethany Brunsman showed – that people are most likely to abandon their own judgment and follow the lead of others.

Many analogies are used to describe this dynamic. "Herding" is the obvious one. Another is "contagion." Sunstein prefers to call it an "informational cascade": The fact that many people believe something convinces more people of that thing, which settles it for still more people, and so on.

Now add the pernicious influence of confirmation bias. Then add news media reporting that not only failed to expose mistaken beliefs but accepted, repeated, and amplified them. And don't forget the many individuals and organizations with a vested interest in how the public perceived real estate risks. In 2008, as air hissed out of the housing bubble and scales fell from eyes across America, the National Association of Realtors launched a $40 million ad campaign promoting the "fact" that, on average, home values nearly double every ten years. Technically true. And totally misleading. That figure, based on data covering the last thirty years, includes the unsustainable growth of the housing bubble. Worse, it isn't adjusted for inflation; do that and most of the increase vanishes.

On and on the information cascade expanded, sweeping over thousands of people, millions, tens of millions. Why did so many people fail to see the real estate bubble for what it was? This is why.

If it seems incredible that a tsunami of error could wash over a society in an era when accurate information is cheap, abundant, and available at the click of a mouse, remember that information technology also makes it easier to get the opinions of others that we find so compelling. Remember also that Google and the Internet only provide what users ask of them, and given the influence of confirmation bias, what most users ask of Google and the Internet is confirmation of what they already believe.

It's easy to fall into despair. If the economic turmoil we are experiencing is rooted in psychology, what can we do about it? Human nature can't be changed. Is there nothing we can do to lessen our vulnerability to economic mania?

In fact, there is. Human nature may be unchangeable but much of the environment in which people live is of our own making. It can be changed. "If we want to prevent things like this from happening again, we have to create tools that are designed for humans and not *Homo economicus*," says Cass Sunstein, whose book *Nudge*, co-written with Richard Thaler, is about how to do just that.

A good place to start is ensuring markets have better information. "We need disclosure requirements that are built for 21st century financial products," Sunstein says. The idea isn't to generate *more* information. The last thing the markets need is more information. It's to simplify and clarify information so that regulators, managers, advisers, bankers, and brokers are less inclined to say "yeah, whatever" and follow the herd. Sunstein calls it "simplified transparency."

The same principle holds for consumers. "The whole catastrophe started because it's very hard to figure out how much mortgage people should take," Dan Ariely says. Mortgage calculators weren't much help because they are typically provided by financial institutions whose interest lies in people taking out bigger mortgages, so they don't factor in possible setbacks – job loss, declining home values – and they don't tell people the *optimum* mortgage they should take. Instead, they tell people the *maximum* mortgage available.

Compounding this problem is "optimism bias," which I mentioned briefly in chapter 11. Very simply, people tend to see themselves in a good light. If they are asked about their driving skills, most will say they are "above average." Intelligence? Above average. Looks? Above average. When it comes to risk, this bias tends to unreasonably diminish the possibility of something bad happening. So if a forty-two-year-old factory worker with a suburban bungalow in a decent neighbourhood is asked how likely it is that a forty-two-year-old factory worker will lose his job, or that a suburban bungalow in a decent neighbourhood will decline in value, he will give a certain estimate. But if he is asked how likely it is that *he* will lose *his* job, or how likely *his* home is to decline in value, he will give a different estimate – a *lower* estimate.

"We don't think about all the things that could go wrong," Ariely says. Because of this bias, and the difficulty people have in figuring out how much mortgage they can reasonably handle, "they borrow way, way too much." Ariely recommends governments provide – or pay third parties to provide – easy-to-use mortgage calculators that give people advice untainted by optimism bias or the self-interest of lenders, mortgage brokers, and real estate agents. Robert Shiller goes further, calling for governments to subsidize independent, disinterested, financial advice for those who cannot afford it. If this had existed a decade ago, Shiller writes, "the crisis might never have occurred."

Perhaps. Of course we'll never know. The one thing we can be sure of is that things went very wrong and the crisis that started in 2008 is very serious. Interviewers have asked me whether this undermines the very hopeful message – "there's never been a better time to be alive" – that closes my book.

The answer is no. Not in the least. It takes only a little historical perspective to see that we are the healthiest and longest-living people in the history of the species. And as people would know if the media had paid attention to those CDC statistics, we're getting healthier and longer-living by the day. Those of us who live in the developed world, along with growing numbers in the developing world, are also the *wealthiest* people who ever lived: In 1900, the average American made $4,748 a year (in 1998 dollars); by 1998, that had risen to $32,444. Over the same period, the hours worked by the average full-time employee fell from 60 per week to 40, while the portion of the average family's budget that went to food fell from 44 per cent to 15 per cent. Even if this economic crisis is severe and a decade of progress is lost, the average American – along with the average Canadian, Briton, Australian, and a lot of other ordinary people on the planet – will still enjoy material prosperity greater than anything royalty could have commanded not so long ago.

Our species has always faced threats – monetary and mortal – and always will. We can be sure that the future will see setbacks, tragedies, disasters, and catastrophes. But barring Armageddon itself – the ultimate low probability–high consequence event – we will not be knocked back so far that our time will cease to be the best time to be alive. Very simply, we will remain the luckiest people who ever lived.

"The future is unknowable," Winston Churchill wrote in 1958, "but the past should give us hope." If we care to look.

ACKNOWLEDGEMENTS

I first met the psychologist Paul Slovic at the Instituto de Astrofisica in the Canary Islands and so it was amid models of the solar system and other astrophysical phantasmagoria that I discovered the psychology of risk perception. The universe is interesting, I concluded. But the mind is fascinating.

It is to Paul Slovic's patience and generosity that I most owe this book. Many thanks. I am similarly indebted to Susan Renouf at McClelland & Stewart, whose enthusiasm for my enthusiasms got the whole thing rolling and kept it going to the end. Peter Bobrowsky, Rudyard Griffiths, Dr. Barry Dworkin, Carl Phillips, and Ron Melchers all contributed mightily.

A special note to my editors at the *Ottawa Citizen*, who have given me freedom and opportunities the like of which most journalists can only dream. Thanks to Neil Reynolds, Scott Anderson, Tina Spencer, Lynn McAuley, and Leonard Stern.

And lastly, I must thank my children, Victoria and Winston, for pulling down my books, scattering my papers, smashing my laptop, shrieking at the most inopportune moments, banging relentlessly on my door, and infecting me with every virus bred in that Petri dish known as junior kindergarten. I have realized that if I can write a book under that onslaught, I can do anything, and so I shall go forward with new confidence. Bless you, darlings.

NOTES

As a journalist writing for a daily newspaper, my usual practice is to provide enough information in the text to allow readers to find my original sources with a quick Google search of names or keywords. In this book, I've generally followed the same approach. These notes are limited to the occasional instances where more information is necessary to find sources, and to provide additional commentary.

CHAPTER ONE

Page 10 "The trends in humanity's political arrangements are also quite positive. . . ." See Adrian Karatnycky, "A Century of Progress," *Journal of Democracy*, January 2000. Note that in 1900 not one country anywhere in the world qualified as a full democracy according to modern standards of universal suffrage.

Page 10 "A major study released later that year by the Human Security Centre at the University of British Columbia. . . ." See *Human Security Report 2005*.

Page 11 "In Europe, where there are more cellphones than people and sales keep climbing, a survey found. . . ." See Eurobarometer/nVision, 2006.

CHAPTER TWO

Page 25 "And evolution has made you what you are. . . ." For a rousing rebuttal of the ghost-in-the-machine view, see Steven Pinker's *The Blank Slate*.

Page 29 "Psychologists found that when they asked students to eat a piece of fudge . . ." Like many of the references to the work of psychologists in this chapter and others that follow, this is drawn from *Heuristics and Biases*, edited by Thomas Gilovich, Dale Griffin, and Daniel Kahneman. Along with the earlier edition of the same work – edited by Paul Slovic, Amos Tversky, and Daniel Kahneman – it is the definitive text on the subject.

Page 35 " . . . if you give it some careful thought . . ." The answer is five cents.

CHAPTER THREE

Page 41 "Those who heard the higher number guessed higher. . . ." For the record, both groups were way off. Gandhi was 79 when he died.

Page 44 " . . . produced an average answer almost 150 per cent greater than a low number." Psychologists Baruch Fischhoff, Sarah Lichtenstein, and Paul Slovic found another use for anchoring numbers in a study that asked people to estimate the toll taken by various causes of death. Without guidance, people's answers were often wildly inaccurate, ranging from one extreme to the other. But when the researchers told people that 50,000 Americans are killed in car crashes each year (a toll that has dropped since the study was conducted), their answers "stabilized dramatically" because they started at 50,000 and adjusted up or down. In later trials, the researchers switched to the anchoring number to 1,000 dead from electrocution – with the predictable result that people's estimates of deaths by other causes dropped enormously.

Page 50 " . . . as even many black men do . . ." For an explanation and tests of unconscious beliefs that anyone can take, see "Project Implicit" at www.implicit.harvard.edu.

Page 61 "There is no 'just' in imagining. . . ." Lottery and casino ads that highlight smiling winners are another form of powerful manipulation. The odds of winning big jackpots are so tiny that almost no one will be able think of winners in their personal lives. But by advertising examples of people who struck it big – often with personal details that make their stories memorable –

lotteries and casinos make it easy for people to recall examples of winners. And that ease of recall boosts Gut's estimate of the likelihood of winning.

Page 67 " . . . only family and friends will hear of a life lost to diabetes . . ." Much of the work of Paul Slovic cited in this book can be found in *The Perception of Risk*, a compilation of decades of Slovic's papers.

CHAPTER FOUR

Page 69 ". . . a conference that brought together some of the world's leading astronomers and geo-scientists to discuss asteroid impacts. . . ." The conference papers were compiled in *Comet/Asteroid Impacts and Human Society*, P. Bobrowsky and H. Rickman eds., Springer Verlag Publishing, New York.

Page 85 " . . . while 'all possible causes' is bland and empty. It leaves Gut cold." See Eric Johnson et al., "Framing, Probability Distortions, and Insurance Decisions," *Journal of Risk and Uncertainty*, 1993.

Page 86 " . . . raising risk estimates by 144 per cent. . . ." See "Affect Generalization and the Perception of Risk," *Journal of Personality and Social Psychology*, 45, 20–31.

Page 88 " . . . beloved grandfathers are not necessary." One of the stranger demonstrations of the mere exposure effect involves asking people to choose which of two images they prefer. One is a photograph of their face the way it actually is. The other is the same image reversed. Most people choose the face that is reversed. Why? Because that's what they see every morning in the mirror.

Page 89 " . . . the Penguins' penalty time rose 50 per cent to 12 minutes a game. . . ." Does the black uniform mean referees perceive the team more negatively and therefore judge them more strictly than they otherwise would? Or does the black uniform inspire players to be more aggressive? Both, the researchers concluded. See "The Dark Side of Social and Self-Perception: Black Uniforms and Aggression in Professional Sport."

Page 92 " . . . bias in favour of the 'lean' beef declined but was still evident." Irwin Levin and Gary Gaeth, "How Consumers Are Affected by the Framing of Attribute Information Before and After Consuming the Product," *The Journal of Consumer Research*, December 1988.

Page 93 "Feeling trumped numbers. It usually does." See Cass Sunstein's *Laws of Fear*.

Page 96 " . . . I won't even think about that" See Robin Hogarth and Howard Kunreuther, "Decision Making Under Ignorance," *Journal of Risk and Uncertainty*, 1995.

CHAPTER FIVE

Page 105 ". . . in a way that the phrase 'almost 3,000 were killed' never can." This summary of the life of Diana O'Connor comes from the remarkable obituaries the *New York Times* prepared of every person who died in the attack. The series ran for months and garnered a huge readership.

Page 108 "Only data – properly collected and analyzed – can do that." The reader will notice that anecdotes abound within this book. My point here is not to dismiss stories, only to note that, however valuable they may be in many circumstances, anecdotes have serious limitations.

Page 110 " . . . 'the deaths of millions is a statistic,' said that expert on death, Joseph Stalin." Psychologists call this the "identifiable victim effect." For a discussion, see, for example, "Statistical, Identifiable and Iconic Victims," George Loewenstein, Deborah Small, and Jeff Strand.

Page 110 " . . . empathetic urge to help generated by the profile of the little girl." Even in relatively unemotional situations – the sort in which we may assume that calm calculation would dominate – numbers have little sway. Psychologists Eugene Borgida and Richard Nisbett set up an experiment in which groups of students at the University of Michigan were asked to look at a list of courses and circle those they thought they might like to take in future. One group did this with no further information. A second group listened to brief comments about the courses delivered in person by students who had taken the courses previously. These presentations had a "substantial impact" on students' choices, the researchers found. Finally, a third group was given the average rating earned by each course in a survey of students who had taken the courses previously: In sharp contrast with the personal anecdotes, the data had no influence at all.

Page 111 " . . . mattered less than the profile." Kahneman and Tversky dubbed this "base-rate neglect."

Page 115 " . . . more about the power of Gut-based judgments than they do about cancer." For a good overview, see Atul Gawande, "The Cancer-Cluster Myth," *The New Yorker*, February 8, 1998.

CHAPTER SIX

Page 126 " . . . go along with the false answers they gave." Robert Baron, Joseph Vandello, and Bethany Brunsman, "The Forgotten Variable in Conformity Research: The Impact of Task Importance on Social Influence," *Journal of Personality and Social Psychology*, 71, 915–27.

Page 129 "The correct rule is actually 'any three numbers in ascending order.'" There are other rules that would also work. What matters is simply that the rule is *not* "even numbers increasing by two."

Page 130 " . . . more convinced that they were right and those who disagreed were wrong." Charles Lord, Lee Ross, Mark Lepper, "Biased Assimilation and Attitude Polarization: The Effects of Prior Theories on Subsequently Considered Evidence," *Journal of Personality and Social Psychology*, 1979.

Page 131 " . . . when they processed neutral or positive information." See Westen's 2007 book *The Political Brain*.

Page 137 " . . . illicit drugs aren't as dangerous as commonly believed." A thorough discussion of the real risks of drugs is outside the scope of this book but readers who wish to pursue it are encouraged to read Jacob Sullum's "Saying Yes."

Page 137 " . . . materials tend to be 'superficial, lurid, excessively negative. . . . '" Why have you never heard of this report? Because the government of the United States successfully buried it. In a May 1995 meeting, according to the WHO's records – and confirmed to me by a WHO spokesman – Neil Boyer, the American representative to the organization, "took the view that . . . (the WHO's) program on substance abuse was headed in the wrong direction. . . . If WHO activities relating to drugs failed to reinforce proven drug-control approaches, funds for the relevant programs should be curtailed." Facing a major loss of funding, the WHO backed down at the last minute. Although a press release announcing the report was issued, the report itself was never officially released. The author has a copy on file.

Page 137 "Higher perceived risk is always better." See, for example, the website of the U.S. Office of National Drug Control Policy (www.whitehousedrugpolicy.gov), where documents routinely tout higher risk perceptions as evidence of success but never – as far as I can see – consider whether those perceptions are out of line with reality.

Page 138 " . . . killed far more people than all the illicit drugs combined." A 2004 article in the *New England Journal of Medicine,* for example, puts the annual death toll inflicted by alcohol at 85,000; all illicit drugs were responsible for 17,000 deaths. See "Actual Causes of Death in the United States 2000." Gaps between the two causes of death are even larger in other countries.

Page 140 " . . . not a problem in the hands of law-abiding citizens." Kahan's research and more is available on the website of the Cultural Cognition Project at the Yale University Law School. http://research.yale.edu/culturalcognition/.

CHAPTER SEVEN

Page 153 " . . . three–quarters of all Americans would be considered 'diseased.'" See "Changing Disease Definitions: Implications for Disease Prevalence," *Effective Clinical Practice,* March/April 1999.

Page 160 " . . . self–interest and sincere belief seldom part company." For a thorough and entertaining look at how the brain is wired for self-justification, see "Mistakes Were Made (But Not By Me): Why We Justify Foolish Beliefs, Bad Decisions, and Hurtful Acts" by Carol Tavris and Elliot Aronson.

Page 167 "One out of eight American children is going hungry *tonight.*'" See *It Ain't Necessarily So: How the Media Make and Unmake the Scientific Picture of Reality,* David Murray, Joel Schwartz, and S. Robert Lichter, 2001.

Page 169 " . . . half–truths, quarter truths, and sort–of–truths." Another fine example is reported in "Is the Tobacco Control Movement Misrepresenting the Acute Cardiovascular Health Effects of Secondhand Smoke Exposure?" in *Epidemiologic Perspectives and Innovations.* The author, Michael Siegel, a professor in the School of Public Health at Boston University, shows how anti-smoking groups promoted smoking bans by exaggerating the danger of second-hand smoke. And another: In the late 1980s and early 1990s, activists and officials struggling to convince people that HIV–AIDS was not only a "gay man's disease" had an unfortunate tendency to spin numbers. The U.S. Centers for Disease Control, for example, reported that "women accounted for 19 per cent of adult/adolescent AIDS cases in 1995, the highest proportion yet reported among women." That frightening news made headlines across the United States. But as David Murray, Joel Schwartz, and Robert Lichter point out in *It Ain't Necessarily So*, the CDC did not include the actual numbers of AIDS cases in the summary that garnered the headlines. Those numbers actually showed a small *decline* in the number of women with AIDS. The *proportion* of AIDS cases involving women had gone up because there had been a much bigger drop in the number of men with AIDS. By the mid-1990s, it was becoming increasingly obvious that activists and agencies had been hyping the risk of heterosexual infection in the United States, the United Kingdom, and elsewhere, but some thought that was just fine. "The Government has lied, and I am glad," wrote Mark Lawson in a 1996 column in *The Guardian*.

Page 174 " . . . I hope that means being both." Many critics of environmentalists have repeated this quotation in a form that cuts off the last several sentences, thereby making it look as if Schneider endorsed scare-mongering. He did not.

Page 176 " . . . may be misleading but it certainly gets the job done." Another technique for making uncertain information exciting is to dispense with the range of possible outcomes that often accompanies uncertainty and instead cite one number. Naturally, the number cited is not the lowest number, nor the average within the range. It is the biggest and scariest. Thus, when former World Bank chief economist Nicholas Stern estimated in 2006 that the costs of climate change to the global economy under a range of scenarios would be 5 to 20 per cent, environmentalists – and far too many journalists – cited it as "up to 20 per cent" or simply "20 per cent."

CHAPTER EIGHT

Page 180 " . . . major U.S. magazines between 1993 and 1997." Wylie Burke, Amy Olsen, Linda Pinsky, Susan Reynolds, and Nancy Press, "Misleading Presentation of Breast Cancer in Popular Magazines," *Effective Clinical Practice*, March/April 2001.

Page 183 " . . . disease got nowhere near coverage proportionate to their death toll." See K. Frost, E. Frank, and E. Maibach, "Relative Risk in the News Media: A Quantification of Misrepresentation," *American Journal of Public Health*, 1997.

Page 190 " . . . not so exciting and alarming is played down or ignored entirely." A handy way to spot sensationalism is to look for the words "danger" and "lurk" in the same sentence – as in "Danger Lurks in Unlikely Corners" (*USA Today*), "Danger Lurks in Yellowstone Park" (Associated Press), "Why Danger Lurks in the High School Parking Lot" (*Metro West Daily News* of Boston), and my favourite, "Dangers Lurk in Dirty Salons," a Fox News story about the little-appreciated threat of improperly cleaned nail files and foot baths.

Page 207 " . . . can be distracted by dramatic stories of no real consequence." A further example: In 1996 and 1997, "flying truck tires" became a major issue in the province of Ontario thanks to a classic feedback loop. Two tragic incidents in which loose tires struck and killed motorists got considerable media attention. The issue became political. Reporting proliferated and even trivial incidents in which no one was endangered made the news. It seemed the roads were in chaos. New safety regulations were passed and, just as quickly as it appeared, the crisis vanished.

So had the regulations put out a real fire? No. The ministry of transportation didn't have a comprehensive incident-collection system in place prior to the crisis, but its partial figures showed there were 18 "wheels-off" incidents and two deaths in 1995, the year the issue started to emerge. Given the millions of vehicles on the road, those numbers are tiny. Then in 1996, the government started to gather better data. The 1996 figures show 41 incidents, and another two deaths. In 1997, there were 215 incidents and no deaths. In 1998, there were 99 incidents. The following year, there were 79, then 87. In 2001, there were 65 incidents and two people were killed. In 2002, there were 66 incidents. In 2003, there were 75 incidents and another person was killed.

Before the panic, tires came loose occasionally and there was a tiny risk to motorists. The same was true during the crisis and afterward. All that changed was appearance and disappearance of the feedback loop.

CHAPTER NINE

Page 215 " . . . so small it can be treated as if it were zero." The term *de minimis* comes from the legal maxim *"de minimis non curat lex"* – the law does not concern itself with trifles.

Page 217 " . . . saying they followed 'very closely' (49 per cent) or 'fairly closely' (30 per cent)." Smart was discovered alive in March 2003. *People* magazine named her one of the "50 Most Beautiful People of 2005."

Page 218 "This astonishingly good news went almost completely unreported. . . ." See "Intimate Partner Violence in the United States," by Shannon Catalano, U.S. Bureau of Justice Statistics.

Page 219 " . . . in newspapers, wrote criminologist Robert Reiner." See Robert Reiner, "Media–Made Criminality: The Representation of Crime in the Mass Media" in *The Oxford Handbook of Criminology*, Oxford University Press, 2007.

Page 219 " . . . debate declined and disappeared virtually unnoticed." In 1999 and 2000, a panic about "home invasions" swept Toronto and Vancouver after numerous incidents in which criminals burst into homes, brutalized the occupants, and grabbed whatever they could take. In one attack, an 85–year–old woman was beaten so badly she later died. Story followed story and it became common knowledge that home invasions were a terrible new threat that was rapidly getting worse. Few reporters mentioned that there was no definition of "home invasion" and therefore no statistics on the crime. They also didn't mention that most recognized categories of crime were falling rapidly, which made it hard to believe that this one form of violent crime was soaring. No matter. Everyone knew it was true and in that inflamed atmosphere a bill stiffening sentences was inevitable. It appeared and passed. And with that, the whole issue faded. But then in 2002, Statistics Canada issued a report that cobbled together two different definitions of "home invasion" and used those to track the crime using existing data. Under the first definition, the rate of "home invasions" had dipped slightly between 1995 and 2000; under the second definition, it had fallen 22 per cent. The report was almost completely ignored by the media.

Page 223 "' . . . rate that was at least six times higher than the actual rate.'" See "Public Opinion, Crime and Criminal Justice" and "Understanding Public Attitudes to Criminal Justice."

Page 234 " . . . the prison population soared from 400,000 in 1980 to 2.1 million by 2000." The latter half of that explosion coincided with a major decline in crime, and people on both sides of the political spectrum concluded that stuffing prisons to the rafters is an effective way to reduce crime. Most criminologists disagree. In *The Great American Crime Decline* – the most exhaustive look at the causes of the crime drop of the 1990s – University of California criminologist Franklin Zimring noted that Canada had not followed the American approach in the 1980s and 1990s and, as a result, a canyon opened between the two countries' incarceration rates: In 1980, the United States imprisoned people at double the rate Canada did; in 2000, the American incarceration rate was *six times* higher than the Canadian rate. Despite this, Canada's crime trends over that entire period were remarkably similar to American trends. In the 1990s, Zimring writes, Canada experienced a drop in crime in the 1990s that "almost perfectly matched the timing of the United States decline and (was) about 70 per cent of its relative magnitude." Zimring rather understatedly concludes this fact is "a challenge" to the conventional view that American politicians not only won elections with promises to "get tough" but won the war on crime, too.

Page 235 " . . . to commit another crime after release than other sorts of criminals." See, for example, "Recidivism Released From Prison In 1994," U.S. Bureau of Justice Statistics, 2003.

Page 235 " . . . less frightening than that unadorned number." See "Online Victimization of Youth: Five Years Later," The Crimes Against Children Research Center, University of New Hampshire, 2006.

Page 237 " . . . civil servants handling the file. 'It's politics,' he told them." This was personally communicated to the author by one of the civil servants present.

Page 239 " . . . the research does not mean what people naturally assume it means – that one in five children on the Internet have been contacted by pedophiles." It's hard to believe these agencies are not aware that the statistic they disseminate is leading people to a false and frightening conclusion. A quick Google search turns up countless blogs and websites where the figure is cited as proof of the threat posed by pedophiles. It appeared in the same context in an article by journalist Caitlin Flanagan in the July/August 2007 issue of *The Atlantic Monthly*. And John Walsh cited the figure as proof of the pedophile menace in an interview on CNN: "The Justice Department says that one in five children receive a sexual solicitation over the Internet. And I think all Americans have seen the 'Dateline' stings with all the different type of pedophiles, doctors, rabbis, priests showing up to have sex with children." As for UNICEF, when I asked a spokesperson for the source behind the agency's statement, he cited the University of New Hampshire study and provided me with a web link to it – even though anyone who actually looked at the document would see that it does not say what UNICEF says it does.

Page 248 " . . . the homicide rates today are among the lowest in eight centuries." Property crime is trickier to track simply because with murders there is usually a corpse and a big fuss, but historians such as James Sharpe of the

University of York have investigated the possibility that violent crime was merely transformed into property crime and they are confident that, no, that did not happen. In the 17th century, as homicide was plummeting in England, property offences fell along with it, Sharpe has concluded. See Manuel Eisner, "Long-Term Historical Trends in Violent Crime," in *Crime and Justice: A Review of Research, Volume 30*, University of Chicago Press, 2003.

CHAPTER TEN

Page 256 "' . . . only form of cancer which shows so definite a tendency," the report noted." See Ronald Bailey, "Silent Spring at 40," *Reason*, June 12, 2002.

Page 257 "The research linking smoking to cancer was new . . ." Suspicions started to mount in the 1940s. In 1950, British scientist Richard Doll studied 20 lung cancer patients and concluded smoking was the only thing they had in common. Doll quit smoking immediately and warned in a paper that the risk of cancer "may be 50 times as great among those who smoke 25 or more cig-arettes a day as among non-smokers." In 1954, a study of 40,000 British doctors came to the same conclusion, and the British government officially advised that smoking and cancer may be related. In 1957, the U.S. Surgeon General Leroy Burney stated his belief that smoking caused cancer. In March 1962, the Royal College of Physicians in Britain issued a report saying the same, and shortly afterward, the Surgeon General created a committee that ultimately led to the famous declaration of 1964 that smoking kills.

Page 260 " . . . thanks to differences in lifestyle." Some important lifestyle factors are far from obvious. The risk of breast cancer, for example, is increased by the hormones involved in ovulation. Thus a woman whose period starts later – perhaps as a result of poor nutrition in childhood – is likely to have a reduced risk of breast cancer. A woman who has her first pregnancy earlier will further reduce her risk. So will a woman who has many babies. Conversely, a woman who received good nutrition in childhood and is in excellent health may start menstruation earlier, which will raise her risk, while a decision to delay having children until later in life, and having only one or two babies, or none, will boost it further. And that description fits most modern, Western women.

Page 262 " . . . who didn't, and so it became hard-wired instinct." Psychologists Paul Rozin and Carol Nemeroff have conducted a series of ingenious expo-sures demonstrating just how tenacious this feeling is. See "Sympathetic

Magical Thinking: The Contagion and Similarity 'Heuristics'" in *Heuristics and Biases*. Any contact with a contaminated object taints the thing, no matter how brief the contact, and neither washing nor even sterilization can entirely remove the taint.

Page 264 " . . . on the list actually cause cancer in humans." For a good overview of these studies and the controversies surrounding them, see Aaron Wildavsky, *But Is It True?*, Harvard University Press, 1995.

Page 270 " . . . are falling but 'much more so for cardiovascular disease." See Statistics Canada, "Mortality, Summary List of Causes, 2004," released April 27, 2007.

Page 276 " . . . it forbids the very steps that it requires." Another example: Nothing could be more in line with the sentiment of "precaution" than doing a biopsy on a growth. After all, the growth may be benign. Surgery would be an unnecessary risk. So a needle is inserted and some cells removed to make sure it's cancerous before treatment proceeds. But in removing cells, there is a tiny risk that cancerous cells be dislodged. These cells may follow the needle track and attach to other tissue. In effect, the biopsy will spread the cancer. This is very unlikely, but it can happen. So if you don't do the biopsy, you may undergo risky treatments unnecessarily, but if you do the biopsy, you could spread the cancer. What does "precaution" mean under those circumstances?

And yet another example: Flame retardants are one variety of chemical that routinely turns up in blood tests; environmentalists want many banned on the grounds that they are suspected of increasing the risk of cancer, hyper-activity disorder in children, and other ills. But how did flame retardants get into our bodies in the first place? As the name suggests, flame retardants are chemicals added to consumer items like children's pajamas and furniture that make them resistant to fire. Some are actually required by law, and for good reason. In 1988, Britain passed a regulation requiring flame retardants in all new furniture. A University of Surrey study commissioned by the government ("Effectiveness of the Furniture and Furnishings Fire Safety Regulations 1988") estimated that in nine years the regulation saved as many as 1,800 lives and prevented 5,700 injuries. So does the precautionary principle say the use of these chemicals should be banned or made mandatory?

Page 277 " . . . there would be little left to eat." The 1996 report was the product of a three-year, peer-reviewed investigation of carcinogens in food. "First, the committee concluded that based upon existing exposure data, the great majority of individual naturally occurring and synthetic chemicals in the diet appears to be present at levels below which any significant adverse biologic effect is likely, and so low that they are unlikely to pose any appreciable cancer risk," the report states. "Second, the committee concluded that natural components of the diet may prove to be of greater concern than synthetic components with respect to cancer risk, although additional evidence is required before definitive conclusions may be drawn."

CHAPTER 11

Page 288 " . . . the 1 in 87,976 annual risk of drowning." Accident statistics come from the National Safety Council's *Injury Facts, 2007.*

Page 291 " . . . attack is probably impossible now." It was even highly unlikely to succeed at the time. The plot was big and complex and, as with any plot of that nature, there were many points at which a failure would collapse the whole thing – which is precisely what happened to an equally ambitious Philippines-based plot broken up several years before 9/11 and a London-based scheme smashed in 2006. And the 9/11 plot *did* experience failures, although the terrorists were repeatedly saved by bad official judgment and dumb luck. For a summary, see Max Bazerman and Michael Watkins, *Predictable Surprises.*

Page 291 " . . . they could inflict the sort of devastation it took armies to accomplish in the past." A critical caveat about "weapons of mass destruction" is often overlooked. In the Cold War, the term was mainly a synonym for nuclear weapons that was gradually expanded to include other unconventional weapons governed by special international agreements – meaning chemical and biological weapons. So it's essentially a legal artifact, which helps explain why many "weapons of mass destruction" are not massively destructive and many weapons that don't qualify as WMDs are. Timothy McVeigh tore an office building in half with a bomb made of fertilizer (which does not qualify as a weapon of mass destruction) while the victims of mustard gas (which is a weapon of mass destruction) typically suffer only agonizing blisters. As for the much-hyped "dirty bomb" – a conventional explosive that also spreads radioactive material – it is usually classed as a WMD because of the radioactive material, but according to the CDC, the levels of radioactivity released by a dirty bomb are unlikely to be high enough to cause severe sickness, let alone death – and so it is the old-fashioned explosive that is the most dangerous part of the device.

Page 302 " . . . referred to terrorism as 'an existential threat to the whole of the human family.'" Most hyperbole about the threat of terrorism puts it on par with the danger posed by the Soviet Union or Nazi Germany. But occasionally, it takes sole possession of the number one spot, as in former governor of Arkansas and Republican presidential hopeful Mike Huckabee's description of "Islamofascism" as "the greatest threat this country's ever faced."

Page 306 " . . . Cheney was invoking the precautionary principle." For a fuller discussion, see Jessica Stern and Jonathan Wiener, "Precaution Against Terrorism," a paper issued by the John F. Kennedy School of Government at Harvard University.

Page 307 " . . . will 'set off a bomb that contains nuclear or biological material.'" The portrayal of WMDs as doomsday weapons, and the obsessive focus on them that follows, can lead even the most sophisticated thinkers to some truly bad conclusions. In November 2007, the esteemed professor of near-eastern studies Bernard Lewis cast the fight against terrorism as the third great fight against totalitarianism, after the struggles against Nazism and Communism. But there is an important difference, Lewis wrote. The Nazis "had no weapons of mass destruction. The Soviets had them, but were deterred from using them by what came to be known as 'mutually assured destruction.' Our present adversaries either have or will soon have weapons of mass destruction, but for them, with their apocalyptic mind-set, mutual assured destruction would not be a deterrent; it would be an inducement." Thus, according to Lewis, neither a genocidal maniac who came within a hair of conquering Europe and dominating the planet nor a superpower capable of snuffing out civilization on 15 minutes' notice were as dangerous as scattered bands of fanatics who may, someday, get their hands on a WMD or two.

Page 308 " . . . of death or 9/11 increased support for the president." See Sheldon Solomon, Jeff Greenberg, and Tom Pyszczynski, *Psychological Science*, December 2004.

Page 310 " . . . war on terrorism is 'the defining conflict of our time,' Giuliani proclaimed." Giuliani's obsessive focus on 9/11 never wavered as the months went by, prompting Democratic Senator Joe Biden to joke that every sentence uttered by the former mayor of New York contains three things: "A noun, a verb, and 9/11."

Page 314 " . . . worldwide economic depression and martial law in America." Clarke's disaster scenario is a little more detailed and extravagant than most but otherwise it's typical of the genre. In *Whose War Is It?*, Canadian historian and security pundit Jack Granatstein opens with a graphic description of an earthquake devastating Vancouver on the morning of February 12, 2008. Seizing the moment, Islamist terrorists detonate a bomb in Montreal and release anthrax in Toronto. "It did not take long before mobs were roughing up anyone who appeared to be of Middle East origin, and women in burkas were punched and kicked." The Canadian military, its meagre resources committed wholly in Afghanistan, is incapable of intervening. Chaos looms. Appalled American politicians close the border. The Toronto Stock Exchange plunges. The economy reels. If it's not already apparent, the central argument of *Whose War Is It?* is that the Canadian military and security services desperately need more funding – and if they don't get it, well, just imagine what could happen.

Page 316 " . . . that this terrible threat is far more likely to happen than logic suggests." One reasonable way to tackle potentially catastrophic scenarios would be to look to real experience of the threats under discussion. But that rarely happened. For all the talk of killer viruses, for example, few mentioned that the last smallpox outbreak in Europe (Yugoslavia, 1972) resulted in only 35 deaths. Nor was much attention given to what happened when an unknown killer virus suddenly appeared in the heart of Europe: It was 1967 and laboratory staff working with African monkeys in the German town of Marburg became infected with what was to be dubbed "Marburg virus," a close relative of Ebola. In the imaginations of journalists or terrorism experts, this incident would undoubtedly end with horrific loss of life, but the reality was considerably less dramatic: There were 32 infections and 7 deaths.

Page 318 " . . . got a tiny fraction of the initial, misleading coverage." Many other cases followed the same trajectory. Most notoriously, when Jose Padilla, an American citizen and Muslim convert, was arrested in May 2002, the Bush administration triumphantly proclaimed that Padilla had been part of a plot to explode a so-called dirty bomb. It was huge news all over the world. Held incommunicado, Padilla sat in limbo. Then, two years later, the Justice Department quietly acknowledged that Padilla had not been planning to explode a dirty bomb. The plot was to turn on the gas in an apartment and ignite it, the department alleged. What had been waved about as proof of terrorists on the cusp of deploying weapons of mass destruction turned out to be nothing more than allegations of a minor, bumbling plot that came to nothing. More time passed. Finally Padilla went to trial and the allegations shrank further: Padilla was alleged to have trained with terrorists in Afghanistan but was not accused of planning any specific attack. And the media? As the allegations got smaller, so did the coverage. By the time Padilla stood trial, he and his case were largely forgotten – leaving intact the impression made years before that the government had narrowly averted a major assault by terrorists armed with a weapon of mass destruction.

The pattern of gross official exaggeration was obvious but still the media didn't hesitate to trumpet new announcements of catastrophes averted. In June 2006, simultaneous press conferences in Washington and Miami were called to announce the arrest of a group of men in Florida who were conspiring to, as the indictment put it, "levy war in the United States" – a phrase echoed by the U.S. attorney general, who said the men intended to launch a "full ground war." Among their plans was the destruction of the Sears Tower in Chicago, reporters were told. Soon, however, it became clear that the men were not quite the highly trained and tenacious terror cell they had been made out to be. In fact, they had no connections with al-Qaeda, no training, no weapons, no equipment, and no plans. An undercover government agent pretending to be with al-Qaeda bought them boots. They were, in short, nothing more than a handful of thuggish malcontents playing "international terrorist" – a reality that, once revealed, did not get a fraction of the media attention garnered by the original press conferences.

Page 320 " . . . In Cohen's mind, there simply is no Door Number Three." It sometimes seems that, in media coverage of terrorism, frightening statements and skeptical scrutiny are inversely correlated. Consider that in September 2007, Ron Kessler, an investigative reporter and author of several books on terrorism, told a reporter with the *Ottawa Citizen* that "it's fairly easy for them [al-Qaeda] to get nuclear devices either out of Russia or from their own scientists." On its face, this is a dubious statement. If it's "fairly easy," why haven't they already done so? But Kessler was not asked this rather self-evident question. His statement was simply passed along unchallenged by the wide-eyed reporter. In 2006, CNN.com even managed to turn literally nothing into a threatening story by noting that al-Qaeda had "gone quiet" – the top leaders had not released video or audio tapes for some time – and speculating on what the silence could mean. In May 2007, *USA Today* found it alarming that al-Qaeda had *not* struck the United States.: "Intelligence analysts say the lack of an al-Qaeda-led strike here may signal that the group is waiting until it can mount an attack that will equal the 9/11 strikes in casualties and publicity value."

Page 321 " . . . the politics had changed and so had Rich's standards about what constituted reliable proof." Similarly, *Mother Jones* – the venerable magazine of the American left – declared terrorism to be a growing menace in March 2007. "The Iraq Effect: War Has Increased Terrorism Sevenfold Worldwide" read the headline about a study commissioned by the magazine that had found a huge spike in "fatal jihadist attacks worldwide." Britain's *Independent* newspaper, reporting with evident delight on the same study, ran the headline: "How the War on Terror Made the World a More Terrifying Place." Buried deep within both stories was the critical fact that the surge in terrorism was in the Middle East and South Asia. The fact that the infinitesimal risk to any one person in America or Europe had not budged was left unmentioned.

Page 326 "' . . . in order to make the generals race there. . . .'" In a September 2007 video, bin Laden also boasted that "nineteen young men" were able to radically change American policy and "the subject of Mujahideen has become an inseparable part of the speech of your leader."

Page 327 " . . . recognize that terrorism is a psychological tactic." As novelist William Gibson put it in an interview, "Terrorism is a con game. It doesn't always work. It depends on the society you are playing it on. It certainly has worked in the United States."

Page 331 " . . . is much lower than it is commonly portrayed, it, too, is real." Oddly, one can plausibly argue that too little money has been spent mitigating the risk of nuclear terrorism – which may be an improbable form of terrorism but is nonetheless the greatest terrorist threat simply by virtue of the number of lives it endangers. At least half the Russian facilities with nuclear materials have still not received security upgrades because American funding for the program that does this work is so limited. Similarly, huge quantities of plutonium that the Russians agreed to destroy were simply put in storage because there was no money to do the job. The UN's International Atomic Energy Agency – the world's nuclear watchdog – has a budget of only $130 million and its director often has to go begging for cash. "The agency constantly risks lagging behind in the technology race because we are forced to make do on a shoestring budget," Mohammed El-Baradei told the Associated Press in 2007. Ted Turner and Warren Buffett became major funders of nuclear security initiatives after the billionaires discovered how the work was being shortchanged by the world's governments.

CHAPTER 12

Page 337 " . . . started inching up. In 1900, it stood at 48 years." See *The Escape From Hunger and Premature Death, 1700–2100*, Robert Fogel.

Page 337 " . . . died before they were five years old." See *Fatal Years* by Samuel Preston and Michael Haines. The authors show that the toll was distributed throughout American society. Losing children was a common experience even for the very wealthy.

Page 338 " . . . life expectancy will rise in every region of the world." See "Projections of Global Mortality and Burdens of Disease from 2002 to 2030," Colin Mather and Dejan Loncar.

Page 341 " . . . to err is human, but, happily for us, we are not human." In a series of experiments, psychologists Emily Pronin, Daniel Lin, and Lee Ross gave Stanford University students booklets describing eight biases identified by psychologists. They then asked how susceptible the "average American" is to each of these biases. The average student at Stanford? You? In every case, the students said the average student was quite susceptible, but they were much less so. The researchers got the same results when they ran a version of the test in the San Francisco International Airport. In more elaborate experiments, Pronin, Lin, and Ross sat people down in pairs and had them take what they said was a "social intelligence" test. The test was bogus. One of the two test–takers – chosen randomly – was given a high score. The other was given a low score. Then they were asked whether they thought the test was an accurate measure of social intelligence. In most cases, the person who got the high score said it was, while the poor guy who got the low score insisted it was not. That's a standard bias at work – psychologists call it the "self–serving bias." But then things got interesting. The researchers explained what the "self–serving bias" is and then they asked whether that bias might have had any influence on their judgment. Why, yes, most said. It *did* influence the other guy's judgment. But me? Not really.

Page 348 " . . . they tend to focus on the negative side of things, for some reason." Just as it is possible to look into the future and imagine horrible things happening, it is possible to dream up wondrous changes. Vaccines for malaria and AIDS would save the lives of hundreds of millions of people. Genetically engineered crops could bring an abundance of cheap food to the world's masses. Hyper–efficient forms of alternative energy may make fossil fuels obsolete and radically mitigate climate change. In combination, they may usher in an unparalleled Golden Age – which is as likely as some of the more outlandish scenarios in Catastrophist writing.

Page 347 " . . . much more confident of those outcomes than the Thomas Friedman of 1985 really was." In 2005, four out of five Canadians agreed that "the world is not as safe a place today as it was when I was growing up." Particularly annoying is that 85 per cent of Canadians born during or prior to the Second World War agreed with that statement. Thus, almost everyone who grew up in an era characterized by the rise of totalitarian nightmares, economic collapse, and world war agreed that the world today is more dangerous than *that*. (See Reginald Bibby, *The Boomer Factor*, 2006.)

Page 351 " . . . satisfied and they changed 'century' to 'hour.'" The full, terrifying title is *Our Final Hour: A Scientist's Warning: How Terror, Error and Environmental Disaster Threaten Humankind's Future in This Century – On Earth and Beyond*. Much of the book is purely speculative. Rees notes, for example, that if nanotechnology got out of control and became self-replicating it could turn the world into "grey goo." This is far beyond any technology humanity has invented or will invent for the foreseeable future, Rees acknowledges, and the only thing making it even a theoretical possibility is the fact that it doesn't violate any laws of physics. As British science writer Oliver Morton wrote in reviewing Rees's book, "If we're to take the risk seriously, we need something more to gnaw on than the fact that it breaks no laws of physics. Neither do invisible rabbits."

BIBLIOGRAPHY

* Essential reading

Allen, Arthur. *Vaccine: The Controversial Story of Medicine's Greatest Lifesaver.*
    New York: Norton, 2007.

Bazerman, Max, and Michael D. Watkins. *Predictable Surprises: The Disasters You
    Should Have Seen Coming and How to Prevent Them.* Boston: Harvard Business
    School Press, 2004.

Best, Joel. *Damned Lies and Statistics: Untangling Numbers from the Media, Politicians,
    and Activists.* Berkeley: University of California Press, 2001.

Bobrowsky, Peter, and Hans Rickman. *Comet /Asteroid Impacts and Human
    Society.* New York: Springer Verlag Publishing, 2007.

Bourke, Joanna. *Fear: A Cultural History.* London: Virago, 2005.

Buss, David M., ed. *The Handbook of Evolutionary Psychology.* Toronto: Wiley, 2005.

Carson, Rachel. *Silent Spring.* New York: Mariner Books, 2002.

Clarke, Lee. *Worst Cases: Terror and Catastrophe in the Popular Imagination.* Chicago,
    IL: University of Chicago Press, 2006.

Clarke, Richard A. *Against All Enemies: Inside America's War on Terror.*
    Washington, DC: Free Press, 2004.

Douglas, Mary, and Aaron Wildavsky. *Risk and Culture: An Essay on the Selection
    of Technological and Environmental Dangers.* Berkeley: University of
    California Press, 1983.

Dunbar, Robin, Louise Barrett, John Lycett. *Evolutionary Psychology.*
    Oxford, UK: OneWorld, 2005.

Flynn, James, Paul Slovic, and Howard Kunreuther, eds. *Risk, Media and Stigma: Understanding Public Challenges to Modern Science and Technology.* London: Earthscan, 2001.

Fogel, Robert William. *The Escape from Hunger and Premature Death: 1700-2100.* Cambridge, UK: Cambridge University Press, 2004.

Furedi, Frank. *Culture of Fear.* London: Continuum, 1997.

*Gilovich, Thomas, Dale Griffin, and Daniel Kahneman, eds. *Heuristics and Biases: The Psychology of Intuitive Judgment.* Cambridge, UK: Cambridge University Press, 2002.

Gladwell, Malcolm. *Blink: The Power of Thinking Without Thinking.* New York: Little, Brown & Company, 2005.

Glassner, Barry. *The Culture of Fear.* New York: Basic Books, 1999.

Goklany, Indur M. *The Improving State of the World.* Washington, DC: Cato Institute, 2007.

Herman, Arthur. *The Idea of Decline in Western History.* Washington, DC: Free Press, 1997.

Jenkins, Brian Michael. *Unconquerable Nation: Knowing Our Enemy, Strengthening Ourselves.* Arlington, VA: RAND, 2006.

*Kahneman, Daniel, Paul Slovic, and Amos Tversky. *Judgment Under Uncertainty: Heuristics and Biases.* Cambridge, UK: Cambridge University Press, 1982.

Keeley, Lawrence H. *War Before Civilization: The Myth of the Peaceful Savage.* New York: Oxford University Press, 1996.

Kida, Thomas E. *Don't Believe Everything You Think: The Six Basic Mistakes We Make in Thinking.* Amherst, NY: Prometheus Books, 2006.

*Lichtenstein, Sarah, and Paul Slovic, eds. *The Construction of Preference.* Cambridge, UK: Cambridge University Press, 2006.

Lichter, S. Robert, and Stanley Rothman. *Environmental Cancer – A Political Disease?* New Haven, CT: Yale University Press, 1999.

Lomborg, Bjorn, ed. *How to Spend $50 Billion to Make the World a Better Place.* Cambridge, UK: Cambridge University Press, 2006.

Lupton, Deborah, ed. *Risk and Sociocultural Theory.* Cambridge, UK: Cambridge University Press, 1999.

Lustick, Ian S. *Trapped in the War on Terror.* Philadelphia, PA: University of Pennsylvania Press, 2006.

Margolis, Howard. *Dealing With Risk: Why the Public and the Experts Disagree on Environmental Issues.* Chicago, IL: University of Chicago Press, 1996.

McGuire, Bill. *Global Catastrophes: A Very Short Introduction.* New York: Oxford University Press, 2002.

Mueller, John. *Overblown: How Politicians and the Terrorism Industry Inflate National Security Threats and Why We Believe Them*. Washington, DC: Free Press, 2006.

Murray, David, Joel Schwartz, and S. Robert Lichter. *It Ain't Necessarily So: How Media Make and Unmake the Scientific Picture of Reality*. Lanham, MD: Rowman and Littlefield, 2001.

Mythen, Gabe. *Ulrich Beck: A Critical Introduction to the Risk Society*. London: Pluto Press, 2004.

Paulos, John Allen. *Innumeracy: Mathematical Illiteracy and Its Consequences*. New York: Hill and Wang, 1988.

——. *A Mathematician Reads the Newspaper*. New York: Anchor Books, 1995.

Piattelli-Palmarini, Massimo. *Inevitable Illusions: How Mistakes of Mind Rule Our Minds*. Toronto: Wiley, 1994.

Pidgeon, Nick, Roger E. Kasperson, and Paul Slovic, eds. *The Social Amplification of Risk*. Cambridge, UK: Cambridge University Press, 2003.

Pinker, Steven. *The Blank Slate: The Modern Denial of Human Nature*. New York and Toronto: Viking, 2002.

Posner, Richard A. *Catastrophe: Risk and Response*. New York: Oxford University Press, 2004.

Richardson, Louise. *What Terrorists Want: Understanding the Enemy, Containing the Threat*. New York: Random House, 2006.

Roberts, Julian V., and Mike Hough. *Understanding Public Attitudes to Criminal Justice*. London: Open University Press, 2005.

——, and Loretta J. Stalans. *Public Opinion, Crime, and Criminal Justice*. San Diego, CA: Westview, 2000.

Robin, Corey. *Fear: The History of a Political Idea*. New York: Oxford University Press, 2004.

Ropeik, David, and George Gray. *Risk: A Practical Guide for Deciding What's Really Safe and What's Really Dangerous in the World Around You*. New York: Houghton Mifflin, 2002.

Rosenthal, Jeffrey S. *Struck by Lightning: The Curious World of Probabilities*. Toronto: HarperCollins, 2005.

Schachter, Daniel L. *The Seven Sins of Memory: How the Mind Forgets and Remembers*. New York: Houghton Mifflin, 2001.

*Slovic, Paul. *The Perception of Risk*. London: Earthscan, 2000.

Stewart, Bernard W., and Paul Keihues, eds. *World Cancer Report*. New York: International Agency for Research on Cancer Press, 2003.

Sullum, Jacob. *Saying Yes: In Defense of Drug Use*. New York: Tarcher Putnam, 2003.

*Sunstein, Cass R. *Risk and Reason: Safety, Law, and the Environment*. Cambridge, UK: Cambridge University Press, 2002.

*——. *Laws of Fear: Beyond the Precautionary Principle.** Cambridge, UK: Cambridge University Press, 2005.

Taleb, Nassim Nicholas. *The Black Swan: The Impact of the Highly Improbable.* Toronto: Random House, 2007.

Tavris, Carol, and Elliot Aaronson. *Mistakes Were Made (But Not By Me): Why We Justify Foolish Beliefs, Bad Decisions, and Hurtful Acts.* Orlando, FL: Harcourt, 2007.

Tetlock, Philip E. *Expert Political Judgment.* Princeton, NJ: Princeton University Press, 2005.

Timbrell, John. *The Poison Paradox: Chemicals as Friends and Foes.* Toronto: Oxford University Press, 2005.

Wildavsky, Aaron. *But Is It True? A Citizen's Guide to Environmental Health and Safety Issues.* Boston: Harvard University Press, 1995.

Workman, Lance, and Will Reader. *Evolutionary Psychology.* Cambridge, UK: Cambridge University Press, 2004.

Zaltman, Gerald. *How Customers Think: Essential Insights Into the Mind of the Market.* Boston: Harvard Business School Press, 2003.

Zimring, Franklin E. *The Great American Crime Drop.* Oxford UK: Oxford University Press, 2007.

INDEX

Rod McIvor

Dan Gardner is a columnist and senior writer for the *Ottawa Citizen*, specializing in criminal justice and other investigative issues. Trained in history and law, Gardner worked as a senior policy adviser to the premier and the minister of education before turning to journalism in 1997. His writing has received numerous awards, including the National Newspaper Award, Amnesty International's Media Award, the Michener Award, and others. He lives in Ottawa with his wife and two children.